**BOB GARNER'S**

# BOOK
# OF
# BARBECUE

JOHN F. BLAIR
P U B L I S H E R
WINSTON-SALEM, NORTH CAROLINA

# BOB GARNER'S
# BOOK OF BARBECUE

## NORTH CAROLINA'S FAVORITE FOOD

BY
BOB GARNER

Published by

# JOHN F. BLAIR
P U B L I S H E R
1406 Plaza Drive
Winston-Salem, North Carolina 27103
www.blairpub.com

*Cover photograph and photographs on pages ii-iii,*
*vi-vii, 15 and 45 © Chezley Royster Photography*
*Rubberstamp on cover by Oxlock used under license from Shutterstock.com*
*Design by Debra Long Hampton*

Library of Congress Cataloging-in-Publication Data

Garner, Bob, 1946-
  Bob Garner's book of barbecue : North Carolina's favorite food / by Bob Garner.
     p.       cm.
  Includes index.
   ISBN 978-0-89587-574-7 (alk. paper) — ISBN 978-0-89587-575-4 (ebook)  1. Bar-
becuing—North Carolina. 2.  Restaurants—North Carolina—Guidebooks.  I. Title.
II. Title: Book of barbecue.
  TX840.B3G362 2012
  641.7'609756—dc23
                              2012007752

10 9 8 7 6 5 4 3 2 1

Facing page: At large barbecues, guests often ate standing up. This shot
is from Braswell Plantation near Rocky Mount, 1944
*Photo by Hemmer, courtesy of the North Carolina State Archives*

*For Ruthie*

Man mopping pit-cooked pigs with a sauce of
vinegar and pepper at a barbecue at
Braswell Plantation near Rocky Mount, 1944
*Photo by Hemmer, courtesy of the*
*North Carolina State Archives*

# NORTH CAROLINA BARBECUE RESTAURANTS

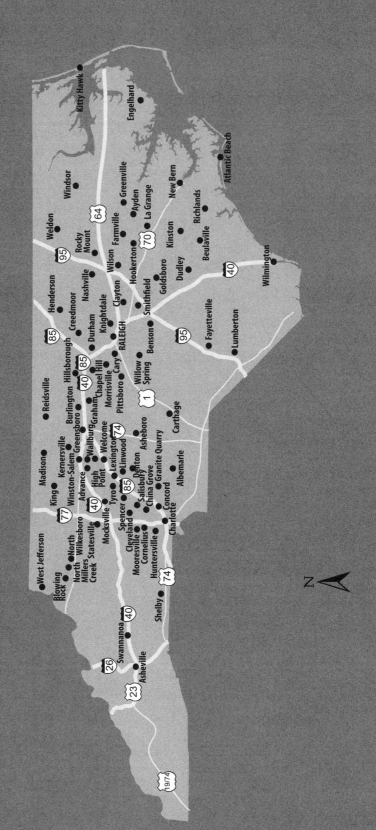

Kitty Hawk

Engelhard

Atlantic Beach

Windsor

Greenville

New Bern

Hayden

La Grange

Richlands

Weldon

Rocky Mount

Kinston

Beulaville

Farmville

Wilson

Goldsboro

Dudley

Wilmington

Henderson

Creedmoor

Nashville

Hookerton

Smithfield

Knightdale

Clayton

RALEIGH

Benson

Fayetteville

Durham

Cary

Hillsborough

Chapel Hill

Pittsboro

Willow Spring

Lumberton

Reidsville

Burlington

Graham

Morrisville

Madison

Wallburg

Asheboro

Carthage

King

Kernersville

Greensboro

Welcome

Linwood

Winston-Salem

Lexington

Granite Quarry

Advance

High Point

Denton

Albemarle

West Jefferson

Tyro

Salisbury

China Grove

Concord

North Millers Creek

Statesville

Mocksville

Spencer

Charlotte

Blowing Rock

North Wilkesboro

Cleveland

Mooresville

Cornelius

Huntersville

Swannanoa

Shelby

Asheville

N

# CONTENTS

Acknowledgments      xv

Introduction      xxi

A Three-Hundred-Year Tradition      3

A North Carolina Barbecue Primer      15

Outside the Restaurant      45

Pork Shoulder or Whole Hog: How to Prepare
   Your Own North Carolina Barbecue      65

Recipes      83

North Carolina Barbecue Restaurants      97

High Cotton Barbeque—Kitty Hawk      98

Martelle's Feed House—Engelhard      99

Moore's Olde Tyme Barbeque—New Bern      101

Oakwood Barbecue—Richlands      103

Sid's Catering—Beulaville      104

Jackson's Big Oak Barbecue—Wilmington      108

Bunn's Barbecue—Windsor      109

Ralph's Barbecue—Weldon      110

Gardner's Barbecue—Rocky Mount      112

Hunter Hill Café & Catering—Rocky Mount      113

Doug Sauls' Barbecue and
   Seafood—Nashville      115

Bill's Barbecue and Chicken—Wilson      116

Cherry's Barbecue and Seafood—Wilson      120

Parker's Barbecue—Wilson      122

B's Barbecue and Grill—Greenville      125

Parker's Barbecue—Greenville      129

Jack Cobb & Son Bar-B-Que—Farmville      131

Bum's Restaurant—Ayden      132

The Skylight Inn—Ayden      136

Morris Barbeque—Hookerton      140

King's Barbecue & Chicken—Kinston      142

B. J.'s Grill and BBQ—La Grange      144

Ken's Grill—La Grange      145

Adams Roadside Bar-B-Que—Goldsboro      147

McCall's Barbecue and Seafood—Goldsboro,
   Clayton      149

Wilber's Barbecue—Goldsboro      151

Grady's Barbecue—Dudley      156

Smithfield's Chicken 'N Bar-B-Q—Locations
   throughout North Carolina      161

White Swan Bar-B-Q & Fried Chicken—
   Smithfield, Benson, Clayton,
   Atlantic Beach      162

Charlie's BBQ & Grille—Clayton      165

Cape Fear Barbecue—Fayetteville      166

The Pik N Pig—Carthage      167

Fuller's Old Fashion BBQ—Lumberton,
   Fayetteville      169

Nelson's Barbecue—Lumberton      171

Village Inn Bar-B-Que and
   Seafood—Lumberton      172

Skipper Forsyth's Bar-B-Q—Henderson      174

Bob's Bar-B-Q—Creedmoor      175

Knightdale Seafood & Barbecue—
   Knightdale      180

Clyde Cooper's BBQ—Raleigh      181

The Pit Authentic Barbecue—Raleigh      186

Danny's Bar-B-Que—Cary, Durham,
   Morrisville      188

Smokey's BBQ Shack—Morrisville      190

Stephenson's Bar-B-Q—Willow Spring      195

Backyard BBQ Pit—Durham      197

Bullock's Bar-B-Cue—Durham      199

Hog Heaven Barbecue—Durham      201

Hillsborough BBQ Company—
   Hillsborough      202

Allen & Son Barbeque—Chapel Hill      204

The Pig—Chapel Hill      208

Allen & Son Bar-B-Que—Pittsboro      210

Hursey's Pig Pickin' Bar-B-Q—Burlington,
   Graham      211

Short Sugar's Pit Bar-B-Q—Reidsville      214

Fuzzy's Pit-Cooked Bar-B-Q—Madison      216

Country Barbeque—Greensboro 219

Stamey's Old Fashioned Barbecue— Greensboro 220

Clark's Barbecue—Kernersville 224

Prissy Polly's Bar-B-Que—Kernersville 225

Stratford Bar-B-Que—King 227

Hill's Lexington Barbecue—Winston-Salem 228

Little Richard's Barbecue—Winston-Salem, Wallburg 229

Mr. Barbecue—Winston-Salem 231

Pig Pickin's of America—Winston-Salem 232

Snook's Old Fashion Barbecue—Advance 234

Deano's Barbecue—Mocksville 235

Red Pig Bar-B-Q House—Mocksville 236

Kepley's Barbecue—High Point 240

Kerley's Barbecue—Welcome 241

Blue Mist Bar-B-Q—Asheboro 242

Troutman's B-B-Q—Denton 243

Bar-B-Q Center—Lexington 245

Cook's Barbecue—Lexington 247

Jimmy's BBQ—Lexington 249

Hendrix Barbecue—Lexington, Salisbury, Spencer 251

Lexington Barbecue—Lexington 253

Smiley's Lexington BBQ—Lexington 257

Smokey Joe's Barbecue—Lexington 258

Speedy Lohr's BBQ of Arcadia—Lexington 261

Tarheel Q—Lexington 262

Stamey's Barbecue of Tyro 264

Backcountry Barbeque—Linwood 265

College Bar-B-Que—Salisbury 266

Richard's Bar-B-Q—Salisbury 268

Wink's: The King of Barbecue—Salisbury 269

Keaton's Barbecue—Cleveland 270

Gary's Bar-B-Q—China Grove 272

M & K Bar-B-Q & Country Cookin'—Granite Quarry 273

Log Cabin BBQ—Albemarle 275

Whispering Pines BBQ—Albemarle 276

Troutman's Bar-B-Q—Concord 277

Lancaster's BBQ—Huntersville, Mooresville 278

Bubba's Barbecue—Charlotte 280

Mac's Speed Shop—Charlotte, Cornelius 282

Old Hickory House Restaurant—Charlotte 284

Carolina Bar-B-Q—Statesville 285

Alston Bridges Barbecue—Shelby 287

Bridges Barbecue Lodge—Shelby 290

The Flying Pig—Shelby 293

Brushy Mountain Smokehouse and Creamery/ Brushy Mountain Café—North Wilkesboro, North Millers Creek 296

Smoky Mountain Barbecue— West Jefferson 297

The Woodlands Barbecue & Pickin' Parlor— Blowing Rock 299

Okie Dokies Smokehouse—Swannanoa 300

Gone but Not Forgotten 303

Postscript 315

Index 316

Denotes "North Carolina Classic" barbecue restaurants which have special legacies, longevity, or historical significances as well as outstanding fare and pit-cooking practices.

*Right:* Clyde Cooper's BBQ, Raleigh

Since the 1500s, when the Spanish introduced them in the South, pigs have been plentiful in North Carolina. Around the Tar Heel State, barbecue is a noun that nearly always refers to chopped or pulled pork.
*Courtesy of the North Carolina State Archives*

# ACKNOWLEDGMENTS

I want to express my sincere appreciation to the many people who helped make this book possible.

First of all, I am grateful to photographer and writer Keith Barnes of Wilson for his incredibly valuable assistance and suggestions, as well as for several wonderful photographs. Keith's input improved this project immeasurably.

I am indebted to the management and staff of UNC-TV, whose support and enthusiasm through the years for my many barbecue segments and programs, as well as my general restaurant reviews, have helped create an entirely new career niche for me. I am particularly appreciative of the assistance of David Hardy, Scott Marsh, Dennis Beiting, and Michael O'Connell with elements of this book. Thanks also to my longtime videographer and friend Mike Oniffrey for the many still photos—including several reproduced in this volume—he has graciously supplied during our more than twenty years of working together.

A special word of appreciation goes to Kim Cumber of the North Carolina State Archives, Keith Longiotti of the North Carolina Collection at the University of North Carolina at Chapel Hill, Catherine Hoffman of the Davidson County Historical Museum,

and Shannon Sweeney of the St. Louis Art Museum.

Thanks to the following persons for valuable assistance with photographs: Woodie Anderson, Michael Pittman, Jes Gearing, Kristin Garcia, Bill Walsh, Bill Stancill, Dwayne Padon, Harry Blair, Will Thorp, Charlie Carden, Randy McNeilly, Amanda Munger, Claire Alley, Marcie Cohen Ferris, Steve Dunning, Don Sturkey, and Mark Johnson.

Finally, I extend my deepest appreciation to my lovely wife, Ruthie, and to my son Everett, both of whom served cheerfully and well as researchers and assistants, and to my children Anna Barrett, Van, Nelson, and Jessica, as well as to all my grandchildren, for their belief in me and their constant support.

Some of what follows was published originally in my first book, *North Carolina Barbecue: Flavored by Time*, although I have vastly expanded the restaurant section to encompass reviews of 101 barbecue joints across North Carolina—one more than the number included in my 2002 book, *Bob Garner's Guide to North Carolina Barbecue*. New and revised material supplements and brings up to date what I have drawn from those previous books.

BBQ

Silver Moon barbecue restaurant near Greensboro, 1937
Courtesy of the North Carolina State Archives

Barbecue has always been the food of celebration in North Carolina. This shot shows attendees eating barbecue at the Sedgefield Hunt in Greensboro.
*Courtesy of the North Carolina State Archives*

Raymond Stith worked on a sharecropper's farm near Rocky Mount during the 1930s. His lithograph
*Southern Barbecue* was produced through an arts program of the Work Projects Administration (WPA),
the largest of the Depression-era New Deal agencies.
*Courtesy of St. Louis Art Museum*

# INTRODUCTION

What is it about barbecue that makes it as enjoyable to talk about as it is to eat—especially here in North Carolina?

For one thing, remembrances associated with barbecue connect us to a three-hundred-year heritage, both real and romanticized. Since the dawn of the automobile era, opinions about who prepares the best barbecue, like political attitudes, have been a legacy handed down solemnly from one generation to the next in the small towns and farming hamlets of eastern and Piedmont North Carolina. (For some reason, the mountain area has never enjoyed much of a barbecue tradition.)

In earlier days, the names of pioneering barbecue restaurateurs were spoken in reverent tones, usually by the males of the family, and the infrequent meal at one of those hallowed establishments was something like worshiping in church, as eyes closed and heads shook slowly and wordlessly back and forth over the evidence of grace bestowed in the form of peppery chopped pork. In the intervals between such rites, frequent reminiscing no doubt elevated the quality of the barbecue to mythical proportions.

The renewed availability of cars and fuel at the end of World War II made searching for the best barbecue a pastime and a popular topic of conversation for returning servicemen and their families. Another new phenomenon, the drive-in restaurant, made sampling and comparison easy. Joint-hopping patrons soon were served thousands of warm, moist, coleslaw-crowned barbecue sandwiches, wrapped in wax paper and brought outside on trays that clamped onto car windows.

But barbecue and its discourse go back even farther. Wispy blue smoke floating above a coppery brown split pig, hissing and crackling over winking coals, drifts back across generations of small farmers, sharecroppers, merchants, and traders, finally reaching the native inhabitants of northeastern North Carolina and Tidewater Virginia, who almost certainly passed along the art of barbecuing to the settlers. It quickly spread throughout the region. But in the aristocracies of those "mountains of conceit," Virginia and South Carolina, barbecuing was often relegated to slaves, its secrets beneath the notice of polite society. However, within North Carolina's "vale of humility," barbecuing was with a few exceptions the occupation of farmers and journeymen, white and black, and its arts, methods, and mysteries were endlessly discussed and debated. That tradition has remained. Today, North Carolinians who barbecue for a hobby or profitable sideline—and there are thousands of them—would list conversation and comparing notes at dozens of festivals and cookoffs at the top of their lists of reasons for practicing their hot, smoky art.

A bottomless saucepot of esoterica and detail is enjoyed by North Carolina barbecue buffs, just as it is by those who engage in the strange barbecue practices of other states. As food writer Craig Claiborne noted in the *New*

Pigs pit-cooked for Bladen County political event, 1939
*Photo by the News & Observer of Raleigh, N.C., courtesy of the North Carolina State Archives*

Barbecue stand operated in Wayne County by John "Jack" Lynch, date unknown
*Courtesy of North Carolina Collection, University of North Carolina at Chapel Hill*

*York Times*, "Differences center on the type of meat used (pork, beef or poultry) or its cut (pork shoulders, spareribs or whole pig); the sauce (tomato based or vinegar with spices); the accompaniments (should coleslaw be tossed with mayonnaise or barbecue sauce?); or which woods impart the best flavor (hickory and/or oak or, more recently, mesquite). Should you baste or not? How do you prefer the meat: chopped, sliced, in chunks? In a sandwich or on a tray?"

Claiborne didn't tackle other differences: Is your pit open or enclosed with a chimney? How far do you place the meat above the coals? Do you cover the meat while it's cooking (to keep ashes from settling on it) or leave it uncovered? Once the meat is cooked, do you leave it on the fire overnight to impart more wood flavor? How finely do you chop the meat? And do you do it by hand, with a cleaver, or by machine?

And then there's the great North Caro-lina barbecue schism between east and west. Because of different settlement patterns, two distinct barbecue styles developed in North Carolina: whole-hog in the coastal plain, shoulders-only in the Piedmont. But that distinction, together with the differences between eastern and western sauces and the regional variations in what are considered appropriate barbecue side dishes, have provided grist for an endlessly revolving mill of barbecue debate. It has also given North Carolina an undeserved national reputation for barbecue schizophrenia that, to outsiders, sullies the state's claim to having the best barbecue on the planet. The *New Yorker*'s Calvin Trillin wrote in his book *Alice, Let's Eat* of being "subjected to stern geographical probings" when he mentioned to former North Carolina residents that he had sampled barbecue in their home state. And in *Southern Food*, John Egerton sniffed, "There are two basic styles of North Carolina barbecue, and

Barbecue has long been the staple food of North Carolina political gatherings.
*Courtesy of the North Carolina State Archives*

proponents of each are so disdainful of the other that doubt is cast on both."

But if the east-west controversy complicates our sales pitch to the outside world, it certainly makes life more interesting at home. If the truth were known, many of those hurling scorn and abuse at their barbecue cousins on the opposite side of Raleigh simply know how to get the most fun out of an argument and are playing a mischievous family tussle for all it's worth. Newspaper, magazine, and television reporters, including this one, are notorious for keeping the argument going long after everyone else is ready to drop it. Sometimes, there's even *intra*regional warfare. In the 1950s, Vernon Sechriest, then editor of the *Rocky Mount Evening Telegram*, and Henry Belk, then editor of the *News-Argus* in Goldsboro, started a friendly rivalry over which of their respective cities served the best barbecue. "No self-respecting pig would wind up as a morsel of vinegar-tainted, half-burned nonsense as that served in Goldsboro," wrote Sechriest. Belk was content to reply smugly that Rocky Mount barbecue "has some resemblance to mush." The mock debate grew so fierce that the Associated Press, deciding to milk the story awhile longer, sent it out over the state wires.

Most of the millions of words written about North Carolina barbecue, however, have revolved around the contest for supremacy between east and west. Author and publisher Jerry Bledsoe, for years a columnist for the former *Greensboro Daily News*, carried on a long-running battle with Dennis Rogers of the *News & Observer*. Each regularly insisted—tongue firmly planted in cheek—that what passed for barbecue in the other's home region was nearly unfit for human consumption. "In the East, you get all these little things in your mouth and wonder what the hell they are," Bledsoe jeered. "They're ground-up skin. That's the only way they have to give the meat any flavor. So what you're getting is roast pork and ground skin with a little vinegar and hot peppers and salt on it." Rogers, taking aim at the Piedmont custom of offering sliced as well as chopped barbecue, answered, "When I am hankering for a big piece of dead hog meat with tomato sauce, I like to follow the advice of my good friend Jerry Bledsoe and head west, where you find lots of it. For some silly reason, Jerry calls that barbecue."

Politicians probably love talking barbecue even more than writers because they feel it's a good way to connect with voters in terms of shared experience. Discussing the finer points of 'cue or tearing off a slab of meat at a pig picking gives a high-born candidate just the right hint of the common touch, while an office seeker from humbler circumstances can proudly out-redneck everyone on the subject.

Barbecue probably became linked to politics in the late 1930s and early 1940s, the heyday of the "political caravan"—a gaggle of campaigning politicians traveling in cars and buses. The caravans would pull into a town for a series of speeches, followed by a barbecue feed and handshaking. Thad Eure, who served as North Carolina's secretary of state for sixty years and who called himself "the oldest rat in the Democratic barn," recalled, "They'd advertise barbecue so much that whenever the caravan would move down the highways and roads in the state, all the pigs and hogs would see them coming and get out of the way."

While barbecue serves a useful political purpose, it can also be taxing on the body and soul over the length of a campaign. But once they're elected, the state's politicians—in Washington and in Raleigh—like nothing better than showing off the delights of their district by hosting a barbecue meal for their colleagues, often forging alliances or resolving differences over barbecue, slaw, and hush puppies or corn sticks brought in for the occasion from some big-name local restaurant.

But the main reason we seldom tire of talking about barbecue is that it represents one of the few remaining antidotes to the mind-numbing homogeneity of the chain restaurants and fast-food joints that sucks the color from our travel today. Nothing comes closer to reflecting local character than a good barbecue place—or at least that is what we would like to believe. In any case, whether we prefer to search for it off the beaten track or carefully choose it because of its longstanding reputation, enthusing about "that great barbecue place" is one of the honest pleasures of life in North Carolina.

For most of us, the tongue fails when it comes to expressing the delights—and the significance—of barbecue. But oh, what might we say if *we* were poets like eastern North Carolina native James Applewhite?

Barbecue Service

I have sought the elusive aroma
Around outlying cornfields, turned
  corners
Near the site of a Civil War surrender.
The transformation may take place
At a pit no wider than a grave,
Behind a single family's barn.
Those weathered ministers
Preside with the simplest of elements;
Vinegar and pepper, split pig and fire.
Underneath a glistening mountain in air,
Something is converted to a savor: the pig
Flesh purified by far atmosphere.
Like the slick-sided sensation from last
  summer,
A fish pulled quick from a creek

By a boy. Like breasts in a motel
With whiskey and twilight
Now a blue smoke in memory.
This smolder draws the soul of our
  longings.

I want to see all the old home folks,
Ones who may not last another year.
We will rock on porches like chapels
And not say anything, their faces
Impenetrable as different barks of trees.
After the brother who drank has been
  buried,
The graveplot stunned by sun
In the woods,
We men still living pass the bottle.
We barbecue pigs.
The tin-roofed sheds with embers
Are smoking their blue sacrifice
Across Carolina.

*Friends of the Library of North Carolina Wesleyan College, 1986*

BOB
GARNER'S
# BOOK
# OF
# BARBECUE

German settlers who journeyed by way of the Great Wagon Road from Pennsylvania ultimately influenced the style of barbecue that developed in the North Carolina Piedmont.

*Courtesy of the North Carolina State Archives*

# A THREE-HUNDRED-YEAR TRADITION

Lovers of genuine North Carolina barbecue sometimes complain, with a slight touch of superiority, that some outside the borders of the state don't seem to understand—as all true Tar Heels do—that the word *barbecue* refers to what is produced on a rack above a bed of coals, and not to the cooking apparatus itself. Someone from New York might say, for example, "Let's cook hot dogs and hamburgers on the barbecue." Even farther afield, Australian actor Paul Hogan became a familiar face to American television viewers even before he starred in the *Crocodile Dundee* films when he appeared in tourism commercials promising prospective visitors that their Australian hosts would "put an extra shrimp on the 'barbie.'"

Sorry, folks, but it looks like the Yankees and the Aussies have us on this one. The staid, old *Oxford English Dictionary* tells us our beloved *b* word comes from the Spanish *barbacoa*. The word originated in the seventeenth century on the island of Hispaniola and was used to describe "a framework of sticks set upon posts," before quickly broadening into a verb to describe the process of cooking on such a framework. Barbecuing was evidently well established among the Indians of the Caribbean because a 1661 book describing Jamaica mentioned native inhabitants who hunted wild game "and their flesh forthwith Barbacu'd and eat."

(Note: Scholars have ridiculed the notion that the word *barbecue* comes from the French expression *barbe à queue*, meaning "beard to tail," saying it's a trivial conjecture suggested merely by the sound of the phrase. But don't tell that to old barbecue hands. The late Walter B. "Pete" Jones of The Skylight Inn in Ayden claimed his family has served the specialty since the mid-1800s. A staunch advocate of whole-hog barbecue, Pete insisted, "The *barb*'s the snout and the tail's the *q*, which means you don't really have barbecue unless you have the whole pig cooked over wood coals—*barb* to *q*." Perhaps early colonists noticed the similarity between the terms and began using them interchangeably, enjoying the play on words and the aptness of the French expression as a description of the way they had seen barbecue being prepared.)

The term followed trade routes from the West Indies and quickly became known in Virginia. Before the end of the 1600s, the colony passed a law banning the shooting of firearms at barbecues. Actually, English colonists in the lower James River settlements may have learned barbecuing from the Indians even before word spread from the Caribbean and were probably the first Europeans in the New World to adopt the practice. Since

Tidewater Virginia and northeastern North Carolina were similar in geography and customs, it's reasonable to assume that eastern North Carolina residents also picked up the roasting method from native inhabitants or their northern neighbors. They were enjoying barbecue well before the beginning of the eighteenth century.

The Indian barbecuing method was to burn a large oak or hickory log on a grate until the coals fell through. The coals were shoveled into a hole in the ground, and the meat was placed on a rack above them to cook. With only minor variations, dressed, split pigs have been roasted over coals in just this way for over three centuries in North Carolina. The practice was so commonplace by 1728 that William Byrd of Virginia took note of it in his chronicle of the surveying of the border between his state and North Carolina. Of eastern North Carolina, Byrd wrote,

Small pigs being barbecued in an open-pit in Hertford County, 1930s
*Courtesy of the North Carolina State Archives*

"The only business here is the raising of hogs, which is managed with the least trouble and affords the diet they are most fond of. The truth of it is, the inhabitants of North Carolina devour so much swine's flesh that it fills them full of gross humors."

Catawba College history professor Gary Freeze has a well-developed, if unproven, theory that the barbecue practices of the Piedmont were heavily influenced by German immigrants who came south from Pennsylvania to North Carolina by way of the Great Wagon Road through Virginia's Shenandoah Valley during the mid- to late eighteenth century. Freeze's research into the hog-butchering practices of the Pennsylvania Germans (which were different from the English methods practiced in the coastal plain) suggests that the pork shoulder was one of their favorite cuts of meat, and that it was usually braised in a fruit-flavored liquid not dissimilar in taste to today's Lexington barbecue sauce. Freeze points out that many of the best-known early barbecue experts in the Piedmont had German names—Weaver, Ridenhour, and Swicegood, for example—and that some of the earliest Piedmont barbecuing was done in heavily German cotton-mill villages.

Since barbecue and Protestant Christianity are both of enormous significance in North Carolina, it is only fitting that a church named after the custom came into being fairly early in the state's history. Barbecue Presbyterian Church was established in Harnett County near Sanford in 1757. The church actually got its name from nearby Barbecue

Creek, named by a Scottish explorer, Red Neil McNeill, who said the mist rising off the stream reminded him of smoke from barbecue pits he had seen in the West Indies.

When one makes the obvious comparison among the catechisms of the various Christian denominations and the dogmas associated with different barbecue styles, it's actually surprising there isn't an Eastern Barbecue Church and a Western Barbecue Church. Certainly, there is no more agreement on the fine points of doctrine between adherents of the two barbecue types than, say, a Hard Shell Baptist and a Presbyterian. But all God's children *are* unified, not only by the central tenets of faith but also by the overarching reality that much of the Lord's work in the state is performed with funds raised from barbecue. In fact, church barbecues are now ubiquitous and have, as the commerce department might say, assumed a vital role in the preparation, distribution, and consumption of barbecue in North Carolina. The two biggest barbecue gatherings in North Carolina are hosted by churches—both of them, coincidentally, in Charlotte. Mallard Creek Presbyterian Church's barbecue has been an annual event since 1929, while Williams Memorial Presbyterian started its yearly fundraiser in 1945. Since both events are held in the fall, patrons must pass through a gauntlet of glad-handing politicians campaigning for office in order to reach the serving lines.

Barbecue may have played a direct role in the establishment of at least one other North Carolina church. In 1775, Henry Evans, a free black Methodist cobbler and preacher, stopped in Fayetteville on his way from Virginia to Charleston. Disturbed by the spiritual condition in which he found the African-Americans of the area, Evans decided to stay and preach. He soon attracted such large crowds that authorities banned him from the city, so Evans began holding clandestine meetings in the woods and sand hills, often moving from place to place to avoid harassment. (The "underground" or "invisible" church was already a Southern tradition among slaves prohibited from attending regular worship services. Those who slipped away to listen to the hours of preaching at these churches were often fed by barbecuing one or two young shoats over flameless beds of coals to prevent detection.) The white Christians of Fayetteville eventually became so impressed by Evans's zeal and the obvious change in his followers that they invited him to preach openly in the city. Local tradition maintains that this change of heart occurred just after white citizens searching the area discovered—and ate—a hastily abandoned pig barbecued at the site of one of Evans's meetings. Whether barbecue was the turning point of this drama or not, a church and later a retirement home were built for Evans in Fayetteville. He died in 1810, having brought Methodism to Cumberland County, the first Methodist church to Fayetteville, and probably the best barbecued pig eaten in the region up to that point.

In Ayden, near Greenville, Pete Jones's great-great-grandfather Skilton M. Dennis is said to have begun barbecuing pigs in the mid-1800s to feed large church camp meetings. He also sold barbecue to the public from a chuck wagon. At that time, Ayden was known as "Ottertown" or "A Den" (as in "a den of thieves"). Jones said that early beginning proved his claim that his family has been in the barbecue business longer than any other in North Carolina. But there is no record of a continuously operating commercial barbecue business since that time. Throughout the nineteenth century, barbecuing pigs was an art practiced largely either by those entertaining friends and family or by itinerant barbecue men who plied their trade part-time at school commencements, camp meetings, fairs, and festivals.

Around 1915, Adam Scott, a black janitor and elevator operator from Goldsboro, cooked his first barbecue for a social gathering of white businessmen. The guests declared it the best 'cue they had ever eaten, and the idea that there might be a future in barbecue was planted in Scott's mind. Although Scott continued to cater occasional parties, it wasn't until almost ten years later, when he was an employee of a local bank, that he started regularly cooking pigs on weekends in a backyard pit and selling the meat. Before long, Scott was serving meals on his back porch. By 1933, he had enclosed the porch and turned it into a dining room—one that would eventually be enlarged three times. Prominent white citizens were soon rubbing elbows with Scott's neighbors and farmers from the countryside. Patrons often had to stand in line in Scott's backyard as they waited to get into his flourishing establishment. One of those who dined on Scott's back

Preparing a barbecue tray at Adam Scott's barbecue restaurant in Goldsboro
*Photo by Sharpe*
*Courtesy of the*
*North Carolina State Archives*

porch, presumably without having to stand in line for too long, was the late governor J. Melville Broughton.

In the late 1940s, Adam Scott turned the restaurant over to his son, Martel Sr., and moved to Winston-Salem to become the personal barbecue chef for R. J. Reynolds Jr. (He also had an active second career as a preacher and revivalist.) Scott's restaurant closed several years back but has now reopened, although only for lunch, and only on a couple of days per week. It is run by Adam's grandson, Martel Jr. The family name has become a household word because of Scott's commercially bottled barbecue sauce, sold in grocery stores across the state.

What may have been the state's first sit-down barbecue restaurant was opened by Bob Melton of Rocky Mount, who died in 1958 at the age of eighty-eight after having been crowned by *Life* magazine as "the king of southern barbecue." Melton was a merchant and horse trader who started cooking barbecue around Rocky Mount as a hobby in 1919. He built a barbecue shed on the Tar River in 1922. Two years later, he constructed a restaurant on the same quiet, shady spot where a rebuilt Melton's stood for many years before the restaurant went out of business around 2002. (That original site was flood-prone. Patrons occasionally had to row to Melton's in boats to pick up orders of

ABOVE: Bob Melton stands on the steps of his restaurant, built adjacent to the flood-prone Tar River.

RIGHT: Rocky Mount's Bob Melton

barbecue.) Melton is also widely considered the man who firmly established the style of preparing barbecue that much of eastern North Carolina later adopted as its own: whole hogs cooked over oak or hickory coals, finely chopped and fairly dry, seasoned before serving with a touch of the same sauce—vinegar, salt, black pepper, and red pepper (finely ground *and* in flakes)—used to baste the roasting pig. Rocky Mount, a railroad and tobacco-market town, was a barbecue center for years before neighboring Wilson. Boasting an even bigger tobacco market, Wilson weighed in with several restaurants such as Braswell's, Sutton's, Godwin's, and eventually Parker's. Goldsboro, thanks to Adam Scott, had long been touting its own barbecue tradition. Even today, those three cities—Rocky Mount, Wilson, and Goldsboro—account for the vast majority of good barbecue restaurants in eastern North Carolina, by almost anyone's reckoning.

A good distance to the west in the town of Lexington, quite a different barbecue heritage was established during the early 1900s. A few barbecuers followed the preferences of their German ancestors in hardwood-roasting pork *shoulders*—as opposed to the whole pig—for special occasions. They started holding occasional public cookouts, dubbing the events "Everybody's Day." Soon, some of these barbecuers began cooking for an entire week at a time when court was being held, since the sessions brought a steady stream of country dwellers to town. In 1919, Sid Weaver and George Ridenhour put up a tent opposite

Barbecue pioneer Sid Weaver cooked shoulders on a pit in his Lexington backyard.
*Courtesy of Davidson County Historical Museum, Lexington, N.C.*

Sid Weaver (*left*) and partner George Ridenhour in front of their early Lexington barbecue stand
*Courtesy of Stamey's Old Fashioned Barbecue, Greensboro, N.C.*

the courthouse that became the first more or less permanent barbecue stand in Lexington. Not long afterward, Jess Swicegood raised a tent directly alongside that one and went into head-to-head competition with Weaver, who had already bought out Ridenhour. Weaver later replaced his tent with a small building, and Swicegood followed suit.

It was at this point that one of North Carolina's most impressive barbecue legacies began to develop. Around 1927, high-school student C. Warner Stamey began working part-time for Jess Swicegood, learning the art of slow-cooking pork shoulders over oak and hickory coals for nine to ten hours, then removing the skin and fat and gently pulling the

Lexington's Jess Swicegood at his original barbecue stand
*Courtesy of Stamey's Old Fashioned Barbecue, Greensboro, N.C.*

meat apart into chunks, the larger ones for slicing, the smaller for chopping. The meat was roasted with no basting but was moistened before serving with ingredients matching the basic eastern sauce, to which a small amount of ketchup and sugar were added.

Stamey dreamed early on of having his own place. In 1930, he moved to Shelby and opened a barbecue restaurant modeled after Swicegood's first stand, a tent with sawdust on the floor. During the next few years, he taught the Lexington method to his wife's brother, Alston Bridges, and to Red Bridges (no relation). When Stamey moved back to Lexington in the mid-1930s, he left behind two men whose Lexington-style barbecue fiefdoms would flourish in Shelby for the next sixty years and whose reputations would extend across the South. Alston Bridges Barbecue and Bridges Barbecue Lodge, Red's place, are still family-run operations serving barbecue cooked according to the secrets patiently passed along by Warner Stamey.

In 1938, Stamey bought the place in Lexington where he had learned his trade from Jess Swicegood. In the early 1950s, he taught his special methods to a young man named Wayne Monk. The longtime owner and oper-

Warner Stamey (*right*) taught Lexington methods to many other successful restaurateurs.
*Courtesy of Davidson County Historical Museum, Lexington, N.C.*

ator of Lexington Barbecue (formerly called Lexington Barbecue #1), Monk is probably the most accomplished and famous barbecue guru in North Carolina today.

But the Stamey influence had not finished spreading. Stamey moved to Greensboro and in 1953 opened a restaurant at a site on High Point Road that is now a landmark opposite the Greensboro Coliseum. About that same time, Stamey—a tireless innovator when it came to pit design, menu modification, and countless other refinements—tried another experiment that changed the North Carolina barbecue experience forever. Be-

fore the 1950s, barbecue had been routinely served on or with white bread or rolls, except for the occasional baked cornbread in the east. Borrowing a feature from the fish camps he had visited, Stamey began serving hush puppies—balls or fingers of deep-fried cornmeal batter—with his barbecue. Today, with very few exceptions, hush puppies are considered the standard accompaniment to barbecue and are served from one end of North Carolina to the other. (Pete Jones's Skylight Inn and B's Barbecue and Grill serve squares of baked corn bread, while several eastern North Carolina establishments offer corn

Stamey's original Greensboro restaurant opened in 1953.
*Courtesy of Stamey's Old Fashioned Barbecue, Greensboro, N.C.*

sticks—long, slender pieces of corn bread that are baked, then deep-fried.)

To this day, rolls are optional with barbecue at Stamey's two Greensboro restaurants and are routinely eaten instead of hush puppies by some old-timers. The original Stamey's drive-in on High Point Road was opened in 1952 and replaced in 1979 by a beautiful ranch-style restaurant. Just inside the front door hangs a portrait of Warner Stamey, the man who spread the gospel of Lexington-style barbecue far and wide.

While some legendary barbecue restaurants are being run by second- and third-generation family members, other well-known places such as Bob Melton's Barbecue and Mebane's A & M Grill have gone out of business in recent years, in some cases because the owners' families weren't interested in carrying on the tradition. But while some among the newer generations of restaurant operators say they aren't willing to invest the long hours and backbreaking work necessary to produce great barbecue, a surprising number of barbecue places have opened in recent years. Some have streamlined the wood-cooking process without abandoning it entirely by moving toward gas- or electric-fired wood smokers. Others have practically guaranteed themselves a tough way of making a living by building old-fashioned over-the-coals pits, which demand much personal attention.

Interest in barbecue has probably never been higher among consumers. The fires are fanned by a plethora of food and cooking shows on cable television, specialized barbecue newsletters, and dozens of pig-cooking contests and festivals spread across North Carolina from Wilmington to Tryon. Back in 1977, columnist Jerry Bledsoe wrote a piece urging the city of Lexington to "bring back 'Everybody's Day,' throw up the tents and have a big annual barbecue festival with music and dancing and other festivities to celebrate this regional delicacy." A few years later, Lexington began doing exactly that. Today, the Lexington Barbecue Festival is the largest such event in the state. Considering the current popularity of what must be considered a dwindling art, we have to face the probability that North Carolina may have fewer really great barbecue places in the years ahead, but that those that remain will thrive for a long time to come.

# A NORTH CAROLINA BARBECUE PRIMER

## The World's Best Barbecue?

I t is an eternally subjective issue, drawing personal taste, regional chauvinism, hyperbole, and friendly boasting into a cacophony of competing claims that will never be settled in our lifetime.

There's no question that some pundits have pronounced North Carolina barbecue the best they've ever eaten. Craig Claiborne, food columnist for the *New York Times*, has eaten in most of the country's best-known barbecue joints over the years and has stated unequivocally that the chopped pork served in North Carolina—both east and west—is definitely his favorite. *National Geographic* picked Pete Jones's Skylight Inn in Ayden

as its world-champion barbecue spot a few years back. And *Southern* magazine recognized Wilber's in Goldsboro as home of "the South's Best Barbecue." (This is even higher praise than it seems at first glance. How much really great barbecue is outside the South anyway?)

Other material can be brought in to support the claim. In the early 1980s, several developments helped gild the state's barbecue reputation, beginning with a well-publicized debate between Congressmen Gene Johnston of North Carolina and John Napier of South Carolina as to which state produced the best barbecue. To settle the issue, several restaurants from the two states each sent twenty to thirty pounds of barbecue to a big contest and barbecue banquet held in Washington. The 1981 event ended in a draw. But in 1982, Short Sugar's of Reidsville was declared the winner of the so-called North–South Carolina Barbecue Bowl. The following year, North Carolina's claim to barbecue superiority was further enhanced when President Ronald Reagan, eager to show off the best in authentic American cuisine, invited Wayne Monk of Lexington Barbecue to feed several European heads of state at a major international economic summit held in Williamsburg, Virginia. And in 1984, Hursey's of Burlington was named champion in the North–South Carolina Barbecue Bowl.

Native North Carolinians can naturally be expected to assert that the best barbecue comes from right here in the Tar Heel State—

especially if they end up moving to another state. In the late 1970s, North Carolina native Barry Farber—a controversial New York City radio talk-show host and unsuccessful mayoral candidate in the Big Apple—arranged with a Times Square restaurant to serve North Carolina barbecue prepared and shipped by Fuzzy's in Madison. Former UNC cheerleader Zacki Murphy of Hillsborough, a veteran model and television spokesperson, was likewise preoccupied for years with the challenge of introducing North Carolina barbecue to New Yorkers. Zacki started out selling PBQ—her term for pit-cooked barbecue—from a vending cart on the streets of New York in between modeling and TV assignments; later, she moved to a small storefront restaurant. Zacki's barbecue, like

An increasing number of North Carolina barbecue restaurants, such as Hillsborough BBQ Company, are offering not only chopped and sliced pork barbecue but also ribs, chicken, turkey, and beef brisket.

Farber's, was pit-cooked by Fuzzy's in Madison, but then it was mixed with her own special Lexington-style sauce and fast-frozen for quick delivery via truck. Although neither of these ventures lasted, Murphy is pursuing her interest in barbecue and in catering back home in North Carolina. New York designer Alexander Julian, a native of Chapel Hill, was fond of quipping that he designed the basketball uniforms for the NBA's former Charlotte Hornets at least partly in exchange for regular shipments of North Carolina barbecue, which he says is unmatched anywhere in the world.

There's something else to this sort of playful barbecue boasting. It has to do with the need to define who we are as individuals in a mass culture. Alan Pridgen, formerly an English professor at Chowan College in northeastern North Carolina, explored this idea in a scholarly paper he once presented to an academic conference on popular culture. He suggested that the urge to seek out and consume the *best* barbecue may be a subconscious search for an identity "rooted in a past of Jeffersonian small farmers who lived out their lives in close-knit families and communities where self-sufficiency, independence and social intimacy and trust were prized." According to Pridgen, "These values are symbolically imbedded in the contemporary North Carolinian's passion for his unique food and his unique culture"— all the more so, he said, since that culture has sometimes been characterized as impoverished and unsophisticated by mainstream America.

Boston butts (the upper half of the pork shoulder) roasting on an enclosed, wood-fired pit typical of the type found in the Piedmont

But if rating barbecue is all tied up in traditional values and pride of place—as well as a sort of reverse snobbery—the experiences of growing up invariably carry the most weight, meaning the best barbecue will probably be found in or near one's own hometown. On the other hand, those city dwellers and suburbanites who discover barbecue later in life have the pleasure of choosing from among various ready-made, secondhand rural identities. Settling on a favorite style of barbecue can be as much fun as dressing up in boots and a cowboy hat or developing a Southern drawl.

The best? It obviously depends on who you talk to. But one thing that *is* certain is that North Carolina barbecue is different from what you'll find everywhere else. I believe it's the only kind of barbecue in which the meat itself—rather than the smoke, the pepper, or the sauce—is the centerpiece. North Carolina pork, barbecued to perfection, has a naturally rich, sweet taste that is delicately flavored by smoke, not overcome by it like something dragged from a burning house. The slow-roasted chopped meat should have an overall light pink to light brown shade, appealingly set off by flecks of dark brown outside meat, and it should not be reddened by a smoke ring. Whether sliced or chopped, North Carolina 'cue at its best is moist (even before sauce) but not laced with fat, meltingly tender but firm in consistency, with the meat shredded into coarse fibers. And it should never be mushy or appear to be held together by congealed fat. Whether the preferred sauce is the peppery eastern va-

riety or the milder, sweeter Lexington-style, it is meant to merely add accent to the meat, not to cling like wallpaper paste or smother it with the taste of liquid hickory smoke, ketchup, molasses, sugar, bell pepper, or chili powder.

Let me point out here that I like the best examples of many types of barbecue from around the country: Memphis-style pulled pig, ribs (basted in sauce or treated with a dry-spice rub), Texas-style beef brisket, chicken, sausage—whatever. But the aroma of pork roasting over hardwood coals—along with the thought of treating my tongue to a warm, yielding barbecue sandwich on a cloud-soft bun, the sweet, tender shreds of pork perfectly complemented by a fiery hint of pepper and vinegar and the piquancy of coleslaw—draws me like a siren song. Unless it's really important to you, I suggest you leave off worrying about which style is better and simply enjoy North Carolina barbecue for what it is, and because it's unlike any other.

## The Great Divide: East Versus West

It could well be that the feuding between the eastern (or coastal plain) and Piedmont portions of the state has cost North Carolina a preeminent position in the nation's barbecue consciousness. Let's face it, we make it tough for someone outside the state to conclude that North Carolina serves the country's best barbecue when we can't even decide among ourselves what good barbecue is. I mean, are we that unsure about it? People from other states may be dead wrong in claiming that their barbecue is better than ours, but at least they usually pull together and argue for *their* native version with a passion and zeal that, in our case, fall exhausted in the dust somewhere between Lexington and Goldsboro.

On the other hand, we North Carolinians can certainly argue that we get more fun out of our barbecue than anyone else in America—not only in the eating experience but also by keeping our barbecue arguments inside the state, where we can enjoy them to the fullest, and to heck with what outsiders think. "You believe they cook better pig in Memphis? Fine. That leaves more of the real stuff for us."

But if you're going to get the most mileage out of the debate, you need to be up on the real differences between the styles of barbecue served in the east and the Piedmont. Actually, the two types are commonly known as "eastern" and either "Lexington" or "western," although the latter is something of a misnomer, since western North Carolina—the mountain area—is practically another state when it comes to barbecue. (You may find something *called* barbecue in some of the tourist destinations in the Smokies, but like the typical feathered Plains Indian style of headdress worn and sold in Cherokee, it isn't authentic to this state, but an import from the West.) For our purposes, "western" refers to the North Carolina Piedmont—from somewhere between Tryon in the west to Raleigh in the east.

You should also be aware that some quite knowledgeable barbecue enthusiasts think there isn't much difference between the two styles. The *New York Times*'s Craig Claiborne wrote, "To an experienced North Carolina barbecue addict, the difference between the Lexington and Down East versions might be pronounced. To me, they were subtle, the main one being the sauce ingredients. And even the absence of a slight tomato tang in the Down East sauce didn't make a whole lot of difference—vinegar is the key factor in both of them."

Much ado about nothing? Or a significant difference between east and west? No matter what you decide, you'll have a wonderful time doing the research.

## Eastern-Style Barbecue

Eastern North Carolina barbecue is *the* original American barbecue. (Even though barbecue probably originated in seventeenth-century Virginia, eastern-style barbecue generally hasn't survived well in the Old Dominion and is difficult to find there.) This coastal-plain barbecue is nearly always prepared from whole hogs. In earlier days, the split pigs were roasted over pits dug in the ground, into which oak or hickory coals were shoveled from a separate fire. Later, the pits were located under shelters or in sheds separated from the main restaurant. These became vertical structures—rectangular boxes of brick or cinder block from two to three feet high, with the grill resting a little below a top covered by a lid that could be raised and

*Top:* Eastern-style barbecue is often served with coleslaw, boiled potatoes, Brunswick stew, and hush puppies.

*Left:* Lexington-style barbecue is sold either chopped or sliced, usually with red "barbecue" coleslaw and hush puppies.

*Photos by Mike Burke*

lowered. The coals were spread at the bottom, around two feet below the grill, where they were fanned by air circulating through vents near the floor. Some eastern pits used to have a metal layer several inches *above* the grill on which coals were spread, so that heat came from both top and bottom, eliminating the need to turn the pig midway through the cooking process. Nowadays, so many eastern North Carolina barbecue houses have begun cooking with gas or electricity that there is hardly a standard pit design in the region. The usual practice in the east is to begin roasting the hogs skin side up for the first few hours, then turn them meat side up. During the cooking process, the meat is often periodically basted with the same sauce used later to season the chopped barbecue.

True eastern North Carolina barbecue sauce is different from what you'll find anywhere else in the United States in that it contains no tomato extracts. It seems seventeenth- and eighteenth-century colonists wouldn't eat tomatoes because of the prevailing belief that they were poisonous. They often prepared their pit-roasted pig with vinegar seasoned with peppers and oysters. This is still the basic sauce used in the east both for basting pigs as they cook and seasoning the barbecue once it's chopped. It consists primarily of vinegar, water, salt, black pepper, red pepper, and both finely ground cayenne and the dried, crushed variety—but no oysters. It is a fiery blend, the chief sensory impression being of hot, salty vinegar. Literally thousands of variations on the basic recipe exist, and favorite sauces are likely to include a dozen other spices, their identities a closely guarded secret. But every eastern sauce at least begins with the vinegar-salt-pepper trinity. A true eastern sauce not only has no tomatoes, it also has no added sugar, molasses, corn syrup, or other sweeteners, although some eastern barbecuers occasionally add some form of sweetener to a "dipping" sauce to be served at a pig picking, leaving it out of the sauce used for basting and seasoning chopped barbecue.

Sometimes, eastern North Carolina barbecue is seasoned "freehand" after it's chopped, meaning that salt, black pepper, and red pepper are sprinkled on and mixed into the chopped meat, which is then moistened with plain vinegar. Barbecue seasoned in this way is likely to find its way to your plate speckled with visible crushed red-pepper flakes or seeds. The importance of sauce or seasonings to the taste of eastern North Carolina barbecue has grown in recent years, as more and more big-name barbecuers have begun roasting their pigs with gas or electricity, rather than cooking over hardwood coals.

Despite the prevalence of basting in the coastal plain, much eastern barbecue also seems to have a drier consistency than that found in the Piedmont. This is partially because of the drier "white" meat from hams and tenderloins that goes into whole-hog barbecue. It may also have something to do with the fact that many high-volume eastern barbecue houses have stopped chopping their cooked pork by hand, opting instead to use machines. These machines not only give a finer "minced" texture to the barbecue but also tend to dry it out a bit. James Vilas, who wrote an article for *Esquire* years ago called "My Pig Beats Your Cow," described the eastern product as "dry, salty barbecue."

The more arid barbecue of the east is superbly complemented by the side dish that most often accompanies it: Brunswick stew, whose sweetness contrasts perfectly with the saltiness of the meat, and whose extravagant moistness balances eastern barbecue's drier texture. Some folks—myself included—enjoy mixing a dollop or two of this thick, reddish orange stew into a serving of eastern barbecue. Originally made with squirrel meat, Brunswick stew today most often contains chicken and/or pork and/or beef. In my opinion, Brunswick stew served with barbecue should contain only boned chicken, tomatoes, potatoes, onions, corn, and lima beans,

plus seasonings. Shredded, cooked pork can be added if the stew is not to be served as an accompaniment to pork, but I still prefer only white meat—no beef—in this dish. If cream-style corn is used, as it often is in the east, no further sweetening is necessary; otherwise, sugar is generally added according to taste. Brunswick stew is less likely to accompany barbecue in the Piedmont. It becomes increasingly rare as you move westward. And when you do find it, it's often a throw-every-thing-into-the-pot mishmash.

Almost as traditional as Brunswick stew as an eastern side dish are the ubiquitous "barbecued" potatoes found throughout the coastal plain. These have a bland or ever-so-slightly sweet taste that perfectly offsets the acidity of the tart, peppery barbecue. They're really nothing more than white potatoes cut

Brunswick stew, which originated in Virginia, is a common accompaniment to whole-hog barbecue in eastern North Carolina. Many families and groups gather during autumn to "cook a stew."

Boiled potatoes are a traditional side dish with barbecue in the coastal plain. These potatoes were being peeled for a huge Rocky Mount–area barbecue in 1944.
*Photo by Hemmer, courtesy of the North Carolina State Archives*

in large chunks and boiled, often with a little onion, tomato sauce, sugar, and bacon drippings added to the water in the pot. But while boiled potatoes are an eastern staple, they pretty much disappear in barbecue spots west of the Raleigh city limits.

Hush puppies are nearly universal in North Carolina barbecue restaurants, but corn sticks are another firmly entrenched eastern barbecue tradition, particularly around Raleigh and Wilson. These slender, eight-inch fingers of corn bread are first baked in a mold, then fried in a deep-fat cooker. The outside of a corn stick has a crunchy texture similar to that of a hush puppy, but the inside is heavier and more dense and has a taste similar to corn bread

prepared without baking powder or flour. As a matter of fact, some eastern barbecue houses such as Pete Jones's Skylight Inn in Ayden and B's in Greenville serve plain baked corn bread—simply cornmeal, salt, eggs, and water—rather than either corn sticks or hush puppies. (One idiosyncrasy of eastern North Carolinians is that they often use *corn bread* as a universal term to refer to all cornmeal-based concoctions, whether baked, griddled, or deep-fried.)

Because Brunswick stew, barbecued potatoes, and even fried chicken are served so often as side dishes in eastern barbecue houses, coleslaw is more of a garnish in the east than it is in the Piedmont, where slaw and hush puppies are likely to be the only accompaniments to the barbecue. The slaw of the east ordinarily contains either mayonnaise or a mayonnaise-mustard mixture, so that it ranges in color from white to bright yellow. Sweet pickle cubes are often included in the eastern version, along with celery seed. Once in a while, you'll run across eastern slaw moistened simply with vinegar and sugar, with no mayonnaise or mustard.

In eastern North Carolina, barbecue has a strong and pleasant association with the region's tobacco culture. In the days before modern bulk curing, when tobacco was still hand-picked, hand-tied onto sticks, and hung in the rafters of curing barns by hand, many farmers celebrated the completion of this exhausting process by holding festive barbecues for the dozens of "hands" who had worked to put in the crop. A pig would be barbecued over an open pit that was often dug beneath the shelter of the tobacco barn, and the meat would be chopped, then served out of a large wooden tub. Today, the conclusion of the harvest is still often marked by barbecues and pig pickings.

It is no coincidence that the best eastern

In eastern North Carolina, pit-roasted whole hogs have traditionally been mopped with vinegar and pepper.
*Photo by Hemmer, courtesy of the North Carolina State Archives*

Those attending tobacco auctions similar to this one at Wilson's Center Brick Warehouse during the 1920s were likely to eat barbecue, which might be sold at a stand, in a restaurant, or even from the back of a wagon.
*Courtesy of Keith Barnes*

North Carolina barbecue was closely tied to the state's tobacco culture. Barbecues were often held to celebrate the end of harvesting and curing.
*Courtesy of the North Carolina State Archives*

barbecue restaurants are in the tobacco-market towns of Rocky Mount, Wilson, and Goldsboro. The *Wilson Mirror* of September 3, 1890, had this to say about the impending opening of that town's tobacco market: "September 10 will be a big day in Wilson, and 5,000 people are expected to be on hand to take part in the sales and to eat the barbecue and trimmings that will be provided by our wide-awake, liberal and generous merchants."

Writer and photographer Keith Barnes of Wilson included that account in his 2007 book, *The World's Greatest Tobacco Market:*

*A Pictorial History of Tobacco in Wilson, North Carolina.* Barnes went on to write in the *Wilson Daily Times* about a "barbecue restaurant row" that grew up across from the South Street warehouse that was home to the Wilson Tobacco Market in the late 1920s and early 1930s. Braswell's (originally operated under a different name), Sutton's, and another eatery stood immediately adjacent to one another, and all primarily served barbecue. Louise Hight of Wilson, who turned one hundred in March 2011, recounted to Barnes that the restaurant owned by her great-uncle

Braswell's Barbecue, part of a "barbecue restaurant row" across the street from a large tobacco warehouse in Wilson, 1931
*Courtesy of Keith Barnes*

David Braswell "had a sawdust floor and oil-cloth on the tables," and that the barbecue was cooked out back behind the building.

"But I mainly remember the good barbecue," Hight told Barnes. "They served nothing but barbecue (no slaw, 'taters or Brunswick stew) along with baked cornbread." Hight added that the three side-by-side barbecue places "were there for the tobacco market. And the barbecue they served was just as good as it is now, maybe better. So far as I know they all did a good business."

David Braswell's great-nephew Doug Braswell told Barnes that his father, Herbert, worked in the family restaurant and that, given the proximity of the tobacco warehouse, the barbecue "sold itself, just like popcorn in the theater."

According to Barnes, the other two restaurants eventually closed, but Braswell's moved to Tarboro Street and later became Godwin's. It thrived for decades and was an important forerunner to Parker's, Bill's, Cherry's, and other Wilson barbecue destinations.

It is still at restaurants like these that farmers often celebrate selling their tobacco with a convivial barbecue meal among friends and associates. In this region more than anywhere else, barbecue is the food that bespeaks good times and is a treat to be savored in the company of others.

## Lexington (Piedmont)-Style Barbecue

In the North Carolina Piedmont, barbecue is nearly universally derived from pork shoulders, rather than from the entire pig. A preference for the shoulder over the whole hog seems to have been noteworthy among German immigrants to the area. Photographs clearly show this regional peculiarity firmly established in the late 1920s. Modern-day experts like Wayne Monk of Lexington Barbecue say shoulders are easier to handle and produce not only juicier barbecue but far less waste than whole pigs. Western-style shoulders are usually slow-cooked for nine to twelve hours and covered with foil or cardboard to keep the ashes off. They're cooked meat side down for the first four hours or so, then turned. In this part of the state, meat is not basted as it cooks, probably because the relatively high fat content of the pork shoulders makes it unnecessary.

The Lexington-style shoulders are often cooked in chimneyed pits that form one wall of the restaurant kitchen. Two rows of metal doors typically provide access—the lower for spreading coals and the upper for adding, turning, and removing the meat. Some Piedmont restaurants, particularly around Stanly and Rowan counties northeast of Charlotte, cook on waist-high pits that simply vent into the open air when their covers are raised—like the ones common in the east. Because of the smoke, these are usually located in buildings separate from the kitchen. Regardless of which type of pit is used, the cooking shed or kitchen has some type of central firebox, often with an opening both to the outside, where wood can be added to the fire, and to the inside, where coals are removed by shovel and sprinkled beneath the cooking shoulders in the pits.

Significant differences exist between east and west in the way barbecued pork is served. Piedmont, or Lexington-style, barbecue is traditionally available chopped, "coarse-chopped" into chunks, or even sliced, whereas eastern barbecue is almost always rather finely chopped. Hand-chopped barbecue in the Piedmont is usually chunkier than the eastern version, except for the machine-shredded variety, which is identical to its eastern counterpart in consistency. It's also interesting to note that in most Lexington-style barbecue houses throughout the Piedmont, you can special-order "outside brown" meat, either chopped or sliced. This is the slightly crusty, chewy, well-browned meat (*not* skin) from the portion of the shoulder where the fat and skin have been stripped away to expose the lean meat before cooking. Many customers in the Piedmont will order no other portion. Personally, "outside brown" is my absolute favorite part of any piece of barbecued pork.

In general, barbecue in the Piedmont seems more moist than the eastern variety, despite its lean appearance on the plate. First of all, shoulders have darker meat and are more marbled with fat than most other parts of the pig; an average fifteen-pound shoulder will slowly drip seven or eight pounds of fat down through the inside of the meat and onto the coals during the nine to ten hours the shoulder is on the pit. But this natural basting isn't the only factor. Since the barbecue is usually not chopped as fine as in the east, the meat retains more of its moisture. Then, too, Lexington-style barbecuers usually serve their meat with more sauce ladled over it than do their eastern cousins. Some Piedmont establishments offer "minced" barbecue—meat that's nearly pulverized, then mixed with copious amounts of sauce to form a sort of sloppy-joe mixture. (You may have deduced that this is not one of my favorites.)

No other variance between the two distinct barbecue regions is as vociferously debated as the difference between eastern and Lexington sauce, although I personally believe it's a distinction in search of a difference. Basically, you take a typical eastern-style vinegar-salt-pepper sauce, add just enough ketchup and maybe a little Worcestershire to darken the sauce to a deep reddish brown, then throw in a little brown sugar—just enough to cut the bite of the vinegar. That's it. That's the big difference all the arguing is about. Oh, a few other spices may be in there, but the basic taste is still vinegar and pepper. For some reason, a lot of people in the east seem to have the mistaken notion that Lexington-style sauce is thick with ketchup and molasses, like the barbecue sauces found in Texas or on supermarket shelves. But while

those who developed Piedmont barbecue obviously were no longer afraid to eat tomatoes, they didn't go hog-wild with them either. Yes, Lexington-style sauce does contain some tomato extracts, but it's usually a relatively thin sauce not much different in color or consistency from the traditional eastern sauce, which is itself usually red from all the ground red pepper that's added. The taste of the sugar is hardly noticeable to most people, since it's overridden by the heat of the black and red peppers. Actually, the biggest difference is the name; most Piedmont barbecue places refer to their particular formulations as "dip," rather than sauce. Piedmont restaurants typically season their barbecue with their regular sauce in the kitchen, then offer a hotter, less-sweet version on the table.

I should mention that not all Piedmont barbecuers think of their product as "Lexington-style." The sauce served over the traditional chopped shoulders in several Rowan County and Stanly County establishments definitely has a vinegar-and-hot-pepper base, with less tomato taste than traditional Lexington dip. And the coleslaw at these places is noticeably more tart. Considering these differences, it's no great surprise to learn of the running disagreement between Lexington and Salisbury, in Rowan County, as to which community was the first to introduce barbecue in a big way. According to local records, John Blackwelder of Salisbury added a barbecue pit to his taxi stand in 1918, one year before Sid Weaver put up his barbecue tent near the Lexington courthouse. The popularity of Blackwelder's barbecue—originally prepared from pork loins rather than shoulders—is said to have quickly spread far and wide due to word-of-mouth reports from the railway workers who became customers as they traveled up and down the line. But of course, the same railway line runs through Lexington, and there is little doubt that the reputation of Lexington's barbecue, if not its quality, soon eclipsed Salisbury's.

The differences between eastern and Piedmont barbecue extend to the side dishes as well. If you were led blindfolded into a barbecue restaurant, then had the blindfold removed at the table, you could easily tell 90 percent of the time whether you were in the east or the Piedmont by one glance at the coleslaw. Western, or Piedmont, slaw is almost always red and has a totally different taste and texture than its eastern cousin. Whereas eastern slaw ranges in texture from shredded to nearly pulverized, Lexington-style slaw is almost always chopped into crunchy bits about the size of BBs. It's basically seasoned with barbecue sauce instead of either mustard or mayonnaise, so it's pepper-hot and vinegar-tangy, and it's also fairly sweet, since more sugar is added than normally goes into the barbecue dip. Some fence-straddling places in Durham, Orange, and Alamance—counties near the dividing line between the Piedmont and the coastal plain—serve western-style barbecue but eastern-style slaw, clear evidence of a sort of barbecue split personality. East met west head-on at the now-defunct A & M Grill in Mebane, which served pit-cooked shoulders with—Lord help us—*pink* coleslaw, dressed with a mixture of mayonnaise and barbecue sauce. Quite a few Piedmont barbecue joints serve both white and red slaw.

Hush puppies are served nearly universally with barbecue in the west, just as they are in the east. The descendants of Warner Stamey claim that he was the first—at least in the Piedmont—to borrow the idea from fish camps, figuring the traditional accompaniment to fried catfish would also go well with barbecue. The hush puppies in the Piedmont seem to be generally skinnier than the ones in the east, but this is probably because most places buy their mechanical hush-puppy-forming machines from the same supplier. Smaller places usually hand-squeeze their hush-puppy batter through a pastry tube into the frying oil, or drop it into the deep fryer by knife, spoon, or scoop. Old menus and photos indicate that rolls and even plain white loaf bread were generally served with barbecue in the 1920s and 1930s. They're both available at some places east *and* west even today.

While you may find sandwiches, hot dogs, and other non-barbecue items on the menu, don't look for Brunswick stew, barbecued potatoes, fried chicken, or vegetables served as accompaniments to barbecue in the west. A barbecue *tray* contains only barbecue, coleslaw, and hush puppies, whereas a barbecue *plate* has all of the above plus French fries. Some of the notable dessert offerings in the Piedmont include banana pudding topped with meringue at Fuzzy's in Madison and Hill's in Winston-Salem, peach cobbler and ice cream at Stamey's in Greensboro, and a variety of outstanding homemade desserts at Allen & Son in Chapel Hill. Bridges Barbecue Lodge in Shelby serves a memorable sherbet pie, which is perfect as a follow-up to the smoky barbecue.

The biggest difference between the two styles is that a lot more places in the Piedmont than in the east sell barbecue that delivers a genuine wood-cooked taste. While recent years have brought a disturbing Piedmont trend toward the use of electric cookers, the expectations about whether or not barbecue is *supposed* to taste of wood smoke is still the great divide that will probably differentiate east and west forever.

## Old-Fashioned Pit Cooking: Does It Really Matter?

There is simply no escaping the fact that thousands and thousands of people across North Carolina smack their lips every day over so-called barbecue that's never been anywhere near a wood-burning pit. North Carolina Department of Agriculture regulations state that pork cooked over gas flames or in an electric cooker cannot be labeled "barbecue" if it's packaged for sale in stores; instead, it must be labeled "cooked pork." However, no such regulations cover what's served in restaurants, and an incredible number of barbecue places—including most of the best-known spots in the east and a growing number in the west—have converted from hardwood to gas or electricity. Others have installed gas- or electric-fired wood smokers, which produce smoke and smoke flavor

but none of the "grill" taste that results from fat dripping directly onto the coals. (In most smokers, the coals are normally offset from the meat itself, so that juice can't drip onto the embers.)

This transformation goes directly to the heart of the matter, to the very definition of barbecue. Can and should meat properly be called "barbecue" if it isn't cooked over wood coals? While a couple of *Webster's* definitions for barbecue describe meat broiled or roasted over an open fire, another says the *verb* barbecue means "to broil or cook meat with a highly seasoned sauce." Old hands will vigorously denounce such a definition, but there it is. And you can hardly deny that, like it or not, it pretty well describes the way things are in many areas in our state; sauce has replaced pit cooking as the defining factor, the key ingredient in barbecue.

Despite all the talk about health department rules being responsible for the change, I haven't found a single case in which a county health department has ever made an existing wood-cooking barbecue place convert to gas or electricity. Even if new restaurants in some counties aren't allowed to build and operate wood-burning pits, existing businesses are almost always covered by so-called grandfather clauses, meaning that they can continue to cook with wood if they so choose.

The plain fact is that a lot of places that built their reputations on real, honest-to-goodness pit-cooked barbecue fall victim to their own success. With a few notable exceptions, real pit cooking is feasible mostly for restaurants doing a small to moderate

Barbecuing pork shoulders for a Lexington political rally around 1930
*Photo by H. Lee Waters, North Carolina Collection, University of North Carolina at Chapel Hill*

volume. Owners become convinced that it will be difficult to expand their business and maximize profits without changing. They feel compelled to switch to a cooking method that will not only allow them to handle increasing volume but also to solve some of the labor problems associated with wood cooking. Nearly all the real open-pit barbecue houses have someone who's been with the business for twenty or thirty years, who's willing to stay up all night or come to work in the wee hours to tend the pits, who performs a hot, dirty, backbreaking job few others are willing to do, and who will be difficult to replace upon retirement. In addition to all that, hardwood,

especially hickory wood, is becoming more expensive and harder to find. The late Pete Jones of the moderately sized Skylight Inn in Ayden used to say he burned between 125 and 200 cords of oak yearly to cook his barbecue. A bigger establishment like Wilber's in Goldsboro—probably the largest open-pit barbecue place in North Carolina—no doubt uses twice that amount.

While the temptations to change to gas or electricity are understandable, why is it that all but a handful of places in the east have made the switch, while a majority of barbecue places in the Piedmont have stuck with the messier, more expensive hardwood pits? My theory is that eastern North Carolinians, with their large-scale-farming mentality, tend to be immensely practical, always ready to find a quicker, more efficient way to do anything. (I've observed this trait firsthand in my two brothers-in-law, who both operate large farms in the northeastern part of the state.) In the Piedmont, on the other hand, I believe the old ways tend to be more carefully preserved, if for no other reason than to provide a comforting and needed contrast to the high technology and frantic pace of the large cities located there.

The really strange thing to me is that, practicality aside, so many eastern North Carolinians, having grown up with world-renowned pit-cooked barbecue, have acquiesced in this wholesale transformation with so little protest. The only possible answer is that Tar Heels from the coastal plain have consumed so much barbecue over the years in restaurants and at catered gatherings of every description that it has gradually become a more or less generic food to them. Somewhere along the line, the requirement that barbecue have a wood-smoked taste was lost, so that the word *barbecue* became subconsciously redefined to describe tender, tasty roast pork well seasoned with salt, vinegar, and a mixture of hot peppers—or, to use the agriculture department's term for the grocery-store stuff in plastic containers, simply *cooked pork*. This is the only possible explanation for the longtime loyalty of customers at well-known eastern restaurants that have switched from open pits to gas or electricity—restaurants like Scott's in Golds-

boro and Bob Melton's in Rocky Mount (both of which, ironically, are now closed, although their closure seems to have had nothing to do with the switch from wood cooking). Patrons' tastes at other eastern establishments that have made the switch can only have evolved as their memories have faded.

Now, let me hasten to say that cooking on an open pit is no guarantee that the end product will be acceptable, and that three of the four things necessary to produce great barbecue can be done very well on a gas or electric cooker. Of the four key factors—tenderness, consistency, wood-smoked taste, and seasoning—only the delicate wood-smoked taste and "grill" flavor obtained from hardwood coals can't be duplicated over gas or electricity. Gas- or electric-fired smokers do give their barbecue smoke flavor and good exterior browning, but in my view, losing the taste imparted by aromatic steam from dripping fat is an important flavor factor. Proponents of gas or electric cookers say the big advantage is that temperature can be controlled precisely at a low level over a long period of time, producing meat that is exceptionally tender because of the extremely slow cooking. However, the owner of Wilber's in Goldsboro—a proponent of open-pit cooking—promotes a different view. Wilber Shirley says, "With a lot of other burners, you cook the hog with the heat on top. Cooking our way, with the fire underneath, the juices drip down through the meat and onto the coals. That dripping makes the meat softer and gives it its flavor."

My own experience has been that much

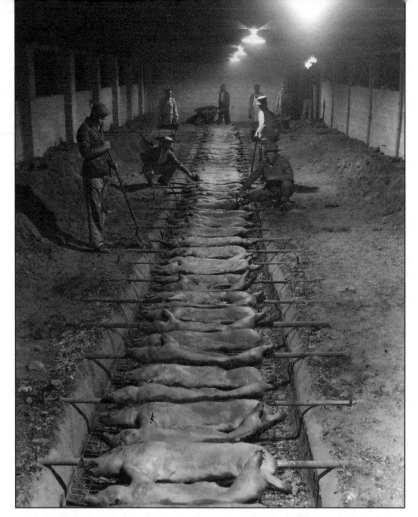

In 1954, Parker's Barbecue in Wilson cooked 155 hogs to help feed the 17,000 people attending the grand opening of the Ralston Purina plant. Income from the event helped Parker's become firmly established.
*Photo by Raines and Cox, courtesy of Keith Barnes*

of the pork cooked on gas or electric cookers *is* extremely tender and juicy without being limp. But with the wood-smoked taste completely absent, the barbecuer has only one remaining ingredient to work with: seasoning. Many gas or electric cooker enthusiasts claim in all earnestness that since the wood-smoke taste was so delicate to begin with, most people won't even notice its absence, provided

the sauce is done just right. A lot of them have tinkered with their sauce ingredients or dry seasonings to the point that they believe they're creating barbecue every bit as tender and flavorful as the original pit-cooked version. And their customers are backing them up by saying things like, "The barbecue tastes just like it always has."

So what's a fellow to do, retreat to a stubbornly held position and refuse to budge, or try to keep an open mind? In a *New York Times* column, Tom Wicker defended the rights of those who switched to gas or electricity, then went on to growl, "But to anyone deeply into barbecue, the idea of cooking it any way but over live coals is repugnant." Personally, I take a more forgiving attitude. While I have tasted some tender, well-seasoned, and extremely tasty chopped roast pork prepared on gas or electric cookers, I'm just not sure I feel comfortable calling it *traditional barbecue.* On the other hand, I've tasted some stringy, tough, dried-out barbecue cooked over hardwood coals. Given a choice, I wouldn't have selected it over the tastier roast pork simply because it was pit-cooked. In the last analysis, I suppose people have a right to define barbecue any way they darn well please. Who am I to say they're wrong? For reasons that may well be emotional as much as taste-oriented, I much prefer a wood-smoked flavor in my barbecue, but I'll concede that some folks out there do a masterful job of seasoning and achieving perfect tenderness and texture. I'll happily consume their barbecue without asking too many questions.

While the number of barbecue places in the Piedmont that have given up pit cooking is growing, every barbecue restaurateur with any kind of aspiration to a regional reputation still has a sizable woodpile outside where it's readily visible. (One or two sneaky souls have switched to electric cookers but keep their woodpiles for camouflage!)

Most barbecue restaurants use a mixture of oak and hickory, a few spots use only hickory, while a few others swear by hardwood charcoal. Some foresters maintain that once hardwood is reduced to coals, it makes no difference what kind it is in terms of the flavor it produces in food. That argument seems to be disproved by the current popularity of mesquite, which lends a distinctive flavor to many grilled foods, although—thankfully—North Carolina barbecue is not among them. (Mesquite is actually more of a large shrub than a genuine hardwood.) My own perception is that hickory imparts a flavor that is at least recognizable, if not superior to that of oak, although oak is probably the wood most commonly used for cooking barbecue in the Piedmont. But having said that, I'm not positive I could consistently pass a blind taste test to discern the difference between barbecue cooked over hickory, oak, or even hardwood charcoal. To my way of thinking, slow-cooking over any of these three types of coals produces outstanding results.

Unfortunately, it seems certain that, with some notable exceptions, the number of barbecue restaurateurs willing to stick with the inconvenience and extra work of pit-cooking is bound to diminish in the years ahead. The late Jimmy Harvey of Jimmy's BBQ in Lexington predicted that nearly everyone would go to gas or electricity in the coming years because cooking with wood is so much work—which is exactly what occurred at Jimmy's. Wayne Monk of Lexington Barbecue has warned that his restaurant, too, may have to take that step one day. Keith Allen of Chapel Hill's Allen & Son, who works as hard as anyone in the state to turn out great hickory-cooked barbecue, put it this way: "The younger generation doesn't want to work that hard; they're more interested in computers and profits. The old way will disappear when the old hearts go out with it."

## Barbecue Outside North Carolina

If you live in North Carolina and have traveled a good bit, you're probably familiar with the differences between traditional North Carolina barbecue and what's served in other states or regions. But for those who have moved to North Carolina from elsewhere, as well as those Tar Heels who haven't ventured far outside our borders, some comparisons with other customs and practices may be helpful. If you're a true enthusiast, one of the most enjoyable parts of the entire barbecue mystique is being able to "speak the lingo" wherever you travel; and in barbecue, as in everything, there's nothing like travel to give you a new appreciation of what you have at home.

For a preview of what awaits, you may want to think of barbecue spreading out from its origins in coastal Virginia and North Carolina more or less westward and southward, like a bucket of water sloshed onto the pavement. Now picture this tide reaching its limit at the southern and western United States borders, then flowing back toward North Carolina, bringing with it much of what it has picked up along the way. Today in North Carolina's cities and suburbs, barbecue restaurants serve not only pork in a thick, sweet,

non-native barbecue sauce but also beef, ribs, and even chicken—imports from other open-pit cuisines that have become a permanent part of our culture. Many recently transplanted North Carolina residents don't even understand the difference between the pit-cooked chopped pork that's our traditional form of barbecue and these other variations. (A business executive who had recently transferred from Seattle was observed in Durham not long ago eyeing a tray of chopped North Carolina barbecue and asking a companion, "What's that gray meat?") In fact, most of us who do know the difference still occasionally enjoy eating beef, ribs, or chicken heavily smoked and slathered with thick, dark red sweet-hot sauce. And if we go into a grocery store to pick up barbecue sauce, we almost always reach for the thick, gooey kind. To us, this barbecue and *real* barbecue are two entirely different things, and we can hardly blame newcomers for being a little confused.

By way of clearing up this confusion, I'll go over some of the regional peculiarities you'll find as you travel across the South—where nearly all the good barbecue is located. First, though, a general observation may be helpful. While most people automatically think *smoke* when they think of barbecue, there is a significant difference between the light smoking directly over hardwood coals given most North Carolina barbecue and the heavy doses of smoke administered to barbecued meat just about everywhere else. In Texas, and in dozens of states that have copied its barbecue, beef brisket, for example, is supposed to come off the pit smoked to a deep blackish brown. This is generally accomplished either by cooking the meat over indirect heat in some type of smoke chamber or by cooking it using soaked wood chunks or green wood in combination with hardwood coals or placed atop electric coils. Slicing the meat is supposed to reveal a "smoke ring" encircling the brisket on all sides—a one-eighth-inch layer of dark pink or red just below the crusty brown edge, which is caused by smoke seeping inside the meat. The smoky taste and aroma are so overpowering that a strong, sweet sauce is needed to balance the flavor and moisten the meat, which is usually dry. This combination of heavily smoked meat and sweet, thick sauce is probably what a majority of Americans think of as barbecue. Aspects of Texas-style barbecue have found their way into most of the regional barbecue variations found nationwide.

Here's a state-by-state rundown on what you might expect to find outside our borders.

North Carolina old-timers are fond of saying, "There's no more barbecue when you reach Virginia." That isn't 100 percent accurate, but it's true enough that you shouldn't worry yourself with learning about Virginia's barbecue practices, because practically none exist. It's a pity, but Virginians are obviously still being made to suffer for William Byrd's snide remark in 1728 that North Carolinians were full of "gross humors" from devouring so much swine flesh. End of discussion.

South Carolina, on the other hand, has a lot of barbecue, some of it whole-hog, some from shoulders. Quite a few places around the edges of the state serve tasty sliced or pork-shoulder barbecue with a slightly thicker version of the tangy Lexington-style sauce. However, the center of South Carolina, around Columbia, is the home of the Palmetto State's most notable barbecue peculiarity: mustard-based sauce. Ranging in color from a startling bright yellow to dull orange, this sauce features either honey or sugar to cut the mustard's pungency, plus vinegar, salt, peppers, spices, and sometimes ketchup. The best places do a fine job of slow-cooking over hardwood coals. Your biggest challenge in enjoying this barbecue variety may be a visual one of seeing the meat turned yellow by the sauce. The other South Carolina specialty, found virtually nowhere else, is barbecue hash, also known as pork hash or liver hash. Served over rice as a popular accompaniment to pork barbecue, this is a thick, meaty gravy devised to use up the organ meats that aren't cooked as barbecue. Brunswick stew is also common in coastal South Carolina.

Georgia, Alabama, and Tennessee all serve mainly pork barbecue, with some beef on the side. Pork ribs in these states are as much in demand as the meat from pork shoulders or hams. If it isn't clinging to a rib, most of the meat is sliced or pulled from shoulders and coated with a thick red sauce ranging from mild to hot. (Not content with *tang*, Ridgewood Barbecue, one of the few outstanding spots in East Tennessee, brags that its sauce "has a *whang* to it.") Although Brunswick stew is still fairly common as a side dish in Georgia, it's found only occasionally in northern Alabama and practically never in Tennessee.

Memphis merits special mention because it's home to the immense "Memphis in May" barbecue festival, which attracts thousands of hungry visitors and features hundreds of teams competing for cooking honors in the barbecuing of whole hogs, shoulders, and pork ribs. Heavy smoking and thick, tangy sauces are the order of the day not only at the festival but also at nearly a hundred Memphis barbecue restaurants that primarily serve Boston butts and ribs. I should note that Memphians can choose from wet ribs (heavily sauced) or dry ribs, which are rubbed before cooking with a mixture of ground pepper and other spices, then slow-cooked over coals. While sauce is served on the side, a lot of folks enjoy the dry ribs with no adornment at all.

Of all the states in the union, Kentucky probably has the oddest collection of barbecue customs, nearly all of them centered in the western end of the state, just across the Ohio River from Illinois and Indiana. As strange as they may seem to us, most of these practices have been around since the 1830s. In the vicinity of Owensboro, which fancies itself "the Bar-B-Q Capital of the World," mutton—the meat of mature sheep—is far and away the most popular type of barbecue, and has been for nearly 170 years, due to the prevalence of sheep farming in the area in the early nineteenth century. Various Catholic parishes have been largely responsible for keeping this unique barbecued meat popular, originally by holding mutton barbecues as social gatherings and more recently by using them as fundraisers. Whole sheep are cut into quarters and slow-roasted over hickory coals for up to sixteen hours, after which the meat is served sliced, either plain or graced by one of three possible sauces: a mild, tomato-based sauce, "black dip" (heavily influenced by Worcestershire), or a peppery hot sauce. Coleslaw is not considered a fit topping for barbecue sandwiches here; instead, they're served with a slice of onion and a pickle. The most popular side dish is Burgoo, a spicy stew similar to Brunswick stew but also containing chopped mutton; no one seems to know how this originated. Owensboro holds a large barbecue festival each May. Sometimes called "the Burning of Owensboro," it features cinder-block barbecue pits built down the middle of a street running alongside the Ohio River.

Arkansas has a distinct east-west barbecue orientation. In the east, pork is the popular choice, with the attention more or less evenly split between shoulders and ribs. Western Arkansas, the part of the state closest to Texas, is better known for its barbecued beef brisket. Thick, red sauce with a kick to it is served on all three barbecue varieties.

Texas concerns itself mostly with beef brisket, although residents also have quite a fondness for pit-smoked pork sausage links. Pork shoulders and chicken are also found occasionally. I've even been to places in Texas that offered barbecued duck. My impression at the time was that it didn't much matter what kind of meat you ordered; it all came to the table smoked to a deep rose hue and tasting about the same under the sweet, hot sauce. I've also had Texas sauce that wasn't as sweet but rather almost a gravy, flavored more with chili pepper and cumin than ketchup and molasses. Beans—both traditional baked beans and ranch-style pintos—are popular in Texas as a barbecue side dish. If coleslaw is served, it is the creamy variety, with lots of mayonnaise and sugar. Bread offered in accompaniment to the barbecue ranges from the occasional thick, grilled Texas toast to the much more common slices of plain loaf bread.

Although I occasionally indulge in the heavily smoked and thickly sauced varieties of barbecue favored in other states, my taste buds always feel vaguely hung over afterward. To me, the difference between these versions and real, traditional North Carolina barbecue is much like the difference between a woman masked by makeup and a lovely, fresh-faced young girl. Here at home, the tenderness and sweet, delicate taste of the pork itself is at the heart of the matter, and little adornment in the way of heavy smoke or sauce is needed to enhance its natural appeal.

## • "The Barbecue Man," or the Accidental Foodie •

The "*Mmmm-mmmm*" exclamation began instinctively but became sort of a trademark. People I meet often ask me to perform it on demand, but I'm no actor. I can do it only after tasting something delicious!
*Photo by Mike Oniffrey*

I never imagined I would become a food writer and restaurant reviewer—or at least the idea never occurred to me until I was nearly fifty. And the concept of writing about barbecue and being recognized as some sort of barbecue "guru" was even more unlikely.

I suppose, though, that I always gravitated toward telling stories. As a child, I routinely led my friends and cousins in putting on little shows or presentations of one sort or another. Ordinary items—a turkey baster, a female friend's toy majorette baton, a drumstick—were likely to double as pretend microphones.

During high school in the Washington, D.C., suburbs, I was bitten briefly by the drama bug and for a time was consumed with the thought of becoming a stage actor. By the time I reached UNC–Chapel Hill, though, I was determined to become a network TV correspondent. I eventually enrolled in the UNC School of Journalism.

Unfortunately, I was not a motivated student, distracted as I was by the social possibilities on campus. I was a cheerleader and loved fraternity parties. The late (and legendary) UNC journalism professor Walter Spearman once told me that of all the Fs he had awarded in fifty years of teaching, mine was the most richly deserved. He was absolutely right, since I had far exceeded the maximum number of allowable "cuts" for his class. I did amass some reporting experience on WUNC radio, which in those pre-NPR days was merely a student radio station crammed into tiny studios in the basement of Swain Hall. My role model became broadcaster Charles Kuralt, who had studied journalism at UNC but left without obtaining a degree. I rationalized that if Kuralt didn't need a bachelor's to become successful in radio and TV journalism, I didn't either. I grew increasingly interested in my part-time job at WDNC, the Durham AM station that was an affiliate of CBS, then the most prestigious name in broadcast news.

During that period, I fell in love with and married fellow UNC student Ruthie Everett, a farm girl from a close family in Halifax County. Although we spent the first couple years of our marriage in Denver, Colorado, where I furthered my radio experience and broke into TV, it became clear with the birth of our first child that Ruthie longed to build a more permanent life in reasonably close proximity to our North Carolina relatives. The attractiveness of being a peripatetic network correspondent—probably based in New York and absent for weeks or months at a time—began to fade.

And so we moved back to North Carolina. I became a WFMY-TV reporter and anchor in Greensboro. I subsequently operated a small advertising and public-relations consulting business and became a freelance film and video producer, eventually returning to television and joining my former WFMY colleagues Ted Harrison and Chancy Kapp at UNC-TV in 1990.

At UNC-TV, I covered the legislature, hosted a weekly journalists' round-table program, produced and anchored documentaries, and was a reporter and producer for *North Carolina Now*, during which time I visited virtually every one of the state's hundred counties. I was eventually assigned to produce several short features on famous North Carolina barbecue restaurants.

The response to those features was startling, to say the least. I had received nominal feedback from viewers during my journalistic career to that point, but I now began receiving scores of telephone calls, letters, and e-mails from audience members who wanted to discuss the finer points of barbecue or tell me about their favorite restaurants. I began writing *North Carolina Barbecue: Flavored by Time* and producing an

I choose my own restaurants for review, but I get suggestions and tips from all quarters: e-mail, letters, telephone calls, in-person recommendations, even social media.

hour-long TV special of the same title—which, if I do say so myself, was an enormous hit on UNC-TV.

I became known, in a strange, totally unanticipated twist of fate, as "the Barbecue Man." People began to recognize me wherever I went. Speaking invitations and requests for me to judge barbecue contests poured in. I produced a couple of hour-long specials expanding from barbecue into the realm of traditional country cooking. In on-camera segments in various restaurants, I developed a largely unconscious mannerism of exclaiming "*Mmmm-mmmm*" after tasting something I found especially delicious

Viewers started stopping me on the street and asking me to deliver the

exclamation and accompanying facial expression on command.

I gradually left the realm of "serious" journalism for full-time food writing—at least in my best-known, most visible work on TV and in books and magazines. I did continue to write about substantive matters during an eleven-year stint as communications director for the North Carolina state office of AARP, and I made occasional TV appearances in that role, moderating discussions on issues related to aging. But as far as most members of the public were concerned, I was primarily still "the Barbecue Man."

Meeting viewers and readers, by the way, has been by far the most enjoyable part of the experience. I'm still primarily a storyteller,

In addition to doing two live cooking shows with Mildred "Mama Dip" Council, I hosted another live cooking program at Bob Timberlake's Lexington studio. Timberlake, a master of marketing, had published a cookbook entitled *Recipes from Home*, which he promoted with the slogan, "I can't cook, but I know folks who can!" Most of the recipes were from the wives of Timberlake's hunting and fishing buddies. *Recipes from Home* is the source of my favorite pie recipe, for "Chocolate Fudge Pie."
*Photo by Mike Oniffrey*

rather than a performer. I'm a fairly introverted and private person, not a natural ham who craves or expects attention for its own sake. So I'm perpetually pleased and amazed that people have responded positively to my food writing and reporting—really, that they have any interest at all in anything I have to say. I appreciate people watching and reading my material, I'm gratified when they want to introduce themselves, and I don't

take it the least bit for granted.

As my food-focused TV work continued, the challenges of eating on camera before an audience of thousands began to manifest themselves. If I took too big a bite, I wouldn't be able to speak at all. If I took a bite, then waited until I properly chewed the food before commenting, the on-camera shots would be full of long pauses. The trick, I found, was taking a small enough bite to be able to chew a couple of times and then talk before masticating the food enough to be swallowed. But this was a ticklish area. While most people seemed to recognize it was necessary to speak before the food was completely chewed, a few wrote to tell me it was disgusting to watch me speak with *any* food in my mouth at all. Recently, I've addressed the problem during the process of editing the video (which I do myself on a laptop computer). While shooting in a restaurant, I've begun taking a bite and reacting visually to the taste but not commenting immediately. After I've swallowed the food, the cameraman will widen or tighten the shot slightly, and I'll then say a few words about the bite I've just eaten. In editing, I'll first include the shot of the bite and the nonverbal reaction, then use an electronic video effect such as a "dissolve" or "spin" to transition to the following shot, in which I comment on the food. It took me only around fifteen years to come up with this simple solution!

People often ask if the food I taste on camera is really as good as I indicate, and how I handle it when I taste something that isn't good.

Actually, I try never to put myself in the position of sampling what may turn out to be unappetizing food. I certainly don't taste something for the first time on camera. Since I am not a restaurant critic, at least in my TV segments, I never do on-camera reviews of places I don't intend to enthusiastically recommend. That means that I have either previously checked out the restaurants or

that they have been highly recommended by sources I trust to give me an honest evaluation. Having employed those filters, I still take time before the camera rolls to taste everything on which I intend to comment. In the relatively rare instances when I find a particular item isn't to my liking, I simply don't make an on-camera comment or recommendation about it.

A slightly different standard applies to the restaurant reviews in this and my previous books. Because all barbecue restaurants are not created equal, and because readers expect some comparison and evaluation of the merits of one place versus another, I include judgments that may not be universally positive. Opinions about the taste and quality of barbecue—as well as considerations of ambiance, history, personal memories, and other factors—are highly subjective. One person's "great" barbecue joint may be only "so-so" in another's book. This actually occurs more often than you might think. The one thing with which I never take issue is someone's personal experience. When I report my own impressions of a particular restaurant, for example, they are just that, and they're no better or more insightful than anyone else's. The idea is for viewers or readers to use my opinions as a starting point and see if they agree or disagree.

There can be little disagreement, though, that my having gradually constructed a professional life of talking and writing about food has produced some memorable experiences.

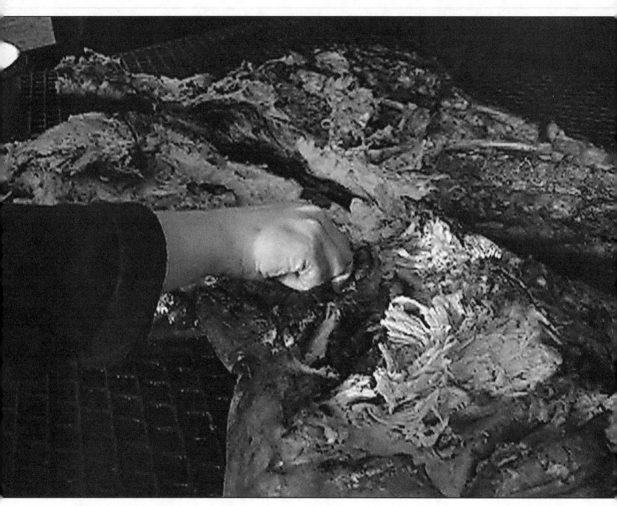

At a pig pickin', you don't have to wait to be served.
*Courtesy of UNC-TV*

# OUTSIDE THE RESTAURANT

## Pig Pickings

P roperly explaining North Carolina barbecue to an out-of-stater can be a tricky business. First, you have to establish the difference between traditional North Carolina barbecue and the oversmoked stuff doused with thick, red, sweet sauce that's called barbecue nearly everywhere today—including some places in our own state. Then you have to deal with the subtle but significant differences between our eastern and Piedmont styles. And you really ought to make it clear to the uninitiated that there is yet another distinct stratum of barbecue lore and enthusiasm in North Carolina. It can be called the "pig picking" culture, and its adherents are those thousands of Tar Heels who enjoy not only eating but cooking barbecue, and who like barbecued pork served directly from someone's grill as much as, if not more than, the barbecue in restaurants.

North Carolinians were attending barbecues for a long time before the opening of any commercial barbecue stands or restaurants. Whether these events were held as purely social occasions or perhaps to celebrate the "putting in" of a tobacco crop, the host would have someone chop the barbecued meat and serve it to his guests, along with corn bread, boiled potatoes, and other dishes.

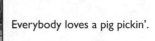
Everybody loves a pig pickin'.

Roy Taylor, former editor of the *Wilson Daily Times*, wrote a weekly column for the newspaper for two years. Having grown up the son of a sharecropper during the Great Depression, he detailed the lives and customs of rural folk in many of his columns, which were eventually compiled into his 1984 book, *Sharecroppers: The Way We Really Were.*

One of his columns that became a chapter in the book is entitled "A Feast on Barbecue." It is so rich in description and so evocative of a long-gone time in our history that I include it here in its entirety:

It is late August and the end of the "putting in backer [tobacco]" season. The "tips" have been pulled from the mass of suckers at the top of the backer stalks and the spindly, small leaves put in the barn to cure. They look gourd-green and spotted as they go in the barns, and they'll probably come out more a green color than anything else.

All the signs point to late summer. In the gardens the collards are showing holes where the terrapin bugs have attacked them and grass has grown tall and seeded out at the end of the rows. Okra stalks have run up and blossoms are at the top of the stalks. Butterflies are flitting around in abundance and hardweeds have grown tall with their small, yellow flowers too insignificant to add beauty to the scene.

But a hard task has been completed when the backer season is finished, and farmers celebrate by holding a barbecue. Those who swap among each other all join in and pay for the pig and each family cooks good things and everybody congregates at one of the houses and they all have a feast.

The barbecue is usually held on a Saturday and it means a whole day of resting and messing around and just doing nothing but stuffing the belly and belching and drinking lemonade and sitting around in the shade and it seems like heaven after seven or eight weeks in the backer fields crapping and looping and hanging and curing backer and getting up every morning in the dark and some mornings soon after midnight when backer has to be taken out.

But the process begins late Friday afternoon. The men kill the pig and get him ready for the pit about sunset, for with no way to refrigerate it, a minimum of hours is allowed for the pig to stay fresh. All the innards are thrown away and the whole mess buried and a cloth is draped over the pig and it is placed on a side table in the kitchen until about 4 o'clock Saturday morning when it is put on the coals.

The pit is usually dug under a backer barn shelter or some place around the backer barns and cleaned out smooth and oak saplings cut and brought up and placed in a pile. The iron rods are taken from the back of the shelter and placed over the pit and everything placed in readiness for cooking the pig.

The large end of the pile of oak wood is set afire in early morning and when there is an accumulation of coals they are put in the pit with the shovel and the entire bottom has to be filled. Then the pig is placed over the coals with the skin side up and soon the grease starts a slow drip, causing little ripples of smoke to rise from the pit.

The green oak is kept burning and some dry chips added if necessary, for it requires a lot of live coals to cook a pig. A jar of vinegar with red pepper cut up in it will be needed

later on to saturate the meat when the pig is turned over. The vinegar is sopped over the meat with a rag tied to a stick.

There is one thing the young 'uns have to do Saturday morning, and that's sweep the yard clean and burn the trash. The yellow chaney [chinaberry] balls that have fallen from the trees have to be taken to the trash pile in the field. But the yard is swept early before the sun gets hot and the tobacco trucks pulled into the yard to be used as tables for the food. They're lined up end on end and placed at the shadiest spot in the yard.

A wooden tub is scrubbed out good and then scalded, for there'll be a tubful of lemonade so everybody can swill down every drop they can drink. There'll even be freezers of homemade ice cream.

While that pig is cooking and the smell filling the neighborhood, the women are flouring those chickens and putting them in hot grease to fry and baking cakes and cooking chocolate syrup to slurp over them.

Fresh cucumbers have been split long ways a day or so earlier and salt and red pepper added so they'll be saturated for the feast. And eggs are boiled and deviled and hoecakes of bread are cooked to go with the barbecue and collards and butterbeans and all the other good things.

Where I lived slaw was not a part of the menu when barbecue was served half a century ago. And neither was cornbread fried in grease as is done today. It was either cooked in a hoecake on top of the stove or baked inside the stove.

That pig is turned over and it's golden brown and sumptuous amounts of vinegar are daubed on the pork and it fries as it hits the cooked meat. Menfolks standing around begin to pull off ribs to taste the delicacy and somebody pulls out the tongue and feasts on it.

The crowd begins to gather at noon and those backer trucks are overlaid with white cloths and the food is placed on the tables and they start fanning flies (just as they do today even without the stables and henhouses and hog pens) and the flies are fanned throughout the meal.

When the skin is good and crisp, the pig is placed in a wood tub and brought to the house for chopping up. The hatchet has been sharpened and the oilcloth removed from the side table and the boards on the table serve as a cutting board. They show marks from former barbecues already. That pig is chopped up fine and toted out to the backer trucks in dishpans and they start loading down the plates.

It's just too good to be true. All that good food and no more backer to "put in" either. Everybody's in a good mood with clean clothes and washed hair and looking good except for the hands that still carry the stain gathered over the barning period. And Saturday night and Sunday coming up too. What a great world!

Large events such as political gatherings typically serve chopped barbecue, while the small, private barbecue has largely evolved into a casual event that yesteryear's hosts might have considered downright barbaric: the "pig picking." Whereas hosts of old wouldn't have laid out a barbecued pig and expected the guests to pick or pull the meat from the bones with their fingers, pig-picking guests who are so inclined are invited to do just that.

Incidentally, the custom of chopping up the cooked pig into what North Carolinians now know as "barbecue" is thought to have grown out of the fact that most people in previous generations began having trouble with or losing their teeth at a much earlier age than is common today. Dentists were relatively few, and their practice was often limited to pulling teeth that were already beyond repair. The host never knew how many teeth any of his guests might bring to the barbecue, and since the oldest members of the families were generally accorded deep respect, he wanted to make sure no one would have difficulty being able to chew the savory roast pork.

As a courtesy, most hosts of pig pickings make sure a quantity of meat has already been pulled from the pig and chopped, ready to be served to those who don't want to roll up their sleeves and dive in. But to most folks, the best part of a pig picking is finding and pulling the most delectable morsels of cooked pork from the pig. The irresistible nibbling of shreds from the ribs or the well-browned "crust" of the meat usually begins among the cooks even before the pig is officially "served," pretty much as Roy Taylor described in his foregoing account.

No one knows exactly why pig pickings evolved (or devolved) from their more refined origins, except that they obviously reflect a widespread trend toward a more casual approach to all types of entertaining. Judging by the name alone, an outsider might consider a pig picking an event designed by and for lowbrows. But nothing could be farther from the truth. Remember, a reverse snobbery is at work in barbecue circles, and it makes pig pickings equally popular among Junior Leaguers and farmers, blue-collar workers

and lawyers. Politicians can't resist them either. When they're spiffed up a bit to include cloth napkins and china plates instead of paper and plastic, pig pickings are increasingly popular at wedding rehearsal dinners and even informal wedding receptions. In their casual attire, they have long been a staple of reunions, church picnics, homecomings, and beer blasts.

In the North Carolina Piedmont, where restaurant barbecue universally comes from pork shoulders, the cooking of whole hogs for parties is relatively unusual. So the pig picking is essentially a ritual of the coastal plain. After all, the whole pig—cooked to a perfect golden brown and laid out on the grill for all to admire—is the star of the show. A barbecue featuring several cooked pork shoulders just wouldn't be quite as appealing, at least from a visual standpoint. However, it is not uncommon for groups of men in the Piedmont to organize parties around the all-night or all-day barbecuing of large quantities of pork shoulders. The meat from these parties is nearly always sold for fundraising purposes, rather than consumed on the spot.

At a down-east pig picking, the cooked pig is typically left spread out belly up on the cooking grate, just as it was arranged during the last third of the cooking, so guests can pass by and serve themselves. The portions that disappear the fastest are the tenderloin—strips of lean white meat on either side of the backbone—and the ribs. But to my taste, the firm, brown outside meat of the shoulders is hard to beat. Once guests have pulled off

Campaigning politicians show up in droves at the Charlotte area's annual Mallard Creek Presbyterian Church barbecue, held in October.
*Photo by Don Sturkey © 1984, Courtesy of North Carolina Collection, University of North Carolina at Chapel Hill*

appetizing servings of meat, they typically splash on a little tangy, vinegar-based sauce and fill up the remainder of their plates with coleslaw, boiled potatoes or Brunswick stew, and hush puppies, perhaps fried fresh on the spot.

My own awareness of pig pickings was born when I married a farm girl from Halifax County, the former Ruthie Everett of Palmyra. Although both my parents grew up in the eastern North Carolina hamlet of Newport—today the pig-cooking-est town in the state—my father left home and became a navy pilot, so I spent my growing-up years first in Florida, then in the northern Virginia suburbs of Washington, D.C. On family visits to North Carolina, we occasionally accompanied my aunt, Meta Peters, to Bob Melton's ramshackle old barbecue place in Rocky

Mount. But I never thought much about pigs, on or off the pit, until I married into a family that not only raised hogs but cooked them as well.

One of my earliest encounters with my future father-in-law should have made it clear that pigs had a place in my future. Ruthie and I met and fell in love while we were students at UNC–Chapel Hill. When I drove to her family's large farm near Scotland Neck so we could jointly inform her parents of our plans to marry, I ended up declaring my intentions to Fate Everett smack in the middle of a pig parlor containing hundreds of malodorous, loudly squealing hogs. Ruthie had tipped him off as to why I was there, so when I stammered out something along the lines of, "Um, I, uh, love your daughter and I, uh, want to marry her," he pretended not to hear me over the deafening racket. Cupping his hand behind his ear, he made me keep repeating myself until, straining to be heard above the insistent hogs, I screamed at the top of my lungs, "I LOVE YOUR DAUGHTER, AND I WANT TO MARRY HER!" Finally, a grin broke across his face. Clapping me on the shoulder, he offered me a cigar. In great relief, I accepted and puffed clumsily away, squinting through the smoke as though I were a seasoned old pig farmer.

Several months later, Ruthie's father and two brothers, Bob and Tad, threw a pig picking for me at my bachelor party. I believe it was the first pig picking I ever attended. I have a dim recollection of a huge old pair of (freshly laundered) women's drawers tied around a stick to make a mop for basting sauce onto the pig. The liquid refreshments flowed freely that night, though, and after more than four decades, my only other recollection of the all-male event is that best man Ed Stoddard and I became swept up in a spirit of oratory and, dressed in nothing but athletic supporters, recited an earthy poem, after which we mooned the entire assembly.

Following our wedding, Ruthie and I lived in Denver, Colorado, for two years, then moved back to North Carolina, where we settled first in Chapel Hill and later in Greensboro, a couple of hours away from her parents' home. Although we had our circle of Greensboro friends, getting together with young couples from Scotland Neck, including Ruthie's brother Tad and his wife, Jayne, to "cook a pig" at the farm became a popular weekend social event, especially since none

of us had much money and the nearest movie theater or nice restaurant was thirty miles away. (We also didn't have to pay for the pigs.)

My other brother-in-law, Bob Everett, lived and worked in Georgia at the time, following his graduation from North Carolina State University, so it was Tad who introduced me to the all-day process of cooking a pig. On one occasion, Tad threw a dressed hog in the trunk of his car and drove to Greensboro to help me put on a pig picking for my newsroom coworkers at WFMY-TV. I remember that he struggled mightily to fully cook the pig on a makeshift outdoor pit, and I recall all of us singing "Shall We Gather at the River" in tipsy hilarity as we passed the hat to cover the costs of the meal. We didn't collect enough the first time around, so we passed the hat (and perhaps a bottle) a second time while singing another verse.

Most of those early pig pickings, though, were at the farm, where Tad, who's also an N.C. State graduate, lived with his wife and farmed with his father. He was equipped with what at the time was considered a fancy trailer-cooker made from a large oil tank. Having slaughtered, cleaned, and dressed a hog the previous evening, we would fire up the cooker with the first bath of glowing coals and get the pig on the grate, meat side down, early on Saturday morning, spreading the coals evenly across the bottom of the cooker. For the remainder of the morning, in between adding some fresh coals every hour or so, we usually occupied ourselves with preparing the sauce or making coleslaw. An hour or so before noon, we would usually throw some venison steaks on the cooker next to the pig so they would be ready for lunch.

After the pig had cooked meat side down for around six hours, it was time to turn it over. This was always an occasion for anxiety because it plainly revealed how well you had done the first half of the job. The idea was to perfectly brown the meat without charring it, a task you had to accomplish without being able to see what you were doing, since the meat faced downward. If you had spread too many coals under the roasting pig, you might turn it to find it had burned, in which case you knew the clear evidence of your lack of skill would be there for all the world to see. In order to avoid this embarrassment, you had to try to control the heat and the rate of browning by avoiding adding too many coals at once, by being careful to keep them spread in a single layer, and by spreading additional coals only under the thick ham and shoulder portions. In fact, after spreading the original layers of coals, we never added any more to the center area under the ribs and loin. We used ears and fingers and eyes to judge whether or not the temperature was about right; as long as we could put an ear next to the cooker and hear the hissing fat drip onto the hot coals, lay our fingers atop the cooker and leave them there for a second or two, and see a faint wisp of smoke coming out of the stack, we knew we were all right. Either heavy smoke or a cooker too hot to the touch, on the other hand, was a sure sign that we had probably added too many coals, and that the pig would be charred if we didn't quickly close all the air vents and get the fire dampened down.

Turning the pig was a matter of placing a second rectangular wire grate, identical to the first, on *top* of the split hog and, with a man on each corner, firmly squeezing together the handles of the top and bottom grates and turning the "sandwiched" pig so that the skin side now rested over the coals. (Why it didn't occur to us to simply cut the hog in two so we could easily turn the halves is beyond me; it was probably simply not considered customary, for whatever reason.) If properly done, the meat-side-down cooking period had not only browned the pig to perfection but gotten it at least three-quarters done. The only remaining jobs were allowing the meat to slowly finish cooking as the skin browned and occasionally basting the meat with sauce.

The hours between the turning of the pig in early to mid-afternoon and the serving of dinner around six were likely to be mischief-filled. You must understand that cooking a pig is a very drawn-out undertaking, with occasional spurts of activity punctuating long periods of sitting around with little to do. As such, it's a perfect way for men to spend a day with friends and neighbors. There's always plenty of yarn spinning; discussing of farming, sports, and politics; and other forms of socializing. It is not unknown, once afternoon arrives, for the participants to "take a drink" as they visit and keep an eye on the cooking pig.

In those days, our callowness and sense of youthful invincibility sometimes allowed our pig-cooking gatherings to get a little out of hand. On one Saturday, after one drink too many, several of us ended up challenging each other to a shooting contest. Standing in a nearby pasture, one of us would toss his cap high in the air, and a challenger would try to blast it with a shotgun. The fact that someone might easily have been hurt or killed makes me shudder as I recall the incident. Another time found a light rain beginning to fall just as guests started to help themselves to the pig. Undaunted (and well lubricated by an afternoon of socializing), we pushed the cooker up the back porch, picked up the entire grill, and regally bore the cooked pig into the house, setting it down on a huge butcher-block table in the kitchen. My brother-in-law Bob was living in the family homeplace as a bachelor at the time, following the death of his mother and the remarriage of his father; otherwise, we never would have either considered or gotten away with such a thing. A lively indoor pig picking and party ensued. However, we all bitterly regretted our foolishness the next day as we nursed our hangovers while scrubbing massive deposits of greasy hog drippings from the kitchen floor.

As my young children began to be more aware of their surroundings (and as I began to grow up a bit, too), I decided my family would be happier and more stable in an alcohol-free environment, so my youthful partying came to an end. My enjoyment of pig pickings, however, continued unabated. Playing at being a gentleman farmer, I moved to a large, old house in the countryside near Burlington and even acquired my own pig cooker. Although I never did any catering, I often organized pig pickings for groups of friends, Sunday-school classes, my sons' Boy Scout troop, and even a group of kids from Belfast, Northern Ireland, who were spend-ing a summer in Greensboro.

One sweltering July evening, I pulled into the driveway with the cooker in tow, a freshly dressed pig already spread-eagled on the grill. The pig was to be cooked the following day. But where could I keep the meat cool in the meantime? Since then, I have learned to slide a dressed pig into a new, large rubber garbage can and to pack bags of ice around it. But at the time, the only thing I could think to do was lay the hog out on the floor of my cellar, the coolest spot in the house. Having no one to help me, I managed to get the pig onto a sheet of clear, heavy plastic and pull it and its heavy load down a short flight of steps to the basement, where I wrapped the plastic around the pig and covered it with bags of ice.

The next morning, anxious to get the pig on the fire, I discovered that I couldn't drag the plastic sheet back up the cellar steps without having the pig slide off onto the floor. I had already sawed off the slender "trotters" so the pig would fit into the cooker, and when I tried to grasp the stumpy legs, my hands slid right off the smooth, clammy skin. Even if I had been able to hoist the 130-pound form onto my shoulder, the cellar ceiling was too low for me to stand upright or even get higher than a backbreaking crouch. Pondering the true meaning of the term *dead weight*, I finally had an inspiration. Dropping to my knees, I was able to get the pig's front legs up over my shoulders. Holding the inert hog to my body with both arms, I struggled to my feet. Looking for all the world like an exhausted marathon dancer, I hugged that lifeless pig for all I was worth as I stumbled backwards up the stairs and into the early-morning sunlight.

Unfortunately, not having thought far enough ahead, I found myself with an armful of cold pig and no clear idea of what to do next. Attempting to rest the front legs on the edge of a table and slither down the pig's body to the back legs so I could shove the whole thing safely onto the flat surface, I dropped the pig, meat side down, onto the ground. For the next two hours, I picked grass, twigs, and bits of soil from the tacky surface of the exposed meat, swearing all the while that this would be the last pig I ever cooked.

It wasn't, though. I've both organized and attended a great many pig pickings since then—all strictly for fun.

## Competitive Whole-Hog Cooking

For many barbecue cooks, the pig pickings that began as a way to pass leisurely Saturdays have been replaced by extremely competitive cooking contests imbued with great seriousness of purpose. Although any pig-cooking hobbyist will tell you that the competition *is* great fun, a lot of hard work, time, and expense are involved, balanced somewhat by the potential for winning big-time cash prizes.

North Carolina hosts an average of twenty-five whole-hog cooking contests of various sizes each year. The field is totally dominated by chefs from the coastal plain, where cooking whole pigs, rather than shoulders, has long been the norm. In fact, all but a couple of the whole-hog cookoffs are held east of

Raleigh, and two more take place in Hillsborough and Graham, which are located more or less on an indistinct line between east and Piedmont in terms of barbecue customs. The North Carolina Championship Pork Cook-Off is a whole-hog state contest held each year by the North Carolina Pork Council. Entrance is open only to winners of various local pig-cooking contests in North Carolina. The state contest and all the local cookoffs are judged under a standard set of criteria developed by the council.

Because potential contestants have been eliminated in earlier contests, the state cookoff has a limited number of cooking teams. The biggest contest of all is one of the local affairs, the renowned Newport Pig Cookin' Contest. Located in flat, sandy Carteret County, Newport is a small tobacco town and bedroom community for the nearby Cherry Point Marine Air Station at Havelock. However, since the early 1970s, it has become famous as the spot where more than one hundred pig-cooking teams gather to compete for barbecue bragging rights and prizes. During the 1950s and early 1960s, I occasionally visited maternal and paternal grandparents in Newport, and I don't recall ever seeing an entire pig barbecued, or even hearing of such a practice. But the festival later grew from its tiny beginnings into a massive event in which a majority of townspeople participate as volunteers. Profits derived from contest entry fees are used for a wide range of civic purposes.

Whereas most pig pickings used to feature hogs roasted over coals in simple cook-

All different types of cookers are used at pig-cooking contests.
*Photo by Mike Burke*

ers made from oil tanks, many of today's competitive pig-cooking teams use sleek, custom-made grills, many of them heated by gas. Proponents of gas cooking say the fuel allows them to precisely control temperatures inside the cooker over a long period of time, which means they can cook a pig at a constant low temperature for up to twelve hours, producing extremely moist, tender meat. But among the latest additions, gas tanks are the least extravagant. Nearly all of the modern grills are outfitted with expensive thermometers, fancy hand or automatic systems for turning the pig, towel-and-utensil racks, cutting boards, smokestacks shaped like pigs, and dozens of other gadgets. Most of them receive gleaming paint jobs, inside and out, before every contest, making them a far cry from the comfortably rusted cooker with the blackened lid that I'm used to.

In fact, if I were to enter a contest with that old cooker, I would be at a distinct disadvantage in cooking with hardwood or charcoal, both because of the increased difficulty of maintaining an even, low temperature with hand-spread coals and because of the emphasis placed by judges on appearance and cleanliness. Not only is the pig expected to be cooked to perfection, but the cooker, the surrounding area, *and the cook* are expected to remain virtually spotless throughout the process. Hardwood coals and charcoal produce fine ash, some of which ends up floating around the cooker, invariably coating the lid, the grill, and even the pig unless it's covered by cardboard or foil. At a noncompetitive pig picking, the chef can claim that any ash falling on the pig "makes it taste better," but in a contest, the same ash would be cause for a deduction of points. I'm delighted to know that these contests still are won occasionally by teams cooking with wood and charcoal, and I salute them for keeping the old ways alive.

When it comes to judging the meat itself, the tiniest details of a cooked pig's appearance are scrutinized by hard-eyed judges and spectators alike. The pig is expected to be roasted to a uniform walnut brown, and any charred spots on the meat, no matter how small, set tongues clucking and scores tumbling. Should the soft, cooked meat separate from the bone or otherwise pull apart as the pig is being turned prior to judging, the chef will have his score lowered accordingly. The pig cannot be cut in half for ease of turning, meaning that elaborate measures are devised for turning the pig without disturbing the wholeness of its skin. And if any cuts are on the meat—as might be made in testing for doneness—the cook can abandon hope of being listed among the contest's winners. Deryll Garner, the longtime mayor of Newport (and a distant relative of mine), jokes about how the town's eye for pig judging may have clouded its reputation. The mayor swears he has heard out-of-staters saying, "They must have some ugly women around here. All I hear is, 'Have you seen that good-lookin' pig of Tom's?' 'Well, no, but I have seen Harry's, and *that's* a pretty pig.' "

The North Carolina Pork Council has a slick DVD with which it begins the training of judges. But other opportunities for training are available, including an annual barbecue judges' school, at which prospective jurists spend an entire afternoon viewing slides and video and poring over the criteria listed on score sheets. "What's wrong with this pig?" calls out one of the school's instructors. Gazing at a blurry slide of a well-browned pig that's slightly blackened around the backbone and ribs, the judges-to-be sing out in unison, "It's burned!"

For the mandatory on-site judging, in which the judges visit each cooking location at a contest, the score sheets guide them in awarding the cooked pigs points in six categories covering appearance and taste. As the evaluation begins, the judges have to answer a crucial question: "Is this pig done?" If the judges determine that the pig is *not* completely cooked, the entry is immediately disqualified.

In the on-site visit, it's ironic that the judges' job is to approach a cooked pig with nary a word to the anxious chef and tear it to pieces as quickly as they can. One judge will lift and turn over each side of the cooked pig, listening for the cracking of crisp skin (highly desired) and probing for soft spots that indicate a lack of uniformity in the crispness. Others wearing rubber gloves will thrust their hands into the cooked meat, pulling bones and tossing chunks of meat here and there as they test for doneness, texture, and moisture. Grabbing a bit of meat from the tenderloin or some other succulent spot, the judges will dunk it into a waiting bowl of sauce and impassively take a bite, avoiding any telltale facial expressions as they jot down their scores. In a few moments, it's all over, and they move on to the next entry, leaving the stunned cook gazing dolefully at the scattered, road-kill-like remains of what had been a really *pretty* pig.

Once the damage has been done, the meat is chopped and seasoned and sometimes submitted for a blind taste test that is an optional component of local contests. (The blind taste-testing is mandatory in the state championship cookoff.) A well-known contestant—perhaps a former champion—could *conceivably* receive higher scores in the on-site judging purely because of his reputation (a highly unlikely occurrence). A blind taste test is supposed to help balance such potential inequities, since each entry is identified only by number and not by name.

Contestants can even choose to be graded in an optional showmanship category, almost always held the day before the actual competition or after the conclusion of the judging. Many teams erect elaborate sets around their cookers—a tobacco-barn scene, for example,

or a country kitchen. Team members are often in costume. The cooks are supposed to demonstrate that they're having a good time as "goodwill ambassadors for pork."

Ironically, no competitive cookoffs—or at least no contests limited in scope to the judging of barbecued pork shoulders—are held for those who prefer to cook Piedmont-style pork shoulders. The Kansas City Barbeque Society, a nationwide organization, does have a category for pork (usually meaning Boston butts or whole shoulders). But a KCBS contest always includes additional categories for ribs, chicken, and beef brisket. A pork shoulder purist could choose to enter *only* the pork category of a KCBS contest, although most competitive cookers enter all categories in order to justify the expense of the entry fee. KCBS has made

In another category of barbecue competition, Tommy Moore of Moore's Olde Tyme Barbeque in New Bern had his crew build the world's largest open-faced barbecue sandwich. Weighing 1,377 pounds, the sandwich earned a place in the *Guinness Book of World Records*. The July 2010 occasion was the three hundredth anniversary of the founding of New Bern. Moore joked, "That little piece of text right there cost me at least twenty-five thousand dollars."

significant inroads in sanctioning barbecue contests in North Carolina in recent years, to the point that there are just as many, if not more, KCBS-sanctioned events in the Tar Heel State as contests devoted to whole-hog cookery. But KCBS normally has no category for whole-hog barbecuing. It is ironic that an increasing number of competitive cookoffs in *eastern* North Carolina are now sanctioned by the out-of-state group and have no guidelines for judging that region's legendary style of barbecue.

One good aspect of the KCBS format, in my opinion, is that no on-site judging is done. All the evaluation is on meat samples anonymously submitted in Styrofoam containers, meaning KCBS judges do not know which contestant's meat they are evaluating. Eliminating on-site judging also eliminates the unnecessary distraction of perfecting the appearance of the cooking site before the judges arrive, leaving contestants free to concentrate on perfecting the actual barbecue they are submitting. On the other hand, one significant shortcoming of KCBS events is that visitors do not have any real opportunity to purchase or taste the entries submitted for judging, whereas North Carolina Pork Council events allow for barbecue to be sampled and sold at the conclusion of judging. KCBS events typically have barbecue *vendors*, but casual visitors aren't ordinarily able to sample the fruits of the contestants' labors.

Tryon, North Carolina, located near the South Carolina line at the foot of the Blue Ridge Mountains, has the largest KCBS cookoff in the state. Visitors to this and dozens of other KCBS contests witness the judging of a *little* North Carolina–style barbecue but also a lot of ribs, beef, and chicken in the thick-sauce-and-heavy-smoke style found from Tennessee westward. Although the Tryon festival is a relative newcomer to the Tar Heel State compared to other cookoffs, its organizers long ago succeeded in having it designated by the governor's office as the Official North Carolina State Barbecue Championship.

## North Carolina's Official Barbecue Festival

While the fiercely competitive eastern North Carolina pig-cooking contests often serve as centerpieces for community-wide celebrations, the state's largest and most successful barbecue festival represents something of a temporary cease-fire among competitors. Bringing together top Lexington-style barbecue restaurateurs to serve their trademark pork shoulder barbecue under a common banner, the Lexington Barbecue Festival is actually a re-creation of an earlier type of event, one that helped begin this Piedmont town's barbecue heritage.

In the early 1900s, public cookouts known as "Everybody's Day" helped introduce barbecue to the folks around Lexington, fanning embers of enthusiasm that later burst into hot flames of passion. It wasn't long before these occasional barbecues were expanded into week-long events designed to serve the crowds attending court sessions. By 1919,

Up to 150,000 people attend the Lexington Barbecue Festival.
*Photo by Mike Burke*

Sid Weaver and George Ridenhour had set up their first barbecue stand a stone's throw from the Davidson County Courthouse.

The original week-long festivals eventually disappeared, but in 1984, the concept of a new "Everybody's Day"—a community-wide celebration of Lexington's legendary barbecue style—was brought back in an expanded form, largely thanks to the vision of Joe Sink Jr., publisher of the Lexington *Dispatch*, and the talents of the late Kay Saintsing, at that time a local organization developer and manager. Since that time, it has attracted visitors in ever-increasing numbers from all over the Southeast.

Lexington, located off Interstate 85 between Greensboro and Charlotte, is a town of 17,000 people but has approximately twenty barbecue restaurants. According to Greg Johnson and Vince Staton's fine book, *Real Barbecue*, Lexington is second among the nation's cities in term of barbecue restaurants per capita, with one barbecue place for every 850 residents. (Ironically, Lexington, Tennessee, with ten restaurants to serve 6,000 residents, took first place.) Obviously, there is a large enough pie in Lexington for all the barbecuers to have a slice. A handful of the top restaurant owners organized the first barbecue festival around the principle of minimizing their differences and promoting Lexington-style barbecue as a distinctive regional delicacy.

Lexington's festival is traditionally held on one of the last two Saturdays in October. But as a warm-up to the big event, all

Part of the crowd on the twenty-fifth anniversary of the founding of the Lexington Barbecue Festival

of October is designated "Barbecue Month." Not content with the time constraints of a one-day festival, organizers fill the October calendar with events such as the Tour de Pig (a cycling race); the 5K Hawg Run; a beauty pageant; golf, tennis, and softball tournaments; and, so help me, the Hawg Shoot Air Rifle Tournament (which emphatically does *not* involve shooting hawgs).

On the morning of the big day, the festivities get under way with the Parade of Pigs. Lest you get a mental image (as I did) of hundreds of unfortunate pigs being herded down Main Street toward their doom by broom-wielding citizens, be reassured that organizers describe the parade as consisting of "a variety of floats and people carrying out the pork-flavor theme." For the festival, an eight-block stretch of Main Street is closed to traffic, and some four hundred exhibitors set up shop, selling everything from crafts to homemade fudge. Musical entertainment, including several concerts by headline acts, is offered throughout the festival, as are a juried art competition and show, a carnival midway, a classic car show, and an area called "Piglet Land" that has rides and entertainment for children.

In 1995, some of the literal and figurative distance between east and Piedmont was bridged when the state pork producers' association voted to accept the city's invitation for the annual North Carolina Championship Pork Cook-Off to be held in conjunction with the Lexington Barbecue Festival. Piedmont residents, used to seeing pits full of pork shoulders, were able to watch the state's top whole-hog experts—nearly all of them from the coastal plain—demonstrate their craft. Such an invasion of whole-hog enthusiasts has not reoccurred since then. Because the Lexington festival does not include a competitive cooking contest, opportunities for interfacing between the adherents of eastern and Lexington-style barbecue is limited at this event.

The real festival action in Lexington is always under two large red-and-white-striped tents on the courthouse square—tents reminiscent of the early shelters set up by Sid Weaver and Jess Swicegood. Here, genuine Lexington-style chopped barbecue sandwiches, slaw, and French fries are served at a furious rate by volunteers and restaurant workers, many of whom also spend the two days prior to the event cooking some fifteen thousand pounds of pork shoulders to feed the expected 130,000-plus in attendance.

Just as rail travel through places like Lexington and Salisbury once helped spread barbecue's reputation, today's Lexington Barbecue Festival is crucial in maintaining the town's standing as a barbecue mecca around Piedmont and western North Carolina. The main route of Interstate 85 between Charlotte and Greensboro now bypasses the city several miles to the east, which means average travelers must have a reason for going into Lexington. Heavy television and newspaper coverage of the festival helps maintain the visibility of the town's twenty barbecue restaurants and gives passersby all the reason they need to take the Lexington exit. Amtrak's Piedmont train, originating from Raleigh, and Carolinian train, originating from Charlotte, make once-a-year stops in Lexington for the festival.

Contests and festivals are important ways of keeping old customs alive, as evidenced by the large crowds attending such disparate North Carolina events as the annual hollerin' contest, the coastal duck decoy festival, and the mountain festival honoring the ramp, a pungent cousin to the onion. The Lexington Barbecue Festival and the dozens of barbecue contests scattered around the state certainly help keep North Carolina's premier food in the public eye. The state pork council has had a barbecue task force since the late 1980s, with the aim of not only promoting contests and festivals but also popularizing pig pickings as a fashionably casual way of re-encountering barbecue up close and personal. Over the past few years, barbecue may have lost a few popularity points to such items as grilled chicken breasts and taco salads as a menu choice. But as a savory symbol of North Carolina's rural heritage, barbecue is as popular and visible as ever—and that's largely due to its being celebrated so widely and so often.

# • Two Minutes of Barbecue Culture •

I explained some of the finer points of North Carolina barbecue to former *Good Morning America* weatherman Spencer Christian during a segment of the ABC program, broadcast live from the Duke University campus.
*Courtesy* Good Morning America

Not long after *North Carolina Barbecue: Flavored by Time* was published, I learned that ABC's *Good Morning America* was planning an on-location (and outdoor) show from the campus of Duke University in Durham. As the new so-called expert on North Carolina barbecue, I was contacted to appear in a live segment showcasing the state's barbecue traditions. Then-weatherman and co-host Spencer Christian would interview me as I showed off a barbecued whole hog, allowed him to sample eastern and Piedmont sauces, and presented a tableful of already-chopped barbecue and the usual accompaniments, including coleslaw, hush puppies, Brunswick

stew, banana pudding, and peach cobbler.

I arranged for a local farmer and barbecuer to cook a pig overnight and show up on the campus for the 8:45 A.M. segment with the freshly roasted hog displayed on the grate of his portable cooker. Meanwhile, I got busy collecting the various foods, tables, and serving implements I would need, including a freshly baked peach cobbler from Stamey's in Greensboro. The late Keith Stamey, co-owner with his brother Charles at the time, ended up baking four cobblers for the show before he turned one out he thought looked nice enough for national TV.

On a bright, freezing-cold winter

morning, I arrived early and began unloading my supplies on Duke's main quadrangle, only to find we had a potential problem with the roasted pig. A couple of twenty-something New York–based associate producers had opened the lid of the portable pit and gazed in horror at the well-browned carcass of the whole hog, which led them to conjure up visions of angry phone calls from PETA and other outraged viewers. The neophyte producers declared flatly that under no circumstances would the cooked hog be seen on TV. Naturally, the farmer who had been up all night cooking it did not take kindly to this development, nor did I, and our vigorous protests led to a series of over-the-headset conversations with other, more senior producers inside the TV truck. After a tense thirty minutes of negotiations, the show's executive producer ruled in our favor, and the potential crisis was averted.

We ended up having to hurriedly move the portable pig cooker, a long table heavily laden with food, a barbecue grill, and other props into place during a two-minute commercial break immediately preceding the feature, since the spot where we had planned to set up ahead of time would have blocked a long, scenic "cover" shot of the quadrangle and Duke Chapel.

As is often the case, we had too much material for the two-minute segment. I rushed through showing Christian the cooked pig (he wisecracked that some of his college dates had been "pig pickings"), letting him taste the fiery eastern vinegar-based sauce ("Whooo-eee!"), and describing the various side dishes and desserts normally consumed with North Carolina barbecue. Short on time, I had no opportunity to show the beautiful cobbler

over which Keith Stamey had labored so intently. But the GMA host was interested and engaged, the main points were well covered, and we made it through the feature with no slip-ups.

As soon as we were counted out of the segment and the cameras went to the next event on the rundown (a live performance of "Gasoline and Fried Chicken" by local band Southern Culture on the Skids), Christian was gone, and I found myself surrounded by famished Duke students. They had been braving the cold for several hours by that point, most had not eaten any breakfast, and they were determined to gobble up every scrap of food pulled together for the demonstration.

Seeing what was coming, the farmer—still peeved at the Yankee producers who had dissed his beautiful cooked pig—quickly locked his hog cooker, hooked it to his pickup, and roared away, depriving the eager students of their only possibility of warm food that morning. Everything else—chopped barbecue, hush puppies, and cobbler included—was bone-cold after a couple of hours in the chilly outdoor temperatures. But the students were not deterred in the slightest. Pushing and shoving, using complimentary Frisbees emblazoned with the Good Morning America logo as plates, and eating with near-frozen fingers, they wolfed down the frigid comestibles with enormous appetite and great appreciation. I wouldn't have thought students at such an expensive university would be attracted to a mound of icy, congealed glop, but most enthusiastically mumbled their thanks for the "free food." Go figure.

Those who help cook the hog get to do some pig pickin' before the guests show up.
*Courtesy of UNC-TV*

# PORK SHOULDER OR WHOLE HOG
## HOW TO PREPARE YOUR OWN NORTH CAROLINA BARBECUE

Barbecue is like a coquettish young woman, favoring only those suitors who ply her with considerable time and attention. Most of us, busy with our everyday lives, pay someone else to spend the long, hot hours required to prepare good barbecue—to carry on the dalliance, if you will—so that we can simply show up at the last minute and reap the rewards. But there are at least a couple of reasons why you occasionally might want to invest some time preparing your own barbecue.

The first is that barbecue is at its absolute peak of perfection when it's pulled straight off the bone, still steaming hot from the pit. Morsels of pork—reddish brown and crusty, creamy white and bursting with just-released juices, or cocoa hued and sweetly tender—will never again delight the senses in exactly the same way as when the bewitching, aromatic vapors from juices hissing onto hot coals rise swirling and wafting around the moist, succulent meat like a cloud of smiling attendants inviting guests to the banquet table. Of course, it is remotely possible to enjoy barbecue this perfect in a restaurant—provided you show up just as it's being freshly chopped, and providing that the fresh batch is intended to be served at once, which is seldom the case. On the other hand, even the best places find it difficult to hold barbecue at its most tender, flavorful point when it has to be kept warm over a period of time.

The other, more important reason—particularly for men—is that the very process of slow-cooking barbecue is a perfect focal point for a day of leisure in the company of others, especially since it also provides a superb meal to be shared at the end of the process. Barbecuing a pork shoulder in a backyard grill can engage the attention of one or two persons for much of a day, while cooking an entire pig is an undertaking suited to a slightly larger group.

Across the rural areas of eastern North Carolina, the all-day (or all-night) ritual of roasting a pig provides a setting for small groups of men to tell jokes, hold serious discussions on the issues of the day . . . and maybe do some sociable tippling. And even among those who don't live in the country, barbecuing a pig is a wonderful way for a group of fast friends to spend time together. But preparing a pig picking can also provide a great social framework for getting acquainted with people you don't really know. Many of those who live in suburban neighborhoods are so engrossed with jobs and child rearing that they hardly know their neighbors up and down the street. Throwing a pig picking is a surefire way to remedy that situation. You can choose four or five men and spend the day getting to know each other through the sharing of a task, all the while preparing a feast for a group of fifty or more. The details involved in actually cooking the pig will provide plenty of conversational material and help bridge any awkward lulls, while the minor mistakes and mishaps that are bound to occur will help cement your budding relationships with laughter. You may decide to furnish the entire meal, getting several people to help you with side dishes such as coleslaw and hush puppies; you might opt to purchase these accompaniments from a restaurant; or you may simply turn the event into a covered-dish buffet, the guests bringing their favorite side dishes and desserts. In any case, the guests will enjoy making a fuss over the gloriously roasted entrée, and you'll be assured of having pulled off a successful party.

If you would prefer to spend a quiet Saturday with your family or a friend or two, barbecuing a pork shoulder in an ordinary covered grill is a low-stress day-long activity that will leave plenty of time for visiting and puttering and provide enough meat to invite several couples over for dinner at the end of the day.

Whether you cook a single shoulder or an entire pig, the barbecue will be as good as any you've ever had in your life—and you'll have pleasant memories of the day you spent preparing it.

## Cooking a Pork Shoulder

While this is a process that doesn't require much work, it does take a good deal of time, so if you want to serve dinner at 6 P.M., you'll need to get started by 9 A.M. You'll need either a six- to seven-pound fresh shoulder picnic or Boston butt (the two halves cut from the twelve- to fifteen-pound whole shoulder, which is what's barbecued by restaurants); a covered kettle-type grill; ten pounds of high-quality hardwood charcoal (I prefer Kingsford); a bag of hickory wood *chunks* (not chips); a second grill or other container for lighting additional coals; a small shovel or scoop; and a pair of heavy-duty rubber gloves.

Begin by generously salting the exposed-meat side of the picnic or Boston butt. Leave it out at room temperature for thirty minutes or so while you're getting the charcoal fire ready. Light five pounds of charcoal in the bottom of the grill and wait until the briquettes are entirely covered with gray ash. When the coals are ready, push the briquettes into two even piles on opposite sides of the grill, leaving six or seven briquettes in a ten-inch circle at the center of the grill so the meat will have some coals to drip on, helping to create the important "grill" component of the taste. Gently place two hickory chunks on top of each pile, being careful not to collapse the mound of briquettes. When the chunks begin to smoke, put the wire cooking grate in place and set the shoulder on it, directly over the circle of coals in the center. Place the picnic or Boston butt meat side down so the fat can drip all the way through the meat and onto the coals; this keeps the meat from drying out. Place the cover on the grill, leaving the ventilation holes completely open.

(Note: With charcoal fires this small, I've found that hickory chips don't work well. If you soak them in water for thirty minutes, as the manufacturer recommends, they often kill the coals when they are placed on the fire. And if you put them atop the briquettes without soaking, they tend to catch fire, causing excessive darkening and drying of the meat. Larger chunks, on the other hand, are slow to burst into flame and usually provide a good thirty minutes of smoke before they need replacing. You won't need to soak them, since they seldom flame up as long as the cover is on the grill.)

As soon as you have the meat on the fire,

light another pile of around twelve briquettes in your secondary grill or fire bucket so they'll be ready to add to the grill in approximately thirty minutes. When the briquettes are completely covered with gray ash, transfer them to the grill, gently adding six briquettes to each pile. Some kettle grills such as the Weber brand have an opening at each side of the wire cooking grate that allows the addition of coals or wood chunks without removing the grate. Lay two more hickory chunks atop the fresh coals on each side, replacing the grill's lid as quickly as possible. One of my favorite outdoor-cooking implements is a folding army-surplus shovel or entrenching tool, which is ideal for transferring lighted coals from one grill to another. Actually, any small shovel or scoop will serve. A pair of barbecue tongs will also do the trick, although using tongs takes a little longer, since you can move only one briquette at a time.

Continue adding six fully lit briquettes and two hickory chunks to each side of the grill every thirty minutes or so. You won't need to add any briquettes to the center, directly under the meat, as it will become deeply browned without any additional coals there. Between the additions of fresh coals, try to resist the temptation to lift the lid to inspect the meat, as this causes significant heat loss and slows the cooking process.

Around three-thirty or four in the afternoon—or after about six hours on the grill—turn the picnic or Boston Butt so the meat side is facing up. At this point, you can reduce the number of coals to four or five on each side if it looks as though the meat is browning too quickly. But it's important to keep adding

Add six briquettes through the grate's side opening every thirty minutes.

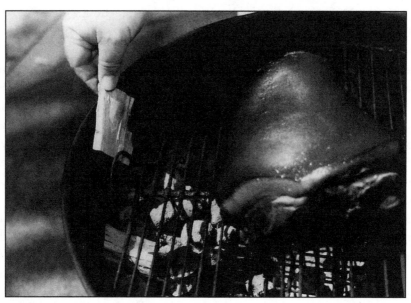

Drop two hickory or oak chunks on top of fresh briquettes.
*Photos by Everett Garner*

coals and wood chunks on a regular basis so the temperature in the kettle grill doesn't get too low.

After another couple of hours of cooking with the skin side down, both the exposed meat and the skin of the shoulder should be a deep reddish brown. Put on your rubber gloves and give the meat a good squeeze with both hands; it should be done enough for you to feel the meat "give" beneath your fingers. While still wearing the rubber gloves, transfer the shoulder from the grill to a pan or a cutting board. The skin covering one entire side of the shoulder should easily lift off in one piece with just a gentle tug. Set the skin aside and use a sharp knife to scrape or cut away any fat that may be clinging to the meat. The remaining lean meat should be tender enough for you to easily tear it off the bone in chunks by hand, although it's all right if you need to use a knife to finish the job.

Arrange the chunks of meat into a pile on the cutting board and chop the cooked pork with a heavy cleaver to the consistency you like. (You may prefer to either slice the meat or continue pulling it into smaller pieces with your fingers.) Liberally splash the meat with a sauce of your choice—a tart, vinegar-tomato Lexington-style sauce would be appropriate— and serve it either on plates accompanied by coleslaw or on warm, soft buns topped with slaw.

## Cooking an Entire Pig

Pig pickings are appropriate at any time of year, although fall and spring are my favorite pig-cooking seasons.

The heat of a summer's day will cause the pig to finish cooking much more quickly. And after tending a hot cooker in summer temperatures all day, you'll end up pretty well "done" yourself by the time dinner is served. Also, most people seem to eat a little more lightly in the summertime than is normal at a pig picking; on the hot, humid summer evenings that are typical in North Carolina, getting anywhere near a heated cooker may be more than most people want to tackle. In the winter, the cold air circulating around the cooker saps the heat and may cause you to have difficulty getting the pig cooked all the way through, unless you're using a sheltered location. You'll also have to arrange to serve—or at least eat—inside once the cooking is done.

The warm, gentle days and cool nights of autumn and spring are perfect for a pig picking. They not only provide a comfortable outdoor environment for cooking but also add a bounce to your step and a keenness to your appetite. In days gone by, pigs were often roasted in late summer or autumn on pits dug under the overhanging shelters of tobacco barns, as farmers celebrated the harvesting and curing of their crops. So fall may be the *most* perfect time for a pig picking. But really, the perfect time comes whenever you have a hankering for some great barbecue and a day of pleasant company.

You can obtain a whole pig for barbecuing from a meat-packing house, a barbecue wholesaler, or a retail supermarket, although you'll want to check to see what kind of advance notice a supermarket requires; it generally ranges from three to seven days. If you're a pig-picking novice, a hog that "dresses out" at 75 to 80 pounds is an easy size to handle and will cook in seven hours. Since the rule of thumb for feeding mixed male and female groups is 1½ pounds of carcass weight per person, a 75- to 80-pound pig will feed a crowd of twenty-five couples or a hungry all-male group of around forty. By comparison, a 100-pound pig will cook in eight hours and feed a mixed group of sixty-five, while a 125-pound pig will take nine hours and feed a mixed crowd of around eighty-five. Don't become confused by the difference between a pig's weight "on the hoof" and the "dressed weight" you'll specify when you order; "dressed weight" means the pig will be completely cleaned and scraped free of bristles, and that its head will have been removed.

(Note: If the cooker you're using has some provision such as a double grate for turning the pig during cooking, you should specify that you want the pig delivered with the backbone split, so the pig will lie flat on the grate, but with the skin left intact. Otherwise, I suggest you have the supplier go ahead and cut the pig in half lengthwise, since the two separate halves will be fairly easy to turn by hand. You can also easily take care of this task yourself.)

A lot of fancy, custom-made pork cookers are available, most of which are designed for use in pig-cooking competitions. All you'll need, though, is a simple cooker of the type made from a 250-gallon oil tank mounted on a two-wheeled trailer. These are generally available for a reasonable rental charge at various locations around the state. If you have trouble finding a source, try asking the meat packer or grocer who's supplying your pig. (The perfect situation, of course, is to have a friend who will let you borrow his cooker.) Your cooker should be outfitted with a wire grate, a door cut into each end for adding coals and supplying ventilation, and a smokestack. If you rent, the agency will expect you to return the cooker in a reasonably clean condition, with the coals and ashes removed and the grate scraped clean of meat and skin.

I use charcoal and either wood chunks or split logs for cooking pigs. I know that purists insist only wood coals can impart the right flavor to barbecued pork, while others swear by the precise temperature control that gas cookers provide. But I'm convinced that high-quality hardwood charcoal briquettes such as the ones made by Kingsford provide just as much taste as wood coals, especially if you add pieces of wood to smolder on top of the charcoal. They also hold their heat much longer, meaning you need fewer coals and don't have to add them as frequently. (Gas is much easier and more precise but in my opinion adds no outdoor-cooked taste at all.) You'll need 60 pounds of charcoal for a 75- to 80-pound pig, 70 pounds for a pig weighing 100 pounds, and 80 pounds for a 125-pound pig. (Note: The alternate method outlined later in this chapter requires considerably less charcoal.)

In addition to a pig, a cooker, and charcoal, you'll need the following items for your pig picking: a kettle-type grill or other

Lighted briquettes are transferred from an ordinary grill, *foreground*, to a pig cooker.
*Courtesy of UNC-TV*

Place hickory or oak chunks on top of lighted charcoal briquettes on the floor of the cooker to produce extra smoke and flavor. Even if they aren't soaked in water, they shouldn't catch fire if the air vents aren't open too wide.
*Courtesy of UNC-TV*

container for lighting additional coals, lighter fluid, a shovel and hoe for transferring and spreading coals, a table to hold your various supplies, paper towels, heavy-duty rubber gloves for handling the pork, a container for sauce and some sort of basting implement, a cleaver and a chopping board if you plan to chop any of the barbecue, chairs for "kicking back," and your favorite cool beverages.

For a seventy-five- to eighty-pound pig that you want to serve at 6 P.M., you should get started by 9 A.M.; this will allow a couple hours more than the recommended seven-hour cooking time to cover setting up, organizing your supplies, and getting your first coals ready. It will also give you a little bit of a "fudge factor" in case you inadvertently let the coals go out or have some other minor problem during the day.

Begin by opening the cooker's lid, removing and setting aside the cooking grate, and placing a twenty-pound bag of charcoal so that it lies flat in the center of the cooker's floor. Rip open the entire top side of the bag and generously soak the briquettes with lighter fluid. Give the fluid a minute to soak in before you light the charcoal. Leave the lid open while the coals are burning down to their desired state.

While you wait on the coals, trim and discard any excess fat or unsightly scraps from the pig. You'll probably also want to use a saw to cut off the hooves, or "trotters," and to get rid of the tail, since some guests won't appreciate any extraneous reminders of the pig's former existence as an actual barnyard animal. Using a large, sharp knife, make a couple of deep cuts parallel to the bone in the exposed-meat side of each shoulder or ham. (In a contest, these cuts would cause points to be deducted under the "appearance" category, but in the real world, most cooks believe they help ensure that the meat gets thoroughly done right down to the bone. They also provide more surface to become browned and chewy.) Generously salt all the exposed meat.

When the briquettes in the cooker are covered with gray ash, use a garden hoe or rake to spread them in an even layer across the entire floor of the cooker so that no coal is resting atop or touching another. Replace the cooking grate and have someone help you carry the pig or its two halves to the cooker. Place it centered—skin side up—on the grate. Make sure the pig is lying flat, then close the lid.

Once the pig is on the grill, take a well-deserved break for a few minutes, then light another five pounds of charcoal in your secondary grill so it will be ready to scatter under the pig about forty-five minutes after it was first placed on the cooker. Once this second batch of coals is ready, divide it evenly and scatter the coals beneath the hams and shoulders only. Use a shovel and reach through the door at each end of the cooker to spread the coals. No additional briquettes will be required under the center of the pig until it is turned skin side down; if you add coals to this area before then, there's a good chance the rib area will be burned when you turn the pig over.

Repeat this process over the course of

To begin, soak an entire twenty-pound bag of briquettes with charcoal lighter.
*Photo by Mike Oniffrey*

Spread five pounds of lit briquettes beneath the hams and shoulders every forty-five minutes.
*Photo by Mike Oniffrey*

the next five hours. Every forty-five minutes or so, evenly spread five pounds of briquettes, covered with gray ash, beneath the hams and shoulders. Periodically check the ventilation door at each end of the cooker; normally, the doors should be cracked open about an inch to allow air circulation over the coals. Avoid lifting the lid to look at the cooking meat, as this causes much of the accumulated heat to be lost. The temperature inside the cooker should remain at a fairly constant level of about 225 degrees. But unlike some of the high-tech competition cookers, yours probably won't have a thermometer, so you'll have to use your hand to estimate the temperature. You should be able to rest your palm on the cooker's closed lid for two seconds (count, "One thousand one, one thousand two"). If you can't leave it there that long, the cooker is too hot. You should also be able to hear just an *occasional* hiss of fat dripping onto the coals and see either heat waves or just a wisp of smoke coming out of the stack. Heavy smoke or continuous "frying" sounds from the grill are sure signs that the cooker is too hot. To cool things down, close the ventilation doors tightly for a few minutes.

The biggest challenge in the entire cooking process comes after five and a half to six hours, when it's time to turn the pig meat side up. The pig essentially will be done by this time, and the difficulty arises in turning the meat without having it fall apart. If you have a second grate, place it upside down on top of the pig so the wire side is resting against the skin and the pig is "sandwiched" between the two grates. Then place one person at each of the four corners. Have the people at the corners squeeze the two grates together and quickly turn the pig over so that it rests skin side down, then remove the extra grate. If you have no second grate, and the pig is in one piece, have four people—wearing gloves—each grasp a ham or a shoulder. When you give the signal, have them lift the pig and roll it toward the front edge of the cooker, allowing the bottom half to fold beneath the top half. Then slide the "folded" pig toward the center and unfold it so that it once again lies flat on the grate, with the meat side facing up. If you had your pig cut in half lengthwise, you should have no trouble turning the two halves, although you'll need to transfer them to opposite sides of the grill so they'll be laid out properly, with the two halves of the split backbone aligned side by side.

Turning the pig is an occasion for anxious anticipation. Cheers inevitably break out when the meat side first comes into view and turns out to be cooked to a perfect shade of reddish brown, with no charred spots. However, if you let your coals get too hot so that your first effort results in the meat being a little too dark, take comfort in the fact that the charred areas can easily be pulled or scraped off—and resolve to back off on the heat the next time.

Once the pig is turned, the work is basically done. Only a few minor tasks remain. First, light a final five to ten pounds of charcoal in the second grill. While you're waiting for the briquettes to be ready, generously brush the entire surface of the meat with melted margarine (or simply squirt it from a

A whole pig is easier to turn if it's split in half. Salt the rib side before putting the pig, rib side down, on the grill.
*Courtesy of UNC-TV*

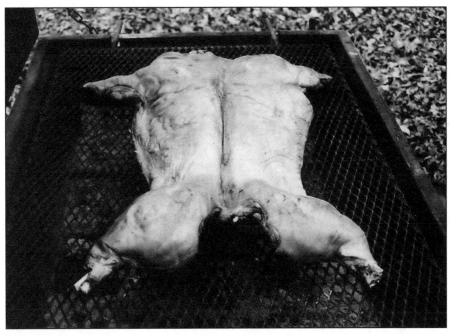

Roast the pig skin side up for the first six hours.
*Photo by Mike Oniffrey*

The two halves of the pig are easy to turn using heavy rubber gloves.
*Courtesy of UNC-TV*

Baste the pig with sauce after it's turned.
*Courtesy of UNC-TV*

squeeze bottle) to help glaze and soften the meat. Next, baste the meat thoroughly with your favorite barbecue sauce, allowing the sauce to reach a depth of one inch in the rib cavities. Some people prefer to use some type of mop to apply the sauce, others shake it out of a bottle onto the pig, and still others use a spoon or ladle to dip the sauce onto the meat; as far as I can tell, one method is as good as another. Once the last pile of coals is covered with gray ash, scatter them in an even layer across the entire floor of the cooker, as was done with the first batch of briquettes. This final layer of charcoal makes the pig's skin brown and crisp; it also finishes cooking the meat and keeps it hot until it's time for dinner to be served.

It's perfectly acceptable for the cooking crew and the first few guests to stand around the cooker and "pick the pig," pulling off the choicest morsels and dipping them in sauce before popping them into their mouths. If your party is an all-male gathering, it's probably acceptable to simply lay out a few knives and large kitchen forks and let guests help themselves to the roasted pork. However, for most groups, you'll need to arrange for one or two persons to help serve meat to the guests. At most eastern North Carolina pig pickings, at least a portion of the pork is taken from the grill and, with the fat and skin removed, chopped to the desired consistency with a heavy cleaver, then seasoned to taste with barbecue sauce. As guests file past the grill with their plates, they have a choice of pulling their own servings of meat from the pig, being helped to slices or chunks of meat by a server, or being served portions of chopped, seasoned barbecue.

Many cooks even in the coastal plain use a basic hot vinegar sauce to season the chopped barbecue but serve more of a Piedmont-style "finishing" sauce—hot vinegar plus tomato and sweetener—for ladling over meat that's to be "picked" from the pig. Your own preferences are all that matter here. I've included several sauce recipes in the recipe section of this chapter. I've also added instructions in the section just ahead on how to season your chopped or pulled barbecue "freehand" before serving it, at which time you can provide bottled sauce for those who want to add to your initial seasoning.

## A Much Easier Alternate Method

The process I've just described is still the way 90 percent of the hogs are cooked over charcoal and wood in North Carolina, and it's the way I did it for thirty years. It will work for you perfectly if you follow the steps I've laid out. It's probably the way to go if you plan to serve in the evening, want to spend the day cooking the pig with your friends, and will enjoy puttering with it every so often.

However, I also want to describe a much easier alternate method that I've begun using during the last decade. It was taught to me by Ed Mitchell, who learned it many years ago from James Kirby of Wilson when Ed was just getting started in the barbecue business. This is by far the easiest procedure if you'll be cooking overnight, chopping and seasoning the meat the next morning, and serving in the middle of the day or early afternoon. If you're looking for an excuse to stay up all night sipping with your buddies, you won't care for this approach. But if you would just as soon put the pig on the fire, go home to bed, and come back to find it done in the morning, here's your answer. Or if you'll be too busy during the day to continuously attend to a pig you want to serve at suppertime, this process will suit you to a T.

In this process, you'll light at once all the charcoal you'll use for cooking the pig, and you won't have to add any more coals except in the rarest of instances. You'll basically be able to put the pig on the fire and forget about it for seven or eight hours.

For a 100- to 120-pound pig, light *two* 20-pound bags of charcoal side by side by cutting open each bag and soaking the charcoal—bags and all—with lighter fluid. Light the bags and let the lighter fluid burn off completely. While the 40 pounds of briquettes are gradually becoming covered with gray ash, use a rake or shovel to arrange them in a line along each of the four sides of the cooker, using approximately ten pounds on each side so you end up with a roughly rectangular shape with the middle fairly empty of coals. Then rake some briquettes—twenty or so—from the rows along the sides into the middle, so you'll have a few live coals for the juice from the pig to drip onto, creating the "grill" flavor you'll want.

When the coals are completely covered with ash, gently lay a length or two of split oak or hickory firewood—or a few large oak or hickory chunks—atop each of the four rows of charcoal, get your grate in place, and put the pig on the middle of the grill skin side up, remembering to salt the "belly side" fairly heavily before laying it over the embers. (Nowadays, I always cut my whole hogs completely into two halves so they'll be easier to handle and so I don't have to worry about performing too many contortions in turning the pig—provided I plan to turn it at all, which I don't always do.) The firewood may blaze up temporarily while you're getting the pig in place, especially if it's dry and well cured, but the flame will become starved of oxygen and will subside as soon as you shut the cooker lid, provided you don't leave too much ventilation. It will, however, continue to smoke heavily, which will add another layer of flavor to the meat during the cooking process. Once you've shut and locked down the cooker's lid, make sure its chimneys are cracked open enough to create a draft, and leave a small opening in any side doors to the pit.

If you want a pig picking in which the entire pig is laid out for people to pinch and pull their own morsels of meat, and if you intend to baste it with sauce for that purpose, plan to turn the pig after five or six hours of cooking. At that point, you'll be able to turn it without its being so completely done that it falls apart when you try to flip it. However, you won't have to add any coals, open the lid, or fuss with it in any other way until you're ready to do the turning. Get your beauty sleep, and when the time comes, simply open the lid and use heavy rubber gloves to turn the two halves, making sure the legs are still pointing toward the outsides of the grate. As quickly as you can, mop the meat with sauce as described previously and shut the lid before too much heat is lost. Cook for another hour or two, and the meat will be falling-apart tender and ready to either pick, pull, or chop.

If, on the other hand, you plan to make chopped or pulled barbecue out of the entire pig and don't intend to have the guests pull the meat off the bone for themselves, you don't have to turn the pig at all while it's cooking. Sleep for an extra hour or two. When you open the lid, the meat should be falling off the bone.

It is conceivable that if you've been cooking in extremely low temperatures, and especially if a strong wind has been blowing, the pig might not be entirely done at the end of seven to eight hours. (You can tell by sticking the point of a knife into the ends of the legs and probing around a little. If you encounter any resistance, the meat isn't yet done and needs to cook a little longer.) In that case, simply light another ten pounds or so of charcoal in a separate grill. When the coals are covered with gray ash, scatter them evenly under the pig with a small shovel. Give it another hour or two of cooking, and you should be in good shape.

Once the pig is completely done, I don't try to turn it over if I haven't turned it earlier, as that would pretty well guarantee it would break apart and make a mess. Instead, I try to gently pull or cut away the skin and set it aside, keeping it as intact as possible. After letting the meat cool to a point at which I can handle it with heavy gloves, I discard bones and excess fat into a trash can and break the remaining meat into large chunks, which I place in long pans. I continue in this way until I've worked my way through all the meat and have accumulated several pans full.

Next, I lay the skin out on the grill in as close to its original shape as possible and scrape the excess fat off with a knife or spatula. In a little while, I'll use the skin as a sort of "serving platter" on the grill, from which guests can use tongs to help themselves to appetizingly prepared and seasoned meat—with no pulling, wrestling, or digging through unappetizing globs of fat!

On a nearby worktable, I use my fingers to shred the pork into hunks, discarding additional fat and bone as I come across it. Sometimes, I chop a portion of it with a cleaver to make some chopped barbecue. Other times, I simply offer the entire pig as "pulled pork," which seems more appropriate when I'm serving it directly from the grill and off the brown, crispy skin.

I like to lightly pre-season my chopped or pulled barbecue while it's still in the pans and before I pile it back onto the pig skin on the grill for serving. I sprinkle the meat liberally with salt, black pepper, vinegar, sugar, and Texas Pete hot sauce, then mix it up with my hands (using plastic gloves) until the seasonings are well incorporated into the meat. I have no particular recipe for this process; I simply taste the meat and decide which of the above ingredients, if any, need to be added. (It's important, though, to get a sufficient amount of salt onto the barbecue so that the flavors really "pop.") Once I have the meat seasoned to taste, I put out bottles of barbecue sauce for guests to add as their taste requires. The initial seasoning tends to sink into the meat quite a bit, so most people want additional sauce.

Side dishes that are particularly well received at a pig picking include coleslaw, hush puppies or baked corn bread, boiled (barbecued) potatoes, Brunswick stew, and either banana pudding or fruit cobbler for dessert. Recipes for some of these dishes are included in the next section. If you want to concentrate your efforts on cooking the pig and minimize additional food preparation, you may decide to simply ask each guest to bring a side dish, a beverage, or a dessert.

## • It's Great Pig, Y'all •

A producer for one of Paula Deen's early TV programs, *Paula's Home Cooking*, called to book me as a guest for a segment on North Carolina barbecue. The premise was that Paula would ostensibly take a road trip to North Carolina to visit me, and I, as the state's "barbecue expert," would explain the background of our east/Piedmont barbecue schism and demonstrate the basics of preparing authentic Tar Heel barbecue on a kettle-style home charcoal grill. But rather than bringing Paula and an entire crew to North Carolina, the New York–based producers flew me to Paula's adopted hometown of Savannah, where each half-hour program was taped in two days' time. We would shoot the supposed North Carolina visit at a local lakeside park. The idea was for Paula to drive up, get out of her vehicle, and greet me as though she had just arrived at some unnamed barbecue demonstration site I had arranged on my home turf.

The schedule was tight. I would fly in the night before, shoot the segment the next morning, and be on a plane home by early

afternoon. I would have no time to cook a pork shoulder on-site for the necessary seven to eight hours, so I would need to bring a precooked joint ready to be reheated on the grill, plus the fixings for coleslaw, hush puppies, and boiled potatoes.

At home, I slow-roasted a hunk of pork to golden brown perfection, froze it, and packed it in a cooler for the flight, which, due to weather delays, didn't arrive in Savannah until nearly midnight. I had thought I would get in early enough for the meat to have plenty of time to thaw before the morning's shoot, but when I reached my hotel, I found that the shoulder was still frozen solid. Not knowing what else to do, I unwrapped it and left it on the bathroom sink to thaw as much as possible during the next few hours.

Not long after daylight, the producer picked me up and drove me to the segment location, where the crew had, at my instruction, set up a Weber charcoal grill and some other equipment and supplies I would need to "make barbecue happen." The shoulder itself still felt partially frozen inside,

Clowning around with Paula Deen on location for *Paula's Home Cooking* in Savannah, Georgia

but it *looked* great for television. I figured I could get enough thawed and warmed meat from the outside of the eight-pound Boston butt to demonstrate how to properly chop and season barbecue and to create a couple of attractive plates for the two of us.

Paula Deen was busy with makeup when I arrived, so we didn't have a chance to meet or chat at first. Clad in utilitarian shorts and T-shirt, I went quickly to work, getting my charcoal going, my pork reheating on the grill, and my cooking table and implements arranged as the TV crew set up lights, reflectors, and a couple of cameras.

By the time I arranged everything and did a quick wardrobe change, Paula was ready to say hello before we began shooting. With a twinkle in her eye, she walked straight up to me, held out her hand, and, repeating a barbecue advertising slogan she had heard somewhere, declared, "Honey, I can't wait to wrap my lips around yo' pig!"

As I stood speechless, mouth wide open, the entire crew burst into laughter. The ice was not only broken but crushed finely enough for a frozen daiquiri. Throughout the subsequent videotaped sequences of her "arriving" and my demonstrating how to cook and prepare barbecue and trimmings, we both had to suppress giggles.

To this day, I have never seen the finished *Paula's Home Cooking* segment (although most of my friends have), but I did come home with a great anecdote to relate at dinner parties.

Boiled potatoes, sometimes flavored with vinegar, ketchup, and pepper, often accompany barbecue in eastern North Carolina. This shot shows a man cooking potatoes for a large barbecue at Braswell Plantation near Rocky Mount, 1944.
*Courtesy of the North Carolina Archives*

# RECIPES

## Barbecue Sauces

North Carolina is practically afloat in barbecue sauce. Even if you've never mixed your own sauce and decide to try one of the recipes listed here, you won't be able to resist adding your own ingredients—which is exactly why so many sauces are out there. Have fun.

### Quick and Easy Basting and Pig-Picking Sauce

1 gallon apple cider vinegar
1 bottle Kraft regular barbecue sauce
½ jar (approximately 1½ ounces) crushed red pepper
3-ounce bottle Texas Pete hot sauce
1 tablespoon salt

1 cup brown or white sugar
1 stick butter or margarine (optional)

Combine all ingredients in a large pot. Bring to a simmer and cook, stirring, until sugar melts.

After basting, pour remaining sauce into small containers to serve with cooked pig.

### Basic Eastern North Carolina–Style Sauce

(Courtesy of the North Carolina Pork Council)

2 quarts apple cider vinegar
1¼ to 1½ ounces crushed red pepper
2 tablespoons salt, or to taste
1 tablespoon black pepper, or to taste

Mix all ingredients well. Use to baste pig and to season chopped barbecue to taste.

### Lexington-Style "Dip"

This sauce has a thousand variations. Be sure to give rein to your creativity even if you follow the basic proportions shown here.

3 cups apple cider vinegar
⅔ cup brown or white sugar
½ cup ketchup
2 tablespoons Texas Pete hot sauce
1 teaspoon salt
1 teaspoon black pepper
1 teaspoon Worcestershire sauce
1 teaspoon onion powder
2 teaspoons Kitchen Bouquet browning sauce

Combine all ingredients in a large pot. Bring to a simmer and cook, stirring, until sugar melts.

Let sit for several hours before serving over chopped or sliced pork shoulder.

## Side Dishes for a Barbecue or Pig Picking

### Eastern North Carolina–Style Coleslaw

This is a recipe from my wife, Ruthie. It's typical of the coleslaw served at pig pickings and fish fries along the Roanoke River in Halifax and Martin counties.

1 medium-sized firm head of cabbage
1½ cups mayonnaise
⅓ cup prepared mustard
¾ cup sweet pickle cubes

2 tablespoons apple cider vinegar
½ cup sugar
1 tablespoon celery seed
1½ teaspoons salt
⅛ teaspoon black pepper

Refrigerate cabbage until ready to use; do not allow it to reach room temperature once you begin. Remove outer leaves and core from cabbage. Cut head in half and finely grate with a food processor or hand grater. In a large bowl, combine cabbage and remaining ingredients. Mix thoroughly. Chill for one hour before serving. Serves 20.

### Piedmont-Style Coleslaw

Here's a tangy, red Piedmont-style coleslaw similar to what is served at Stamey's in Greensboro and Fuzzy's in Madison. This has a bite to it!

1 medium-sized firm head of cabbage
½ cup apple cider vinegar
½ cup sugar
⅔ cup ketchup
2 teaspoons salt
2 teaspoons black pepper
2 teaspoons Texas Pete hot sauce

Refrigerate cabbage until ready to use. Remove outer leaves and core from cabbage. Cut head in half and coarsely grate with a food processor or hand grater so cabbage bits are about the size of BBs. Return cabbage to refrigerator. In a small mixing bowl, combine vinegar, sugar, ketchup, and seasonings and mix well. Remove cabbage from refrigerator and pour this mixture over it. Mix with a large spoon until well blended. (Note: This may look dry at first, but there's plenty of liquid to moisten the cabbage thoroughly if you keep mixing.) Refrigerate 1 hour before serving. Serves 20.

## Tad's Barbecue Potatoes

My brother-in-law Tad Everett's recipe is a slight variation on the boiled potatoes found in most eastern North Carolina barbecue restaurants, but the folks around Palmyra, Hobgood, and Oak City always go for these in a big way!

5 pounds potatoes
4 large yellow onions
¼ cup bacon drippings
20-ounce bottle ketchup
¼ to ½ cup Texas Pete hot sauce, according to taste
⅓ cup sugar
salt and pepper to taste

Peel potatoes and onions and cut into large chunks. Place in a large pot and cover with water. Add remaining ingredients, stir to blend, and bring potatoes to a boil. Reduce heat and simmer for 30 to 40 minutes until potatoes are soft. Let potatoes sit over low heat, stirring occasionally, until ready to serve. Serves 20.

## Bob Garner's Barbecue Beans

1 medium onion
1 green bell pepper
1½ tablespoons vegetable oil
2 14.5-ounce cans baked beans or pork and beans, drained
1½ 14.5-ounce cans kidney beans (light red, dark red, or one of each), drained
1½ 14.5-ounce cans black beans, drained
1 tablespoon chili powder
1 tablespoon cumin
½ teaspoon salt
1 tablespoon apple cider vinegar
1 cup sugar

Dice onion and green pepper and sauté in vegetable oil until soft. Add beans and remaining ingredients and simmer over low heat until heated through, stirring frequently to prevent sticking. Serves 20.

## Hush Puppies

Several good hush puppy mixes are on the market, but this is a recipe from scratch that I developed. My friends tell me these 'pups are as good as any they've ever tasted.

3 cups self-rising white cornmeal
1 cup all-purpose flour
1 tablespoon sugar
1 teaspoon baking powder
1 teaspoon onion powder or 1 medium onion, chopped fine (optional)
2¼ cups buttermilk
2 tablespoons bacon drippings

Combine dry ingredients (along with chopped onion, if desired) in a large mixing

Hush puppies fry up perfectly at 350 to 370 degrees. You can squeeze the dough from a pastry bag or simply scoop it with a spoon.
*Courtesy of UNC-TV*

bowl. Add buttermilk and bacon drippings, stirring until well blended. Heat oil to 350 degrees in a deep fryer or Dutch oven. Spread batter evenly, ½ inch thick, on flat surface of a pancake turner or spatula. Use a sharp knife to trim excess from sides and end of turner. Holding spatula over hot oil, cut straight down through batter, then push ½-inch-wide "fingers" of batter sideways off end of turner and into hot oil. Cook only a few at a time. You'll need to keep "reloading" the end of the pancake turner with batter, rather than working your way all the way down to the handle. As hush puppies float, turn them so they brown evenly. Drain on paper towels. Makes about 3 dozen.

**Skillet Corn Bread**

Some people prefer baked corn bread, rather than hush puppies, with barbecue. Here's an easy recipe that produces a tasty, rather flat corn bread with a crispy crust and top.

2 tablespoons bacon drippings
1½ cups self-rising cornmeal
½ teaspoon salt
1¼ cups whole milk

Preheat oven to 500 degrees. Place bacon drippings in a well-seasoned cast-iron skillet and put skillet in oven for 3 to 4 minutes. While skillet is heating, combine cornmeal, salt, and milk in a bowl, stirring until well blended. When drippings are very hot, remove skillet from oven (using a thick oven mitt) and pour drippings into batter, quickly stirring to blend. Quickly pour batter into skillet; mixture should sizzle. Place skillet in oven and immediately reduce heat to 450 degrees. Bake approximately 20 minutes until golden brown. Cut in wedges to serve. Serves 6 to 8.

## Brunswick Stew

Many residents of rural eastern North Carolina pride themselves on their Brunswick stew recipes. Getting together on a winter weekend to "cook a stew" in a large iron wash pot is an activity that, like a pig picking, usually involves several families and consumes an entire Saturday. Most recipes are for seventy to eighty quarts of stew, which are typically divided among the participating families and frozen. Many churches and organizations also make and sell Brunswick stew to raise funds.

The following recipe is a little more manageable; it makes around seven quarts. It's similar to the wonderful Brunswick stew once sold at Scotland Neck's Whitaker's Barbecue, which was open only on weekends and was more commonly known simply as "the Barbecue Stand." You'll notice that this stew does not contain green beans, garden peas, carrots, okra, or other extraneous vegetables commonly added to stews in Piedmont North Carolina.

Even though this recipe is designed to be made in a kitchen rather than over a fire in the backyard, the work will be lighter and you'll have more fun if you invite a friend over for the day to help you make it.

2 quarts water
3½ - to 4-pound chicken, cut up
14.5-ounce can baby lima beans, undrained
8-ounce can baby lima beans, undrained
2 28-ounce cans whole tomatoes, undrained and chopped
16-ounce package frozen baby lima beans
3 medium potatoes, peeled and diced
1 large yellow onion, diced
2 14.5-ounce cans cream-style white corn
¼ cup sugar
½ stick unsalted butter or margarine
1 tablespoon salt
1 teaspoon pepper
2 teaspoons hot sauce

Bring water and chicken to a boil in a Dutch oven. Reduce heat and simmer for 40 minutes or until chicken is tender. Remove chicken and set aside. Reserve 3 cups broth in Dutch oven. Pour canned lima beans and liquid through a wire-mesh strainer into Dutch oven. Reserve beans. Add tomatoes to Dutch oven. Bring to a boil over medium-high heat. Cook, stirring often, for 40 minutes or until liquid is reduced by ⅓.

Skin, bone, and shred chicken. Mash reserved beans with a potato masher. Add chicken, mashed and frozen beans, potatoes, and onions to Dutch oven. Cook over low heat, stirring often, for 3½ hours. (To avoid having to stir, place covered pot in a 300-degree oven for the same period.) Stir in corn and remaining ingredients. Cook over low heat on stovetop or in a 300-degree oven for 1 additional hour, stirring often if on stovetop. Serves approximately 30.

For the summer version of banana pudding, arrange a layer of cookies, one of bananas, one of custard, and one of whipped cream, then repeat. For the winter version, arrange two successive layers of cookies, bananas, and custard, then spread meringue on top.
*Courtesy of UNC-TV*

## Desserts

### Banana Pudding

Banana pudding is the most widely served dessert in North Carolina's barbecue restaurants, probably because it's relatively quick and easy and because the creamy taste and soft texture provide a pleasant contrast to the tangy bite of the barbecue and/or cole-slaw. Even though most restaurants make a simple version using instant vanilla pudding instead of real custard, the extra trouble required to follow the following two recipes from my wife, Ruthie, will be amply rewarded when you serve your guests. I've included a winter version with a rich golden meringue topping and a refrigerated summer version crowned by whipped cream.

### Winter Banana Pudding

8 eggs
2 tablespoons flour
1¾ cups sugar, divided
scant ¼ teaspoon salt
4 cups whole milk
1½ teaspoons vanilla
pinch of freshly ground nutmeg
½ teaspoon cream of tartar
1 box Nabisco Nilla Wafers
7 medium to large firm, ripe bananas, sliced

### Custard:

Separate eggs. Put egg whites in refrigerator to chill. Beat egg yolks by hand until smooth, then gradually whisk in flour, 1¼ cups of the sugar, and salt. Gradually add milk, stirring constantly. Slowly bring to a near boil over moderate heat, stirring constantly. Cook about 10 minutes until thickened. Remove custard from heat and stir in vanilla and nutmeg.

### Meringue:

Beat egg whites and cream of tartar with an electric mixer until soft peaks form. Slowly add remaining ½ cup sugar, continuing to beat until stiff peaks form.

Line bottom and sides of a 9-by-12-inch baking dish with Nilla Wafers. Cover wafers with a layer of sliced bananas, using around 3½ bananas. Spead ½ of custard over bananas. Make another layer of remaining Nilla Wafers, remaining 3½ bananas, and remaining custard. Spread meringue over top of custard, making sure to push it all the way to the edges and to "seal" it so it doesn't shrink. Bake at 425 degrees for 5 minutes or until meringue is browned, then let sit at room temperature for several hours before serving to allow ingredients to blend and soften. Serves 10 to 12.

## Summer Banana Pudding

8 egg yolks
2 tablespoons flour
1¾ cups sugar, divided

scant ¼ teaspoon salt
4 cups whole milk
1½ teaspoons vanilla
pinch of freshly ground nutmeg
1 pint whipping cream
1 box Nabisco Nilla Wafers
7 medium to large firm, ripe bananas, sliced

### Custard:

Beat egg yolks by hand until smooth, then gradually whisk in flour, 1¼ cups of the sugar, and salt. Gradually add milk, stirring constantly. Slowly bring to a near boil over moderate heat, stirring constantly. Cook about 10 minutes until thickened. Remove custard from heat and stir in vanilla and nutmeg.

### Whipped Cream:

Beat whipping cream at high speed with an electric mixer until it begins to thicken. Continue beating while slowly adding remaining ½ cup sugar. Beat until soft peaks form. Set aside.

Line bottom and sides of a 9-by-12-inch baking dish with Nilla Wafers. Cover wafers with a layer of sliced bananas, using around 3½ bananas. Spead ½ of custard over bananas. Spread ½ of the whipped cream over the custard. Make another layer of remaining Nilla Wafers (reserving a handful to crush for garnish, if desired), remaining bananas, and remaining custard. Spread remaining whipped cream over top.

Refrigerate for several hours. If desired, garnish with crushed vanilla wafers. Serves 10 to 12.

**Peach Cobbler**

Next to banana pudding, peach cobbler is the dessert that seems to go best with barbecue. Chip Stamey of Stamey's in Greensboro prepares two outstanding fruit cobblers (usually served topped with vanilla ice cream), but they say peach outsells cherry by about ten to one. He was understandably reluctant to share Stamey's recipe, which uses canned peaches, but Ruthie Garner's version, with either frozen or fresh fruit, is also a triumphant finale for a pig picking . . . or any other meal.

3 cups plus 4 tablespoons flour, divided
1½ teaspoons salt
2 sticks (1 cup) softened butter, cut into ½-inch slices
7 to 8 teaspoons ice water
3 1-pound bags frozen unsweetened peaches, thawed, or 7 cups sliced fresh peaches
2 cups sugar
⅓ cup melted butter
zest of 1 small lemon
juice of 1 small lemon

**Crust:**

Sift 3 cups of the flour and mix with salt. Using a pastry cutter, fork, or just your fingers, cut or work softened butter into flour

Lemon juice and lemon zest add a delicious touch to peach cobbler. I prefer fresh or frozen peaches to the canned version, and I like pie pastry, rather than biscuit-dough topping.
*Courtesy of UNC-TV*

until mixture is in even bits about the size of small peas. Gradually add ice water and mix lightly with a fork until mixture begins to form into a ball. Wrap ball in plastic wrap and chill in freezer for 5 minutes. (If you prefer a more biscuit-like crust, substitute self-rising flour for regular flour, add 4 tablespoons sugar to the flour, and eliminate the salt. Substitute milk for ice water but otherwise prepare the pastry as described above.)

### Filling:

In a mixing bowl, combine peaches, sugar, remaining 4 tablespoons flour, melted butter, lemon zest, and lemon juice. Mix thoroughly. Spread ½ of filling mixture in the bottom of a 9-by-12-inch glass baking dish.

Remove pastry from freezer and divide into 2 pieces. Roll or pat out 1 piece to a normal piecrust thickness and cut into ½-inch strips. Lay strips across peaches in baking dish. Roll out remaining pastry and cut it into strips. Pour remaining fruit into baking dish and lay remaining pastry strips atop the fruit. Bake at 425 degrees for 10 minutes, then reduce heat to 350 degrees and bake an additional 50 minutes until golden brown.

Let cobbler cool. Serve topped with vanilla ice cream or whipped cream. Serves 10.

I know that several of these recipes probably look a little intimidating or complicated for our hurry-up age, but let me remind you that these are meant to be leisure-day dishes prepared for the pure fun of it—or perhaps as a way of quietly paying tribute to a less-hectic time. They have delighted the palates of Tar Heels for generations. For me, learning to prepare them has been a lot like learning to cook barbecue—a satisfying way to participate in our collective experience as North Carolinians.

# • Flay-ed in the Backyard •

The producers of Bobby Flay's *FoodNation*, another early Food Network program, called to have me help put together a segment on North Carolina barbecue. Bobby and his crew were going to be in Charlotte for one day. They wanted the barbecue feature to be one of three different pieces— making up an entire half-hour episode of the show—that could be shot that day. (The others were a profile of a Charlotte soul-food restaurant, The Coffee Cup, and a segment to be filmed at the home of an up-and-coming Charlotte chef.) Ours was to be the last shoot of the afternoon, after which Bobby and the crew would board their motor coach and travel overnight to Kentucky, where they would tape another three features the *next* day. Don't let anyone tell you that putting together these shows is all glamour; it's hard, slogging work.

The concept was to arrange a backyard pig picking for a sizable group of guests, during which I would demonstrate not only the eastern North Carolina custom of roasting an entire pig but also the Piedmont practice of barbecuing pork shoulders. We would showcase the preparation of barbecue, Brunswick stew, and deep-fried hush puppies, ultimately providing recipes, and the producers would arrange for a local band to close out the segment with a song as the "party" began. My daughter and son-in-law, Anna Barrett and Van Smith, lived in Charlotte at the time, and their neighbors agreed to let their spacious backyard be the location

for the segment. Invitations were sent to fifty guests, all of whom agreed to bring a covered dish to supplement the food that would be prepared on-camera. My younger son, Everett—the one of my three children who inherited my love for cooking and especially for preparing barbecue—would assist me.

The day of the event dawned bright and sunny. Everett and I spent the entire morning getting a whole hog and several shoulders roasting in our portable charcoal-fired pig cooker and setting up the equipment and ingredients for cooking a pot of Brunswick stew and frying corn bread. At midafternoon, *FoodNation*'s huge tour bus pulled into the quiet residential street, and a crew of cameramen, lighting and audio technicians, producers, and the director piled out. Bobby Flay, who had already taken part in two previous setups since early morning, remained on the bus to catch a nap.

Once the camera equipment was in place and the shots and sequences had been blocked out, Bobby Flay showed up. He was friendly, personable, and ready to get down to work. We began with the stew, and the shooting progressed smoothly as Bobby, Everett, and I chatted about the history of Brunswick stew, chopped onions and potatoes, boned and shredded already-cooked whole chickens, mixed in baby lima beans, tomatoes, and corn, and stirred the mixture to avoid sticking.

We moved on to the portable pit, where I explained how the earliest East

My son Everett and I introduced Food Network's Bobby Flay to a backyard North Carolina barbecue on a 2003 episode of Flay's former show *FoodNation*.
*Courtesy of Food Network*

Coast settlers had found Native Americans barbecuing wild pigs over pits of hardwood coals and how those pig roasts—later to become known as pig pickings—had become the centerpieces of a great many eastern North Carolina social gatherings. The three of us used our fingers to pull crispy morsels from the beautifully browned pig, and Everett pulled apart the meat from one of the well-done shoulders and demonstrated how a heavy cleaver is used to turn the pulled pork into chopped barbecue. Flay got quite a chuckle from our explanation that the custom of chopping barbecue began two centuries ago, when thoughtful hosts realized that many of their guests didn't have enough of their teeth left to handle the pork unless it was served more or less "pre-chewed."

As the sun dipped lower in the sky, it became apparent that the weary crew was ready to wrap up the day's shooting. By then, the guests had all arrived, so we taped them going through the food line and sat everyone down for a group shot. Flay delivered some closing lines thanking Everett and me for our efforts. The producers prompted all the guests to shout one particular phrase in unison to close the show—I can't remember for the life of me what it was—and the band struck up as everyone began eating.

Before everyone got to the dessert course, the twenty-person crew was packed up and gone, headed for Louisville, where it would start again early the next morning.

# • A North Carolina Pig Pickin' •

My son Everett also collaborated with me on one of my own productions, an hour-long special for UNC-TV called *A North Carolina Pig Pickin'*. Featuring the late former governor Bob Scott (the biggest promoter of barbecue among all North Carolina governors), former *News & Observer* columnist Dennis Rogers, and Tom Green (a hilarious friend and barbecue expert), the show became my personal favorite among all the programs of my career.

The premise was simple. My son would help me put a pig on the fire to roast all day, demonstrating the proper steps. Scott, Rogers, and Green would join me in sitting around the cooker and talking barbecue lore as the hog cooked. Viewers would observe me preparing the dishes to be served with the barbecue, including boiled "barbecue" potatoes, coleslaw, hush puppies, peach cobbler, and banana pudding. I would join my all-day companions in "picking" the pig once it was done (and before the guests arrived). A bluegrass band would show up. We would end by serving the food and enjoying the music. Simple, huh?

We booked Wing Tip Farm, a scenic party venue outside Raleigh, to serve as the location. Even though the events in the program would appear to have taken place in a single day, the various segments were actually taped on four separate days spanning a period of several months. One entire day was devoted to getting shots of preparing a whole pig for barbecuing, getting it on the fire, and, later, obtaining close-up "beauty" shots of the browned meat. Another day was taken up with shooting the preparation of side dishes, both in the Wing Tip Farm kitchen and at an outdoor setup. A third day was consumed in taping the conversational segments as we sat around the pig cooker discussing the importance of barbecue to North Carolina's history, politics, church life, and other social institutions. The fourth day was filled by the filming of the pig-picking "party" itself, including many retakes of musical performances by the bluegrass band.

We ended up cooking three entire pigs: one for demonstrating the process of putting a hog on to cook and, later that day, getting the vital "make 'em hungry" shots of browning meat, dripping fat, swirling smoke, and glowing coals; one for a series of shots of the former governor, Dennis Rogers, and Tom Green picking off morsels of roast pig and salaciously dropping them into their mouths while moaning with joy; and the third to serve to the guests at the actual pig picking.

I was especially happy about the "barbecue reminiscences" portion of the program.

Even though Bob Scott, son of Governor W. Kerr Scott, served only one term as governor, he did more than any other of the state's chief executives to promote North Carolina's barbecue heritage. It was Scott who in 1972 proclaimed North Carolina the "Pig Picking Capital of the World."

The former governor was delighted to be asked to appear in the show. He provided wonderful anecdotes about the countless

The late former governor Bob Scott proclaimed North Carolina "the Pig Pickin' Capital of the World."
*Courtesy of UNC-TV*

Former governor Bob Scott, longtime friend Tom Greene of Scotland Neck, and former *News & Observer* columnist Dennis Rogers joined me to talk North Carolina barbecue lore in *A North Carolina Pig Pickin'*.
*Courtesy of UNC-TV*

My friend David Farrior of Burgaw, an incredibly talented musician, wrote a song called "It's Pig Pickin' Time" for the show. *Courtesy of UNC-TV*

political barbecues he had attended during his various campaigns and his terms as both lieutenant governor and governor. He took particular delight in ribbing Rufus Edmisten, a fellow Democrat from the North Carolina mountains, who claimed to have lost the 1984 gubernatorial race because he made the mistake of characterizing barbecue to a group of reporters as "damnable stuff." "It's true that no man is ever elected governor of North Carolina without eating more barbecue than is good for him," chuckled Scott, "but Rufus should have known better than to say such a thing, no matter how much barbecue he had been forced to consume during the campaign. He lost the race because of it, and he certainly deserved to lose."

Dennis Rogers was selected for the panel because of his description of barbecue as North Carolina's "Holy Grub" and because of his frequent acerbic in-print exchanges with *Greensboro Daily News* columnist (and later true-crime author) Jerry Bledsoe over the relative merits of eastern whole-hog barbecue, which Rogers favored, and tomato-sauced Lexington-style barbecue of the type praised by Bledsoe.

Tom Green, a John Deere farm equipment dealer from my wife's hometown of Scotland Neck, was relatively unknown outside Halifax County. But on his home turf, he had a reputation as a masterful whole-hog chef and was regarded as one of the funniest men anyone has ever met. Green had impeccable comedic timing and an eerie ability to mimic others' speech. His anecdotes about pig-picking adventures and misadventures in northeastern North Carolina were delicious. His close friends, including me, considered him a naturally gifted comedian in the Jerry Clower tradition. As he related during the show, Green was fond of corralling Yankees to invite to pig pickings in the woods, convincing them that the proper dress for such events was a coat and tie. "All the rest of us show up looking like characters from *Deliverance* and watch this poor guy trying to keep his silk tie out of the sauce pooled in the pig's belly," Green chortled.

All the disparate pieces of the show came together well, a big crowd turned out for the "party" portion of the show, the bluegrass band got the guests fired up and clapping from a makeshift stage on a flatbed trailer, and the barbecue and fixings received positive reviews from the hungry guests.

# NORTH CAROLINA BARBECUE RESTAURANTS

I n the pages that follow, I present my personal choices of the 101 best places to eat barbecue in North Carolina. Obviously, almost every single reader would have made a few different choices. And on anybody's list of the 101 best *anything*, probably 10 to 15 entries could have been replaced by an equal number that weren't included. If I've left out your favorite barbecue spot, what's really important is that you make an effort to let the folks there know how much *you* appreciate them. I don't consider myself a restaurant critic, since I recognize that my opinion is no better than anyone else's. So rather than say something uncomplimentary about a place, I'd rather say nothing at all and let it go at that. Let me urge you, however, not to conclude that a restaurant is substandard because it isn't included here. I could easily have made an honest mistake (and probably have somewhere).

After I began doing barbecue segments for UNC-TV, I started to receive phone calls, letters, and e-mails recommending certain places. I also asked around, eavesdropped, and quietly stopped into places I had seen or heard about, usually without identifying myself, until I determined they were restaurants that warranted further exploration.

I do believe that all the restaurants included here have something significant to recommend them. The places with special legacies, longevity, or historical significance, as well as those with particularly outstanding fare and pit-cooking practices, are identified as "North Carolina Classic" barbecue restaurants. This designation includes a few newer restaurants that have gone to special lengths to maintain our weighty barbecue traditions and to utilize best practices.

My most sincere wishes are that you'll have fun referring to this guide, and that it will help you come up with your own list of North Carolina's top 101 barbecue places. That's the only list that really counts.

Now, go forth and enjoy some good pig!

## High Cotton Barbeque

5230 Virginia Dare Trail North
Kitty Hawk, N.C. 27949-5934
252-255-2275
http://www.highcottonbbq.com
Open for lunch and dinner seasonally

Matt Cooper and Will Thorp's High Cotton Barbeque in Kitty Hawk caters to more patrons from out of state than from North Carolina. The two walk a bit of a tightrope, trying to strike the proper balance between giving people what they expect and are accustomed to and educating them on the delights of authentic eastern North Carolina barbecue.

"People come in and ask if we have ribs or brisket, and we answer, 'Yes, but we also have barbecue,'" Thorp grins. A Rocky Mount native, he stayed true to the eastern barbecue tradition he grew up with even while attending culinary school in Asheville. Now, he's working to transplant some of his barbecue heritage into the sandy soil of the Outer Banks.

Thorp grew up on whole-hog barbecue

cooked over wood coals by such legendary Rocky Mount restaurateurs as Bob Melton, Josh Bullock, and Buck Overton. He and Cooper, who runs the kitchen, are determined to create some of that magic for their coastal customers. They use a Southern Pride smoker, which employs a gas flame to get hickory logs smoldering and producing swirls of smoke, through which rotating, Ferris wheel–like racks of Boston butts, racks of ribs, beef briskets, and chicken circulate. The pork for the chopped barbecue ends up with lots of extraordinarily smoky, brown, chewy bits of outside meat, which lend tremendous flavor to the 'cue. Add some tangy traditional eastern North Carolina sauce to that, and you're in business—provided you can get "newbies" to try the vinegar-based dressing they may have heard about but have never actually experienced.

"A lot of people from outside North Carolina have it firmly in their mind that they don't like vinegar-based sauce, even though they've never tasted our sauce or our barbecue. But once we ever get them to sample it,

High Cotton Barbeque,
Kitty Hawk

they almost always end up not only ordering it but coming back for more," says Cooper. "That sauce has endured for three hundred years for a reason, and people generally get on board in a hurry once they're used to it."

A thick, sweet, red sauce *is* on hand at High Cotton, as you might expect out there on the vinegar frontier. It goes quite well with the restaurant's pork ribs, the nicely cooked brisket, and even the house "smoked" chicken. It's a tasty, well-flavored example of a western, tomato-enhanced sauce. I particularly enjoyed it with the chicken, which had a near-perfect consistency.

High Cotton also does a good job with fried chicken, as it does with chicken 'n' pastry, a traditional dish in all regions of North Carolina. The restaurant's version is served with a good, rich chicken broth, pleasing highlights of celery, and nice, fluffy pastry. "Pulled" chicken is also available.

Be sure to try the "Sugar Pig's chess pies," all of which are made with the traditional chess pie recipe that features a splash of vinegar and a pinch of cornmeal. High Cotton has chocolate, pecan, lemon, and coconut varieties.

My grandson Sadler, who was seven years old at the time, made a brief on-camera appearance for a UNC-TV *North Carolina Weekend* restaurant review at High Cotton. Doing a flattering imitation, he took a bite of barbecue sandwich and proclaimed, "The bread's soft . . . the slaw has nice texture . . . and the hot sauce makes it really 'flavory.' *Ummm-ummm*." Not bad—except that maybe I should repeat that the barbecue in the sandwich was pretty doggone good as well.

## Martelle's Feed House

33301 U.S. 264
Engelhard, N.C. 27824
252-925-1799
http://www.martellesfeedhouse.com
Lunch and dinner are served Tuesday through Saturday. Lunch is offered on Sunday.

A full-service restaurant and catering operation, Martelle's is particularly well known for its barbecue—which makes it *the* best-known, and maybe the only, spot for barbecue around the Lake Mattamuskeet area and throughout sparsely populated Hyde County.

The place serves lean, chopped, slow-roasted pork with an intense pit-cooked flavor that comes from being cooked over live coals. The barbecue is complemented by delicious, crispy hush puppies and eastern-style coleslaw. The sauce is strictly eastern-style, which is no surprise when you consider that it's difficult to get much farther east than Engelhard, North Carolina. This is good, solid flatland fare. With equal ease and aplomb, the folks at Martelle's can serve single, generous plates of barbecue in the restaurant or a barbecue feed for a hundred, complete with all the fixings.

Martelle and Veronica Marshall and their sons, Brandon, Justin, and Brian, all help operate the restaurant at various times during the year. Martelle is mainly responsible for cooking meat—not only the barbecued pork but also the steaks for which the

Martelle Marshall personally cooks the barbecue and ribs at Martelle's, which is also known for its steaks and its oyster bar.

place is equally well known. When it comes to beef, the restaurant is most noted for rib-eye steaks; it will cut any size hunk a customer desires, as long as it's above fourteen ounces. (A twenty-ounce rib-eye was on special when I visited.) Martelle obviously knows what he's doing when it comes to grilling as well as slow-cooking on a barbecue pit. The steaks come to the table full of juice and flavor, with a nice, brown, crusty exterior. As an accompaniment to my savory steak, I had a tasty, rich baked sweet potato attractively slathered with butter and brown sugar.

Crab cakes are another house specialty. They're absolutely chock-full of sweet, rich Hyde County crabmeat.

Five years after opening in 1997, Martelle's added a gift shop, as well as an oyster bar, which has become a favorite hangout for the duck and goose hunters who frequent Lake Mattamuskeet. Hyde County oysters are considered some of the best in North Carolina. Brandon Marshall says the bivalves shucked at Martelle's are as "fresh as you can get." Harvested every day during the season by Mattamuskeet Seafood, they're plump, firm, salty, and absolutely delicious. (I took home a bushel of these big, premium oysters after going through a couple of dozen, lightly steamed, at Martelle's.) The hefty peel-and-eat shrimp and the blackened tuna-bite appetizers—served with a tangy house dipping sauce—are also first-class.

Few, if any, places in North Carolina serve barbecue this good and also offer such high-quality food of other types.

## Moore's Olde Tyme Barbeque

3711 Dr. M. L. King Jr. Boulevard (U.S. 17 South)
New Bern, N.C. 28562
252-638-3937
http://www.mooresbarbeque.com
Lunch and dinner, Monday through Saturday

After passing a string of chain restaurants on New Bern's Dr. M. L. King Jr. Boulevard, it's good to see the no-nonsense building housing Moore's loom into sight and to smell the wood smoke in the air. Moore's has what must be the biggest woodpile in the entire state—the place looks like a sawmill. Even though the barbecue at Moore's is now cooked part of the time over wood coals and part of the time in an electric pit, the process still produces barbecue that's worth going out of the way for.

At its present site since 1973, Moore's actually had six previous locations around New Bern. Owner Tommy Moore says his father, Big John Moore, started in the barbecue business in 1945 before he had any location at all. The elder Moore borrowed thirty-five dollars to buy a pig and pay someone to cook it over a pit dug into the ground, with the idea that after he sold the barbecue and paid off the cook, he could buy another pig and keep going. The scheme worked, although Moore was nearly run out of business right off the bat when the pig escaped before he could get it slaughtered. Fortunately for us all, he caught and cooked that first porker, sold the barbecue, bought another, and plowed the profits back into the business until he was able to open up shop in a converted gas station. Try to imagine someone building a respectable business from the ground up in that way today.

Moore's has always been a modest, no-frills kind of place. The kitchen and order

Tommy Moore has one of the most impressive woodpiles in North Carolina.

counter are in the center. Customers carry their food to plain dining rooms on either side. Tommy Moore expanded one of the dining rooms considerably in 2002, but the place is still fairly basic—just the spot to enjoy honest-to-goodness whole-hog barbecue.

Moore's serves its pork finely chopped and tender with tiny bits of crisped skin mixed in. The sauce is a typical eastern vinegar-and-red-pepper mixture blended for today's tastes—meaning that, unlike the traditional eastern sauce of bygone years, it has some added sugar to cut the acidity. The chopped 'cue is served with finely chopped white coleslaw seasoned mostly with vinegar and sugar and hush puppies that are exactly what the puffs of fried corn bread are supposed to be—perfectly light and golden brown, and not too sweet-tasting either.

The place is also well known for its seafood—mainly shrimp, flounder, and trout—and for its fried chicken. Several regulars told me that the barbecued chicken is superb as well. Ribs are prepared each Saturday and served with the thick, red sauce that now seems to be expected with that particular cut of meat.

In 2010, as part of the celebration of the three hundredth anniversary of the founding of New Bern, Tommy Moore cooked up the idea of preparing a *Guinness Book of World Records*–sized barbecue sandwich. Unfortunately, *Guinness* already had a listing for a traditional barbecue sandwich. So rather than try and top an existing record, Moore set out to create a new world record for the planet's largest *open-faced* barbecue sand-wich. The finished product, served on July 3, 2010, consisted of a fifteen-foot bottom bun covered with barbecue and finished off with a layer of coleslaw. It weighed 1,377 pounds.

Tommy Moore ended up getting an inch-and-a-half entry in the *Guinness Book of World Records* for the effort, which took months of planning and the construction of a special oven in which to bake the bun. "That little piece of text right there cost me at least twenty-five thousand dollars," Moore told me. "I wouldn't do it again, that's for sure. It was a mess."

After all the hard work, the book ended up mistakenly describing the mammoth sandwich as having been constructed to commemorate the three hundredth anniversary of *Moore's Barbeque*, rather than that of the city of New Bern. On the bright side, Tommy now owns a supply of baseball caps reading "Moore's Barbeque: *Guinness Book of World Records* Holder."

More importantly, Moore's was included in a 1988 book detailing the authors' picks of the top hundred barbecue places in America. While all such lists (including that in this book) are arbitrary, you can bet that Moore's should stay on your must-go list until you have a chance to see and taste for yourself.

Oakwood Barbecue, Richlands

## Oakwood Barbecue

113 Westside Lane
Richlands, N.C. 28574
910-324-4930
http://www.oakwoodbbqnc.com
Open Friday and Saturday from 11 A.M. until
barbecue runs out. Takeout only.

One day, I was driving along a rural highway in Onslow County with a UNC-TV cameraman when I spotted a roadside sign for this enterprise. Turning onto a side road, we drove a quarter-mile and discovered a little outbuilding located behind a private residence. It was a spanking-new takeout kitchen and barbecue pit, the longtime dream of Morris Thompson. Morris had always wanted a barbecue place of his own, and after years in other pursuits, he finally made it happen. With the help of his wife, Judy, and some other folks, Morris sells his quintessentially eastern North Carolina whole-hog barbecue Friday and Saturday from eleven in the morning until the 'cue runs out.

As the name of the place indicates, this barbecue is cooked only over wood coals. "I've never cooked a pig with gas," says Morris, "and I've been doing it for a long time as a hobby. There's no question—wood is better."

Most of the best things in life are simple, and the Thompsons are wise enough not to go against this piece of folk wisdom. They serve just-cooked, freshly chopped barbecue, eastern-style white coleslaw, hush puppies, and canned soft drinks. Period. They figure that if real barbecue fans aren't happy with that, they aren't real barbecue fans and probably wouldn't be happy with anything. I found the barbecue to be wonderfully seasoned, flavored with a clean oak-wood taste, and absolutely delicious.

Although Morris had to jump through hoops with permits to build a place for wood-cooking barbecue, he was undeterred. "I was determined," he declares. "I've always wanted my own place, and I was going to have it."

Morris has an old-fashioned burn barrel under a shelter behind the pit. He uses a little charcoal to help get the split hardwood fire going strong, but after that, it's all wood—mostly oak, with a little pecan wood thrown in for subtle flavoring. When he shovels the coals that fall through the grate at the bottom of the barrel under the roasting hogs, the inevitable magic happens—and at least one small part of the world beats a path to his door.

When you walk into Morris's place, you're likely to find him behind the takeout counter, beaming with pride at what he's managed to pull off. That alone is all the reason you need to pay him a visit. From Jacksonville, follow U.S. 258 West/N.C. 24 West (Richlands Highway). Turn left on N.C. 111 toward Catherine Lake, then turn right on Westside Lane, portions of which are unpaved.

## Sid's Catering

*North Carolina Classic*

455 South Railroad Avenue
Beulaville, N.C. 28518
910-298-3549
Lunch is served on Saturday from 9:30 A.M. until
  the barbecue runs out.

Sid's is one of those great little places you'd never know about unless you live nearby or unless someone told you, which is how I got the tip.

This combination restaurant, takeout kitchen, and catering service is housed in a large wood building that's considerably nicer than the quarters occupied by many barbecue places. But you'd never know it was there unless, well, you *already* knew it was there.

It sits completely hidden behind an ordinary brick ranch-style home on the outskirts of Beulaville in Duplin County. You have to turn into the driveway and get completely past the house before you even catch sight of the place. I drove past three times. When I finally arrived out back, the parking area was jammed with vehicles.

All the cooking is done by Sid Blizzard Sr. and Sid Blizzard Jr. Sid Sr.'s wife, Ann, and a couple of grandchildren also lend a major helping hand. Since the takeout and restaurant business is Saturday only, Sid Jr. is able to pursue his vocation as a full-time schoolteacher and still follow in the footsteps of his father, a former farmer, who began selling his home-cooked barbecue out of the back of a camper in 1977. The elder Blizzards built a small cookhouse behind their home, then enlarged the facility while rebuilding after Hurricane Fran.

Whole-hog pork barbecue and barbecued chicken are the mainstays of the Blizzards' menu. Both are so outstanding that customers begin showing up before 9 A.M. on Saturday morning, not just to get takeout but to sit down and eat barbecue for breakfast or brunch. "Well, the crowd gets pretty big early in the day, and when they run out of fresh barbecue, they close, so we just choose to eat early to make sure we don't miss out," one customer told me.

Sid's serves a piece of crispy, pit-flavored pork skin with every order of chopped pork barbecue or barbecued chicken. Holding the skin in one hand and eating the chopped barbecue with the other will let you combine the

Three generations of
the Blizzard family with
customers at Sid's

perfect amount of each in every bite. The skin stays crispier and more tasty than if it were chopped and incorporated into the barbecue.

Sid's serves a straightforward eastern-style sauce with a bit of sugar added. The well-balanced blend is sold in bottles on the premises.

The business is called Sid's Catering because serving groups has provided the lion's share of the proceeds over the years. In fact, Sid's was preparing to serve a group of ninety the day after I visited. Next to catering, the bulk of the business comes from the takeout trade, although more and more people are deciding to eat on the premises. I've found that in North Carolina small towns with weekend-only barbecue stands, eating barbecue and fixin's for the Saturday noon meal is a tradition for many families. Seeing so many people consuming barbecue *before* lunch was something I had not previously encountered. It seems that half the town's residents, as well as a sizable group of people from miles away, find their way up the circular driveway and dash inside to claim their carry-out orders.

If you're planning a visit, be sure to arrive early enough to enjoy both the pork *and* the chicken! From downtown Beulaville, turn west on N.C. 24 toward Kenansville. Turn left on South Railroad Avenue and go 0.3 mile to number 455, on the left. The restaurant is hidden behind the brick house.

Sid's Catering is hidden
behind a private residence,
but the parking lot is jammed
on Saturday mornings.

# • Travels with Buzz •

In 2009, my wife, Ruthie, and I celebrated twenty years of owning Boston terriers. We love their intelligence, curiosity, and social warmth. Our first Boston became not only an incredibly well-traveled companion but also a minor star in two of my hour-long UNC-TV specials, *North Carolina Country Cookin'* and *More North Carolina Country Cookin'*.

Buzz was already a road veteran before he began traveling with our UNC-TV crews. For four years, he attended every home football game at James Madison University in Harrisonburg, Virginia, where my son Nelson was a place-kicker and punter. Buzz made the eight-hour round trips between our home in Burlington and JMU's Shenandoah Valley campus while napping on a pillow in Ruthie's lap. He would join us for the pregame tailgate with other football parents, wait patiently in the car during the games, then be allowed to race excitedly around the Bridgeforth Stadium turf once the crowd had mostly exited the stadium. The JMU band marched and performed following every home game. Hearing the drums and the music, Buzz would always know the game was over and would be gazing expectantly out the car window, waiting for us to return to the parking lot to collect him and sneak him into the now-unguarded stadium, where Nelson would be waiting to put him through his paces. Buzz also made the road trip to the annual Blue-Gray college all-star game in Montgomery, Alabama, in which Nelson played

on Christmas Day in 1997. Buzz ran the field as usual once the final whistle sounded. As we did practically everywhere we traveled, we smuggled him into the hotel, tipping the bellman to look the other way.

For the *Country Cookin'* shows, we used Buzz as a visual transitional device. After I finished my on-camera explorations of the food at down-home restaurants, we would work him into the transition to the next restaurant on the list. There might be a shot of him riding in the UNC-TV van with his nose stuck out the window. He might walk into the foreground of a shot of the restaurant to be reviewed. Viewers might see him being held up to peer through a restaurant window. Or he might stand on top of a highway map, sniffing the route from one town to the next (after I had dribbled a little meat juice along the path I wanted him to sniff). We also included him in other miscellaneous shots, including one in which we used a stopwatch to see how long it would take him to wolf down a molasses-filled sweet potato biscuit from one particular diner (3.7 seconds).

For the ending sequence and the credit roll of the first *Country Cookin'* program, we used a shot of Buzz and me walking on a treadmill, ostensibly to work off the pounds we had gained while filming the show. We thought the moving belt of the treadmill might frighten or confuse Buzz, but he hopped aboard without any apparent concern.

Festival 2000!   Please Call
UNC·TV  1-800-984-9090
www.unctv.org

My Boston terrier, Buzz, and I walked on a treadmill, ostensibly to lose weight gained during filming of UNC-TV's *North Carolina Country Cookin'* but in actuality to provide an engaging closing shot. Buzz performed like a treadmill veteran, although he had never seen one before.
*Courtesy of UNC-TV*

Once I turned the machine on, he trotted contentedly along as though he were on the most ordinary of afternoon walks.

Viewers all over North Carolina still ask me about my "little dog."

Buzz was with us for fourteen years before he died. We now have a second Boston, Lucy, who has a totally different facial expression and temperament. Lucy has never taken up television, but she is an incredibly skilled self-taught soccer player who entertains at halftime of kids' soccer matches, dressed in a pink, dog-sized soccer jersey. And like Buzz, she's allowed to run around athletic fields following Nelson's

games. He's now a high-school soccer coach. His players (as well as the players and parents from visiting teams) get a kick out of his bringing Lucy onto the turf following matches. Whereas Buzz only ran dizzying laps around the perimeter of the field to work off energy, Lucy dribbles soccer balls, using alternating sides of her head to maintain perfect pacing and control. She also "traps" balls from out of the air by smothering them with her body and paws as they strike the ground, without allowing them to bounce away out of control.

Still, the only place she's appeared on camera is YouTube.

Jackson's Big Oak Barbecue,
Wilmington
*Photo by Claire Alley*

## Jackson's Big Oak Barbecue

920 South Kerr Avenue
Wilmington, N.C. 28403
910-799-1581
http://jacksonsbigoak.com
Lunch and dinner, Monday through Saturday

The motto at Jackson's Big Oak Barbecue is, "We ain't fancy, but we sure are good." In truth, Jackson's is the best place in Wilmington for a comforting dose of eastern-style barbecue.

The "Big Oak" in the restaurant's name refers to a landmark tree on the property, not to the presence of a woodpile. Jackson's approaches barbecue much like most other places in the coastal plain, in that the right combination of vinegar, salt, peppers, and spices, rather than wood-smoked flavor, is considered its defining characteristic.

Actually, a tacitly accepted system of romantic self-delusion about pit cooking has emerged in the region. A July 2001 editorial in the *Wilmington Morning Star*, for example, described eastern barbecue thusly: "It is to be caressed for seven or eight hours in the aromatic warmth of smoldering hickory." The writer likely made those remarks knowing that no restaurant anywhere *near* Wilm-

ington cooked barbecue in that fashion.

In carefully chosen words, Jackson's says its barbecue "is slowly cooked and hickory smoked every night." This means it's cooked in electric pits with bits of wood added to produce smoke. What the heck! In a corner of the state where vinegar seems to be the be-all and end-all, let's give Jackson's credit for even trying to infuse the meat with a little smoke. The end product is tender and well seasoned, with crispy brown bits mixed with the lean meat for flavor.

Jackson's is a cheerful, busy place with wood paneling and pictures of local football players and other sports notables on the walls. The menu features the barbecue basics—chopped pork, slaw, barbecued chicken, ribs, Brunswick stew, eastern-style barbecue potatoes, hush puppies, and corn sticks. The nice selection of home-style vegetables includes baked beans, potato salad, candied yams, green beans, black-eyed peas, fried okra, and, best of all, collards.

This may not be exactly a premier barbecue destination, but it's a good little place to stop when you're in the neighborhood—which is not far from UNC-Wilmington.

Bunn's Barbecue, Windsor

## Bunn's Barbecue

127 North King Street
Windsor, N.C. 27983
252-794-2274
Lunch and dinner are served until 5 P.M. on Monday, Tuesday, Thursday, and Friday. Lunch is offered until 2 P.M. on Wednesday and Saturday.

This intriguing little barbecue joint, located in a quaint mid-1800s building in historic downtown Windsor, has been selling barbecue since 1938, although not under its present name. It's a tiny place but one with self-confident owners, as evidenced by the fact that it advertises its barbecue as "the World's Best."

Grace and Wilbur Russell bought the restaurant in 1969 and operate it with their sons, Russ and Randy. It seems that because the previous owner was originally from the town of Bunn in Franklin County, he was nicknamed "Bunn." Since everyone in Windsor was accustomed to that name on the restaurant, the Russells decided to keep it.

Bunn's was flooded in 2010 and 2011, but the number of friends and customers who showed up to help the family members clean up and reopen is a testament to their local popularity.

Inside the one-time service station are a few tables where customers can sit at lunchtime, but the dinner trade is mostly takeout. The barbecue, served with a spicy, vinegary sauce, is quintessential eastern-style, except that it's made from pork shoulders. The vinegar-based slaw and authentic Brunswick stew are popular. But instead of hush puppies, the really big deal here is the baked corn bread. Everyone wants a corner piece because of the crispy edges.

Barbecued chicken is available on Tuesday. The Russells prepare chicken 'n' pastry, an eastern North Carolina favorite, on Thursday. The restaurant is also known for its hot dogs, which are available all the time, and for its homemade pies, including sweet potato, chocolate, and coconut.

Ralph's, Weldon

## Ralph's Barbecue

1400 Julian R. Allsbrook Highway (U.S. 158)
Weldon, N.C. 27890
252-536-2102
Lunch and dinner daily

For many years after its founding in 1941, Ralph's—now one of the oldest barbecue places in North Carolina, if not *the* oldest—was located on a side street in Roanoke Rapids. The place became known far and wide. Nowadays, the business sits in the middle of a one-acre parking lot on U.S. 158 between Roanoke Rapids and Weldon, just off Interstate 95. The large, barn-roofed building is just the right size to accommodate crowds of local patrons and interstate travelers. It's gussied up nicely with a green-canopied entrance, green awnings, and a row of pink neon pigs across the front.

Patrons come to enjoy the expansive barbecue and country-cooking buffet, order off the menu, or visit the busy takeout section. With its carpeting and gray-and-green interior color scheme, Ralph's looks more like a Holiday Inn restaurant that a venerable bar-

becue joint, but the food is still good, if not quite what it once was.

The menu consists basically of barbecue—which is served with Brunswick stew, coleslaw, and hush puppies—and various sandwiches. The takeout counter offers sandwiches, barbecue and fixings, seafood, fried and roasted chicken, vegetables, and desserts. The buffet seems to attract most of the action at Ralph's.

This restaurant doesn't really serve chopped barbecue. The pork comes either minced or pulled, which the proprietors call "sliced." The minced version is one step beyond chopped and is much too fine for my personal taste, although I found the seasoning to be spot-on. The very effective eastern-style sauce is a simple mixture of vinegar, salt, and pepper, with a little sugar added for balance. The so-called sliced barbecue is actually pulled apart in hunks, as it would be at a pig picking. It's highly appealing. If a whole hog is properly cooked, the meat falls easily into pieces with the touch of a hand, so there's no need to bring a sharp knife into the process, unless it's to cut the pork into bite-sized pieces on the plate. It's actually more fun to simply pick it up with your fingers and take a bite.

The chunks of slow-roasted pork at Ralph's are tender and moist. I highly recommend them, rather than the minced alternative. On the day I visited, one pan of pulled pork on the buffet was slathered with a thick, sweet, red sauce, undoubtedly with the goal of keeping traveling Northerners in their barbecue comfort zone. The other pan was simply seasoned with eastern sauce and was very good, even though any evidence of wood-cooked taste was notably absent. The eastern-style pulled pork is a big plus at Ralph's. A lot of other coastal plain establishments would probably do well to imitate it.

On previous visits, I have found the Brunswick stew here to be delicious and to have a great balance between sweet and savory. Unlike the Piedmont version, much of the Brunswick stew cooked in the eastern third of North Carolina is fairly sweet, probably because it's meant to balance the salty vinegar taste that characterizes the barbecue alongside which it is normally served. Eastern cooks include or leave out cubed potatoes according to their tastes. This version has no potatoes.

Highlights on the buffet the day of my visit included delicious cabbage, flavored with chunks of smoked sausage, and a wonderful smothered chicken. You seldom find chicken baked or stewed in a rich gravy in restaurants any longer. I thought Ralph's falling-off-the-bone poultry was memorable.

The fried chicken was tasty and suitably juicy on the inside, although the batter-dipped coating (as opposed to dredging in a dry breading) was not to my personal taste. However, I heard several people praising the fried chicken, and their view should be given as much weight as mine.

In my opinion, some of the other items on the buffet were not quite up to the standard I have encountered on previous visits to Ralph's. The restaurant's version of eastern-style "barbecued" or "red" potatoes proved to be tiny canned potatoes in what tasted like Campbell's tomato soup. The macaroni and cheese looked and tasted as though it was made with a dried cheese sauce, rather than actual melted cheese. To be fair, I didn't get to sample the real stewed potatoes and good-looking navy beans. And the slices of deep-fried fatback were a nice touch to accompany the barbecue, in place of crispy bits of skin.

The only two desserts on the buffet the day I visited were rice pudding and banana pudding, the latter seemingly made with banana-flavored instant pudding, which has an unmistakable chemical taste, especially when compared with simple egg custard. The banana pudding was topped with a nice baked meringue. If you're going to break eggs to gather enough whites to make a meringue, why not use the separated yolks to make a proper custard? I'm just sayin' . . .

In my view, Ralph's has built up too much history and goodwill in over seventy years of existence to be using the sort of shortcuts it seems to be taking in some—but not all—of its offerings, especially on the buffet. Overall, the food is still good, and the place is still worth visiting. But I challenge the owners to "step it up" in order to maintain the restaurant's proud reputation.

## Gardner's Barbecue

1331 North Wesleyan Boulevard (U.S. 301)
Rocky Mount, N.C. 27804
252-446-2983
http://www.gardnerfoods.com
Lunch and dinner daily

Other locations:
3651 Sunset Avenue
Rocky Mount, N.C. 27804
252-443-3996

841 Fairview Road
Rocky Mount, N.C. 27801
252-442-5522

The menu here once said, "Gardner's Barbecue Voted North Carolina's Best," without specifying where or when this referendum occurred. While disagreement would undoubtedly arise over whether this place deserves quite *that* high an honor, most people would probably go along with a claim that stated, "Gardner's Barbecue Voted Pretty Decent."

The barbecue at Gardner's contains no hint that the meat has ever been anywhere near wood coals, which means customers depend upon the eastern-style sauce to turn the very, *very* finely chopped roast pork into barbecue. The sauce is mainstream for the coastal plain, and regulars do seem to like it a lot. Those watching their cholesterol might try the chopped turkey barbecue, which is drier than the pork barbecue due to the lower fat content. Again, turn to the sauce to add interest. The taste of either type of barbecue is enhanced immensely by being eaten in tandem with Gardner's very mustardy, very sweet coleslaw, which is the type I like best out of all the varieties spread across North Carolina.

The crisp-skinned, flavorful fried chicken at Gardner's is a definite treat, the baked chicken (no longer called "barbecued") a little less so. If chicken is among your favorite dishes, you can also get fried chicken livers and gizzards. I found the chicken 'n' pastry quite tasty and authentic.

As a matter of fact, the chicken 'n' pastry turned out to be my favorite dish, along with the sweet, not-overcooked cabbage. Although I have enjoyed the collards at Gardner's in the past, I found them too sweet and not seasoned to my personal taste on my last visit. However, I do like the very fine texture to which they are chopped.

In my opinion, Gardner's Brunswick stew is not representative of the best the Rocky Mount area has to offer. It contains a spice I couldn't identify and didn't recognize as authentic for this particular dish.

One item I found to be tasty was the "corn nuggets"—little fritters of sweet, cream-style corn. They're crisp on the outside and soft on the inside. I'm guessing the staff has to bring the little scoops of creamed corn to an almost-frozen state in order to get them battered and deep-fried without coming apart.

The desserts at Gardner's are mostly middling. I like the fact that the restaurant uses pie pastry, rather than cake or biscuit

Gardner's Barbecue, Rocky Mount

dough, as topping on the cobblers, but the fillings are *way* overloaded with cornstarch. When I visited, the banana pudding had such an artificial appearance that I wasn't tempted in the slightest to try it.

The sweet tea is too sweet by half, but customers have the option of ordering "half-and-half," which I overheard several doing.

You won't feel you've been to barbecue mecca when you leave Gardner's, but you'll certainly leave well freighted with food that, for the most part, has no real surprises, good or bad.

## Hunter Hill Café & Catering

501 Old Mill Road
Rocky Mount, N.C. 27804
252-443-1311
http://www.hunterhillcafe.com
Lunch (until 2:30 P.M.) and dinner (from 5 P.M. to 8 P.M.) are served Monday through Friday. Lunch is offered until 4 P.M. on Sunday.

Hunter Hill Café brought smoked barbecue back to Rocky Mount after a long absence. While more prominence seems to be accorded the restaurant's beef brisket, ribs, and barbecued chicken than the chopped barbecue, all its meats get high marks for flavor, tenderness, and texture. The side dishes are excellent, the staff is friendly and engaging, and the place has obviously developed a large, loyal following. Hunter Hill uses rotating charcoal and wood smokers that provide lots of wood-cooked taste. Although the cooking meat does not drip juices onto the coals in these types of smokers, the end product is delicious nonetheless. I'll go out on a limb and classify this as Rocky Mount's best barbecue at present.

Now just off U.S. 301 near the town's Stone Park, the restaurant occupied a location near Benvenue Country Club for several years before the building burned. The present structure once housed Bob Melton's Barbecue, after that longtime iconic restaurant left its location beside the Tar River. But Melton's was unable to weather the relocation and closed several years ago. Actually, Hunter Hill serves much better barbecue and country-style sides and desserts than Melton's did toward the end of its history, so the present occupants are carrying on the city's rich barbecue tradition.

The barbecue—which comes from shoulders, rather than the whole hog—is chopped coarsely, which I like, and has bits of chewy, brown "bark" and some attractive reddish coloring from the smoke. It's juicy, moist, and nicely seasoned with vinegar, salt, red and black pepper, and sugar. Hunter Hill also has a homemade "rib-style" sauce that is meant to go on ribs, brisket, and even its barbecued chicken.

The restaurant is proud of its beef brisket. When I arrived in the cafeteria-style serving line, an employee asked if I had been there before and was quick to offer me a sample of the tender sliced beef. The meat is served fairly heavily coated with the tomato-based sauce, which is thick and fairly sweet but still has a strong vinegar tang. I found the brisket to be comparable to the best examples I sampled the next day in a barbecue competition.

The barbecued chicken has a nice, smooth texture, which is normally achieved through soaking the chicken pieces in a brine solution containing both salt and sugar. (The chicken comes shrink-wrapped from the restaurant's food distributor, and I think it probably already contains a brine solution.) In any case, the texture and "bite" of the chicken are pleasant even in the breast meat, which is the hardest to keep moist and juicy. The chicken has a good, strong smoke flavor. While the sauce is a little more heavily tomato-based than that used on most examples of traditional eastern-style barbecued chicken, it works well overall.

I sampled the collard greens, the macaroni and cheese, and the rutabagas, and all were absolutely delicious. Hunter Hill uses cabbage collards—which I find to be more tender than the common Georgia variety—and seasons and chops them to near perfection. The rutabagas were rich and sweet. The mac 'n' cheese was the baked variety and had a thick layer of sharp cheddar on top. The macaroni elbows could have been cooked a slight bit less for more of an al dente feel, but that's nitpicking, to be honest. It's top drawer mac 'n' cheese by almost anyone's standard.

The homemade chocolate cake, pineapple cake, and rich banana pudding were up to the quality of everything else I sampled.

You'll easily spot the five-foot green lettering on the huge, bright yellow Hunter Hill catering trailer, parked immediately adjacent to the restaurant. There's a story behind the eye-popping paint job on the trailer. Owners David, Kim, and Cathy Eilers will probably get a kick out of telling it to you if you can catch them in a free moment.

## Doug Sauls' Barbecue and Seafood

813 Western Avenue
Nashville, N.C. 27856
252-459-4247
Lunch and dinner, Tuesday through Saturday

This small, locally owned place with the slogan "Your Place or Mine" has been in business for over three decades. The second generation of the Sauls family now runs things very ably. Between the small but bustling restaurant and a sizable catering operation, Sauls' has managed to serve a wide swath of the population around the "Triangle East" area between Raleigh and Rocky Mount, as well as innumerable passers-through, including former president Bill Clinton.

Situated in an attractive setting just off U.S. 64 Alternate (Western Avenue) on the outskirts of Nashville, the Nash County seat, the restaurant is modest. The L-shaped dining room inside the simple cinder-block building holds around fifteen small tables. The food is brought out once customers have placed their orders at the counter, then picked up their own silverware and beverages. The place is simply decorated with toy cars, vintage soft-drink machines, old bottles, antique tools, and ceramic and stuffed animals clustered around a small fireplace. The busy takeout counter has its own entrance to the side.

The barbecue here has been praised online as "some of the best in eastern North Carolina." I discerned no smoke flavor at all, leading me to surmise that it's cooked on electric or gas pits. But it was lean, clean barbecue, chopped finely and having a traditional, strong vinegar-pepper flavor. Although I

Doug Sauls' Barbecue and Seafood, Nashville

ordered a plate, I can imagine that the 'cue and the fine-textured, creamy, sweet-tart slaw work together well on a sandwich. Actually, the chopped pork is exactly what most people imagine when they think of eastern North Carolina barbecue. It will fall comfortably in the "comfort food" range for most barbecue fans.

I personally found the delicious home-style vegetables to be even more memorable than the barbecue. I luxuriated in servings of soft, savory country-style cabbage and some of the region's typical stewed potatoes, delicately flavored with paprika but not tangy with vinegar, sugar, and ketchup, as are many eastern "BBQ" or "red" potatoes. The Brunswick stew tasted fairly authentic at first bite, although I soon discovered that it contained baked beans, which are certainly not unpleasant but also not authentic in stew, at least in this region of the state. Hairsplitting aside, the slightly sweet stew went well with the vinegary barbecue, and I'm sure the dish has been accepted and indeed embraced by Sauls' loyal customers over the decades. The hush puppies here actually resemble onion rings. They're quite tasty, if not the crispiest I've ever eaten.

The fried pork chop I sampled, however, *was* appealingly crispy, with a light homemade-tasting coating. It's hard to find tasty fried pork chops in home-cooking restaurants. I will definitely visit Sauls' in the future just to enjoy its version of this classic.

Another dish I found to be authentic and well worth ordering again was the country-style steak, which was clearly a piece of round steak, pounded or cubed, browned in oil, then slowly braised until the meat fibers relaxed into tenderness. The brown gravy, containing sliced onions, tasted entirely homemade, with none of the savory but slightly artificial taste common to many dried brown gravy mixes. I've heard good things as well about the chicken 'n' pastry and the fried chicken.

Seafood is obviously a big deal here. Although I didn't sample any on my visit, I observed a Friday-afternoon crowd at the takeout counter carrying away impressive amounts of crispy deep-fried flounder, trout, shrimp, and oysters.

Doug Sauls' Barbecue and Seafood is a cheerful, worthwhile lunch or dinner destination, serving barbecue and fixings, plus a wider range of country meats and vegetables finely tuned to customers' tastes over the years. You'll enjoy it.

## Bill's Barbecue and Chicken

3007 Downing Street
Wilson, N.C. 27893
252-237-4372
http://www.bills-bbq.com
Lunch and dinner, Tuesday through Sunday

Bill's isn't a barbecue place—it's an empire.

In the early 1960s, Bill Ellis bought a run-down country drive-in with a reputation as a less-than-wholesome teenage hangout. The sprawling white-brick restaurant that grew out of that early drive-in was destroyed by the floodwaters of Hurricane Floyd in 1999. But by then, it had managed to build a rep-

Bill Ellis has rebuilt the restaurant building destroyed by Hurricane Floyd, part of a complex on the site.
*Photo by Keith Barnes*

utation commensurate with its nearly four decades in business under Ellis's direction. During the dozen years following that disaster, Bill's complex south of Wilson came to include a more recently built barbecue buffet restaurant, a spacious convention center, a walk-in, drive-up takeout building (complete with a fast-food-type ordering kiosk), a suite of offices, and a garage. What it did *not* include until 2012 was the rebuilt version of the original restaurant, now once more the visual centerpiece of the Ellis hospitality empire.

Before and after the hurricane, Ellis's complex has included dozens of catering trucks of all sizes, including several seventy-five-foot tractor-trailers. All the vehicles are emblazoned with his logo (a bright red sil-

houette of the state of North Carolina with the words *BILL ELLIS, Wilson, N.C.,* in white and blue) and his slogan ("We doos 'em right!"). The trucks advertise "World Famous Barbecue and Fried Chicken, Anywhere, Anytime."

The logo looks a bit like a campaign sign, which is not inappropriate, considering the thousands of political gatherings and state-government functions Ellis has catered over the decades. In fact, on many occasions, Ellis and his food-service teams have traveled out of state to cater functions organized by North Carolina's recruiters of new business and industry. Years ago, the Ellis team took an eighteen-wheeler all the way to Palm Springs, California, for such a function. Ellis has proudly advertised "coast-to-coast catering" ever since.

Inside the bustling original restaurant, and later in the buffet restaurant Ellis built to replace the damaged structure, the red, white, and blue logo could be seen on T-shirts and hats for sale in the lobby and in dozens of color pictures of NASCAR-type racecars sponsored by Ellis. Those cars looked for all the world like really fast barbecue delivery vehicles. Another Ellis passion, softball, was evidenced by scores of trophies and team photographs, with hundreds of uniformed chests bearing his ubiquitous visual trademark.

The size and visibility of the catering business aside, Bill's various restaurants offer eastern North Carolina–style barbecue that almost perfectly defines the coastal plain cuisine. While his barbecue and side dishes cannot really be described as distinguished or truly memorable, they are consistent. Patrons know exactly what to expect each and every time they walk through the door. What Bill's serves up is comfort food, and meal hours always find his expansive parking lot jammed with folks who need comforting. Ellis has created a huge success in serving people what they want and enjoy. And you cannot argue with success.

Bill's serves quintessential eastern barbecue, strongly flavored by salt, vinegar, and red pepper, with crushed pepper flakes and seeds readily visible throughout the chopped meat. I discovered, happily, that Bill's does not chop the barbecue superfine, unlike some other prominent eastern establishments; instead,

the meat has an attractive shredded texture. You'll find no discernible wood-smoke taste in this barbecue. However, open-pit taste is not a characteristic many easterners seem to prize any longer in their barbecue, so Bill's is on safe ground in primarily cooking with gas. Bill's version contains little fat or gristle, although it is heavily laced with bits of finely chopped skin. Some people swear that good barbecue *must* have skin chopped up in it, while others don't like it at all; personal preference is everything here. The pork is flavorful and tender, partly due to being slow-cooked at precisely controlled temperatures and partly to the fact that Bill's has its own enormous hog farm, where the pigs' diet and other factors are tightly controlled.

Ellis's barbecue buffet restaurant pays tribute to the eastern North Carolina tradition by featuring a whole cooked pig laid out on a brick mock-up of a real pit. Of course, plenty of chopped barbecue is already prepared and seasoned, but patrons can also use tongs to pull their own succulent, moist hunks of meat off the whole pig. This form of presentation helps hold freshness and natural juices within the meat, thus avoiding the ravages quickly inflicted on most chopped barbecue by steam tables. On the other hand, the pig is presented skin side up, which unfortunately doesn't show off its most appetizing side—the browned and crispy underbelly. Both fried strips of fatback and pieces of crispy pork skin are available to provide extra crunch and to counterbalance the silky texture of the interior meat.

Boiled potatoes almost always accompany Bill's barbecue as a side dish. While some barbecue cooks around the coastal plain add a fair amount of red pepper and/or tomato sauce to the water in which the potatoes boil, Bill's version shows little or no evidence of this. The potatoes seem to be intentionally left a bit on the bland side to help balance the acidity of the barbecue. But they're very pleasing, with only a little salt and just a hint of pork drippings or other similar seasoning.

Bill's coleslaw is minced fine, its predominant flavors coming from vinegar, sugar, and mustard; it appears to contain little or no mayonnaise. This is both a sweet and tart slaw, with the characteristic eastern North Carolina yellow hue.

Other options include tender, full-flavored collards of the heirloom "cabbage collard" variety grown in the immediate area, as well as sweet, pleasing steamed cabbage. The chicken 'n' pastry is tasty and seems fairly authentic. The "barbecued" chicken is oven-cooked in thick red barbecue sauce and bears no evidence of any pit-cooked taste, but it is acceptably tender.

Frankly, I have been disappointed on several occasions with Bill's Brunswick stew, which I find to be too dark in color, dry, and relatively tasteless, except for having a gritty paprika-type flavor. Most people in the coastal plain seem to like sweet Brunswick stew, but Bill's stew has no discernible hint of sugar or other sweetener. In addition to larger-than-optimum lima beans (rather than baby butter beans) and large-kernel yellow corn, the stew contains copious helpings of green beans—something you might expect to find

in the Piedmont but certainly not in the heart of eastern North Carolina barbecue-and-stew country. Most of the folks who flock to Bill's were raised on Brunswick stew, and it seems unbelievable that his restaurant can turn out a consistently marginal version of this dish without the reputation of the place being damaged. But I have to acknowledge that such has obviously not been the case.

Luckily, the shortcomings of the Brunswick stew are more than balanced by the delicious crispness of Bill's corn sticks, which are lighter than other versions I've encountered. The crust is satisfyingly crunchy all the way around, while the center is reminiscent of good, honest, flat-baked corn bread or corn pone, with a straightforward taste of white cornmeal. During my visits, I've found Bill's hush puppies to be tasty and light, if not particularly crispy.

Bill's is also famous for fried chicken, a staple of his catered meals. The large breast I was served more than lived up to my expectations. The skin was golden and crisp but not brittle, while the white meat was tender and dotted in places with beads of juice. I've heard that the chicken can vary in greasiness, but I have not personally experienced any shortcomings.

The desserts, frankly, seem to be little more than an afterthought. The overly sweet apple, cherry, and peach cobblers all feature canned fruit or canned pie filling, and all have a gummy, unidentifiable crust that seems to have started out as a biscuit-type pastry, rather than flakier pie pastry. The banana pudding apparently is made with artificial-tasting banana-flavored instant pudding, rather than with real custard, and no meringue or whipped cream is in evidence.

In keeping with the tastes of the region, the tea is very, very sweet. But it's a well-brewed, clear, and mild beverage.

You might say that Bill's barbecue and fixings occupy the safe, comfortable middle, rather than the exhilarating but precarious edge. While some may characterize Bill's as "the Golden Corral of barbecue," you'll find little, if anything, to strongly criticize among the menu items. You'll definitely enjoy soaking up the eastern North Carolina ambiance of the place, as well as knowing that you're dining with one of the biggest (or at least most tirelessly promoted) names in North Carolina barbecue.

## Cherry's Barbecue and Seafood

5139 Webb Lake Road
Wilson, N.C. 27893
252-237-2070
Lunch and dinner, Wednesday through Sunday

"Watch the plates and see what comes back to the kitchen uneaten or barely touched. Keep working to perfect those dishes until hardly anything comes back."

That's the watchword for Robbie Woodard, who has owned Cherry's with his wife, Karen, since 2006. He says the dishwasher has one of the most important jobs in his restaurant because of his ability to discern what the customers like best—and see firsthand what they obviously *don't* like best. Woodard

has continued to burnish the reputation of this barbecue and country-cooking restaurant, in business since 1965.

To be perfectly fair, I sampled the chopped barbecue at Cherry's in midafternoon, when it had been sitting on a buffet line for several hours, which generally does nothing to improve the flavor and texture of the meat. Still, even under those less-than-ideal circumstances, I found it quite good: lean and nicely seasoned. I liked the sauce, which was the traditional dressing one would expect throughout the coastal plain of North Carolina but with a slightly heavier touch of sugar than some, which offset the tartness of the vinegar in a well-balanced way. I can well imagine that if the whole-hog barbecue is still this good after sitting on a steam table for a long while, it is probably exceptional when served and eaten fresh off the cooker. The whole pigs are cooked on a gas cooker. And since Cherry's has refined the seasoning to a science, the end product is of high quality. Woodard says catering averages out to be roughly a third of his business year-round.

Now, to the rest of the wonderful delights at Cherry's!

The fried (actually sautéed and steamed) cabbage was far and away the best I've ever tasted and may be the best vegetable I've ever had the pleasure of sampling. I like underdone and crunchy vegetables as well as the next person, and I often whip up a batch of al dente green beans or downright crunchy fresh broccoli, cooked only long enough to deepen the color. But there is also a great deal to be said for cabbage cooked down to a wonderful, silky, palate-caressing state the way it's done at Cherry's. Considering the otherworldly flavor, you have to figure some pork is in there somewhere, so it may not be the healthiest cabbage you've ever eaten, but I guarantee it will be among the most delicious. Treat yourself.

The yellow-green cabbage collards were also cooked to the peak of perfection, which explains why Cherry's sells loads of them by the quart, especially around the Thanksgiving and Christmas holidays, which are among the best times for collards anyway.

Slowly braised pork backbone, finished off with fluffy strips of dumpling pastry, was originally a dish designed to make something worthwhile out of bony scraps, thereby stretching the available supply of food. The humble backbone may live adjacent to the succulent tenderloin, but whereas the relatively small-diameter "backstrap" of the pig can be considered the meat of the affluent, the backbone itself has always been consid-

ered food for poor folks. But try this heavenly dish at Cherry's and you'll think you've made your way to the king's table. The meat is exquisite, the dumpling strips are feather light, and the rich, thick broth is truly fit for royalty.

I also sampled superlative stewed potatoes, tender, flavorful butter beans, delicate chicken stew (Cherry's name for what most people call chicken 'n' pastry), and a tasty, cheesy potato casserole with ground beef and onions.

Cherry's has a Wilson address, but it seems way out in the country, despite being within just a few miles of town. A nearby sign proclaims, "End of Earth 4 miles, Cherry's Barbecue 6 miles." How, you might ask, does a restaurant find success this far out in a rural area?

One answer is that several churches are nearby. The busiest time of the week is Sunday dinner, right after services let out. The restaurant business is risky enough as it is, and it helps to be on the side of the Almighty

Grady Roberts prepares collards at Cherry's Barbecue.
*Photo by Keith Barnes*

in providing Sabbath sustenance.

The other answer, of course, is that if you produce food this delicious, word will inevitably spread, and folks will find their way to your door.

## Parker's Barbecue
2514 U.S. 301 South
Wilson, N.C. 27893
252-237-0972
Lunch and dinner daily

U.S. 301 used to be the main north-south artery through eastern North Carolina—the equivalent of today's Interstate 95 for those traveling from the Northeast toward Florida. In 1946, at the beginning of the post–World War II transportation explosion, Parker's opened alongside U.S. 301 as a barbecue-and-fried-chicken restaurant; a motor court was added later. Considering this fortuitous meeting of time, place, and great food, it isn't surprising that today Parker's is one of the best-known names in eastern North Carolina dining. Even though I-95, which roughly parallels U.S. 301, passes seven miles to the west, plenty of travelers still detour off the interstate to eat at the restaurant, which advertised itself for years as "North Carolina's Famous Eating Place."

The tobacco market in Wilson was just as important as the transportation explosion in helping build Parker's reputation. In North Carolina's flue-cured-tobacco belt, barbecue has always been associated with celebrating the harvesting and curing of the yearly crop of the golden leaf. Farmers not only organized barbecues for those who had helped them pick and "put in" their crop but often celebrated the sale of their tobacco at the warehouse auctions by joining friends and family for a barbecue meal at a place like Parker's. A large photographic mural of workers outside a tobacco barn hangs on one wall at Parker's, acknowledging the importance of the former tobacco culture to the restaurant's success. Despite the disappearance of the tobacco auction system in recent years, the crop—now largely grown under contract—can still be found within a stone's throw of Parker's barbecue pits.

Brothers Graham and Ralph Parker and a cousin, Henry Parker Brewer, founded Parker's, building the restaurant with timber floated up the Tar River from the family farm in Pitt County. It took about ten years for the place to become established. The turning point occurred when Ralston Purina opened a large plant in the area in 1955 and contracted Parker's to feed over seventeen thousand people—for seventy-five cents each—at the grand opening. The day of the big feed, which took place at the county fairgrounds, was the only time in its fifty-year history that Parker's has been closed for business.

Henry Brewer died in 1987, the same year Graham and Ralph decided to retire and sell the original Wilson restaurant to Bobby Woodard and Don Williams, both longtime Parker's employees. Woodard died in 1996, leaving Williams as the sole owner. Kevin Lamm and Eric Lippard, two other former employees, have since joined the ownership team. (The Parker's locations in Greenville are owned by a brother and nephew of Graham and Ralph but are run as an entirely separate business.)

A meal at Parker's is all about custom and continuity, rather than adventure. Most people know exactly what they'll order even before they arrive: chopped barbecue, fried chicken, coleslaw, boiled potatoes, Brunswick stew, corn sticks, and iced tea. Unless you plan to spend the afternoon sawing logs or chopping cotton, eating this repast at noon will almost certainly put you out of commission for the rest of the day. But then, I've noticed that a great many of Parker's customers have attained an age and level of wisdom at which a dignified afternoon nap is not considered out of the ordinary. Many of these customers have dined regularly at Parker's for forty years or more. Their meals here seem like quiet observances of the changing

Eric Lippard, Donald Williams, and Kevin Lamm of Parker's

Current Parker's owners Donald Williams, Kevin Lamm, and Eric Lippard with original co-owner and founder Ralph Parker *(seated front)*, who still visits the restaurant regularly
*Photos by Keith Barnes*

of the seasons and the orderly passage of the years—rites celebrating the slow, ceaseless rhythms of life on the flat, sandy coastal plain.

Like all the similar restaurants of its era, Parker's used to pit-cook its barbecue over oak coals. In recent years, the Wilson restaurant has been mildly criticized for supposedly cooking its pigs with gas. This criticism is not entirely accurate, partly due to some confusion about the cooking practices at the different Parker's locations. It's true that gas hoods have been installed over the regular pits at the Wilson restaurant, but they're used only at the end of the cooking process, basically just to brown and crisp the skin. During most of the eight to ten hours that the whole hogs are on the pits, they're roasting over hardwood charcoal—which, in my opinion, is virtually indistinguishable from oak or hickory coals in terms of the taste it adds to the barbecue. Hardwood charcoal is also used by several other outstanding eastern restaurants, including The Pit in Raleigh, Stephenson's in rural Johnston County south of Raleigh, B's in Greenville, and Sid's Catering in Beulaville. The gas burners at Parker's allow the pigs to crisp up and finish cooking without having to be turned skin side down for the final couple of hours. In my judgment, that's a fair compromise between tradition and labor-saving technology.

Like its crosstown competition, Bill's Barbecue, Parker's has raised its own hogs since the 1970s. The tenderness and flavor of pork have much to do with a hog's diet and the conditions under which it is raised. The folks at Parker's think that improved meat quality is a significant enough goal to keep several employees, a manager, and a veterinarian on their hog-farm payroll full-time.

Parker's barbecue is squarely in the eastern North Carolina mainstream: finely chopped, lightly sprinkled throughout with crushed red pepper flakes and seeds, and seasoned with salt, vinegar, and peppers. The relatively high proportion of white meat from the hams and loins makes this a fairly lean and dry barbecue, although it's served well moistened with sauce. And of course, extra sauce is always on the table. Although the vinegar-and-pepper mixture is called "mild," enough red pepper flakes are floating around in it to tip you off that this is not a condiment to be trifled with.

Boiled potatoes and a sweet yellow coleslaw help to soothe the palate between bites of liberally sauced barbecue, while the restaurant's golden corn sticks, which are baked and then deep-fried, offer a satisfying heft and crunch in contrast to the soft textures of the other foods. Another interesting taste contrast occurs between the tart, salty barbecue and Parker's Brunswick stew, which, according to eastern North Carolina tradition, is served moderately sweet. Now, thousands of individuals and groups from this region frequently cook their own large quantities of Brunswick stew, either as a hobby or for fundraisers, mostly according to recipes handed down from one generation to the next. These local chefs, who are invariably rigid about their methods of preparation, deride any restaurant stew as institutional tasting at best or inedible at worst. I have heard many comments of this sort about Parker's stew simply because the restaurant enjoys such a high visibility. But I personally think it's pretty good—although, not surprisingly, it's not up to private small-batch standards.

Parker's fried chicken is also famous throughout the area. The restaurant sells as much chicken as it does barbecue. Hundreds of churches, civic organizations, family reunions, and other groups within a fifty-mile range regularly place orders for large quantities of chicken. And that doesn't count what's prepared and consumed through Parker's sizable catering operation. Parker's joins Bill's, the White Swan, and Bum's in Ayden in offering eastern North Carolina's finest fried chicken. I'd be hard-pressed to find anything negative to say about the chicken at those places, just as I'd have trouble finding much of a difference in the way it's prepared at the various spots.

In terms of ambiance, Parker's is about as vanilla as it gets. The exterior is simple white clapboard, while the interior features sheet-paneled walls, Formica-topped tables, and no-nonsense wooden chairs. Parker's hires young men in high school and college to wait on tables—no waitresses. They all wear white aprons and white-paper drive-in-style hats as they scurry about with loaded food trays, lending an entirely appropriate 1950s aura to the place.

## B's Barbecue and Grill

751 B's Barbeque Road
Greenville, N.C. 27834
Lunch, Tuesday to Saturday (until the barbecue runs out)

Due to road widening and the inexorable march of progress, B's has changed on the outside. But among the important things, not much has been altered, and that's great news.

In previous years, barbecue lovers were not able to visit B's without having three images indelibly imprinted on their memories. Some have changed, some haven't.

The first was the cars and trucks jamming the dusty, unpaved parking lot and spilling out along the sides of both N.C. 43 and B's Barbeque Road, which form a T-intersection right beside the restaurant. B's lot had no neatly lined parking spaces, and customers in a hurry constantly pulled in and out, leaving their vehicles sitting any which way while they dashed to the takeout window. Since that threw the rest of the parking lot into chaos as well, many customers simply chose to park on the highway shoulders, on the theory that they would be exposed to side-swiping from only one direction, rather than all four. The amazing thing is that Greenville and Pitt County officials didn't complain about the cars and trucks on the shoulders. As co-owner Peggy McLawhorn sweetly explained, "They all like to eat here, too." (The fact that the secondary road beside B's is named for the restaurant also tells you a little something.)

Now, N.C. 43 has been widened to four

B's as it appeared in the 1960s. Most of the space in front of the building is now gone, due to road widening.
*Courtesy of the North Carolina State Archives*

lanes, and curbs on both sides prevent parking on the shoulders. Parking is no longer available on the front side of B's; the few feet that remain of the front space, as well as the side parking lot, have been paved.

The second mental image was—and still is—that of the high proportion of well-dressed professional men and women among the clientele, either standing in the line snaking out the front door of this former country store or waiting their turn for the takeout window in a single file that on nice days forms between picnic tables full of al fresco diners. Oh, the restaurant has always drawn plenty of working folks, too, in coveralls, jeans, plaid shirts, and boots. But B's is located just a mile north of the Pitt Memorial regional medical complex, and many of the doctors and other health professionals who would warn *you* about the risks of eating too much barbecue still regularly slip away to B's, as they have for a long, long time.

The third picture you would have taken away from B's was of four of the hardest-working women in eastern North Carolina. Peggy McLawhorn and her three daughters—Tammy, Donna, and Judy—ran B's for many years. Peggy has now retired and left her daughters to keep the tradition going. On any given day, customers used to find at least three of the four behind the cafeteria-style counter, dressed in baseball caps and T-shirts, cheerfully frazzled and dishing up barbecue and chicken dinners like women possessed. The frantic energy of the restaurant was on display when I first visited the place to tape a segment for UNC-TV's *North Carolina Now.* Since B's has no telephone, I was unable to make the usual advance arrangements. When I showed up unannounced with a television crew, Peggy and her daughters were so busy serving the usual lunchtime mob that they hardly noticed my cameraman, Jerome Moore, moving around the kitchen area, practically underfoot, to get the shots he needed. After the crowd thinned, the crew set up lights around one of the booths, and we taped a long sequence of shots of me eating and commenting on B's delicious chopped-pork barbecue and barbecued chicken. Only when we had finished shooting the entire segment and were packing up the equipment around 2 P.M. did Peggy have a chance to get out from behind the counter long enough to come over and ask, "Who *are* you people, anyway?"

Now, visitors aren't likely to see Peggy at the restaurant, but the daughters are as much in evidence as always, still working as hard as ever.

The overwhelming success of B's was sort of a happy accident for the McLawhorn family. Eighteen years ago, the late Bill McLawhorn and his wife, Peggy, decided to get out of farming and look for another line of work. Bill had barbecued pigs and chickens more or less as a hobby for years, and he thought he had a pretty good sauce recipe, so the couple decided to look into the barbecue business. "There wasn't any kind of restaurant out on 43," Peggy remembers, "so we bought this old country store and fixed it up the best we could." A brother-in-law named Bob was a partner originally, and since the letter *B* could stand for both Bill and Bob, the restaurant simply became "B's." The McLawhorns built a screened shed behind the restaurant and installed open pits. Today, the smoke from the roasting pork and chicken still billows in waves through the screens and across the yard, where it settles over the customers busily eating at the red-painted picnic tables, infusing their clothing with a faint, delightful aroma that reminds them for the rest of the afternoon of the great meal they enjoyed.

B's could probably double its volume if the McLawhorn women could find time to expand. But for years, they've just been trying to keep their heads above water in dealing with the current trade. "We sure never thought this business would turn out anything like it has," said Peggy, "and it's probably going to get bigger with all the building that's going on out this way." Indeed, the farmland on B's side of Greenville is rapidly being transformed into a suburban landscape, with

Donna McLawhorn, Judy Drach, and Tammy Godley are the "face" of B's Barbecue.
*Photo by Keith Barnes*

apartment complexes, condominiums, and large new homes crowding out the tobacco barns and open fields that have characterized the region for decades.

When the road widening occurred, rumors circulated that B's would close its doors. But the McLawhorn daughters decided to stay on. They put a new sign on top of the building, even though it was the free kind provided by soft-drink companies. B's hasn't been fancy at any time in its history, and the family obviously didn't think it was the time to start putting on airs. The parking-lot paving did bring a fresh look to the exterior, but the overall impression is still no-nonsense.

A couple of key pit men and cooks have passed away over the years, along with founder Bill McLawhorn. And following Peggy's retirement, the place has a slightly different feel. Still, customers swear there's no way the food could get any better than it is at this moment.

B's serves tender, hand-chopped pork barbecue from whole hogs, which are pit-cooked over hardwood charcoal. The barbecue is woodsy-flavored from the charcoal but only lightly seasoned, so you'll probably want to add a splash of the restaurant's vinegar-and-pepper sauce. B's doesn't waste a lot of time, attention, or money on frills. At one time, the sauce on the tables was likely to be bottled in any kind of container the McLawhorns could get their hands on. On several of my early visits, quite a few of the tables were outfitted with Canadian Club whiskey decanters filled with the light red sauce, although Canadian Club was almost certainly

*not* one of the ingredients.

Since B's cooks whole hogs, rather than shoulders, ribs are available, but they aren't sold in individual orders. Instead, you'll have to buy a whole set—all the ribs from an entire pig—which is enough to fill a large, four-inch-deep foil pan. These are unbasted, unsauced, slow-cooked ribs with slabs of tender meat still attached. They are, quite simply, out of this world.

B's is as famous for its barbecued chicken as it is for its pork barbecue. The half-chickens grill for hours over a low charcoal fire and are immersed, just before they're served, in a vinegar-based sauce similar to the one for the chopped pig. The chicken is not overcooked so that it slides off the bones, and the vinegar flavor is not overwhelming, as it is in many versions of eastern-style barbecued chicken. Even after the chicken is soaked briefly in the sauce, the skin remains crisp, and the meat has just the right firmness and texture. You won't find better grilled chicken inside the borders of North Carolina—and perhaps not anywhere else either.

The side dishes at B's are traditional but not extensive. In addition to the standard coleslaw, B's serves eastern North Carolina boiled potatoes and home-style green beans, so it's possible to put together a chicken dinner that's a relatively healthy, low-fat meal. Hush puppies have been replaced here by squares of traditional, flat-as-a-pancake baked corn bread, which is a delicious and refreshing change of pace.

The chicken, pork barbecue, and side dishes at B's are all good enough to put the restaurant at or near the top of the list of the state's best barbecue spots. And we should all feel relieved that B's didn't join the group of important barbecue restaurants that have closed in recent years.

## Parker's Barbecue

http://www.parkersbbq.com
Lunch and dinner daily

3109 South Memorial Drive (N.C. 11)
Greenville, N.C. 27834
252-756-2388

Second location:
    2020 Greenville Boulevard Southeast
    Greenville, N.C. 27858
    252-758-9215

Many years ago, the Parkers divided up the family barbecue business. Former em-ployees now run the Parker's in Wilson, while Parker kinfolks operate the two locations in Greenville. The menus are similar in the two towns, but the restaurants are under totally different management and are not at all the same.

Parker's has become a household name in eastern North Carolina because people know what to expect every time they visit. As a result, the Greenville Parker's locations, like the one in Wilson, do a tremendous business. The location on busy South Memorial Drive in Greenville actually has five dining areas—one in the center of the building and two each on either end—so private parties of just about any size can be accommodated easily. The functional décor features white walls and white and green chairs. When I visited most recently, a manager was circling the room to check on every table and make sure everyone was satisfied, and I noticed that my server left

Parker's Barbecue, South Memorial Drive, Greenville

behind an entire pitcher of iced tea; both of these were really good touches.

Parker's is what I call a "filling station," offering safe, predictable food—and lots of it—to people who don't like to get too adventurous with their dining. I found the Greenville restaurant considerably improved since my previous visit. The place specializes in barbecue dinners, which include the pork itself, two vegetables, and both hush puppies and corn sticks. You can also get a barbecue plate, which includes only barbecue, coleslaw, and corn sticks/hush puppies. You can add chicken to the barbecue dinner and make it a combination family-style dinner, with barbecue, fried *and* barbecued chicken, coleslaw, green beans, boiled potatoes, and corn bread.

Since wood-cooked flavor is not expected of barbecue very often in eastern North Carolina, the customers at the Parker's in Greenville have no problem with the fact that the meat isn't pit-cooked and doesn't taste the least bit smoky. It has a strong vinegar flavor, particularly if you add a little of the house sauce. This sauce has both ground red pepper and crushed red pepper flakes, balanced with more sweetness than I remember from my previous visit several years ago.

I found the Brunswick stew fairly authentic. It had a good, strong flavor, although it wasn't as sweet as some found farther north, closer to the Virginia state line. It had a clear corn taste. The stew contained green beans, which aren't a traditional ingredient. But in truth, they didn't change the flavor profile at all.

The hush puppies were really tasty and held their crispness well. The ubiquitous eastern boiled potatoes, served with a dash of paprika, admirably balanced the tartness of the barbecue—which is no doubt why our forebears started serving these spuds with spicy barbecue. Parker's crunchy corn sticks are ten-inch bars of corn bread that are first baked, then deep-fried. The potatoes and corn sticks are among the best dishes on the menu. Whereas last time I thought the fried chicken was only so-so, this time I found it good enough to make me want to keep eating after a sample bite or two.

The mac 'n' cheese had a sort of floury cheese sauce. It was not memorable, homestyle macaroni and cheese—the kind that holds together firmly and has crunchy, baked bits. In all honesty, it's difficult to hold that kind of "Grandma's" mac 'n' cheese on a serving line such as the one required to feed everyone in a place the size of Parker's.

Slices of various kinds of cake are available for dessert. A new addition to the menu provides an excellent sweet touch, in my opinion—the apple-cinnamon "Crispito," a flour tortilla rolled around the fruit filling, then deep-fried. Delicious!

Overall, my opinion of Parker's in Greenville went up after my most recent visit. But the restaurant already had a legion of loyal fans to begin with.

## Jack Cobb & Son Bar-B-Que

3883 South Main Street
Farmville, N.C. 27828
252-753-5128
Lunch and dinner, Wednesday, Friday, and Saturday. Takeout only.

Jack Cobb & Son Bar-B-Que dates back to the 1940s, when current owner Rudy Cobb was a boy and his father, Jack, worked at a local tobacco company in Farmville. Jack Cobb established a little side business, selling barbecue to his black fellow workers. Word about the excellent barbecue quickly spread, and whites began to show interest in becoming customers of Jack's as well—although, things being the way they were at the time, none of them felt comfortable coming over to Jack's place to buy it. Jack ended up getting a white friend to sell the barbecue for him.

Meanwhile, Rudy learned the marketing side of the business in a direct way. His father would load up the family car with barbecue plates and park it in a strategic location, from which Rudy could use it as a staging area from which to sell the barbecue plates door to door throughout the African-American community.

Jack and Rudy worked hard to establish a loyal customer base among blacks and whites alike. While times of racial tension occasionally brought opposition to the business from both races, no sign of any of that lingers today. A steady stream of patrons, white and black, comes to Rudy's takeout-only location on Farmville's South Main Street to get genuine whole-hog barbecue, cooked for eighteen hours over wood coals. (The wood comes from construction scraps, hardwood trees downed by storms, and other sources. The smoke from all of it does an excellent job of flavoring this eastern-style 'cue.) The restaurant also serves barbecued chicken and turkey barbecue, which seems to be a hit, considering the number of orders I saw being placed. These essentials are accompanied by a very sweet coleslaw with lots of mustard and good, crispy hush puppies. The barbecue

The woodpile and the pit house around back are the "business" side of Jack Cobb & Son Bar-B-Que in Farmville.

is "lean and clean," with less fat and skin than in the meat at some nearby eastern establishments. It has a good, subtle wood-smoke flavor and matches up well with the peppery sauce.

I found the barbecued chicken to have a nice char and a relaxed feel, but when I broke a piece open, I noted plenty of droplets of juice inside, too. This is the vinegar-flavored, clear-sauce chicken popular in the region, and it's terrific. I also thoroughly enjoyed the sandwich I sampled containing turkey barbecue and slaw. The texture and taste were similar to the pork barbecue, but my twinges of guilt were considerably less, considering the lower fat content. Upon hearing several customers ordering portions of mixed pork and turkey barbecue, I was amused that I didn't have a single thought that this was some sort of heresy.

The other item at Jack Cobb & Son that I would put in the "essential" category is the collard greens. Farmville is located in that magical area of the state where the tender heirloom variety known as "cabbage collards" thrives—the same type as in nearby Ayden, which bills itself as "the Collard Capital of the World," with good reason. The day I visited, two different vendors were selling loose cabbage collards by the pound at stands outside Rudy's establishment. But of course, I was most interested in the fact that Rudy Cobb was cooking the same collards *inside*.

The greens were, quite simply, sublime. They were meltingly tender, subtly flavored with pork, and a bit on the sweet side. If you're near Jack Cobb & Son during collard

season—fall or mid- to late spring—I strongly recommend including a serving or two in your to-go barbecue order. You may find yourself eating them with your fingers in the car, then walking into the house picking telltale bits of collards out of your teeth.

I also enjoyed the sweet potato and pecan tarts that Rudy includes on the menu for "a little something sweet."

Be advised that you'll find absolutely nothing fancy about Rudy's place, and that you'll have nowhere to sit while you wait for your order. It's sparse, but it's authentic. Believe me, that's enough.

## Bum's Restaurant

North Carolina Classic

566 Third Street
Ayden, N.C. 28513
252-746-6880
Breakfast and lunch are served Tuesday and Saturday. Breakfast, lunch, and dinner are served Monday and Wednesday through Friday.

Bum's Restaurant in downtown Ayden, ten miles south of Greenville, is the undisputed gathering place for this Pitt County town of five thousand. It features outstanding eastern North Carolina whole-hog barbecue, pit-cooked over wood coals, and carries on a family barbecue-cooking legacy that goes back more than 150 years. It is as good an example as North Carolina has to offer of a restaurant that excels not only in its barbecue but also in a wide range of wonderful homestyle cooking.

Named for Latham "Bum" Dennis, who

Early BBQ pit man John Bill Dennis, founder of the J. B. Dennis Café, which later became Bum's Restaurant
*Courtesy of the Dennis family*

bought the restaurant from a cousin in 1966, Bum's serves breakfast, lunch, and dinner cafeteria-style. The place opens as early as four in the morning during deer season and has a "coffee club" of retired state employees and other regulars who gather early to discuss world and local affairs and help themselves from the coffeepot. The location on Ayden's main downtown street, across from the town hall, ensures that a great many townspeople stop in at some time during a typical day. A small, core group partakes of every one of the sixteen meals a week served at the restaurant. The Dennis family members call nearly all the locals by their first names and treat the many out-of-towners, attracted by Bum's reputation or the town's annual Collard Festival, with the same warmth as they do townspeople. A cheerful, bustling place with two large public rooms and a private dining room, it's

as much a perpetual town meeting place as it is a restaurant.

Out behind Bum's is a cookhouse, where whole pigs are slow-roasted for hours on simple brick pits covered by sheets of tin. After split hardwood is burned down to embers in the fireplace, the live coals are sprinkled one shovelful at a time through the iron pit gratings (rather than through a separate opening below the grate) so that they come to rest around the edges of the pit, with some rolling directly under the roasting pig. The smoke swirls all around the meat, the juices drip onto the coals, creating flavorful swirls of steam, and the aroma is absolutely incomparable.

Once the meat has reached a state of relaxed tenderness that allows the bones to be pulled cleanly, it's fragmented by hand into holding pans for later chopping and seasoning in small quantities as needed, so that it will remain fresh-tasting. Typically, a pan of pulled barbecue will contain a bottom layer of inside meat, a layer of well-browned "bark" or "outside brown," and a layer of crispy skin. When one of the employees is ready to chop and season a finished batch of barbecue, he or she can scoop straight down into the pan and come up with a perfect mixture of different types of meat and varied textures. Chopped by hand and seasoned with the Dennis sauce of vinegar, salt, peppers, and sugar, the finished product is probably virtually identical to the barbecue served by six generations of Dennis family members over a span of a century and a half.

Ancestor Skilten Dennis, born in the early 1840s, is said to have sold barbecue and fed large church groups in the Ayden area out of the back of a covered wagon. His son, Skilten M. Dennis, and his grandson, Bill Dennis, carried on the barbecue business. Grandson Bill eventually ended up selling the barbecue from a booth rented from the town in a curb-market setting. Whenever Bill Dennis saw that he would need more barbecue to sell at the booth, his wife, Susan, would kill, dress, and barbecue a thirty- to fifty-pound pig at home on their farm. She cooked the meat on a wire grate resting over a pit dug into the ground, into which coals from an oak fire were spread beneath the pig. Susan Dennis would then send the cooked barbecue to town in a wagon so Bill and his young son, John Bill, could continue serving customers.

John Bill, the fourth generation of Dennis pit masters, carried on what he learned from his father, selling trays of barbecue and wife Bettie's corn bread from a couple of locations before building a seventeen-foot trailer in 1941 on the site of the present-day Bum's. He constructed a chimney and pit on the back of the lot and sold barbecue out of the trailer for seven years before building a permanent restaurant, the J. B. Dennis Café, which eventually totally surrounded the trailer. He envisioned the larger restaurant as a place for serving a wider menu than simply barbecue. When the restaurant was eventually completed, the trailer was dismantled and carried out the back door one piece at a time. Dennis never missed even one day of selling barbecue during the construction process. Now, he could begin to cook and serve the home-style meals he dreamed of.

John Bill's son Bobby worked at the café as a boy but later decided to pursue another career. So in 1960, John Bill hired Latham "Bum" Dennis, a cousin who was just coming out of the service and who already had many years of experience working for other cousins, the Jones family, at an already-established and famous Ayden barbecue joint, The Skylight Inn. Bum Dennis worked for John Bill for three years, rented a place of his own for another three, and eventually bought the J. B. Dennis Café from John Bill in 1966, renaming it Bum's Restaurant. Bum Dennis and his wife, Shirley, have worked together for more than forty-five years to make the place what it is today: a restaurant serving absolutely outstanding barbecue that also offers the best of the *rest* of country cooking.

Bum's son Larry, a member of the sixth generation of Dennis barbecue experts, has now come back into the business with his father and mother, joined by his wife, Teresa, and their daughters, Emily Dunn, Jessica Dennis, and Leah Dennis. Larry is a jovial bundle of energy with an infectious enthusiasm for his work. He considers himself the luckiest man alive and claims there's nowhere he would rather be on any given day than at the restaurant "cookin." He works close to a hundred hours a week but still finds time to not only tirelessly and inventively promote Bum's on Facebook but also to interact personally with nearly every customer, getting direct feedback on the preparation and seasoning of the home-style dishes that have helped make Bum's famous. "People around here were raised up on this kind of food," he says, "and if I'm a little off on the salt or black pepper or sugar or something, they'll let me know."

Ayden bills itself as "the Collard Capital of the World," and Bum's collard greens may well be the best on planet earth. He grows all the collards served in the restaurant in his own large garden and delivers them personally to the café every morning. The yellowish green cabbage collards are an especially tender heirloom variety not often found outside Pitt County. Larry Dennis has taken over the daily task of giving them the special family touch. In one pot, he boils the collards until they're soft, while in another he creates a complex seasoning stock. "I put in some fresh ham, some tenderized ham, and some country ham, and I add a lot of different kind of sauces to it. I boil it until the ham is as soft as butter, then pour the stock over the collards," Larry says. The collards are put through a commercial chopper so that the greens, the tender chunks of ham, and the heavy stock

Larry Dennis prepares Bum's famous sweet potato muffins.

are all worked together into a rich, silky, palate-caressing mash.

Bum's is also notable for its fluffy rutabagas, savory cabbage, complex Brunswick stew, black-eyed peas, soft stewed potatoes, rich sweet potatoes, and other vegetable delights. In addition to the succulent pit-cooked barbecue, Larry and the staff offer incredible, moist fried chicken (which my daughter calls the best she's ever tasted), barbecued beef, beef stew, pit-cooked barbecued chicken, fried and stewed seafood, chicken and pastry, boiled country ham, and country-style steak. Thin, extra-crispy baked corn bread, Bum's signature sweet potato muffins, deep-fried corn sticks, and warm, meringue-topped banana pudding hang a resplendent halo over all these heavenly choices.

The warm glow you'll experience at Bum's will be only partly due to post-meal contentment; the rest will come from fellowship perfected through nearly a half-century of practice.

## The Skylight Inn

North Carolina Classic

4617 South Lee Street
Ayden, N.C. 28513
252-746-4113
Lunch and dinner, Monday through Saturday

Okay, here's the plan. You live your whole life in this little town of several thousand people. You don't go off to college, and you don't seek an executive position with a fast-track company offering excellent chances for advancement. You just stay right here

The Skylight Inn is topped by a scaled-down replica of the dome atop the United States Capitol.

and work. You open a little place—nothing fancy or even very noticeable, not even on the main highway. You put in day after day of long, inconvenient hours doing hot, dirty, greasy, back-hurting, splinter-in-your-finger, eye-stinging, foot-aching work. And you do it all again the next day. And the next.

After thirty years, you're famous in your field. You've received dozens of awards. You're praised in national magazines and on network television. Presidents try your product and offer their compliments. And people from all over beat a path to your little, unsophisticated town—it calls itself "the Collard Capital of the World," for Pete's sake—just to buy your product. They even tell you they're fixing to transport it halfway around the world, to Turkey or someplace. You've never had an advertising agency or public-relations campaign. Shoot, for years, you didn't even have a sign out front. Just word of mouth. And the next thing you know, "Oh, Pete,

BBQ

The Skylight Inn's barbecue tray is topped with a slab of corn bread and a tray of slaw.

*Southern Living*'s on the phone. Can you talk to them?"

Got it? Okay, on three—down, set . . . hut—hut—hut!

Ayden, located in Pitt County twelve miles south of Greenville, is well known in the region for some state-championship-caliber 1-A football over at Ayden-Grifton High School. But the local team never pulled off a play as big as *that*. Something that unlikely, that American, could happen only in the world of barbecue, where the thing that matters ultimately is the verdict the public renders on your work. No use just to plan it or talk about it. You've got to produce—every day.

Founder Walter B. "Pete" Jones (who never used the Walter B.) died in 2005. He never wanted to do anything else. "I'd sit in school, as far back as the fifth or sixth grade, and daydream about having my own bar-

becue place," he remembered. After high school, while acquaintances with stars in their eyes were daydreaming about little else but getting out of Ayden, Pete went to work cooking barbecue for his uncle, then finally opened a business of his own in 1947. Nearly forty years later, he found someone to build a silver-painted wooden dome—vaguely like the one atop the United States Capitol, but smaller—on top of his otherwise undistinguished brick building. *National Geographic* had just identified his place as the barbecue capital of the *world*. Considering all his previous awards, and since the restaurant was a little off the beaten track, he figured he might as well make it easier for people to know this was the place. The capital.

Anyone who knows barbecue knows that family and heritage are important. You have to love feeding people and love watching them enjoy your food. You also have to be fiercely determined to keep those happy looks on their faces. At least part of that seems to be passed along in the blood. Pete's great-great-grandfather began selling barbecue in Ayden out of the back of a covered wagon sometime in the mid-1800s, and while the barbecue business hasn't run continuously all that time, his family has been at it a great many years. Illustrative of Pete's no-nonsense attitude about what it took to become successful was the fact that the place didn't have *any* kind of sign for a long time. As word about Pete's barbecue spread around Ayden, Grifton, Winterville, and Greenville, everyone simply called the place "Pete Jones's." And as Pete said pointedly years ago, "A place like this don't need any sign."

Don't come to The Skylight—now operated by Pete's son Bruce, his nephew Jeff, and Bruce's son Samuel—expecting gingham tablecloths and cutesy little pig cutouts. The décor can perhaps best be described as absent. The Skylight has no menus, and the tables are bare, adorned only with bottles of Texas Pete, pepper vinegar, and toothpicks. You'll find no waitresses either. If you want to eat at The Skylight, you go up to the counter, order, pay, and carry your food to a table like everybody else, thank you. For a long time, this was probably the only barbecue place in the known world that didn't have sweet iced tea—or *any* iced tea. Everything to drink came in a bottle—the sixteen-ounce soft-drink variety. When Pete heard the soft-drink companies were phasing out bottles, he bought three tractor-trailer loads of bot-

tled Pepsis just so he wouldn't have to put in a newfangled fountain-drink machine. The place had to go to fountain drinks not long ago. It now has a tea dispenser as well. It may be a mercy that Pete didn't live to see it, given his antipathy to such "improvements."

Although The Skylight has offered barbecued chicken as a catering item for a long time, it never served it in the restaurant until recently. It still prepares potato salad and desserts only for catered events. The barbecued chicken is just about the only menu addition in recent memory, other than the beverages.

And really, you don't come to The Skylight to experience change anyhow. You come for a barbecue sandwich on a bun, topped with yellow coleslaw. (It was many years before Pete stopped using plain, white loaf bread—light bread—in favor of hamburger-type buns.) Or you come for a paper tray of chopped barbecue, a square slab of baked corn bread, and a little dish of slaw. That's the way it's served, too—tray of barbecue on the bottom, sheet of restaurant tissue, piece of corn bread sitting on top of that, more tissue, and the paper container of slaw with a plastic fork stuck into it on top of the stack. That way, you can pick the whole thing up in one hand and have the other free for your drink. For a long time, Pete had no cash register, just a pile of currency and coins under the counter from which he made change. He also kept a loaded pistol down there.

When you get to your table, you survey your three or four items, counting the beverage. That's it—no French fries, no potato salad, no baked beans, and, right smack in the middle of the Collard Capital of the World, no collard greens or other vegetables.

All of this points to the fact that the business end of this enterprise isn't up front in the kitchen or dining room. It's out back. That's where you'll find the wood lot of oak and hickory big enough to remind you of a small lumberyard, and the detached cinder-block building where tending the fires and cooking have long been Jeff's responsibility. Out of an ordinary open fireplace, Jeff shovels live coals and scatters them under the whole split pigs roasting in three-foot-high pits. He works from the top, dropping the coals through the metal bars on which the meat rests, maneuvering the shovel around the sides of the meat. In the gloom of the unlit building, a shaft of white sunlight streaming through an open door reveals floating particles of fine ash, which, together with the billowing smoke and the scraping of the shovel, make the whole scene look like what we called "the bad place" when I was growing up. I visited in February; imagine this in August.

The roasted, falling-apart-tender pigs are transported to the kitchen, where skin and fat are separated from the lean meat. But they aren't separated for long, because as the meat is sprinkled with Texas Pete and salt (but no other sauce) and thoroughly chopped, a fair amount of the fat and skin is chopped and mixed back in with the shredded, crunchy, reddish brown outside meat and the white or light brown meat from the shoulders, hams, and loin. And that's a good thing. Now, some would shudder at the fat content of The Skylight's barbecue. But those people probably wouldn't be caught dead in any kind of barbecue place to begin with—not even those places in the Piedmont that produce a much leaner blend. If we can all agree that eating barbecue is like firing a cholesterol bullet straight into our hearts, we can simply note that The Skylight's merely packs a heftier slug, along with a clearly superior—a downright awesome—flavor. (A little bit of the cooked pig finds its way into the restaurant's signature baked corn bread, too. The square baking pans get a dollop of liquefied pork fat—euphemistically called "drippings"—before the batter is ladled in. If you peer into the oven, you can see the hot grease bubbling merrily over the edges of the dense, inch-and-a-half-thick corn bread.)

The Skylight Inn's barbecue is simply unlike any other, and certainly different from most eastern barbecue, which tends to be a little drier and have a more pronounced vinegar-pepper tang. Since it's the fat that carries the flavor of the seasoning through barbecue, or most any food, The Skylight gets more of the wood-smoke taste in its meat than just about any other place I've found in the east. The texture is moist and luxuriant to the tongue without being over-sauced. The bits of crispy skin provide a bewitching crackle and crunch. All in all, it's wonderful but powerful stuff that probably should carry a disclaimer stamped onto each paper tray—"Warning: Causes drowsiness. Do not eat before driving or operating heavy machinery." My UNC-TV cameraman, Jeff Anderson, normally a bundle of nervous energy, smacked his lips through a tray of The Skylight's barbecue, then climbed back into the van, mumbled something about wanting to lie down, and slept throughout the two-hour return trip to the studio.

The Skylight Inn really is world-famous on the barbecue circuit. Although reputations in the restaurant business can be queerly and swiftly made, the legacy of Pete—and now Bruce, Jeff, and Samuel—has held up long enough to be taken seriously. Whether you end up pronouncing the barbecue the absolute best you've ever tasted or characterize it as merely an interesting regional oddity, it's well worth going out of your way to visit The Skylight Inn. But cut way down on your fat intake for a week before you do.

## Morris Barbeque

North Carolina Classic

891 Morris BBQ Road
Hookerton, N.C. 28538
252-747-2254
http://morrisbarbeque.com
Open Saturday from 8 A.M. to 2 P.M., or until barbecue sells out

Morris Barbeque represents a true, if disappearing, slice of Americana and an unusual glimpse of community life in bucolic Greene County and most of rural eastern North Carolina. The following history of the family business was written for the Greene County Historical Association by Ashley Morris, great-granddaughter of the founder.

When the folks of Greene County think of good food, most think of good barbeque, and the name Morris Barbeque has become synonymous with that thought.

Willie McKinley Morris, whom the older generation may know as "Pop," and his wife Frances (Frankie) Hartsfield Dail Morris, lovingly called "Nannie" by her family, started Morris Barbeque in 1956. But even before that, "Pop" peddled his barbeque down the streets of Hookerton on his mule and cart. At that time it was cooked under his tobacco shelter, on iron rods over a pit filled with charcoal, corncobs, and oak wood. That would have been in the days when Hoover was president. However, in February of 1956, he decided to make his restaurant a more stationary one, and he built what is still standing today as Morris Barbeque.

What is now the "pit" is actually a building that once served as a chicken coop on the farm. The buildings may be old but that is what gives them the character and appeal they have today. During those early days "Pop" also ran a small store stocked with cleaning supplies, staple grocery goods, and cigarettes. The store served as a hang-out for the people of "Pop's" generation. Many would gather together outside of the store to fellowship and hear "Pop" play his steel guitar. Music and laughter must have filled the air during the weekdays only to be replaced on Saturday mornings with the sounds of meat cleavers chopping that delicious, hot-off-the-grill barbeque and the whirr of the crushed ice machine used to cut the slaw.

The smells had to have been wonderful, too! Imagine the scent of fried hush puppies, delicious pork, and even the tasty desserts that "Nannie" would sometimes whip up to sell at the store. But even better than the sounds and smells had to be the tastes! Cool, crisp, sweet slaw; hot, crunchy, slightly sweet hush puppies; warm, moist, vinegar and red pepper–seasoned barbeque; crunchy pork

Morris Barbeque, Hookerton

skins; and tasty ribs: those were the items that were and still are on the menu at Morris Barbeque.

For many years, "Pop" raised his own hogs and continued to cook with charcoal. In later years he switched to gas, but the recipe was still every bit as delicious as before! The restaurant was a family affair, with many family members filling different positions over the years. When dear "Pop" passed on to his heavenly home on December 19, 1991, preceded in death by his dear wife "Nannie" on April 29, 1974, the family business was left to his grandson William Franklin Morris, Jr. Today the tradition continues with very little change in the recipe and methods that "Pop" used. And it is still a family affair, continued today by grandson William Morris and great-granddaughter Ashley. They both enjoy hearing a new story every Saturday from someone who once knew "Pop" or stopped by to buy his barbeque.

Many hold trips to Morris Barbeque as a dear memory within their hearts and continue to return years later even though many have moved to other states and can only make it home to Greene County occasionally. But the people do not hesitate to let it be known that they just had to visit once again to taste that barbeque and to recall wonderful memories of their past.

The pig-cooking practices of this family business, whose roots extend deep into the soil of Greene County, confound one of the cornerstones of North Carolina dogma—that barbecue must be cooked over live coals to be considered truly fine. On the contrary, the lean, finely chopped pork at this humble establishment—cooked on gas, without a hint of wood smoke—is, quite simply, some of the best I have ever tasted.

William Morris and his daughter Ashley, who run the Saturday-only business and keep the memories alive, clearly understand the concept of complementary tastes. The 'cue is not only as perfectly seasoned as any I have ever encountered, it also flawlessly brings out the flavor and texture of the sweet, finely

William Morris is interviewed by an oral-history team outside his pit building as daughter Ashley listens.

cut coleslaw (or vice versa). The Morris family doesn't chop crispy bits of pork skin into the barbecue itself. Instead, every scrap of the crunchy skin is broken into saltine cracker–sized pieces for sale, as are the crispy ribs and even the pig bones—with succulent bits of meat still attached.

I encourage you to pick up a square of this heavenly pork skin, judiciously pile barbecue and coleslaw on top to make it into a country canapé, and take a moderately sized bite. Before you do too much chewing, quickly add a small bite of well-browned hush puppy to what you already have in your mouth. Now, chew it all together—and roll your eyes in delight. Follow this simple barbecue meal with an incredible slice of red velvet, German chocolate, or chocolate pecan cake, all lovingly baked by Ashley to help preserve the dessert-making legacy of her great-grandmother Frankie ("Nannie").

I visited Morris Barbeque at ten o'clock on a Saturday morning intending to sample a few bites from a small barbecue plate. But I simply couldn't stop eating. Even at that early hour, I soon consumed the entire plateful. I rest my case.

Whatever you do, don't miss this place. Three ring-tailed monkeys used to hang around the premises and sometimes sit on the hogs' backs. Unfortunately, none of them is still alive. On the other hand, you'll receive deep satisfaction in meeting William and Ashley, as well as the half-dozen or so loyal employees who clearly love being part of the living history at Morris Barbeque.

## King's Barbecue & Chicken
405 East New Bern Road
Kinston, N.C. 28504
252-527-2101
Lunch and dinner are served Monday through Friday. Breakfast, lunch, and dinner are offered Saturday and Sunday; a special Sunday buffet is served in a separate room.

King's Barbecue & Chicken has been a familiar landmark to millions of travelers up and down U.S. 70, including generations of beach vacationers, who sometimes combine a visit with a stop at the nearby Neuse Sports Shoppe. This place has been around since 1936, when Frank King Sr. owned a country store on the site. A poolroom in the back became the first restaurant when King started heating canned foods from the store on a potbelly stove to feed the pool players. During the 1950s, the site was a teen hangout. The back parking lot was said to be the biggest lovers' lane in the area.

Now, King's is one of the largest restaurants in the South, seating eight hundred and serving an average of eight thousand pounds of barbecue, six thousand pounds of chicken, and fifteen hundred pounds of collard greens each month—and that's with collards appearing on the menu only at certain times. I find it amusing that King's restaurant sign is mounted on the same tall poles as the sign for the adjacent Piggly Wiggly supermarket. The Piggly Wiggly "smiling pig" logo appears to serve double duty for both the barbecue restaurant and the grocery.

King's has several large, clean, attractive rooms that are opened or closed according to traffic at any particular time. The dining room used most often has red-checked tablecloths on the booths around the walls and the tables in the central area.

I was gratified to find that my plate of pork barbecue was moist and flavorful, glistening with a delicious eastern North Carolina vinegar-and-pepper sauce. I had especially crisp, tasty French fries, which were even better after being sprinkled with some of the barbecue sauce. The barbecued chicken on my combination plate had a fairly thick red sauce, unusual in this part of the state, where thin vinegar mixtures are usually used to baste and dress barbecued chicken, but it was good nonetheless. For dessert, I tried a serving of King's appetizing banana pudding, topped with meringue and served in an edible waffle bowl, but I noticed the nice-looking array of pies as well.

No matter what you're hungry for, you have a good chance of finding it at King's. Along with pork barbecue and barbecued

King's is known far and wide for its "Pig in a Puppy" sandwich.

chicken, there's barbecued turkey, beef brisket, pork ribs, seafood platters, down-home favorites such as hamburger steak, country ham, and pork chops, and even grilled steak. The daily specials include such dishes as chicken and pastry, meat loaf, stew beef, and roast chicken. Many seasonal vegetable choices are available as well. Finally, the large sandwich menu includes "Pig in a Puppy"— pork barbecue piled between halves of a bun-sized hush puppy.

Overall, King's serves high-quality food of every type and does a wonderful job of merchandising everything from its barbecue sauce and other packaged items to its "Oink Express" barbecue shipping service, through which customers can send dry-ice-packaged barbecue and fixings just about anywhere by calling 1-800-322-OINK.

## B. J.'s Grill and BBQ

7823 U.S. 70 East
La Grange, N.C. 28551
252-566-4702
Breakfast and lunch are served Monday through Thursday and Saturday. Breakfast, lunch, and dinner are offered on Friday. Barbecue is served on Wednesday and Saturday only!

If you can't find what you're hungry for at B. J.'s Grill and BBQ, you may be just too darn hard to please. This neat-as-a-pin spot beside U.S. 70 has a menu that's absolutely covered with fine print—one third of a tri-fold sheet just for breakfast (served from 4 A.M. on) and the other two-thirds for daily lunch specials,

barbecue, the Friday-night dinner menu, and sandwiches. The children's menu and desserts are on the back.

B. J.'s didn't open until 1980, but by 1986 it had already won the contest for "Best Barbecue Down East," sponsored by the area's NBC affiliate, WITN-TV. The whole-hog pork is extremely lean and, unlike some eastern North Carolina barbecue, is hand-chopped only to a fairly coarse consistency, which, in my opinion, helps retain the meat's moisture and tenderness.

B. J.'s serves its barbecue with a wonderful mild, sweet sauce that's equally popular around the restaurant as a dressing for steak, collard greens, pizza, and other foods. Referring to the sauce, owner B. J. Thigpen—a hardworking, no-nonsense woman—says confidently, "That'll be my retirement." Her husband, Darrell, who helps run the place, introduced me to an interesting twist, serving me a small plate of barbecue moistened with sauce and mingled with chopped raw onion. He had already discovered what I found— that the tastes somehow balance perfectly. (I'm not sure yet whether this is true of other barbecue or just that at B. J.'s, but I'm conducting further research.)

On Thursday, B. J.'s prepares barbecued chickens and whole thirty- to forty-pound barbecued turkeys, which are chopped and seasoned just like pork barbecue. The same sweet vinegar-based sauce is used to season these foods as well.

For dessert, be sure to try one of the homemade apple jacks, made with dried apples.

B. J.'s Grill and BBQ,
La Grange

Remember, if you're looking for pork barbecue, plan to be at B. J.'s on either Wednesday or Saturday, since those are the only days it's served.

## Ken's Grill

7645 U.S. 70 West
La Grange, N.C. 28551
252-566-4765
Breakfast, lunch, and dinner are served Monday through Saturday. Barbecue is offered on Wednesday and Saturday only.

Ken's Grill is an unobtrusive little place, the kind of spot you might blow right past without noticing as you travel U.S. 70 to Morehead City or Beaufort. Before I had a chance to visit, I received several phone calls about the barbecue at Ken's over a period of several months. I finally found myself passing through the area on a Wednesday—one of only two days of the week that Ken's prepares barbecue, the other being Saturday. I decided to pick up a sandwich for the road. I thought

the meat from Ken's was in a class all its own: firm, chunky, tender, and perfectly seasoned, with a delightful, savory aftertaste that lingered pleasantly on the tongue.

Only after arriving at Ken's with a UNC-TV camera crew several months later did I discover that his barbecue is not cooked over a wood-fired pit, as I had supposed, but in an electric cooker. Now, I can be pretty stubborn about some things, but when presented with incontrovertible evidence by Ken Eason and his brother David that it is possible to produce superior barbecue cooked in a manner other than over hardwood coals, I decided to relax my thinking and go with the flow. Not many people are able to get the results Ken achieves without the wood, but there's no denying his barbecue is simply delicious. I consider myself fortunate to have some of it whenever I'm in the neighborhood.

The other thing I liked about Ken Eason's place during that first visit was this modest, unassuming man's air of flattered surprise at being singled out for recognition. When our camera crew arrived, we found the

Ken's is often packed with locals and U.S. 70 travelers.

little restaurant shined up spick-and-span. Both the older women and the fresh-faced teenage girls working there were proudly and identically turned out in neat, matching shorts, white cotton blouses, perky white-paper hats, and sharp, obviously new navy-blue aprons. Many of Ken's regular customers from around La Grange were on hand, too, and most of them were quick to offer unsolicited testimonials about the consistent quality of the food. The restaurant is quite a community gathering place, the bulk of Eason's business coming from his neighbors. However, beginning with Easter weekend and stretching through spring and summer, the grill gets a lot of beach traffic on Fridays and Saturdays.

Over the years, I have become a regular visitor, not only because of the warm greeting I always receive from Ken and David but also because of several dishes in addition to barbecue that this place prepares as well as anyone on the planet. The restaurant is always packed when I stop in, which, admittedly, is usually on a Friday or Saturday.

The Eason brothers have an infectious enthusiasm about their place, which carries on a tradition begun when their father owned and operated "Skin's" Drive-In nearby. The elder Eason began cooking and selling barbecue on Saturdays only. When Ken took over the operation upon his father's death in 1974, he continued the practice, then expanded to Wednesdays after he built the present seventy-seat restaurant in 1980. Ken still uses his father's secret sauce recipe, which is obviously what elevates his barbecue from the ordinary to the realm of the sublime. Several local residents—who aren't exactly in the Sahara when it comes to the availability of fine barbecue—pronounce it the best they've ever eaten. The hand-chopped pork is served in sandwiches and on paper trays, accompanied by mayonnaise-based coleslaw and, as long as they last, a piece or two of crispy fried pork skin.

The method of forming hush puppies at Ken's is something I hadn't observed before. The cook piles the thick batter on the blade of a long metal turner as though she's laying mortar, trowels it flat on the top and sides with a knife, then, in a blur of speed, cuts straight down through the batter, pushing one-inch-wide "fingers" of the mixture off the end of the turner and into the hot cooking oil.

Besides barbecue, Ken's offers thick, hand-pattied burgers, which are typically served country-style—topped with cheese, slaw, mustard, and awesome homemade chili. A different special is offered every day. On Fridays, Ken's serves its version of the thick fish stew that's probably the number-one local delicacy, surpassing even barbecue. This tomato-based stew containing fish, bacon, potatoes, onions, and poached eggs, plus lots of pepper, has every seat in the restaurant filled on the appointed day.

Ken's Grill serves delicious pieces of homemade cake prepared by Ken's wife, Teresa, from recipes that have been in her grandma's box for many years. I tried lemon cake and fudge cake and found them both to be moist and delicious. Teresa has a new bake shop called Sweetie Pies, which offers not only pies, cakes, and other desserts but also homemade bread.

Ken's occupies a small, square building on the south side of U.S. 70 outside La Grange, roughly halfway between Goldsboro and Kinston. Don't judge this particular book by its cover, because if you ever stop the first time, you will undoubtedly be back often.

## Adams Roadside Bar-B-Q

3445 U.S. 70 West
Goldsboro, N.C. 27530
919-739-3859
http://www.adamsroadsidebbq.com
Lunch and dinner, Wednesday through Saturday

Second location:
1813 Berkeley Boulevard (U.S. 13 North)
Goldsboro, N.C. 27534
919-751-0270

"Where would this country be if no one ever took a chance?"

That was Scott Adams's answer to my question about the degree of confidence required for him to open a new barbecue restaurant in Goldsboro, which already has—and has had—several barbecue joints approaching legendary status. Scott's and Wilber's have been big names for decades, and McCall's, a more recent addition, does a healthy business as well. Now, Adams has joined the mix, offering pretty traditional and very tasty eastern North Carolina chopped barbecue, *plus* versions of pork ribs, beef brisket, and barbecued chicken that will appeal to the ever-increasing number of non–North Carolinians in the

Ken Eason's wife, Teresa, makes homemade cakes using recipes from her grandma.

Scott Adams cooks whole pigs, cutting them into pieces to fit into his cooker.

area, who tend to gravitate toward the thicker, sweeter sauces of Memphis and Kansas City. There really is something for everyone here. People with varying barbecue loyalties will be too busy eating to do much finger pointing or arguing.

The location on U.S. 70 eight miles west of Goldsboro is a takeout stop, although a few picnic tables are available next door for outside dining in pleasant weather. That's where I tasted a flavorful, moist, and tender offering of chopped 'cue, dressed with a mainstream eastern-style sauce—plenty of vinegar, salt, and pepper, but with a hint of sweetness as well. If you're died-in-the-wool eastern-leaning in your barbecue preference, you'll be happy with this barbecue. It has a good, albeit delicate, smoke flavor, too, which you don't always find in eastern 'cue these days.

Over at the eat-in location on Berkeley Boulevard (which also has a pedestrian take-out window), I sampled the pork ribs, which are unashamedly served in the Memphis "wet" ribs style, meaning they come to the table not only with a good crust of brown meat, spices, and sugar but also a glazing of thick, red sauce. Now, I believe North Carolinians like this type of ribs as well as anyone in the country. The fact is, we've been barbecuing ribs and putting thick, sweet sauce on them for years—even though we don't generally refer to ribs as "barbecue," for which we have a different sauce-and-seasoning concept altogether. That said, the ribs I sampled were exceptionally well cooked—plenty of moisture, good tenderness, attractive appearance, and good resistance to the teeth when bitten. Personally, I tend to prefer slightly more of a vinegar tang even in a thick rib sauce. But although this one was sweeter than I would concoct in my own kitchen, I enjoyed it immensely. I would order these ribs again anytime, and lick my lips over them.

The symmetrical slices of beef brisket I tasted also had favorable tenderness and moisture, along with a nice reddish smoke ring. The meat was cooked with hickory and mesquite wood, a combination that goes well with beef but not so much with pork.

The barbecued chicken had kept a strong golden brown color throughout the cooking cycle and had some nice darker charred spots and appealing grill marks on the skin. Most people in this area expect barbecued chicken to be more "falling off the bone" than this version, and they tend to like more of a vinegar-based sauce. However, the meat was plenty tender and yielding, and the thick, sweet sauce matched up well with the deep, wood-cooked flavor that permeated the skin and outer meat. It makes a highly appealing alternative for folks who love barbecued chicken but just don't care for vinegar—bless their hearts.

I sampled a good, strong mac 'n' cheese with a crispy coating, good binding to hold the noodles together, a nice golden color, and plenty of cheese melted throughout. The baked beans were interesting, offering more of a vinegar tang than one normally finds, which helped to balance the brown sugar and spices.

I heard enthusiastic compliments about Adams Roadside Bar-B-Q before I ever had a chance to try it myself, and I was favorably impressed, for sure. Purists for barbecue made from the whole hog, cooked directly over wood coals, will probably prefer Wilber's. But Scott Adams and his crew are filling a market demand and doing it very well indeed. I'll be back.

## McCall's Barbecue and Seafood

http://www.mccallsbbq.com
Lunch and dinner daily

139 Millers Chapel Road
Goldsboro, N.C. 27534
919-751-0072

Second location:
10365 U.S. 70 West
Clayton, N.C. 27520
919-550-3877

McCall's Barbecue and Seafood is a relative newcomer, having been in business only since 1989. Old friends Randy McCall and Worth Westbrook used to talk of owning their own business back when they worked as feed salesmen for Ralston Purina. The two men ended up founding McCall's, although they did it in a rather unconventional way.

Back in the 1970s, a man named Elmer Davis started a little, one-day-a-week pit-cooked barbecue operation near the community of Pikeville, a few miles north of Goldsboro. (Pikeville is known as the birthplace of Charles B. Aycock, a former governor of North Carolina.) Davis would take advance orders for barbecue or chicken plates early each week, to be served on Fridays, then go back to his pit and prepare the amount of each type of food needed to fill the orders. In many eastern North Carolina farming communities, popular foods such as chopped

McCall's Barbecue and Seafood, Goldsboro

barbecue, fried fish, and barbecued chicken are often sold "by the plate" in this way—not only by enterprising individuals but also by groups like volunteer fire departments, PTSA organizations, and local churches. Around Goldsboro and Kinston, for example, fish stew is a favorite local delicacy. Before a particular batch is even prepared, it has often been completely sold—by the bowl—in advance, the orders to be filled between certain hours on a given day. Davis's business prospered in a modest way. The people around Pikeville began to look forward to eating his barbecue on Fridays. Davis finally reached the point of cooking several whole pigs and scores of chickens each Friday, week in and week out, over a period of several years.

Meanwhile, McCall and Westbrook, who lived nearby, were looking for a suitable business to enter. Randy McCall and his wife made the first move, figuring that if they took on Davis's part-time barbecue business, they could generate enough income for McCall's wife, an accountant, to be able to stay home one day a week. The McCalls bought Davis's barbecue operation, and Worth Westbrook soon joined them in the business.

After continuing to serve Pikeville for a time, the partners decided to expand. They bought an empty building just off U.S. 70 east of Goldsboro. The building had housed several other restaurant ventures, none of them successful. Their original concept was to open a new eatery featuring barbecue and seafood, the barbecue to be pit-cooked over oak coals at the small pit in Pikeville, then transported to the restaurant in Goldsboro. They renovated the building and opened Mc-Call's with a flourish in 1989. However, the restaurant's second day in business came close to being its last when the Pikeville barbecue pit caught fire and burned. (Although they had previously caused only minor damage, McCall and Westbrook ruefully admit that they had managed to catch the pit on fire several times before this incident, when they were selling barbecue to the Pikeville community.) The two partners were rescued by the nearby Nahunta Volunteer Fire Department, which offered the use of its barbecue pits until Randy and Worth could rebuild.

What the two initiated afterward was unique at the time, although it has since become something of a pattern for many new barbecue restaurants. In addition to constructing three conventional pits for cooking with hardwood coals or charcoal, the partners contracted with a Midwestern firm, Old Hickory Pits, to modify a new cooker design to meet their needs. The invention consisted of a Ferris wheel–like contraption of five baskets, each containing five separate racks. Inside a ten-foot-square stainless-steel oven, the "Ferris wheel" would turn baskets loaded with either quartered pigs, pork shoulders, or chicken sections. In a cylindrical fire chamber designed to radiate heat at the back of the oven, gas flames would combust either wood or charcoal, and the smoke thus generated would billow through vents in the fire chamber and into the oven, where the meat-laden racks would rotate. Nowadays, similar smokers are used in quite a few restaurants across the state.

Quartered whole pigs or pork shoulders are cooked for ten or eleven hours in McCall's smoker, after which they're placed over oak coals or charcoal on a conventional pit and cooked for another couple of hours. (The cooking times are different for chickens.) The results are excellent. The chopped eastern North Carolina–style barbecue has a distinct wood-cooked flavor without being overly smoked, and the meat is as tender as could possibly be desired. (I'm told that any bone will pull cleanly from the meat by the time it has finished cooking.) The barbecue is cooked fresh daily and seasoned according to taste rather than predetermined measurements, since "every pig is different," according to Westbrook. The partners point out

that the pigs are intentionally cooked until they're a little on the dry side because their customers seem to prefer barbecue without a lot of moisture. To my taste, McCall's barbecue doesn't seem at all too dry. The barbecued chicken comes out golden brown and tender, with a slight bit of charring that offers eye appeal and an attractive crunchiness to the skin.

McCall's is a big, bustling restaurant that offers seafood and both a lunch and dinner buffet, in addition to barbecue plates and sandwiches. But don't let the size fool you. The barbecue is reminiscent of the type you'd expect at a much smaller establishment.

Chopped barbecue is included on the buffet, along with barbecued chicken and a tray of pork skins and ribs. But because of the difficulty of holding peak texture and flavor in meat on a steam table, I recommend you order your barbecue off the menu in order to enjoy it at its freshest. The buffet does have an excellent selection of vegetables, as well as entrées such as pork chops, fried chicken, and several seafood choices.

## Wilber's Barbecue
4172 U.S. 70 East
Goldsboro, N.C. 27534
919-778-5218
http://www.wilbersbarbecue.com
Breakfast, lunch, and dinner daily

Wilber's is one of the biggest names in barbecue in eastern North Carolina. Unlike a few other famous places in the coastal plain, this is a restaurant where the name above the door still means *exactly* what it did when Wilber Shirley bought the former Hill's Barbecue and opened it under his own name in 1962.

Wilber's is one of only a handful of remaining restaurants anywhere in the eastern part of the state where barbecue is cooked entirely over hardwood coals. Many other places still trade on the names and reputations of men who took the trouble to cook barbecue the old, slow way—the way it was meant to be cooked—but behind the scenes, their owners have quietly gotten rid of the wood, the pits, the smoke, the shovels, and the mess of pit cooking. Not Wilber. He points out that tradition comes with a hefty price tag, a fact he knows well, since his crew cuts and splits wood year-round. But he says, "I think the finished product is worth the effort. I think that I've been successful with it, and I firmly believe that's the way to cook it."

There are larger barbecue operations, if you count catering and wholesale distribution. But few, if any, barbecue restaurants in North Carolina serve more customers than Wilber's. And he not only manages to prepare his barbecue the old-fashioned way, he does it without making a big fuss about it. The fact that his staff cooks up to 130 entire pigs on a busy Labor Day weekend hasn't caused him to start looking anxiously into electric or gas cookers. For that reason alone, lovers of real pit-cooked barbecue ought to stop by his place and shake his hand. Wilber says that salesmen have tried to sell him electric- or gas-fired pits. He jokes that he tells them that not only will he not buy one, but to please park their display models around back during their sales call, so his customers won't see them and get the wrong idea.

The three most important things in real estate are location, location, and *location*. Being well situated sure doesn't hurt in the barbecue business either. U.S. 70, which passes directly in front of Wilber's place east of

Wilber Shirley

Goldsboro, is usually clogged with day traffic between Raleigh and Kinston. Perhaps more importantly, it's also one of the three main routes to the ocean in North Carolina. Nearly everyone from the mountains, the western Piedmont, the Triad, and the Triangle who is headed for Emerald Isle, Pine Knoll Shores, Atlantic Beach, Beaufort, Ocracoke, or Hatteras passes within thirty yards of Wilber's front door. Most of the fighter jets at nearby Seymour Johnson Air Force Base also pass pretty close overhead, since the restaurant is squarely beneath the landing pattern. On more than one occasion after stepping out of my car in Wilber's parking lot, I've been startled out of my wits by a positively ground-shaking, screaming blast from some swept-wing fighter hurtling from out of nowhere directly over my head, a few hundred feet off the ground.

Beneath the continuing air show, Wilber's lot is nearly always crowded, especially during the vacation months, when he has a produce stand right in front of the restaurant. All in one stop, customers can eat lunch or dinner and pick up the fresh tomatoes, cucumbers, and peaches they'll need at the beach cottage.

For many years, Wilber's has had the same homey, laid-back feel: red brick and white trim on the outside, knotty pine paneling and red-checked tablecloths inside. A lunch counter and bustling takeout area are in the center of the sprawling building, with tables to the right and left. Big, open dining rooms are located at either end, allowing Wilber to seat more than three hundred

at peak periods, which occur basically every Friday and Sunday. Plaques in the foyer proclaiming "South's Best Barbecue" and framed book excerpts and magazine articles hanging inside the restaurant provide quiet testimony to the reputation Wilber Shirley has built among barbecue aficionados not only in North Carolina but across the country.

However, that reputation wasn't made inside the restaurant—which is, frankly, pretty ordinary looking. It came as the result of endless hours—long, slow, middle-of-the-night hours—at the barbecue pits behind the main building. The man who put in a great many of those hours was the late Ike Green, a patient, affable man who cooked pigs for Wilber Shirley for more than thirty years before he passed away. Others have taken his place, of course, but I particularly remember—and find instructive—an evening visit with Green in the mid-1990s.

Green's domain encompassed a hundred-foot woodpile, an open-air fireplace with a straight wooden chair pulled up beside it, and a long cinder-block building with hip-high open pits running the length of each side. Each evening, just a hundred yards or so from the eighteen-wheelers roaring up and down U.S. 70, Green would build a fire of stacked oak logs in the fireplace. He let the fire burn down to coals for an hour or so as he trundled a wheelbarrow between the pit house and the restaurant building, loading the forty or fifty half-pigs he would cook that night onto the pits, where they would slow-roast for nine hours.

On that particular cool evening years ago,

having straightened the last side of pork on the cooking grate, and waiting for the fire to burn down, Green pulled the straight-backed chair up to the fire, leaned back on the spindly rear legs, and reflected on his beginnings in the pig-cooking business. It seems that when he was around thirteen, Green went to an older friend's house one evening during the Christmas holiday to help him cook a pig on a backyard pit dug into the ground. The older man drank too much and went to sleep, but young Ike stayed up all night tending the coals. When the man's wife came out the next morning, she pronounced the cooked pig "pretty" and praised the dogged teenager for the good job he had done. "You give a child praise, and he'll think he's done something great," Ike said. "And that's what started me cookin' 'em, and I've been cookin' 'em ever since."

Green glanced at the fire, rose from the chair, and picked up a shovel leaning against the pit-house wall. He rapped the burning logs with the back of the shovel to break them up, causing the embers to fall to the bottom of the fireplace, then pushed the flat implement into the red-orange mound and straightened up with a shovelful of flickering coals. Trailing sparks, he walked at an unhurried pace across the hard-packed dirt and into the pit house, stopping at the nearest pit. Pushing back a low, sliding door, he inserted the shovel through the opening and scattered the embers in a perfectly even cascade beneath the meat lying two feet above. He then walked back outside and over to the fireplace, scraped up another shovelful of coals, and re-peated the process. He trudged steadily back and forth for twenty minutes between the fire and the increasingly smoky pit house as he worked his way down the pits to the end of the building. Then, leaning his shovel back against the wall, he moved slowly to his chair and eased himself down.

"I like sittin' out here, takin' my time," he said quietly. "There ain't nobody much to bother you. Once in a while, somebody'll come along actin' strange, and I'll send them on their way. But if somebody comes by and acts right, I'll sit and talk with him. When I get the pigs done and turn 'em, maybe I'll give him a rib. But I can't work if I got to watch somebody too close."

In an ironic foreshadowing, considering Green's death not many years afterward, I wondered aloud what would happen to Wilber Shirley when Green retired or got too old to work. "Well, he might have to close up," Green said with perfect seriousness, "because he likely ain't going to get nobody. . . . I mean, I haven't seen nobody yet from this younger generation . . . that's faithful, you know, and will work and stay right here with it like I do."

*That*, friends, will prove to be the epitaph for many barbecue places. Fortunately for Wilber's, other faithful men *have* stepped up in the years since Green's death to keep the fires alive during the long nights. But there's little question that finding such workers is becoming increasingly difficult.

Wilber Shirley himself is no slouch when it comes to hard work. He's usually at the restaurant twelve or thirteen hours a day, six days a week. But he says that after all his years

of owning the place (and several years of working for the former Griffin's Barbecue in Goldsboro before that), he still loves coming in every morning. He has a son-in-law who's been with the business for many years now, so he's confident the operation will remain in family hands.

In any case, since you never know what's going to happen, I advise you to enjoy Wilber's tender, juicy, wood-smoked barbecue while you can, and for as long as you can. Shirley says eastern-style barbecue is unique because it combines several parts of the pig, all with slightly different tastes and textures. "It's kind of like making a cake with different ingredients," he observes. "You mix meat from the hams, the shoulders, the loin, and the side, and all of them are a little bit different, so you end up with a blend." He makes his particular blend a little more moist than some whole-hog chopped barbecue by adding extra dark meat from several shoulders he's barbecued on the side. This innovation also allows him to include more shreds of dark brown, chewy outside meat, making the mixture appealing to the eye as well as the palate. In my opinion,

most eastern North Carolina houses end up with too fine a texture for their barbecue by using machines to chop it. Wilber's still does this time-honored task by hand, which helps maintain the moisture of the meat and provides a pleasingly chunky texture.

Wilber's barbecue is seasoned to taste with salt and ground pepper after it's chopped, but most people will want to add a splash of his special sauce. The sauce is served in cruets at the table and is also for sale in bottles at the cash register. Like all eastern sauces, it contains vinegar, salt, red pepper, black pepper, and spices (the mystery ingredients). But Wilber's sauce is perhaps the most complex blend of this general type that I've tasted. Unknown earth-toned spices give the sauce an unusual reddish brown shade. I suspect that several distinct varieties of finely ground dried red peppers are in the sauce, but the taste is spicy and flavorful, not searingly hot. Wilber's is one of several eastern sauces that needs frequent shaking to loosen and blend the extremely fine sediment of spices that settles to the bottom of the bottle, like minute grains of sand settling on a riverbed.

Of all the barbecue places I've visited across the state, I've never been to any besides Wilber's that serves potato salad with barbecue. Not that there's anything unusual about potato salad in eastern North Carolina, but it's usually served with a cold meat, like sliced, boiled ham. Although it's a little jarring to see it sitting on a plate beside a serving of barbecue, the potato salad is quite good, featuring a smoother consistency and more of a vinegar bite than some recipes. Some people refer to his special version as *mashed potato salad*.

Another extremely popular dish at Wilber's is the country-style barbecued chicken. I call it "country-style" because it comes to the table attractively covered with a fairly thick, light-colored gravy flavored with vinegar-based barbecue sauce. It's sort of a smothered fricasseed or stewed chicken, but with a definite barbecue flavor. I've never encountered barbecued chicken like it anywhere else. Wilber tells me that the former Griffin's Barbecue invented the recipe. Veteran Wilber's customers who are "in the know" are fond of ordering a dish of this chicken gravy for dipping their hush puppies and French fries.

Wilber's serves combination plates featuring barbecue and either fried or pit-barbecued chicken alongside potato salad, Brunswick stew, coleslaw, and hush puppies. Some seafood selections are available as well. These side offerings all get high marks for quality and consistency, but the main thing you'll remember after a visit to Wilber's is the barbecue itself, which is absolutely superb.

## Grady's Barbecue

3096 Arrington Bridge Road
Dudley, N.C. 28333
919-735-7243
Breakfast and lunch are served Monday through Friday. Breakfast, lunch, and dinner (until 6 P.M.) are offered on Saturday.

Put on a tape of the Coasters oldie "Searchin' " as you set out across the coun-tryside south of Goldsboro on a truly adventurous search for this jewel of a place. After checking your turns and distances carefully, and after enjoying some beautiful rural countryside, you'll finally round a corner, pick up an evocative aroma of roasting pork, and see a haze of blue-white smoke emanating from the barbecue pits behind a small, nondescript, white-painted structure nestled between the arms of two seemingly lonesome rural roads that merge beside the building. The crossroads will seem lonesome only for a moment, though, as you realize there's actually quite a bit of local traffic, nearly all of it turning into Grady's (pronounced "Graddy's").

Until the last few years, Grady's was, quite simply, one of the best-kept secrets in North Carolina. The locals knew about it, of course, and probably took part in a good-natured conspiracy to keep the rest of us from finding out too much, lest outsiders overwhelm the place. In fact, it really is so far off the beaten track that average barbecue lovers would have practically no chance of ever stumbling across it. However, the word is now out among barbecue die-hards, and Grady's is receiving ever-increasing attention, recognition, and appreciation. Stephen Grady even serves on the board of the North Carolina Barbecue Society.

If you're armed with directions and in the mood for a pleasant cross-country mission, some of the best pit-cooked barbecue in eastern North Carolina, if not the entire state, will be your reward for locating Grady's. Stephen Grady, a quiet, dignified black gentleman, opened the place in 1986. He worked

Stephen Grady cooks whole hogs with wood and charcoal.

for a sawmill at the time. When the mill owner promised all the free wood he could use, Grady thought he saw a great opportunity to build a business for his wife, Gerri, to run. He figured he could get the hogs on the fire early each morning, then turn things over to Gerri while he went off to saw lumber the rest of the day. Well, Stephen Grady left the sawmill several years ago, finding that the barbecue and catering business was enough to keep both him and Gerri busy full-time.

Grady's serves absolutely superb wood-cooked whole-hog barbecue in a tiny dining room that seats no more than twenty. The tender, delectable meat has a subtle but unmistakable wood-smoke taste, is attractively laced with bits of crispy, tasty skin, and is moistened by a well-mannered vinegar-based sauce that does contain some sugar. Simple boiled potatoes and a sweet white coleslaw complement the barbecue perfectly, as do large hush puppies that are light, crispy, and not overly sweet. The place also serves top-notch iced tea, dark and robust.

Grady's offers hearty daily specials (I sampled country-style cabbage, black-eyed peas, and a wonderful hamburger steak with gravy), plus a variety of sandwiches. It opens early every day but Sunday for breakfast. Local residents arrive in a steady stream throughout the day for takeout orders.

An article in the November 2000 issue of *GQ* magazine gave Grady's a "Best Barbecue" rating, proving that excellence will generally make itself known, even if it's practiced at an out-of-the-way rural North Carolina crossroad.

Plan a trip to meet Stephen and his cheery, outgoing wife and to experience some memorable barbecue. And do so at your earliest convenience, since Stephen is making noises about leaving the business soon to "go fishin'."

# • Spotting a Rising Star •

I was asked to speak at the 2002 annual Southern Foodways Alliance Symposium on the campus of the University of Mississippi in Oxford. It is one of the biggest gatherings of chefs, restaurateurs, food journalists, and cookbook authors in the country. The topic that year was "Barbecue: Smoke, Sauce and History," and of course I was slated to speak on the history and heritage of North Carolina barbecue. I would also participate in a book signing for my recently published *North Carolina Barbecue: Flavored by Time*, enjoy barbecue-oriented lunches prepared by some of the top chefs in the country (including Ben and Karen Barker of Durham's Magnolia Grill), partake of a fried catfish dinner at run-down-but-colorful Taylor Grocery outside Oxford, and attend the closing address by novelist and food writer Calvin Trillin. But the most interesting gathering would be a "friendly" cookoff between barbecue pit masters from Alabama, South Carolina, and North Carolina, who would provide the entrées for a large, outdoor dinner party. While there was to be no crowning of an official champion, everyone knew that the representatives from the various states would be competing for the hearts and souls (to say nothing of the written evaluations) of some of the most influential and pickiest barbecue eaters on the planet.

Southern Foodways Alliance executive director (and prolific food writer) John T. Edge telephoned me several months before the symposium to seek my recommendation for a pit master to represent North Carolina. With little hesitation, I suggested Ed Mitchell of Wilson, who at the time was operating a small barbecue restaurant in what could only be called a tough market. The Wilson barbecue scene was—and is—dominated by Parker's and Bill's, two well-known establishments, and Mitchell's was considered by many to be on the "wrong side of town." But I had encountered real magic at his barbecue/soul-food restaurant, and I felt that Ed Mitchell—a genial African American with an open smile, a white beard, and a deft hand with barbecuing whole hogs—would represent the Tar Heel State wonderfully well.

Ruthie and I almost didn't make it to the symposium. We had booked our flight to Memphis out of Greensboro, but for some unaccountable reason we drove from our home in Burlington to Raleigh-Durham International Airport a couple of hours before our scheduled departure, whereupon we discovered our mistake. Although we could not rebook a flight without major additional expense, the agent was able to move us to a later flight from Greensboro in order to buy us a little time. We jumped in our car and drove the ninety miles from RDU to Piedmont Triad International Airport at a hazardous clip, making our rescheduled departure with only a minute or two to spare.

Between the confusion over the flight and some nervousness about my upcoming talk, I had forgotten all about Ed Mitchell until I ran into him in Oxford at lunch the day before the cookoff. He was visibly worried because his truck driver had gotten lost

This photo of Wilson's Ed Mitchell in the *New York Times* helped launch his career as a regionally and nationally known pit master. I arranged his appearance at the 2000 Southern Foodways Alliance annual symposium in Oxford, Mississippi.
*Photo by Marcie Cohen Ferris, Chapel Hill, N.C.*

somewhere between North Carolina and Mississippi and hadn't yet shown up with his two portable pig cookers. My lecture went smoothly that afternoon. In a gush of relief, I headed off to the Jack Daniel's–sponsored catfish dinner without giving another thought to Mitchell's potential equipment problem.

The truck driver did finally materialize with the pits, although not until the next morning, and not until a couple of hours *after* Mitchell wanted to have his hogs on the fire. To make matters worse, a steady rain had set in. The other pit masters were equipped with slick competition-style barbecue rigs, complete with lacquered cookers and fancy canopies, but Ed Mitchell had not thought to

bring any kind of shelter. He and his brother Aubrey noticed a large oak tree still in full leaf. As they rolled their rusty portable pits toward the partial shelter afforded by the overhanging branches, they noticed the other pit masters laughing.

Ed told me later that all his confidence deserted him in that moment, and that he was temporarily overtaken by a paralyzing fog. Aubrey, however, stepped up. "I didn't come all this way to be laughed at by a bunch of guys who don't know what we know about cooking barbecue," he snarled to Ed. "Let's get these coals going and show them something."

"If it hadn't been for Aubrey stiffening his spine at that moment, I'm not sure what might have happened," confessed Ed.

Within a few hours, Mitchell's two whole hogs were on the fire, someone had shown up with a canopy for him, and the skies were brightening—in fact, more than he knew at the moment. At the end of the symposium's Saturday-afternoon session, Marcie Cohen Ferris of the University of North Carolina faculty walked over to the town park where the barbecuing was taking place, camera in hand. There, she happened upon Ed Mitchell dressed farmer-style in overalls, raising the lid of the smoking pig cooker to inspect the nicely browning pig on the cooking grate. A front-page story about the barbecue symposium in the *New York Times* included Ferris's photo of Ed gazing beneficently down at the roasting pig. The story and photo helped launch Ed Mitchell's national career, making him the subject of numerous national television features and landing him in magazines such as *Gourmet* and *Bon Appétit*.

And Marcie Cohen Ferris wasn't the only symposium attendee who took notice of Mitchell. At dinner that evening, after the participants had an opportunity to sample the offerings from the various pit masters, a particularly large crowd gathered at the Mitchell brothers' marquee. Having politely sampled ribs and pulled Boston butt (anointed with a strange Alabama *white* barbecue sauce) elsewhere on the grounds, they were positively transported by Ed's succulent, smoky chopped whole-hog barbecue laced with flavorful bits of perfectly crisped skin and lightly anointed with a well-balanced vinegar-and-pepper sauce.

"Those ribs were a little tough," I overheard one man mutter. "At an event like this, you sure don't expect to be fighting against any *meat*. But now this . . . This is something else."

By the end of the evening, a discernable buzz was running through the crowd, and the name that was repeatedly whispered was *Mitchell.*

Following an all-pie-and-Coca-Cola breakfast Sunday morning, barbecue guru Calvin Trillin hung a glittering star at the top of Mitchell's Christmas tree during the symposium's closing baccalaureate session. Normally a devotee of Kansas City pork ribs and beef brisket, Trillin was succinct in his praise of Mitchell's eastern North Carolina vinegar-sauced pork. He had previously mused in one of his books that finding good North Carolina barbecue "seemed to depend on which side of Rocky Mount you find yourself." But in Oxford, after experiencing Ed's pit skills for the first time, he pronounced Mitchell's the best North Carolina barbecue he had ever tasted "in *any* direction from Rocky Mount."

One of the greatest pleasures of my career has been playing a small part in pit master Ed Mitchell's being recognized on the national barbecue stage. He has gone on to such TV shows as *Man v. Food* and *Throwdown! with Bobby Flay*; he's been featured on NBC's *Today*; and he was the subject of a *Gourmet* magazine–inspired TV show, *Diary of a Foodie.* He's a regular at New York City's annual Big Apple Barbecue Block Party and has plans to open a new restaurant in the Triangle area.

I'd like to think it all shifted into high gear with his triumph at the Southern Foodways Alliance event in Oxford, and that my recommendation had a little something to do with that.

## Smithfield's Chicken 'N Bar-B-Q

Locations throughout North Carolina
http://scnbnc.com
Lunch and dinner daily

I have to admit that I avoided Smithfield's for a long time because it's a chain and because I'm more interested in family-run places that have interesting stories surrounding them.

The fact is, though, that these folks serve eastern-style barbecue that's every bit as good as that in some of the most famous barbecue houses of the coastal plain—perhaps better than some. Here, you'll find barbecue prepared without a hint of wood smoke, but it's tender, perfectly seasoned, and, most importantly, not chopped too finely. The meat has an attractive chunky texture that allows it to retain its natural moisture. As a result, it is quite pleasant al dente (to the tooth). The vinegar sauce is right on target, considering that this is very much an eastern North Carolina chain. And the portions are more than generous.

I enjoyed the sweet yellow slaw that accompanies the barbecue. While my other side dish, potato salad, had perhaps a bit too much mayonnaise for my personal taste, it still came across as tangy and appealing. The hush puppies at Smithfield's are fresh, hot, and not too sweet.

I'm happy to report that the fried chicken matches the pork barbecue in quality. It has a crispy coating and skin, a moist and juicy interior, and perfect seasonings. At the time I visited, the Smithfield's restaurants were also offering whole deep-fried turkey breasts. Although I did not sample this dish, I imagine it is excellent as well, considering the superior taste of the chicken.

I found the iced tea to be superb. In fact, it was better than that served at many of the "name" barbecue joints. However, the prepackaged desserts are merely a concession to convenience and are not worth your time.

Smithfield's "Chicken Breader" and barbecue sauce are sold at each location.

For consistently high quality of food, generous portions, reasonable prices, and cleanliness, Smithfield's gets a good, strong B-plus or even an A-minus in my grade book. I look forward to going back.

## White Swan Bar-B-Q & Fried Chicken

http://www.whiteswanbarbeque.com
Lunch and dinner daily

3198 U.S. 301 South
Smithfield, N.C. 27577
919-934-8913

Other locations:
105 North Honeycutt Street
Benson, N.C. 27504
919-894-4446

11960 N.C. 210
Benson, N.C. 27504
919-989-9299

3103 U.S. 70 East
Smithfield, N.C. 27577
919-202-5932

3655 Wilsons Mills Road
Smithfield, N.C. 27577
919-989-6500

549 N.C. 42 West
Clayton, N.C. 27520
919-553-7450

2500 West Fort Macon Road
Atlantic Beach, N.C. 28512
252-726-9607

The original White Swan restaurant is one of those tiny, unprepossessing places off the beaten track that you'll feel really smug about discovering. Of course, it's off the beaten track only for those who don't live around

Smithfield, and not far off the track at that—just a mile and a half from Interstate 95. For area residents, though, it's not only a place with consistently delicious eastern-style barbecue, superb fried chicken, and championship-caliber hush puppies, it's a place with a colorful past and a reputation.

Having established the White Swan's credentials up front, I want to say a little about the history of the place before getting down to the details of the dining experience. You'll enjoy sitting in the tiny, wood-paneled dining room, sipping some truly wonderful iced tea, and anticipating the arrival of your order as you let the atmosphere soak in and imagine the Swan in its earlier days.

Just across the parking lot from the present barbecue restaurant stood the infamous Flowers' Tavern, a two-story roadhouse and tourist court dating to the late 1920s. It was apparently sort of a Tennessee Williams kind of place. You can almost hear the duet between the faint, bluesy wail of a saxophone and the rhythmic humming of the cicadas as you imagine what the place was like on a sultry summer evening:

*Dark automobiles huddle untidily in the building's shadow, their windshields and chrome bumpers reflecting the bright red and blue of a flashing neon sign. Pale golden rectangles of light fall from the windows and cut sharply across a dusty parking lot. Inside, the insistent thump of the drums is the only fragment of the jukebox's blare that manages to cut through the discordant babble of voices and the clink of glasses. From the dusky gloom comes the chunk of a car door opening. A deep, rich female laugh floats through the purple*

Linwood Parker is the driving force behind the growing White Swan barbecue operation.

*evening and across the dark highway, disappearing into the black cloak of the woods.*

Ava Gardner, the movie star, grew up in, and is buried in, Smithfield. You can easily combine an excursion to the White Swan with a visit to the Ava Gardner Museum downtown. Even before she became famous, the raven-haired beauty with the throaty voice is said to have had a fondness for nightlife. There's no evidence that the Flowers joint may have been one of the spots she frequented. But the rumors fly thick and fast even today that Flowers' Tavern was known for the availability of bootleg whiskey and, well, female companionship.

In 1951, Cleveland Holly bought the place and tore down all but four of the sixteen tourist-court cabins that stood in a row along U.S. 301, then one of the main north-south routes through eastern North Carolina. He replaced the freestanding cabins with a long, one-story brick motel, demolished the second story of the old tavern building, and remodeled the ground floor into a brick-veneered restaurant. Most importantly, he

changed the name of the place to the White Swan, perhaps thinking of the large number of those graceful birds in the swamps surrounding the Neuse River and nearby Holt Lake. Holly later built a small barbecue-pit building a few feet from the restaurant. For years, diners could choose between a hearty country-type meal in the dining room or barbecue and hush puppies next door at the pit. Holly lived in the motel, which he operated along with the restaurant and barbecue stand until his death in 1977. Evidently, he mistrusted banks, because the accumulated cash earnings of many years were found stashed all around his lodgings on the morning he died peacefully in his sleep.

Following Holly's death, the Swan was taken over by a brother-in-law, who is credited with adding fried chicken to the barbecue-pit menu. In 1988, the business was bought by Linwood Parker, a Smithfield accountant, and one of his clients, J. D. Heath. Parker and Heath added a small dining room to the barbecue-pit building, created a catering business, and expanded the menu to include Brunswick stew, baked beans, and boiled potatoes, all of which are White Swan staples today. Heath died in 1994, but Parker continues to operate the Swan.

The original restaurant was for a while open only for breakfast but is now back to offering a full menu of country-type food, although Parker leases it out to another operator. Meanwhile, the expanded barbecue stand next door is a bustling business. In addition to a couple of tables in the original eating area, it has seating for thirty in the intimate dining room, a cheerful place with a varnished wood ceiling and walls and curved wood-slat benches. Despite the limited seating, the restaurant serves from six hundred to a thousand people a day, thanks in part to a healthy takeout business. A weekend-only, walk-up barbecue window is on one side of the building.

Linwood Parker—at this writing the mayor of Four Oaks and a past chairman of the Johnston County GOP—answers with the smoothness of a veteran politician when asked why the White Swan quit cooking its barbecue over hardwood coals and began using electric cookers. It seems, says Parker with a straight face, that some of his customers were complaining about the smoky taste of the barbecue. Given that kind of audacity, Parker could move smoothly into a higher elective office. But I have to admit that the White Swan is one of those rare places where the barbecue seems to have suffered little from the transition. While I never had the opportunity to taste the work of Raymond Massengill, the veteran Swan pit man who shoveled oak and hickory coals at the restau-

rant for forty-one years, I found the modern, electric-cooked version soft and moist, yet crunchy, with brown outside bits and an attractive, if mild, seasoning. The White Swan is one of only two places I've run across that, as an added attraction, routinely garnish a barbecue plate with a crunchy, brown piece of fried pork skin, a toothsome accompaniment to the tender chopped meat.

The house barbecue sauce is a hot, salty vinegar mixture. The average diner will want to add a few dashes to his or her serving of chopped barbecue. A former United States senator who was a frequent customer once ordered a bottle of the sauce to bring home. Not wanting to take advantage of his position, the senator insisted on paying for the bottle. But for years afterward, he ragged Parker unmercifully about charging him five dollars for "fifteen cents' worth of vinegar and pepper." The Swan's coleslaw is eastern-style, lightly dressed with mayonnaise and appealingly sprinkled through with bits of chopped sweet pickle.

You won't be able to stay out of the basket of hush puppies brought to your table at the Swan. Some reviewers have pronounced them the best they've ever eaten, and they certainly deserve to be at the top of anyone's list. They're extremely light, crispy, and faintly sweet, with that perfect golden brown color that results from years of frying experience, along with oil that's heated to an exact temperature. Oddly enough, Parker is quick to mention that the hush puppies are made from an Atkinson's Mill mix available in area stores. If you can cook them half as well as the ladies at the Swan do, my hat's off to you.

Fried chicken is a popular accompaniment to barbecue in the coastal plain. To me, only three or four places down east manage to keep it moist and juicy inside, with a crisp, perfectly browned skin. The White Swan is one of them. Its chicken doesn't have one of those extra-crispy batter-type coatings that showers crumbs everywhere when you bite in. If you pinch off a bite of this chicken, the rest of the piece stays together. The inside meat is as flavorful as the skin, and the chicken has no greasy feel at all. The folks here must be doing something right—the White Swan cooks six hundred to a thousand chickens a week at the original location alone, which is a lot for a restaurant with such a limited seating capacity.

Parker says the secret to the White Swan's popularity is "consistency with people who like your barbecue." I've stopped on several occasions and have found that the offerings are indeed consistently good.

Parker has significantly expanded his operation, opening a half-dozen satellite locations that sell his signature barbecue and chicken under the White Swan banner. The base facility has a large commercial kitchen for cooking large quantities of barbecue to supply those restaurants, vacuum-sealing the 'cue in pouches to maintain freshness.

You'll enjoy meeting the gregarious Parker if he happens to be around the original restaurant when you stop in. But even if you miss him, I'm fairly certain you'll consider your meal memorable.

## Charlie's BBQ & Grille

8948 Cleveland Road
Clayton, N.C. 27520
919-934-0093
http://www.charliesbbqandgrille.org
Lunch and dinner, Tuesday through Saturday

Charlie Carden spent thirty years in the North Carolina Highway Patrol, his wife, Kim, at his side during his entire career. They were stationed at different locations around the state, from east to west, so they became familiar with the state's regional barbecue styles. What could be a more natural progression for a couple of barbecue lovers than to decide to open their own restaurant?

Charlie had one more thing going for him: the fact that he already considered himself a "people person" before deciding to go into a retail business venture. "You have to be a people person to be successful in either career," he says. "Here, interacting with customers and the general public every day. There, having to learn to handle people, calm them down, and defuse potentially stressful or even dangerous situations. You just can't make it unless you can deal with people."

Charlie, his hair a little longer and more stylishly cut than during his highway patrol days, is working as hard in "retirement" as he ever did in the patrol. But it's clear that he relishes being more or less in charge of his own destiny. His small, bustling restaurant in a commercial strip several miles outside Clayton serves up barbecue that pays homage not only to the various regions of North Carolina but also to locales farther west. It takes a lot of

Charlie and Kim Carden of
Charlie's BBQ & Grille

time and attention to see that the barbecued meats are cooked "low and slow" enough to make them moist, tender, and flavorful and that the side dishes are both interesting and inventive.

The Cardens serve wood-smoked pork shoulder, pork ribs, beef brisket, and barbecued chicken, all roasted for hours in a smoker that gets its heat from electricity but generates its smoke from hickory wood. Their sauces recognize the vinegar-based tradition of the coastal plain, the vinegar-tomato-sugar "dip" of the Piedmont, and the thicker, even more tomato-based sauces commonly found nowadays in the foothills and mountains.

The chopped pork has a definite smoky flavor and goes well with any of the sauces. The pork ribs I sampled were served with a nice exterior char, good tenderness, and a sufficient resistance to the bite to keep the meat from sliding off and dangling from the bone. The brisket seemed just slightly overdone. It may be that I happened along at a time when Charlie's was almost out of good, firm, slice-able brisket and was down to the ends, which are almost always more fibrous than the rest of the cut. In any case, it was delicious, if not contest-winning purely in terms of appearance. The barbecued chicken had a very "relaxed" look and texture that told me it was well done before I even bit into it, and the skin had a good, deep char and color.

Charlie's makes its own crispy potato chips in two versions—sweet potato, with cinnamon and brown sugar, and white potato, with salt and garlic. Both are appealing and unusual to find in a barbecue joint.

The signature dessert I sampled was a Kim Carden creation—a wonderful, homemade butter pecan cake. In a banana-pudding world, it was a delightful change of pace.

Charlie's isn't absolutely redolent of visual atmosphere, since it's located in a fairly bland commercial space, but it has plenty of human warmth nevertheless—something that happens only when a real people person is running things.

## Cape Fear Barbecue

523 Grove Street
Fayetteville, N.C. 28301
910-483-1884
http://www.capefearbbq.com
Lunch and dinner daily

This popular minority-owned place used to be a Smithfield's location but changed hands in 1999. The menu is similar to that of the eastern North Carolina chain, and the food is generally tasty and plentiful. In fact, it's good enough that then-candidate Obama paid a visit for barbecue during the 2008 campaign.

Barack Obama campaigning for president in 2008 at Cape Fear Barbecue
*Photo by David Katz, Courtesy of Obama for America*

The restaurant is decorated with banners, athletic jerseys, and other memorabilia from Cape Fear High School. The presence of a plaque expressing appreciation from the school's PTSA suggests a special relationship between the owners and the high school. Having followed (and helped to finance) the activities of three children as they moved through secondary school, I like to see this kind of spirit and support, so I personally would go out of my way to patronize such a community-minded place.

Barbecue and fried chicken are the mainstays of the menu here. My barbecue sandwich was piled high with a generous serving of pork, which tasted spicy and fresh and looked hand-chopped but wasn't wood-cooked. The Brunswick stew contained meaty chunks of pork and was acceptable, but I found it a little on the watery side. I also wondered about the inclusion of green beans, which—excuse me—just *don't* belong in

Brunswick stew! The fried chicken, I'm happy to report, was right on target: crispy on the outside, tender, juicy, and well seasoned on the inside.

Cape Fear Barbecue is obviously run by enthusiastic, hardworking people who realize that life is about more than just business. I think you'll have a pleasant barbecue experience here.

## The Pik N Pig

194 Gilliam-McConnell Road
Carthage, N.C. 28327
910-947-7591
http://www.pik-n-pig.com
Lunch and dinner are served Tuesday through
    Saturday. Lunch is offered Sunday.

Several years ago, the owner of the Gilliam-McConnell general aviation airport, located outside the Sandhills community of Carthage, talked the Sheppard family into opening a barbecue restaurant in a rustic building immediately adjacent to the runway. It was a strange experiment that turned out better than anyone could possibly have imagined. Today, locals, pilots from all over central North Carolina, and other travelers and foodies proclaim that the place has some of the best barbecue they've ever tasted.

Strictly speaking, it isn't *exactly* traditional North Carolina barbecue. But the pulled pork is better in a lot of people's minds than what *has* been served up as traditional in the region. It's wonderful, no matter how you characterize it. The Pik N Pig smokes pulled pork, ribs, chicken, and even pork

Crusty, smoky pulled pork at The Pik N Pig
*Photo by Woodie Anderson*

chops all night over hardwood coals. Whereas the traditional method in North Carolina is to cook meat directly over the coals, where juice and fat can drip onto the embers and impart another layer of taste, The Pik N Pig uses a rotating-shelf type of smoker, in which the meat spends all its time in an offset smoke chamber, rather than on a grate above the embers. The subtle difference in taste between this indirect method and the long-practiced over-the-wood style is, in truth, lost on many people. More and more restaurants are using these types of wood smokers nowadays in order to provide a traditional wood-cooked taste without someone having to continuously shovel coals from a fireplace under the cooking meat. Most barbecue patrons have come to appreciate the effort involved in not simply cooking the pork on a gas or electric pit and trying to cover the resulting flavor deficiency with sauce, as many restaurants do. When it comes to carping about the subtle differences between "authentic" and "inau-thentic" methods of wood cooking, well, "it isn't polite to talk with your mouth full," as the Sheppards say in promoting their restaurant.

The airport and The Pik N Pig have become popular destinations for pilots looking to get in some flight hours, have a good meal, and socialize with other fliers. The restaurant has a covered outdoor porch that is the preferred seating spot during fine weather. But the rambling, low-ceilinged interior does just great when the temperature drops or when precipitation threatens. After landing, it takes just a few minutes for a pilot to taxi near the restaurant, get passengers or bystanders to help push his plane off the taxiway onto the grass apron, find a table, and put in a barbecue order. Is this a great country or what?

The pulled pork here has a deep brown crust and a fair amount of pink color from the smoke. It stays moist during its overnight hours on the smoker, which means it gets tender and yields nicely to the teeth. It's generally served with a smoky, tomato-based sauce that includes a lot of onion flavor, but purists will also enjoy it without any sauce whatsoever. If someone happened to bring in a bottle of thinner, Lexington-style dip to dress this pulled pork, he or she would find the end result very close to what's sold in that Davidson County barbecue mecca.

Pork ribs are a Saturday-night-only specialty at The Pik N Pig. It's a good idea to call ahead and reserve them, as the air traffic picks up significantly on Saturday rib nights. Quite a few pilots land just long enough to pick up a take-away rib order before getting back into the air. The ribs are firm enough not to be sloppy and are full of wood-smoke taste. They would win awards in most competitions, in my opinion. In a word, they're fabulous.

The barbecued chicken here is referred to as "smoked" chicken. It comes to the table with a great-looking deep brown color, a crispy skin, and an incredibly juicy interior. I can truthfully say this is one of the most moist, flavorful examples of smoked or barbecued chicken I've ever tasted.

I also sampled a nicely smoked slice of boneless pork loin—a barbecued pork chop, if you will. I thought it was delicious—nearly perfect in texture without being either too chewy or too fall-apart tender.

The hush puppies and corn muffins with an interesting jalapeño butter add quite a bit of interest, as do the crispy fried pickle chips with ranch dressing. The side dishes—including coleslaw, potato salad, and green beans—are fairly bland, in my opinion, and the Brunswick stew contains okra, an inauthentic touch, at least in North Carolina. I didn't sample the baked sweet potato, but it looked appetizing on several other customers' plates, with lots of butter and brown sugar.

And the desserts! Oh, my. Over my protestations, the staff brought out samples of chocolate *and* vanilla "Better Than Sex Cake," "Coca-Cola Cake," Key lime pie, banana pudding, and coconut pie. All were very, very good. The fudgy, chewy chocolate cake, topped with whipped cream, came out on top as my personal favorite.

## Fuller's Old Fashion BBQ

http://www.fullersbbq.com
Lunch and dinner are served Monday through Saturday. Lunch is offered until 4 P.M. on Sunday.

3201 Roberts Avenue
Lumberton, N.C. 28306
910-738-8694

Second location:
113 North Eastern Boulevard
Fayetteville, N.C. 28301
910-484-5109

For several years after its founding in 1986, Fuller's established a reputation for serving what some customers called "the best country food in a fifty-mile radius." In addition to whole-hog barbecue cooked off-site in a wood-burning pit at owner Fuller Locklear's farm, the place features an enormous buffet of artery-clogging selections and a small, lonely salad bar.

The restaurant moved to larger quarters several years ago and also added a second location, in Fayetteville. Whether or not the meats, seafood, breads, vegetables, and desserts are as good as they've always been or only in the above-average category seems to depend on the day of the week, the time of day, the alignment of the stars, and the individual opinions of the customers. You can order off the menu or opt for the buffet. Since barbecue and many other foods do not take well to being held for long periods on a steam table, where oxidation takes a toll on freshness, the menu may be the best option for rendering judgment on the quality of the food. On the other hand, especially when it comes to vegetables like collards and cabbage that do pretty well on a buffet line, the sumptuous spread at Fuller's is awfully hard to resist when you're really hungry and a little impatient to be fed. A lot, too, depends on how recently the food was set out or replenished on the buffet.

There seems to be widespread agree-ment that the pit-cooked pig, whether hand-chopped or pulled, is extremely good. It has a smoky taste and the pleasing mixture of textures that results from using the whole hog, with its variety of white and dark meat, velvety interior sections, crispy or chewy outside brown bits, and morsels of skin. The 'cue comes from the kitchen fairly heavily sauced with a vinegar-pepper mixture typical for southeastern North Carolina, so you won't need much additional sauce, if any. Of course, a lot of folks passing through on Interstate 95 aren't all that crazy about our iconic vinegar-based sauce, so Fuller's more or less *has* to put some of the thick, red Memphis- or Kansas City–style stuff out as well, just to keep the peace. It's okay if you're into that sort of thing, I guess.

The hush puppies deserve high marks, especially if you don't get them off the buffet, where they tend to become a little soggy. The round, fried corn bread cakes are pretty dog-gone good as well.

In my opinion, nearly all buffets struggle when it comes to keeping desserts fresh and homemade-tasting, especially when the restaurant's volume is significant. Some die-hard Fuller's devotees will vehemently disagree with me, and I'm not saying my opinion is any better than theirs, but to my taste, I don't think the restaurant's desserts are in the same category as the best of its other offerings.

As long as you choose wisely and somewhat selectively when you visit, in consideration of some of the factors I've mentioned, Fuller's provides a positive dining experience.

## Nelson's Barbecue

4880 Kahn Drive
Lumberton, N.C. 28358
910-739-3350
http://nelsonsbarbecue.com
Lunch and dinner, Tuesday through Saturday

Owner-operator Andy Price grew up in Lumberton, but his family is originally from near Goldsboro and has a strong attachment to the barbecue produced at famous Wayne County institutions like Griffin's Barbecue and later Wilber's. It isn't surprising, then, that Price approached Wilber Shirley when he was searching for a barbecue mentor. Price offered to help Shirley for free if Wilber would let him be a "shadow."

When Shirley asked Price why he wanted to be in the barbecue business, Price told him, "I want to be just like you."

"He liked that, so the deal was on," remembers Price.

It was ten years after his brief apprenticeship when circumstances finally allowed Price to open his own place in Lumberton. But even after that long an interval, the influence of Wilber Shirley is evident.

Nelson's—named for Andy's dad—serves delicious, moist, fresh barbecue that comes from a combination of whole hogs and pork shoulders, the method also used by Shirley to obtain maximum yield. The meat is cooked over charcoal, with a generous amount of hickory wood added for extra flavor. The hours the meat spends slowly roasting over live coals add immeasurably to the taste. I noticed that both the whole hogs and the shoulders I observed on the pits had unusually well-crisped skin, which is a sure sign of experience in barbecuing. The chopped pork is superbly seasoned in the kitchen and can be further enhanced at the table with a well-balanced vinegar-based finishing sauce. This is high-quality barbecue indeed.

The equally tasty barbecued chicken is reminiscent of the charcoal-cooked chicken served at B's in Greenville. The crisp skin is absolutely full of charcoal flavor, and the meat is tender and yielding. As soon as the chickens come off the grill, the pieces are dunked in an eastern-style finishing sauce. As the chicken "rests," the sauce has plenty of opportunity to seep into the meat before it reaches the customer.

Nelson's also serves pit-cooked ribs, as seems to be a growing trend across the state. The ribs are on a par with the chopped barbecue and the chicken. The meat is soft and flavorful without being mushy, and the exterior

Pit man Chris Allen (*left*) and Nelson's owner, Andy Price

has an attractive char and "crust." To go with the ribs, Nelson's has a thicker western-style sauce.

I was impressed with the Brunswick stew at Nelson's. The ingredients are authentic—chicken, limas, corn, tomatoes, potatoes—and the texture is nice and thick. I thought the stew could have used a little more salt, but Andy Price told me up front that the staff is trying to hold down the salt level in several of the foods. The same is true of the eastern-style coleslaw, which tends toward the yellow hue popular in the flatlands. The slaw complements the barbecue, chicken, and ribs very well.

I sampled the banana pudding, made from Andy Price's own recipe, and found it exceptional, with a particularly silky texture. This version is served cool, its whipped-cream topping attractively garnished with crushed vanilla wafers.

Nelson's opened in late December 2011, so it's a newcomer on the barbecue scene. But it's obvious that the folks here have a deep regard for tradition and cooking practices that go far back into our history. I predict the restaurant will become a favorite—especially since it's located almost immediately adjacent to Interstate 95 and its steady stream of potential customers. Those who check out Nelson's will not be disappointed in the least.

### Village Inn Bar-B-Que and Seafood
3345 Martin Luther King Junior Drive
Lumberton, N.C. 28358
910-739-2050
Lunch and dinner, Thursday through Saturday

This place began in the 1950s as a little barbecue takeout stand across the road from the current location. I talked to an eighty-one-year-old man who told me he still remembers how good the barbecue was in those days. The restaurant was previously known as Hayes Barbecue. In the late 1970s, the name was changed to Village Inn Bar-B-Que and Seafood when the business moved to its current location.

Dewey Stone, the owner since the late 1990s, found himself an accomplished cook and has managed to hold onto him for years. That's the reason this restaurant, which has no real décor or ambiance to speak of, is so popular. It's open only Thursday through Saturday, which gives customers a purposeful, on-a-mission air when they visit. There's no nonsense in the surroundings, which to tell the truth are sort of dark and forbidding. But when the food arrives, it's as though the dining room is suddenly filled with light and Dewey himself is greeting everyone with a warm smile and a hug, shouting, "Welcome!"

The barbecue is either very finely chopped or almost ground, depending on your choice of terms. A tart, peppery, but still rather sweet sauce is added for seasoning in the kitchen. You can also get the pork shoulder sliced with a good proportion of outside brown "bark" mixed in. The meat is cooked on an electric pit for several hours and is then finished over charcoal. The charcoal taste adds a pleasant, positive note in both the sliced and chopped/minced meat. The white slaw and perfectly shaped, airy hush puppies take the meal to a high level.

To be perfectly honest, I don't know that I would drive fifty miles for the barbecue alone, although it's certainly good. But I'd drive twice that distance for the seafood. Even I can say, "Man does not live by barbecue alone." I highly recommend that you plan to experience the Village Inn's flavorful, exquisitely lightly-breaded specialty. Fish, shrimp, scallops, oysters, deviled crab—it doesn't much matter which is your favorite. They're all cooked by someone with a gift.

It would be unusual for a person with such a knack for frying seafood to mess up fried chicken. Indeed, the crispy, juicy poultry

Village Inn owner Dewey Stone serves terrific seafood and barbecue.
*Photo by Amanda Munger*

meets the same standard of excellence.

The sweet tea at Village Bar-B-Que and Seafood is exceptional. Yes, it's as sweet and any Southern tea I've ever had, but there's more to it than the sugar, I think. In any case, you'll want several glasses.

Okay, maybe the place is plain and will never receive awards for interior decoration. Who cares? This is a "Yum-yum, eat 'em up" spot if there ever was one, so don't miss it.

## Skipper Forsyth's Bar-B-Q

2362 North Garnett Street
Henderson, N.C. 27537
252-438-5228
http://www.skipperforsythsbbq.com
Lunch and dinner, Tuesday through Saturday

Although it isn't widely known outside the Henderson area, this place—also known as Skipper's Family Restaurant—is actually among the state's oldest barbecue restaurants. It has been in continuous operation since 1946. Regina Ellis, the granddaughter of founder Skipper Forsyth, now operates the restaurant, together with her son. In addition to barbecue, Forsyth's is popular for a wide range of country-style favorites and some delicious desserts.

The large, bright dining area is furnished with booths around the outside and tables in the middle. The place is frequently bustling with a crowd that seems to lean a little toward the white-collar side.

Finely shredded pork shoulder, heavily mixed with a tangy, tomato-leaning family sauce, is one of the main attractions, along with the Brunswick stew, which was originally made at home by Regina's grandmother. Restaurants are no longer allowed to serve home-prepared food, so the stew is made on the premises these days, but it's apparently as popular as ever. Regina used to help stir the stew in her grandmother's kitchen as a little girl. She also played on the woodpile behind the original restaurant's pits. There is little evidence of any wood cooking at the restaurant today. But served on a warm, soft bun and topped with Forsyth's sweet-pickle-laden coleslaw, the chopped barbecue is very, very tasty, and the locals swear by it. Ellis says the recipe for the sauce was given to her grandfather by a local doctor, who advised that the ingredients in the secret mixture "would never hurt anyone."

The hush puppies at Skipper Forsyth's— thin, crispy, and on the sweet side—are very appealing, to my taste. And speaking of sweet, the iced tea seems laced with sugar in a proportion designed to cool palates overstimulated by the signature tangy barbecue sauce. Unfortunately, this probably more than balances out any healthy characteristics of the sauce itself, but the tea is undeniably appealing.

As you might expect at a family restaurant, some good-sounding daily specials are offered. And from the looks of the photos on the restaurant's Facebook page, the townspeople turn out in large numbers to enjoy them. At the time of this writing, Tuesday featured chicken and dumplings and baked spaghetti; the Wednesday special was beef

Skipper Forsyth's Bar-B-Q, Henderson

tips on rice; Thursday was the day for baked turkey and dressing; Friday was devoted to BBQ pork ribs and meat loaf; and Saturday's special was barbecue and Brunswick stew. Hamburger steak is a favorite available every day, and the fried chicken—a menu staple—gets strong reviews from regulars. Vegetables regularly include cabbage, collards, stewed tomatoes, and boiled potatoes.

Most all the desserts are homemade, including banana pudding, chocolate meringue pie, pineapple and piña colada cakes, and cool, delicious Snickers pie, drizzled with chocolate syrup. Oddly, the fruit cobblers are not made at the restaurant. Most restaurants of this type *begin* their dessert offerings with homemade cobbler.

Skipper Forsyth's is no more than a couple of miles off I-85; take the northbound exit for U.S. 158 Bypass. It's a very worthwhile lunch or dinner destination.

## Bob's Bar-B-Q
1589 Lake Road (N.C. 56)
Creedmoor, N.C. 27522
919-528-2081

When Nita Whitfield and her husband, Bobby, built Bob's Bar-B-Q in 1970, it seemed way out in the country. At that time, Interstate 85 hadn't been completed in the Creedmoor-Butner area, twelve miles north of Durham, but the Whitfields knew it soon would be. Today, Bob's location on N.C. 56 is just a couple hundred yards from the busy north-south artery. Since the long-ago arrival of the interstate, the whole region has become a center of commerce. The area around Exit 191 has filled up with several motels, a strip shopping center, and all the major fast-food franchises. The community of Butner, just down the road, has experienced virtually constant expansion in recent years due to the presence of a state mental hospital, a center for the mentally handicapped, an alcohol-treatment facility, and a federal prison. Several new plants and corporate campuses have also been built in the area. And it seems that the people who work at these places are all fond of eating at Bob's Bar-B-Q, where they mingle with a steady stream of local residents and I-85 travelers.

The joint, as they say, is jumpin'.

Not only do customers like the food at Bob's, they are also served quickly. Many local workers have but thirty minutes for lunch, counting traveling time. They can pop into Bob's and get something really good to eat and still make it back to their jobs on time. Customers at Bob's pick up a tray and go through a mini-cafeteria line. Barbecue and other ready-to-go dishes are served on the spot, while orders for hamburgers, seafood, and other menu selections go back to the kitchen and are delivered to the table.

Bob's is actually named for Nita's father, Bob Whitt, who died in 1985. A longtime

deputy sheriff in nearby Roxboro, Whitt opened a barbecue stand there relatively late in life and ran it for fifteen years before retiring. But retirement didn't really suit Whitt, so his only daughter, Nita, and her husband built the present restaurant basically to give her father something to do. Bob Whitt ran the place for ten years until his health began to fail. Now, Nita handles most of the responsibilities of operation, with occasional input from her husband. She employs a couple of men to take care of the meat and a mostly female staff to prepare and serve the rest of the food. Nita says she has the best group of workers in Granville County. One thing's for sure: the employees are proud of the restaurant. One longtime staffer pulled me aside and looked me straight in the eye as she asked, "You do understand? This place is an institution."

Nita says that before her father opened his Roxboro place in 1957, he went all over the state researching various methods of cooking barbecue. At the outset, Bob Whitt decided to go with an electric pit, rather than messing with wood. He bought one of the first electric pits anywhere in the area. The pork shoulders at Bob's are still cooked that way, although the original cooker has long since been replaced. If any complaints have been voiced about the lack of a wood-smoked taste in this barbecue, they certainly haven't affected the restaurant's popularity. I've been contacted by several people who wanted to recommend the place. One fellow from Virginia told me it's his favorite North Carolina barbecue restaurant.

Bob's Bar-B-Q, Creedmoor

The barbecue at Bob's is hand chopped, tender, and fresh tasting. It comes to the table already well moistened by a mild, sweet sauce that contains little evidence of pepper. No skin or fat is chopped up into the barbecue, so you're basically getting pure, lean meat. This is good, solid, middle-of-the-road 'cue, prepared according to Bob Whitt's carefully considered way of doing things. It's the kind of barbecue that would win awards for consistently pleasing taste, rather than for excitement. And let's face it, a lot of people say excitement is the last thing they want to encounter in any restaurant, especially a barbecue place. The barbecue is accompanied by a mild, pleasing mayonnaise-based coleslaw and fresh, crisp hush puppies.

Brunswick stew is a big deal at Bob's. The restaurant makes forty gallons at a time, four or five days a week. The mixture is sweet and perfectly seasoned, although in my judgment it could stand to be a slight bit thicker. Chicken, pork, and beef are all used in this recipe,

but the vegetables are limited—as they properly should be—to tomatoes, potatoes, butter beans, cream-style corn, and onions. Thankfully, Bob's version contains no green beans, garden peas, okra, or any of the dozens of other extraneous ingredients that often find their way into the so-called Brunswick stew found in the Piedmont.

Bob's is one of those places on or near the dividing line between two schools of thought regarding barbecue. In response to my question, Nita said she wasn't sure whether Creedmoor is located in the east or the Piedmont. I'm not sure myself. Customers find an interesting blend of the two regional styles at Bob's. Piedmont-style pork shoulders are accompanied by mayonnaise-based slaw and Brunswick stew, which are both ordinarily confined to the eastern region. No one seems to find the anomaly the slightest bit unusual.

Another of the restaurant's specialties known far and wide is its homemade chicken salad, made from Nita's mother-in-law's recipe.

As you might expect, the salad is often purchased in large quantities for bridesmaids' luncheons, teas, and other predominantly female social gatherings. Between eight and twelve large stewing hens are simmered every day until the meat is ready to drop off the bones. Bob's makes the salad in pots so big that the workers have to stand on tiptoe to see inside. This chicken salad has a substantial consistency—containing hand-chopped, boned chicken, rather than the minced or pulverized stuff that goes into commercial chicken salad—so in addition to being a standard for ladies' events, it's plenty hearty for a man's appetite, too.

Pork ribs and chicken 'n' dumplings have been added on the serving line at Bob's, along with an array of appealing country-style vegetables.

The thing at Bob's that will stick in your memory more than anything else, though, is the homemade pie. Chocolate cream pie. Chocolate chess pie. Sweet potato pie. Forty to fifty pies a day, all made on the premises. In September, when Bob's obtains its yearly supply of sweet potatoes, the staffers peel sixty bushels to go into the pie-filling mixture, which is prepared, then frozen. Bob's has eight large chest freezers, and a good deal of the space in them is taken up by sweet potato pie filling. Those who work at Bob's do not want to run out of sweet potato pie. "If we give out of that, we might as well just pack it up and go home," say the servers, shaking their heads in awe and fear at the very thought. "People get angry if you tell them you're out—not just irritated, angry!"

You may want to avoid Bob's busiest day, Friday, when five different groups meet at the restaurant.

## • Death of a Pig Cooker •

There used to be a place in Burlington, where I made my home for many years, that had several pig cookers for rent.

It was a run-down little car wash. The retired man who ran the business for its owner had been a well-known barbecuer of whole hogs in his younger days. He had amassed a collection of relatively crude portable pits made from the kind of metal tanks used to hold home heating oil. The owner allowed him to store them at the car wash, where he occasionally rented them out to earn extra income. I had rented cookers on several previous occasions and had always found it much harder work to scrub off the cooking grate and clean the ashes out of the pit afterward (in order to get my cleaning deposit back from the fussy old gentleman) than to actually roast the pig.

On one fateful occasion, I needed a cooker so my college-aged son Everett could handle a catered Saturday pig picking on my behalf for a group of fraternity boys at the University of North Carolina at Greensboro. When I stopped by the car wash on Friday evening to pick one up, the business was closed and the caretaker was absent. However, the pig cookers were accessible, as the length of chain fastening them all together—to discourage would-be thieves—had no padlock to secure it. As a relatively regular customer, I figured I would pay the

My younger son, Everett, shares my love for cooking, but he's much better at it.

rental when I returned the cooker. I simply helped myself, hitched up the pit-on-wheels, and left with it.

The next morning, Everett set off for Greensboro with the cooker in tow. It wasn't long before I received a cell phone call. Everett stammered a brief, horrid tale. At seventy miles per hour, the aged trailer frame had come loose from the towing tongue, and the old pit had careened out of control and—fortunately—onto the bumpy shoulder of I-85, where it literally came to pieces, strewing a trail of rusty debris along a half-mile stretch of highway apron. All that was left was the trailer tongue itself, still dragging behind the towing hitch.

After a frantic couple of hours, I was able to locate a replacement cooker, send Everett on his way to the catering event, and dispatch a truck to collect the remains of the collapsed cooker from the roadside. But I soon discovered a much bigger problem.

Still unable to find the retired pit purveyor at the car wash, I called his home to explain what had happened and make arrangements to pay for the damage. When his wife answered and I asked to speak to him, she tearfully informed me that he had passed away during the night!

Now, at that point, I still hadn't identified myself, and I sorrowfully admit to entertaining a fleeting temptation to say, "Oh, I'm so sorry," and simply hang up without giving my name, thereby extricating myself from the problem of the purloined pit. However, conscience quickly took hold, and I began to wrestle with the delicate challenge of composing an artful letter combining (a) an expression of condolence, (b) an explanation for having stolen, then destroyed the property of the deceased and, by extension, his grieving family, and (c) an offer to pay for the loss.

Throughout a forty-year journalistic career, I doubt I ever had a knottier writing assignment.

Months afterward, I received a phone call from the amused owner of the car wash, to whom the letter of condolence/apology/restitution had been forwarded by the pit man's widow. He breezily told me I could forget making any compensation for the damages and that the decrepit pig-cooking pit had no doubt been on its last legs when I absconded with it. "Sounds like you've already been through enough trouble on this deal," he chuckled.

He was more right than he knew. Everett and I were never able to collect the four-hundred-dollar catering fee for the fraternity pig picking that occasioned all the trouble. So in the end, we paid our cosmic debt in full.

Knightdale Seafood & Barbecue, Knightdale

## Knightdale Seafood & Barbecue

706 Money Court
Knightdale, N.C. 27545
919-266-4447
http://www.knightdaleseafoodandbbq.com
Lunch and dinner daily

Knightdale Seafood & Barbecue began operation in 1988 and has been in a new location since 2003. Founders and current operators Larry and Phyllis Addleton lived in an upstairs apartment over the original location for eleven years (after thinking they would be there for only six months) and kept the restaurant in its original quarters another four years. For quite a period of time at both the old and new locations, Knightdale offered not only conventional eastern-style barbecue, steaks, and prime rib but also exotic dishes such as buffalo stew and ostrich steak. Nowadays, though, a good-sized oyster bar and seafood selection serve to balance out the homier barbecue and country-cooking side of the equation.

Besides barbecue and fried or barbecued chicken, patrons can also sample chicken 'n' pastry, meat loaf, country-style steak, hamburger steak, country-cooked pork chops, ribs, burgers, sandwiches, and steaks up to sixteen ounces. The vegetables tend to be very good. I sampled well-seasoned and tender collards and traditional boiled potatoes, although these were red potatoes with the skins left on.

I found the barbecue to be good, if not traditionally pit-cooked. It was lean and had some smoky taste, probably from an electric or gas smoker using hardwood for flavor. It was rather moist and well sauced. The sauce had a light vinegar touch. I thought I could tell that some of the natural pork juices had been mixed back into the barbecue as well, which is always a good thing. The meat seemed to be holding its texture and tenderness well, and appetizing brown bits were sprinkled throughout.

I think the Brunswick stew at Knightdale

used to have more of a conventional taste than it does now. For me, this stew needs to be just a touch on the sweet and velvety side to balance out the acidity of the tomatoes, which is why it has traditionally contained creamed corn and potatoes, both of which tend to be mellowing agents. However, I found Knightdale's stew to be too tart-tasting, and it contained nontraditional ingredients such as green beans and black-eyed peas. Many people eat stew and barbecue together. But in order for that to be enjoyable, the Brunswick stew has to have enough of a sweet touch to counterbalance the piquancy of the barbecue. In my opinion, this stew is too acidic for a barbecue side dish.

The hush puppies, served very hot, were outstanding.

Knightdale Seafood & Barbecue won *Spectator*'s 2000 "Best Barbecue in the Triangle" award, as well as an AOL "City's Best" recognition in 2005 for "Best Southern Cooking." A broad selection of appetizing food is available here. No matter what sort of mood you're in, you'll almost certainly like something on the menu.

## Clyde Cooper's BBQ

109 East Davie Street
Raleigh, N.C. 27601
919-832-7614
http://clydecoopersbbq.com
Lunch and dinner (until 6 P.M.), Monday through
  Saturday

The restaurant opened by the late Clyde Cooper near the corner of Davie and Wilm-

ington streets has been *the* place for Raleigh barbecue since 1938—or at least it was until 2007, when The Pit at the other end of Davie Street started offering some serious competition. Clyde Cooper's BBQ is now the oldest surviving barbecue restaurant in North Carolina. It has long served a clientele largely made up of lawyers, judges, politicians, and businessmen. The eastern-style chopped pork isn't pit-cooked and would go totally unnoticed by most in any blind taste test. But barbecue in Raleigh—and in much of the rest of the state, for that matter—has been as much about ritual as about flavor until fairly recently. There's something almost sacramental about a visit to Cooper's two long, narrow rooms with the stamped-tin ceilings and the "Rainbow Gasoline and Motor Oil" pump decorating a corner.

The food here is unadorned and straight

Interior of Clyde Cooper's BBQ

Cooper's has been located on Raleigh's East Davie Street since 1931.

from the heart of tobacco country: vinegar-splashed barbecue, Brunswick stew, coleslaw, boiled potatoes, hush puppies, and pork skins. It's what former *News & Observer* columnist Dennis Rogers used to call "the Holy Grub." Sure, you can also find ribs and barbecued chicken, along with some pretty good vegetables such as collards and corn 'n' butterbeans, but the backbone of the business is the traditional barbecue plate or dinner.

Patrons can order their barbecue chopped coarse (similar to "pulled") or sliced. No matter what style they choose, it will be flavored with lots of salt, red pepper, and vinegar, but it will have absolutely no smoky taste.

Cooper's Brunswick stew has a good, robust taste and is suitably sweet for this region of the state. However, the stew has random green beans and pinto beans floating around in it. The owners should know better.

A barbecue plate includes both pork skins and hush puppies. The corn bread is smooth-textured and sweet, although it isn't crispy enough for my taste. On the other hand, the pork skins provide enough added crunch to make up for it. The slaw contains no mayonnaise or mustard—just cabbage, vinegar, sugar, and a little minced carrot.

Cooper's iced tea is worth a refill or three, but don't bother with the desserts. They're store-bought and not worth the trouble.

Because of the number of "suits" who often fill the place, people in Raleigh refer to Cooper's fare as "power barbecue." But this is still just a barbecue joint, after all, so whatever you want to wear will be fine.

My grandson Sadler Smith, born in South Korea, appeared at the age of nine in a *North Carolina Weekend* segment about Korean barbecue. He had already appeared in two previous segments, the first at a traditional North Carolina barbecue restaurant. At the time of this taping, Sadler was already well on his way to becoming an enthusiastic "foodie." *Courtesy of UNC-TV*

About a million people have told me they want my job when I retire.

Maybe a million more have asked if they can be my assistant. "You must need somebody to tote the camera equipment or drive you around," they say. "I want to put in an application."

Perception is reality to most people, even if the perception and the reality don't actually match up. Some people reason that if I'm eating every time they see me on TV, it must follow that I'm always eating, even when I'm not on TV. Many of the same people reason that if the only thing they ever see me doing is reviewing restaurants, that must be my entire job—and what a glorious job it must be!

They are absolutely right that it's a great job, one that I am extraordinarily grateful for. I realize full well how fortunate I am to be able to do work that I enjoy and that seems to please others, and I don't take it for granted in the slightest.

However, most don't understand that the restaurant reviewing I do for UNC-TV's *North Carolina Weekend* is only one of the three or four jobs I have, and that my television work is freelance, part-time, and done almost entirely on weekends, when others are relaxing. I have worked full-time Monday through Friday at occupations *off* the UNC-TV payroll since 1997. My book and magazine writing—my second job—is done on my own time, outside my regular working hours devoted either to my employers or— during one two-year period—to my role as

Wayne Waters telephoned to arrange a book signing and ended up introducing me to Jack Cobb & Son Bar-B-Que in Farmville. Proprietor Rudy Cobb is at right.
*Courtesy of Pete Bell*

a self-employed, independent producer of full-length programs. So, when added to my other undertakings, the restaurant reviews—my *third* job—subtract from the weekend time I might otherwise have to attend ball games, camp in the mountains, attend my grandchildren's soccer games and swim meets, or just stay at home and cook for fun. Nearly all the *North Carolina Weekend* features are shot on Saturdays and Sundays (since, after all, they introduce viewers to various potential weekend activities), and my restaurant visits are no exception.

Typically, I arrange a TV shoot every four to six weeks. Together with an assigned cameraman, I arrange two restaurant visits on Saturday and one on Sunday, which usually means an out-of-town overnight stay. I try to keep all three reviews in one fairly compact geographical area of the state so we'll have the maximum time for shooting and less devoted to driving. Once the third segment, which usually takes place at lunchtime on Sunday, is completed, we normally invest the

hour or so necessary to download all the accumulated digital clips from the camera to my computer hard drive. At home, either after work or on *another* weekend, I review the footage, write a script, record my voice-over narrations, and edit the features on my MacBook Pro laptop using an industry-standard editing program, Final Cut Pro. This process eliminates my having to drive to the UNC-TV studios in Research Triangle Park to use the in-house editing facilities. When my features are completed, I upload them to a UNC-TV server via an Internet protocol known as FTP. All this means that I seldom have to actually visit the UNC-TV premises, which saves a lot of time.

I think most people assume my role is only to appear in the segments, after which other editors and producers convert them into finished television products. Not so. But even taking into account the factors that most folks don't consider, it's still a wonderful job. People often make it clear they think they would like to trade places. My friend Keith

Barnes used this as fodder for a column in the *Wilson Daily Times* in 2001:

Where would you really like to work?

I read a survey in the news last week about job ratings that included categories like most respected jobs, most dangerous jobs, highest-paying jobs, etc.

Chances are that if you've lived a normal adult life you've had several different occupations.

Even if you haven't, I imagine you have at least thought about doing something else and maybe dreamed of that perfect job.

Some jobs I would love to try include the following. Let's call it "My Top 10 List of Jobs I'd Like To Have."

Included on Barnes's list was the following:

• Bob Garner—Garner works for UNC Center for Public Television, and his job involves, among other things, traveling all over the state in an RV and sampling the food at popular restaurants. When he's not visiting barbecue houses he's usually found in places that specialize in country-style all-you-can-eat type meat-and-taters cuisine.

In each restaurant, with a video camera set up before him, Garner sits down to a table with a huge spread of food and reports to us how good the stuff is he's sampling.

After each bite of fried chicken, barbecue, collards, biscuits or whatever, he closes his eyes, nods his head slowly back and forth and says something like, "Uummm, that's really tasty." I can't believe he's actually paid to do this.

Barnes went on to say in the column (later published in his book *Whatever Happened to the Milkman?*) that he picked my job number one, which meant it rated more highly than occupations such as astronaut, reporter for *Roller Coaster Magazine*, and photographer for *National Geographic*!

Just for the record, UNC-TV has never provided me with an RV. But it's still a great job.

I have visited practically every barbecue joint in North Carolina. UNC-TV videographer Mark Stroupe captured some of the magic of the wood-fired pits at Hillsborough BBQ Company.

The Pit, Raleigh
*Photo by Scott LeVoyer*

## The Pit Authentic Barbecue

328 West Davie Street
Raleigh, N.C. 27601
919-890-4500
http://www.thepit-raleigh.com
Lunch and dinner daily

Although The Pit is probably North Carolina's most unusual barbecue restaurant in terms of style and ambiance, its whole-hog eastern-style barbecue and traditional side dishes pay homage to the state's three-century barbecue heritage, as does the brief history of North Carolina barbecue printed on the back of the dinner menu. Acclaimed for preserving historic buildings in downtown Raleigh and elsewhere, owner Greg Hatem exhibits a corresponding passion for preserving the state's traditional foodways—particularly its barbecue culture.

Housed in a 1930s former meat-packing plant in downtown Raleigh's warehouse district, The Pit nicely balances weathered brick walls and a largely traditional menu with con-

temporary lighting, sleek décor, and a lively bar area. An enormous, ceiling-high glass room divider separating the entrance corridor from an adjoining dining room is etched with a huge, labeled drawing of a pig divided into its component parts, titled with the legend, "Everything But the Squeal." The U-shaped bar and several cocktail-height tables occupy the lower level up front, while three distinct seating areas, a private dining room, and the semi-open kitchen are two steps up from entry level. A bustling restaurant with a lot of energy, it's often very busy. The Pit has seating for 250 and frequently does 1,000 "covers" per night. There's almost always a wait for a table, especially from Thursday through the weekend. The restaurant has managed to tap into an obvious Raleigh hankering for authentic pit-cooked barbecue. But customers also clearly enjoy dining on those time-honored victuals in a rather upscale setting.

The Pit roasts whole hogs over wood

and charcoal right in the kitchen, with the freestanding metal pits open to the view of customers. An elaborate and expensive hood-and-exhaust system efficiently vents the heavy smoke. The barbecue is served pulled and chopped, with the chopping done in small batches throughout the day. The chopped version is seasoned with salt, black pepper, red pepper, vinegar, and sugar, and moistened with savory reserved juices. Customers can add extra "eastern" sauce from cruets at the tables. The succulent pulled pork—also prepared in small batches—is very lightly seasoned so that customers can dress it the way they like at the table, using either the eastern sauce or a thicker western version. The meat is noticeably smoke-flavored and fall-apart tender, yet it maintains an ever-so-slightly chewy texture.

The restaurant serves meat from pastured pigs raised outdoors on family farms, which are audited and certified by the Animal Welfare Approved program. Pigs roast all

night at the restaurant. As soon as they're removed from the grates first thing in the morning, the pits are cleaned and refired, ready to take on full loads of half-chickens and racks of ribs, both of which are exceptionally popular. The tender barbecued chicken acquires a lovely, light char and a deep smoke flavoring, and the ribs—not overly spiced or exotically flavored—taste much closer to a rack of ribs directly off a whole, roasted pig than do those served in most rib places. Both baby back and larger, meatier "Carolina-style" ribs are available. Unless customers request otherwise, the chicken and ribs come to the table brushed with The Pit's western North Carolina sauce, which is characterized by a substantial vinegar flavor and is not overly sweet.

The Pit also serves a well-received, meltingly tender smoked beef brisket, delicious turkey barbecue, and even a flavorful—and surprisingly popular—barbecued tofu. But don't read too much into that. Pulled and chopped whole-hog barbecue and pit-cooked

Barbecue sandwich at
The Pit, Raleigh
*Photo by Scott LeVoyer*

ribs are still overwhelmingly the biggest sellers.

The selection of sides at the restaurant reflects a commitment to celebrating North Carolina's best-loved home-cooking favorites. They include well-seasoned, traditional creamed corn and cheesy bacon grits (at dinner only), heirloom yellow cabbage collards, bacon 'n' beer–flavored BBQ baked beans, moist but crispy fried okra, a substantial and crusty baked mac 'n' cheese, black-eyed peas, and, of course, creamy coleslaw. Light, sweet hush puppies and fluffy biscuits accompany all plates. An unusual and delicious skillet corn bread that changes slightly according to the season can be ordered as a starter.

Other starters give a major hat tip to tradition. Pimento cheese is available in coated and deep-fried "poppers." Attractive hand-battered onion rings are served with a tangy Oak Island sauce featuring whole-grain mustard. Additional appetizer favorites include crispy pulled-pork-and-collard egg rolls and bruschetta garnished with house-smoked hog jowl bacon.

The Pit has a wide selection of micro-brewed and craft beers, premium and small-batch bourbons, and a very respectable wine list. Traditionally, most barbecue restaurants in North Carolina serve nothing stronger than sweet tea, despite the ironic fact that the cooking and eating of whole pigs across the coastal plain during the past three centuries has nearly always involved the consumption of some sort of spirits. The Pit has brought this heretofore unacknowledged, back-of-the-pickup practice into the open at its lively but well-behaved bar. Patrons have embraced it enthusiastically, without its seeming to have any effect on the family-friendly nature of the place.

Empire Eats, a subsidiary of Greg Hatem's real-estate operation, Empire Properties, operates four other restaurants in downtown Raleigh: The Raleigh Times is a full-service casual restaurant and tavern featuring classic bar-fare favorites; the Morning Times is a coffee shop with sandwiches and desserts; Sitti offers traditional fare from Lebanon, home of Hatem's forebears (*sitti* is the affectionate term for *grandmother* in Lebanese); and Gravy is an intimate eatery offering traditional Italian fare. Hatem grew up in the northeastern coastal plain community of Roanoke Rapids, where the surrounding farm country nourished his early attachment to traditional whole-hog barbecue. It isn't surprising that The Pit is by far the largest of his restaurants.

Open only since 2008, The Pit has quickly become one of the most popular barbecue restaurants in central North Carolina, as well as a favorite downtown Raleigh watering hole.

## Danny's Bar-B-Que

http://www.dannysbarbque.com

311 Asheville Avenue, #G
Cary, N.C. 27518
919-851-5541
Lunch and dinner, Monday through Saturday

Danny's offers pulled pork, ribs, brisket, and chicken.

Other locations:

2945 Miami Boulevard, #118
Durham, N.C. 27703
919-806-1965
Lunch, Monday through Friday

9561 Chapel Hill Road
Morrisville, N.C. 27560
919-468-3995
Lunch and dinner, Monday through Saturday

Let's acknowledge right up front that this is basically Texas-style barbecue brought to Wake County by way of the Jacksonville, Florida, area, where the owner of Danny's Bar-B-Que lived with his family before moving to Cary in 1989. A note in the menu says that after their arrival, the family members went in search of the barbecue they were used to— "real pit, hickory smoked BBQ"—but could find only "shredded pork with vinegar sauce." Hence, Danny's Bar-B-Que came into being, serving pork, pork ribs (spareribs and baby backs), chicken, and beef cooked in an electric smoker with some hickory wood added.

First of all, Danny's family probably *did* have trouble finding traditional pit-cooked North Carolina barbecue in the Capital City area *at that time*, since only a couple of places in the immediate vicinity were still cooking over live coals. Folks have settled for what I call "generic" barbecue, flavored only by the sauce (which often provides little flavor at all), for so long in the eastern portion of the state that they should be willing to accept a fair criticism.

However, had Danny's family members ventured just a short distance to the west (say, to Allen & Son in Chapel Hill), they would have discovered the first of many places that cook over a *real* hickory or oak pit, not its modern-day electric-smoking counterpart, which is probably what *they* settled for back home in Jacksonville. Let's give them a C-minus for incomplete research.

Danny's really packs in the crowds. I had a twenty-minute wait the day I was there. The viewers of WRAL-TV voted its barbecue "Best in Wake County" in 1997, so the restaurant should be given due respect. On the other hand, it's probably only because the family moved to an area that at that time was relatively lacking in the *best* North Carolina barbecue that their restaurant is in business at all—a circumstance that probably explains the award, too.

All kidding aside, I've enjoyed every meal I've ever had at Danny's, and I've had several. I find that the meats, which are served without sauce, are lean, pleasantly smoke-ringed and smoke-flavored, and tasty. The sauces, offered on the side, include a dark, thick, molasses-flavored number; a thick, mustard-based, South Carolina–inspired sauce; a spicy-hot, thick sauce that's reddish orange in color; and a weak version of eastern-style sauce that needs more pepper.

The pork at Danny's doesn't quite have the falling-apart tenderness and juiciness that result when whole shoulders or butts (the upper half of the shoulder) are cooked extremely slowly. The pinkish color and flavor that come from merely *smoking* meat are also different from when the meat is both smoked *and* grilled by being cooked directly over live coals. That's because, in the former case, it's missing the unique flavor that comes only from fat dripping onto hot coals, which produces an aromatic steam that envelops the meat.

Academic discussions aside, Danny's barbecued meats and well-prepared side dishes offer a refreshing change of pace, yet provide an experience that's not totally off the reservation in terms of what North Carolinians enjoy about the state's best barbecue. If

the ambiance at Danny's clean, modern facility isn't the same as at some dilapidated barbecue shack out in the country, more's the pity. But the atmosphere *is* friendly. And the family members deserve for all of us to go by and give them a pat on the back for having sense enough to move to North Carolina.

## Smokey's BBQ Shack

10800 Chapel Hill Road (N.C. 54)
Morrisville, N.C. 27560
919-469-1724
http://www.smokeysshack.com
Lunch is served Monday through Saturday.
Dinner is offered Thursday through Saturday.

When you think of this place, think *Smokey* as in *Great Smoky Mountains*, because the restaurant has a definite western North Carolina vibe. That said, the electric-fired wood smoker used to prepare the pulled pork, ribs, brisket, and chicken does a good job of imparting a nice wood-cooked flavor and an attractive texture to the meat. What appears to be an old, unused wood-burning pit building sits behind the restaurant, and I noticed smoke coming from a stainless-steel smokestack atop the kitchen, so the smoked meats are obviously prepared on one of the newfangled smoker setups.

One slogan here is, "All dry rubbed and slow smoked to perfection." (Another is, "This place rocks, and so do most of the tables.") But since traditional North Carolina pork barbecue isn't ever dry-rubbed with anything other than maybe some salt—and most times

Smokey's
BBQ Shack,
Morrisville

not even that—it's easy to tell that some barbecue fusion is going on at Smokey's.

Not to worry. It's pretty good stuff by just about anyone's measure.

I had an appetizing barbecue sandwich, served on a high-quality twist-top roll. Our native 'cue is nearly always served on the cheapest of hamburger rolls (not that there's anything wrong with that!), so the quality of the bread alone was another dead giveaway that this barbecue has roots in soil other than our own—maybe across the state line in East Tennessee. (One clue: I happen to know the owner is a big Volunteers fan.)

The meat on my sandwich was chunky, moist, and nicely textured and had what I call a good, firm "bite" to it, along with plenty of outside brown bits. The creamy slaw had a good flavor, but the barbecue itself exhibited little taste of any prior seasoning or dry-rubbing; it had a pretty straightforward pork flavor, albeit with a nice touch of smokiness. The thick, red western-type sauce (available in bottles) was served in a little tub on the side. Since the sandwich was piled high with meat, it took more than one tub to really give it any kick. I personally think the barbecue

would benefit from at least a light salting before being placed on a plate or sandwich. All in all, though, the Boston butt came off the smoker in good shape indeed. Most people will find the meat tasty and toothsome.

The side dishes at Smokey's—which I wasn't able to sample—include Brunswick stew, French fries, fried okra, potato salad, mac 'n' cheese, green beans, baked beans, and mixed greens.

The restaurant occupies a modest, perhaps even ramshackle, cinder-block building with a twelve-table enclosed front porch and a back room that contains the order counter and a couple more tables. I loved the smart-alecky signs posted here and there: "Due to budget cuts, the light at the end of the tunnel has been turned off"; "Sexual harassment will not be tolerated—However it will be graded"; "Sarcasm—Just one of the services I offer."

Smokey's is located in a fast-growing area of Morrisville near I-540 and the Raleigh-Durham airport. Considering all the office parks and housing developments springing up, it's hard to predict how long the restaurant will maintain its current, appealing rural-road feel.

This photo helped lead me to a firm resolve to lose weight.
*Photo by Keith Barnes*

I get a lot of questions and comments about my weight and body size, which isn't a surprise considering that every time viewers see me on television, I'm eating. Even though they may intellectually know I'm eating only long enough for the camera to document my sampling of various dishes, another part of their brains leaps to the conclusion that I eat constantly, camera or no camera.

For a long time, my weight more or less supported that conclusion. Now, I'm quite a bit trimmer than I once was (although not as trim as I'd like to be), and the weight questions and comments tend to follow a couple of familiar patterns.

"You look a lot bigger on TV than you do in person," someone will remark. The fact is that in some of the old segments that are still occasionally rerun, I *was* a lot bigger than I now appear, either in person or on camera.

"With all that food I see laid out on the table, I'm surprised you don't weigh five hundred pounds," another will wisecrack. Here, I explain that I eat just a bite or two of each item—only enough to get a satisfactory take—and that the rest goes unconsumed except in the rare instances when I can persuade my cameramen to sample a particularly luscious dish; most of them are too intent on their photography to be distracted by food, at least until the job is over. While I like to *show* many different dishes in order to give viewers a comprehensive preview of a restaurant, I don't sample all of them, and I certainly don't eat more than a tiny bit of each dish I try. Actually, eating a bite or two of several different dishes adds up quickly to what should be a normal-sized meal.

I admit that, for many years, I *did* eat a whole lot more than I do now, whether in private life or on television. This is no big revelation to anyone who remembers that I used to weigh around a hundred pounds more than I do at present. My waist size has shrunk from forty-six to thirty-six.

For years, I tried every diet and weight-loss method known to man, without much success. I went on exercise regimens with limited success, but I was never able to approach what doctors told me was a normal weight for someone with my bone structure. And as a man who describes food in great detail, in a way calculated to make others hungry, and as someone who dearly loves to cook and experiment with different dishes, eating miserly portions of uninteresting food was never something I could keep up for long.

Still, with three children and several grandchildren for whom I want to be around as long as possible, I knew I was shaving years off my life by remaining overweight. I was taking three blood pressure medications, and my bad cholesterol measurements were not headed in the right direction. I suffered from obstructive sleep apnea, joint pain, and plantar

As this caricature indicates, I had at least two chins at the time of my 2006 "Bob Garner Eats" series of articles for *Our State* magazine. *By Travis Foster, courtesy of* Our State *magazine*

I had lost over a hundred pounds by the time I joined The Pit Authentic Barbecue in Raleigh in mid-2011. At left is the owner of The Pit, Greg Hatem. At right is Wilber Shirley of Wilber's Barbecue in Goldsboro, guest of honor at The Pit's 2011 Barbecue Heritage Dinner celebrating Shirley's many years in the business.

fasciitis, which caused severe heel pain.

Finally, I decided to undergo gastric bypass surgery. A fellow member in my church had undergone the surgery, slimmed down amazingly, and talked in glowing terms about her positive experience with the bariatric surgery program at Wake Forest University Baptist Medical Center in Winston-Salem. After requesting information and attending several orientation sessions, I made the decision to move forward. But it was to be a full two years between the time I first considered weight-loss surgery and the actual operation. One notable holdup: my medical insurance required that I undergo a more conventional six-month diet program, closely supervised by my physician, before I could be approved for the surgery. Another delay revolved around my primary physician's initial opposition to my undergoing general anesthesia—which always presents a certain risk—for what he considered a nonessential operation.

In due time, all the delays, cautions, and reservations were resolved or overcome, and I had the surgery in June 2010.

While my experience has been extraordinarily positive, those considering bariatric surgery should realize that it is not by any means a magic bullet. Most programs require significant weight loss before the operation is performed. Permanent dietary and lifestyle changes including proper nutrition and nutritional supplementation are required, as is a psychological evaluation. Many of those who undergo gastric bypass are obliged to permanently give up consumption of all but the tiniest amounts of sugar and fried or especially fatty foods, and many also find that their consumption of alcohol must

be severely limited. (That's because alcohol is metabolized much more slowly following so-called Roux-en-Y surgery, which causes food to bypass a major portion of the small intestine, thereby limiting caloric absorption but reducing tolerance for and absorption of certain foods and beverages.) Fairly expensive specialized vitamin supplements are prescribed for life following such surgery.

As a result of the procedure, I have a great deal more energy and feel much less fatigued, I have brought my blood pressure down to a normal level without medication, and I have maintained the same weight for a long period. Statistics show that the average bariatric surgery patient can expect to lose between 70 and 80 percent of excess body weight during the first year following surgery, and that has mirrored my personal experience almost exactly.

I am much more fortunate than many bariatric patients in that I can eat just about anything following my surgery—just not very much of it, and not nearly as quickly as I once did. My stomach was reduced in size to approximately the dimensions of a jumbo-sized egg, with the opening from stomach to intestine shaved down to the diameter of a tube of lip balm. I have learned to eat much more slowly and to chew each bite approximately thirty times. Meals that I used to bolt in five minutes now take half an hour.

But the bottom line is that I was able to lose a significant amount of weight and immeasurably improve my health, yet still maintain my appetite, my taste, my enjoyment of food, and the wherewithal to sample almost anything in modest quantity. That is a great gift, and I am everlastingly grateful.

## Stephenson's Bar-B-Q

11964 N.C. 50 North
Willow Spring, N.C. 27592
919-894-4530
Lunch and dinner, Monday through Saturday

First of all, you may have trouble finding the Wake County community of Willow Spring on a map. Second, a lot of maps spell it Willow *Springs*, which the post office swears is wrong. Third, Stephenson's, except for mail delivery purposes, isn't even in Willow Spring but rather ten miles away in Johnston County. Actually, the restaurant is smack in the middle of a rural no man's land where Wake, Harnett, and Johnston counties meet about halfway between Benson and Garner, and midway between Fuquay-Varina and Smithfield. But regardless of being well off the beaten track, Stephenson's is usually packed at lunch and dinner, which tells you pretty much everything you need to know right up front.

Back in the mid-1950s, the late Paul Stephenson was a farmer—as well as a talented bluegrass musician—who didn't have any barbecue experience. One day, a man showed up and bought fourteen of his hogs for eleven cents a pound. "I got to thinking, who's making the money on these pigs?" Stephenson remembered. "He was going to chop 'em up into sandwiches and come out smelling like roses. And I decided I'd a whole lot rather smell like roses than what I smelled like at the time, so I really started thinking hard about getting into the barbecue business."

In due time, Stephenson managed to get out of farming and into the business of serving the public. The new restaurant seemed like a perfect place to teach the values he wanted to pass along to his young family. When Paul's two sons, Andy and Wayne, were growing up and playing baseball, their father convinced them that chopping barbecue would build up their hand and arm muscles, giving them more heat on their fastball and a better break on their curve. The two obviously embraced that notion wholeheartedly, as the center of the restaurant's old butcher block, now on display in the vestibule, is hollowed out like a wooden bowl from all the spirited barbecue chopping it absorbed. The training must have

Stephenson's Bar-B-Q,
Willow Spring

Stephenson's original chopping block is on display in the foyer.

worked pretty well, since Wayne went on to become an all-state high-school pitcher.

That early chopping paid off for Andy, too. After several years in the family nursery business adjacent to the restaurant (which Wayne now operates), he has run the restaurant following the retirement, then the death, of his father. Andy's wife, Lynn, also has a major role at the restaurant. "The best thing about our restaurant," Lynn says, "is the family atmosphere among the owners, workers, and customers. We're down-to-earth, and the people who eat here are, too." Most of the kitchen workers have been at Stephenson's for many years. Tending the heavy pork shoulders on the hot, smoky pits has always been considered a man's job. The ladies in the kitchen are responsible for the home-cooked vegetables and the weekly specials—like spareribs and chicken and pastry—that have made Stephenson's famous in the area.

Stephenson's uses hardwood charcoal in its pits, rather than oak or hickory coals. Andy is convinced that the charcoal actually gives the meat a smokier flavor and better taste than could be attained from wood. The pork shoulders begin cooking during the day,

but Andy has learned that the meat absorbs an extra measure of wood-smoked taste if it's left on the pits overnight to continue roasting very slowly as the charcoal briquettes burn out.

Even though it's prepared from pork shoulders rather than the whole hog, and even though it isn't as finely chopped as some of the barbecue in the region, the 'cue here is eastern-style in its salt, vinegar, and pepper seasoning. Andy tends to chop the lean, light-colored chunks of what the family calls "beautiful meat" from the shoulder fairly coarsely, while the crusty, brown outside layer is more finely chopped to add flavor and texture throughout the mixture. A small amount of fat scraped from the inside of the skin is also added, since this is where most of the wood-smoked flavor is concentrated. But by anyone's standard, this is still very lean barbecue. The typical Stephenson's barbecue plate is accompanied by coleslaw, boiled potatoes in a mild, tomato-flavored base, and hush puppies with a touch of onion, all well prepared and appetizing.

As good as the barbecue is at Stephenson's, you'll be missing out if you don't also explore the other menu offerings. Neither the barbecued chicken (prepared every day) nor the pork ribs (prepared Thursday through Saturday) are pit-cooked. Instead, they're slowly roasted in the oven and smothered in flavorful tomato-based sauce until the meat can easily be cut with a fork alone. These specialties are available with a wide range of country-style vegetables, depending on the season.

To enjoy Stephenson's biggest hit aside from the barbecue, you'll want to seek out the restaurant on a Thursday—the day of the week when chicken and pastry has been served for nearly thirty years. Stewing hens are slowly cooked in a large pot, then taken from the stock so the skin and bones can be removed. The chicken is then shredded, added back into the delicious broth, and layered with strips of hand-rolled pastry. This is simply some of the best chicken and pastry you will ever experience.

Stephenson's is a simple, cheerful place with red-checked tablecloths. All the food is served on real plates, rather than on paper or plastic, as is the custom in most barbecue restaurants. Picture windows opening onto a well-landscaped garden area add a peaceful touch to the larger of the two dining rooms. A thriving trade has pushed Stephenson's seating capacity to the limit, and peak periods can be a little hectic, leading to talk of expansion. But in the meantime, the quality of the food and the friendly atmosphere are worth any crowded conditions you might encounter.

## Backyard BBQ Pit
North Carolina Classic

5122 N.C. 55
Durham, N.C. 27713
919-544-9911
http://www.sweetribs.com
Lunch and dinner, Monday through Saturday

First of all, owner Melvin Simmons and his staff want everyone to know that real wood smoke is involved in cooking the authentic eastern North Carolina–style barbecue at Durham's Backyard BBQ Pit. The signage proudly identifies this place as a "smokehouse," and the woodpile and real pits around back further classify it as a genuine, old-fashioned kind of restaurant, with the meat cooking in pits directly over hardwood coals.

The selection of country side dishes and the wide array of fried fish choices also identify the restaurant as sort of a soul-food headquarters, which, together with the tangy, smoky barbecue, ensures that the Backyard BBQ Pit is really, really busy most of the time.

Simmons, who grew up in the community of Belhaven in far eastern North Carolina, cooks that region's whole-hog barbecue in spirit and approach, if not in actual fact, due to some logistical considerations and the size of his pits. While the circumstances of his location demand cooking shoulders and hams, everything else about his barbecue shouts "coastal plain" loud and clear. The 'cue is served *very* well moistened with a well-balanced vinegar-based sauce that has visible flakes of crushed red pepper and a nice touch of sweetness to mellow out its bite. And whereas whole-hog barbecue, with its

mixture of white and dark meat, can tend to be on the dry side without proper care and treatment, the slightly higher fat content of Simmons's shoulders and the amount of sauce used in the kitchen help his barbecue really "cling" together in a pleasant way. An added benefit is the higher-than-normal proportion of chewy bits of "outside brown" meat than is normally found in eastern North Carolina whole-hog barbecue. I can tell you that the combination of outside brown shoulder meat and good eastern sauce makes for a heavenly experience. Melvin Simmons provides a superb example of how good eastern North Carolina–seasoned barbecue can be when it's also cooked over actual wood coals, a practice that is regrettably in decline in the coastal plain but is alive and well at Melvin's place.

You'll find absolutely nothing of note about the décor, ambiance, or cafeteria-line service of the Backyard BBQ Pit, except that

notes, testimonials, and autographs are written on practically every square inch of the walls—which actually gets first-time customers more excited and into an anticipatory mood than any decorating scheme possibly could.

If customers wrote nothing on the walls but accolades about the side dishes, there still wouldn't be any space left. At the time I visited, side dishes included fried cabbage, sweet and white potatoes, fried okra, potato salad, coleslaw, macaroni and cheese, collards, green beans, and—ho-hum—French fries. The fries are quickly forgiven, though, in the pure, unadulterated excellence of the real vegetables and the mac 'n' cheese. While you might expect homemade macaroni and cheese to be baked to the point at which it is well browned and sort of crusty in places, this dish works because of its pure cheesiness. Even though the macaroni is cooked beyond the al dente stage, and even though it doesn't have much of a crunchy topping, the amount of thick, golden, chewy actual melted cheese—not cheese sauce—guarantees raves. Think of the look and texture of a thickly covered and perfectly melted piece of cheese toast and you'll get the idea. Awesome!

The fried cabbage is, if possible, on an even more exalted plane. It's called "fried" because the cabbage is sautéed in some kind of wonderful pork drippings or other health hazard, then further seasoned and simmered/steamed until it's golden in color and has turned to absolute magic on the tongue. Sweet, soft, savory . . . This is cabbage over which you could shed tears of joy.

In addition to barbecue and expertly cooked fried seafood, the restaurant offers smoked chicken (coated with a western-style sauce), tender, country-style beef ribs, and a wonderful-looking fried pork chop dinner I can't wait to sample personally. When I've visited, quite a few people among the mixed Research Triangle Park/blue-collar/family crowd have ordered the pork chops, which tells me everything I need to know about that particular dish.

Neither the Styrofoam takeout containers in which everything is served (whether takeout *or* eat-in) nor the napkin-and-plastic-dinnerware packets nor even the fact that the restaurant is thinking about hooking up with a local vineyard to offer "Swine Wine" detract in the slightest from the terrific and authentic food experience at the Backyard BBQ Pit.

## Bullock's Bar-B-Cue

3330 Quebec Street
Durham, N.C. 27705
919-383-3211
http://www.bullocksbbq.com
Lunch and dinner, Tuesday through Saturday

It's a tribute to the power of the word *barbecue* that an owner will often use it in his restaurant's name even if barbecue is only one among sixty or seventy items he serves. I knew one man who ran a place called Jack's Barbecue that didn't serve barbecue at all.

Since owner Tommy Bullock has specialized for years in catering pig pickings, the word is certainly appropriate for his restaurant. However, Bullock's is more of an emporium of all types of Southern comfort food than it is a barbecue joint. The restaurant's varied, down-home menu is obviously on target because a big crowd is usually waiting for the place to open for lunch. In fact, Bullock's has enjoyed heavy patronage practically since it opened in 1952.

Bullock's has two large dining rooms, plus a glassed-in porch. I have never visited when all three rooms weren't pretty well packed. Despite the constant hubbub in the place, a veteran waitress will quickly bring your drink, run through the daily specials, explain various choices, and take your order with the businesslike voice of a blackjack dealer.

Beginning with North Carolina pork barbecue and barbecued chicken and beef, the menu is extensive. It covers the whole range of country cooking: greens and vegetables of every description, chicken pie, country-style

Bulllock's Bar-B-Cue, Durham

steak, ham, meat loaf, beef tips . . . you name it. You can also order lasagna, roast beef, a number of fried or broiled seafood choices, sandwiches of all types, salads, and more desserts than any of us needs to consider.

Bullock's serves typical eastern-style barbecue, which is finely chopped. Because it isn't pit-cooked, it has no smoky taste. Customers can add the fiery vinegar-and-red-pepper sauce to satisfy their own tastes. Many end up adding salt as well. Sweet, white coleslaw and moderately sweet, onion-flavored hush puppies accompany the barbecue. You can have these same side dishes when you order a plate dinner of crisp, tasty fried chicken or Brunswick stew.

Among the most popular desserts at Bullock's are homemade coconut pie and chocolate pie. The chocolate pie has a deca-

dently rich, smooth filling, a flaky bottom crust, and a gorgeously browned, crisp meringue. The pie alone makes Bullock's worth a try.

After many visits, I have found that the barbecue and other dishes at Bullock's are of a consistently high quality overall. If very little is truly memorable (with the exception of that chocolate pie), I'm always pretty sure that nothing will fall short of the mark either. Although the locals consistently give Bullock's an average score of around seventy-five points out of a possible hundred, you have to remember that practically every time the doors swing open at eleven-thirty in the morning, a crowd is waiting to get in.

## Hog Heaven Barbecue

2419 Guess Road
Durham, N.C. 27705
919-286-7447
http://www.hogheavenbarbecue.com
Lunch and dinner, Monday through Saturday

Hog Heaven, which opened in 2003, is the domain of Mark Johnson, who cut his barbecue teeth in competitive cookoffs. He was a Hillsborough Hog Days winner in 2005 and has several other trophies on display in the restaurant as well, just in case anyone is inclined to question his credentials. They probably wouldn't anyway, and certainly not after reading that Hog Heaven won the City Search Best Triangle Barbecue distinction in 2004 and 2005 and the City Search Best Catering Award in 2007.

Mark understands what holding barbecue on a steam table can do to its freshness. Keeping the barbecue tasting like it just came off the pit is a big deal to him. "You can't chop fifty pounds of barbecue at a time and expect it to be at its best, so we only chop one shoulder at a time, as needed," says Johnson. "You just can't let it sit on the line."

This is unabashedly eastern-style barbecue, even though Mark cooks shoulders rather than whole hogs for space reasons and keeps a Lexington-oriented "dip" on the tables. As seasoned in the kitchen, the 'cue is spicy, tangy, and properly salty. (It's amazing how many restaurateurs don't bother to properly season and salt their barbecue as it's chopped. This really needs to be done, in my opinion, even in restaurants where customers can add more sauce at the table, according to their tastes. If they add sauce to barbecue without enough salt, it still won't taste right.)

Hog Heaven serves traditional eastern boiled potatoes, which Mark Johnson calls "Granny potatoes." Even though they don't have the red pepper or tomato that's sometimes added in the east, they're still the perfect, neutral "pillow" for the piquant barbecue. I also sampled the terrific turnip greens, which were not the least bit bitter, as is sometimes the case.

I had heard through the grapevine that someone from the National Barbecue

Association said Hog Heaven's fried chicken was the best he had ever eaten, so I was expecting a lot—and I wasn't disappointed. The skin and the breading were right, the interior moisture was right, and the texture and "bite" were right—meaning Hog Heaven's bird can get a man in a celebratory mood in a hurry.

And the love that Hog Heaven shows chicken doesn't stop there. The restaurant serves a tasty and popular barbecued chicken *and* something you won't find on every corner: real chicken 'n' pastry. Mark says he can't imagine opening a barbecue restaurant without having chicken 'n' pastry on the menu. But the fact is that even though it's on the menu, there may not be any left in the kitchen for those who dawdle, since Hog Heaven sells out almost every day before closing. This is melt-in-your-mouth chicken wrapped in a cloud.

Johnson also brought over some exceptionally fresh-tasting fried shrimp for me to sample. The light breading and perfect seasoning brought a smile to my face and a heartfelt "Mmmm-mmmm" from my lips, especially since the shrimp weren't overcooked in the slightest.

My experience was topped off with an absolutely delicious banana pudding—homemade, of course.

Being on the barbecue competition circuit helps keep a restaurant operator sharp and on his toes, and the clear beneficiary is the customer. You can't please everyone, but I don't think many will be disappointed in this place.

## Hillsborough BBQ Company

*North Carolina Classic*

236 South Nash Street
Hillsborough, N.C. 27278
919-732-4647
http://hillsboroughbbq.com
Lunch and dinner are served Tuesday through Saturday. Lunch is offered until 3 P.M. on Sunday.

No shortcuts were planned in the launching of Hillsborough BBQ Company. The concept was, from the beginning, to cook barbecue the old-fashioned way, over hardwood coals. Wayne Monk of the legendary Lexington Barbecue invited Hillsborough BBQ founders Tommy Stann and Matt Fox over to look at the design of his pits when they were planning their new restaurant. Today, their brick front-opening pits are similar to Monk's, if smaller. As at Lexington Barbecue, split logs are burned down to coals in a fireplace, and the embers are periodically spread directly beneath the slow-roasting Boston butts, pork ribs, half-chickens, beef briskets, and turkey breasts.

Hillsborough BBQ Company occupies a relatively small storefront space in an old commercial section several blocks from downtown Hillsborough. Although the attractive upscale bar is a break from tradition, the walls are decorated with historic North Carolina barbecue photos. In keeping with those traditional pictures, the place serves authentic Lexington-style barbecued pork shoulder and barbecued chicken but also throws in the ribs and beef brisket in acknowledgment of the increasingly well-

Hillsborough BBQ Company has an inviting interior and is one of only a few North Carolina barbecue restaurants with bar service.

traveled tastes of so many barbecue fans.

The hand-chopped meat from the Boston butts—the upper half of the pork shoulder—has the incomparable taste that comes only when fat and juices from the meat drip directly onto the winking coals below, adding a layer of "grill" flavor to the intense smoky taste. Much of what is billed as wood-cooked or wood-fired barbecue today amounts to "smoking," whereby the meat is cooked in a chamber filled with smoke and heat that is offset from the actual coals, so there's none of that wonderful hissing and dripping. Hillsborough BBQ Company's traditional North Carolina pit uses direct heat, rather than indirect, and the flavor of the pork is improved immeasurably as a result. Patrons can choose either creamy white coleslaw or the "kickier" red variety to complement their barbecue plates or sandwiches.

The high-quality pork ribs are served with a good char and a thick glaze of sweet barbecue sauce. When you bite into one of them, the remaining meat will stay in place on the bone, rather than falling onto the table or your shirt. I give the restaurant high marks for flavor, consistency, and appearance.

The attractive beef brisket slices are tender but hold together well and are absolutely loaded with smoke and grill flavor from the wood pits. Since brisket is something of a Western and Midwestern specialty, it's only appropriate that Hillsborough offers what it calls a "Midwestern" sauce to go with it.

The barbecued chicken is also cooked to an extremely tender stage without becoming dried out, so that plenty of juice still flows when you cut or bite into it.

The side dishes are a real plus at this restaurant. I particularly enjoyed the over-roasted green beans, a tasty Southern corn pudding (not often found except on home tables), sweet, meat-seasoned collard greens, and a macaroni and cheese that really held together well, thanks to copious amounts of white cheddar. Some unusual touches are available as well, such as a wedge salad topped with crumbled Gorgonzola cheese and crunchy bits of pork skin.

The homemade desserts are another high point at Hillsborough BBQ Company. I sampled an awesome Key lime pie, a dark, complex pecan pie, strawberry-rhubarb pie (one of my personal favorites), and a seasonal peach pie. The banana pudding is also delectable.

Stann and Fox also have part-ownership in an appealing beverage gallery, deli, and gift shop known as The Depot, located down the street from their barbecue restaurant. Specialty sandwiches at The Depot feature meats that are smoked on their barbecue pits.

Stann and Fox have cooked in barbecue competitions. They remain committed to cooking with real wood coals, which is a lot more work and is more time consuming than other methods of producing acceptable barbecue. It's really encouraging to see barbecue restaurants opening in our hurried culture that are devoted to a way of cooking that absolutely can't be rushed. I highly recommend Hillsborough BBQ Company.

## Allen & Son Barbeque

6203 Millhouse Road (at N.C. 86)
Chapel Hill, N.C. 27516
919-942-7576
Lunch and dinner, Tuesday through Saturday

What makes a guy like Keith Allen keep the faith? No man in North Carolina works any harder to produce superb barbecue, and the fact that he hasn't reaped the financial rewards or basked in the praise afforded some other, better-known restaurateurs has never deterred him from his single-minded purity of purpose. No shortcuts. "This business of cooking barbecue has to be done a certain way—it has to be done *right*," he insists. "When we get so that we can't do it the right way, we'll just pull the name off the sign and go home."

Allen stands about six-foot-three and has the shoulders of a frontiersman, broad enough to carry the burden of doing what others will not in his pursuit of excellence. Almost any barbecue man will tell you that the hickory wood required to slow-cook pork to perfection is increasingly hard to find. Allen came to that realization many years ago, so he started searching for the wood and cutting and hauling it himself, a brutally demanding labor of love that continues today. That still leaves the chore of reducing the pile of hickory logs he accumulates out back—tree trunks, really—into pieces small enough to work with.

"We split it ourselves," Allen told me on my first visit.

"With what," I wanted to know, "a log splitter?"

"Yeah, this is our log splitter right here," Allen chuckled, picking up a steel wedge and a maul—a cross between an ax and a sledgehammer. See who we're dealing with here? A guy who cuts and splits his barbecue-cooking wood *by hand*. And once it's split, he gathers it up by the armful and carries it twenty or thirty feet to the big fireplace between the two pits, where the forty-inch sections burn down into coals suitable for shoveling periodically beneath the cooking meat. Allen has had help at certain times with this task and has done it by himself at others, but it has always been done the same way.

A couple of other places have borne the Allen & Son name, but the rather unprepos-

Allen & Son Barbeque, Chapel Hill

sessing site on N.C. 86 six miles north of Chapel Hill toward Hillsborough is the spot where the real art is created. The original Allen & Son restaurant, founded by Keith's father, is located on U.S. 15-501 south of Chapel Hill near Bynum. Now leased out under separate management, it serves electrically cooked barbecue. A former Allen & Son location on N.C. 54 just south of Interstate 85 at Graham has been closed for many years. "We just couldn't cook with wood and keep all the places open. It's too much work," says Keith Allen. "We decided to concentrate on really doing it right at this one place."

Allen worked in the original restaurant as a youngster. He was attending UNC–Chapel Hill and working part-time as a meat cutter when he heard that the former Turner's Barbecue was for sale. "I came out, looked around, and bought this place on my lunch hour from the A&P," he remembers, "and then I went back and told my father that I had a barbecue place, too." He's been here for over four decades. While the location on

N.C. 86 between Chapel Hill and Hillsborough is not exactly prime in terms of traffic, Allen has built up a nationally legendary business, which you might not know simply by surveying the day-to-day customer flow. Hardly a week goes by that some food writer, broadcast producer, or blogger doesn't fly into Raleigh-Durham from New York or elsewhere in the Northeast and head immediately to Allen & Son, either purely for a barbecue fix or to gather material for a story. Keith has been featured and interviewed by practically everyone by now. His old-fashioned methods have made him a North Carolina barbecue icon.

The propane tanks on Allen's portable barbecue cookers might lead his party patrons to the erroneous conclusion that he has opted for this easier cooking method. But in fact, the gas burners simply serve to keep the barbecued pigs warm at catering sites. In this crossover area between east and Piedmont, whole or half hogs are still in demand for catered pig pickings. Along with the pork shoulders preferred for the chopped barbecue served in the restaurant, whole and half hogs are lovingly cooked over pure hickory coals on the restaurant's pits. Both are tended on an innovative roll-out rack, which greatly simplifies the task of turning the meat during the cooking process. Some barbecuers like to mix a little green hickory or oak with their dry wood, but Allen is strictly a dry-wood man. He likes to shovel in and smooth out his first bed of coals of the day and get the pit hot before he ever rolls the rack containing the meat over the embers. From then on, he sprinkles coals sparingly under the shoulders about every thirty minutes. Because the pit is preheated, his pork is usually falling off the bone in around seven hours. While the shoulders are transformed almost instantly into chopped, seasoned barbecue while they're still smoking hot from the pit, a roasted whole or half hog for a pig picking must present an attractive, appetizing appearance to party guests. It's here that Allen displays the fruits of his experience, proudly pulling from the pit's smoky darkness a crusty, mahogany-hued side of pork without a single charred spot, guaranteed to delight even the most hard-eyed judge of the barbecuer's craft.

Allen & Son occupies the corner of a wooded lot. The small cinder-block building has a gravel parking lot and a weathered metal sign. Though a bit weathered as well, the interior décor is comfortable, with cream-colored walls, dark green tablecloths, and touches of pine paneling. It looks much the same as it always has, despite some rebuilding after a fire years ago.

The barbecue plates—chopped barbecue, coleslaw, and hush puppies—are available with or without French fries. I recommend you order your meal *with*, because they aren't the usual frozen steak fries or crinkle-cuts. Instead, wonder of wonders, they're the real thing: homemade, chunky, skin-on strips cut from large baking-type potatoes and deep-fried to a wonderful shade of brown that's about thirty seconds past the "golden" stage. The generous mound of glistening fries spilling off the plate is reason enough for a trip to Allen & Son. But they're just a warm-up for the barbecue, which is coarsely chopped into meltingly tender chunks, sprinkled through with shreds of deep brown, chewy outside meat, not skin. The wood-smoke taste from pure hickory seems to be a touch more intense than that from other hardwoods such as oak, and Allen's barbecue has a manly robustness without being overly smoky. The peppery sauce mixed into the chopped meat is thin, dark red, and slightly sweet, but the tang of the vinegar is softened by a slight touch of melted butter or shortening, giving the barbecue an attractive, slightly shiny glaze. No tomato is in the sauce, even though it resembles a Lexington-style "dip" in appearance. The taste, however, says eastern North Carolina.

Keith Allen has the most aggressive barbecue-chopping style I've ever witnessed. Working with insulated rubber gloves, he carries the shoulders from the pits to the kitchen and quickly strips steaming-hot meat from five or six shoulders at a time, until he has a pyramid of pork chunks perhaps three feet across and a foot high. Seizing two machete-shaped cleavers called "lamb break-ers"—slightly longer and narrower than the usual barbecue-chopping implements—Allen plants his feet in a wide stance and begins chopping with both arms in a rapid, rhythmic cadence, never slowing or faltering until the entire mound of meat has been turned into chopped barbecue ready for seasoning. Whether from weightlifting or years of handling the heavy steel cleavers, Allen's arms and shoulders are thickly muscled. It takes him only a few minutes to chop an entire day's supply of barbecue.

Allen serves one of the tastiest and most authentic versions of Brunswick stew I've run across. I don't like most of the Brunswick stew available in the Piedmont, especially the stuff sold by churches and other fundraising groups, although I usually buy it just to be supportive. To my way of thinking, far too many extraneous meats and vegetables—mostly canned—find their way into these free-spirited concoctions. But Allen stays with the traditional ingredients: chicken, beef, tomatoes, potatoes, corn, and lima beans. His stew is properly thick and satisfying, and the vegetables are not cooked into an unidentifiable mush, as is often the case. Brunswick stew is often slightly sweet, usually because of the use of cream-style corn, but Allen's version is straightforward meat and vegetables, with no detectable added sugar. His recipe offers a slight but interesting change from the stew that's a common side dish in barbecue houses east of Raleigh.

*Don't* fill up on hush puppies at Allen & Son, because they can't hold a candle to Keith Allen's delectable homemade desserts. Most barbecue places I've visited offer banana pudding and fruit cobblers, and some truly outstanding examples of each are sold around the state. But Allen's dessert list is unique among barbecue restaurants. I sampled pecan pie with a perfect flaky crust and a rich, moist, not-too-sticky filling that was obviously freshly made. The pie was topped with a scoop of homemade vanilla ice cream that had a delightfully icy, almost grainy texture, assuring me that only fresh milk, cream, eggs, sugar, and vanilla went into it, not the tree sap known as guar gum or xanthan gum that commercial ice-cream producers include to produce a bland, phony smoothness. Allen also offers cream cheese pound cake (with cream cheese icing), chess and blueberry pies, cobblers, and a seldom-seen item that's one of my personal favorites at home—bread pudding, moistened bread baked into a rich custard, with plenty of plump, juicy raisins.

If Keith Allen were interested in volume or profits alone, he would have opted out of the barbecue business long ago. In fact, he has other business interests that allow him to keep cooking barbecue in the time-honored way he loves. His devotion to tradition has made him famous in the insular world of barbecue writers and enthusiasts from all around the country, where he is probably better known than in his own backyard. But in fact, *any* barbecue lover who would like to pass along a nod of appreciation for hard work and tradition should make Allen & Son a regular stopping place.

## The Pig

630 Weaver Dairy Road, #101
Chapel Hill, N.C. 27514
919-942-1133
http://www.thepigrestaurant.com
Lunch and dinner, Monday through Saturday

At first glance, The Pig has a little too much of a suburban look to be perceived as a traditional barbecue joint. But the whole-hog barbecue, roasted in hunks in an electric smoker, is actually a tasty and pretty mainstream example of eastern North Carolina 'cue. In the barbecue tray I sampled, the meat was tender, moist, and pleasantly textured and had quite a few dark brown, chewy bits mixed in. It had a nice but not overpowering smoky taste without being overly reddened, as sometimes happens in wood-chip smokers. The slightly sweetened vinegar sauce, which had no discernable tomato added, provided a finish that would be well received in any small town or rural stretch of the coastal plain.

The pork comes from North Carolina pasture-raised, Animal Welfare Approved pigs, free of hormones and antibiotics.

The personable young owner of The Pig, Sam Suchoff, has created a blend of traditional and artsy menu touches that's hardly unexpected in a town like Chapel Hill. The coleslaw, for example, is a straightforward white slaw that's a little less sweet than most; it offers a nice balance to the barbecue and sauce. But the other normal accompaniment on a tray of barbecue at The Pig—a pile of sweet, crispy pickle slices—is seldom found elsewhere in North Carolina, or indeed any-

where this side of Kentucky. The pickles, incidentally, are a holdover from The Barbecue Joint, a previous restaurant in the building. They much more closely resemble fresh cucumber slices than do most pickles.

The tiny hush puppies are light and airy—almost like fried dumplings or dough-nut holes—and have less discernable corn-meal taste than most. They're a pleasant alternative to their more substantial cousins at other barbecue places.

Side dishes include traditional offerings such as macaroni and cheese, baked beans, fried okra, French fries, potato salad, and collards. But you can also get a serving of crunchy sprouts 'n' 'shrooms or fried green tomatoes. The collards, served leafy rather than chopped, are cooked in a stock that contains smoked pigs' feet and pig tails, universally considered prime flavoring agents for collards. They're tender and delicious.

The Pig is also known for its all-pork hot dogs, cooked in the smoker. On Wednesdays and Saturdays at the Carrboro Farmers' Market, The Pig serves these signature dogs on buns baked fresh by another market vendor. They're served on commercial buns at the restaurant.

The well-used smoker at The Pig also turns out beef brisket, ribs, cola-marinated pork belly (which makes a terrific sandwich), and barbecued tempeh. Tempeh is made from cooked and slightly fermented soybeans. Formed in a patty, it's similar to a firm veggie burger. Tempeh has a mild, nutty flavor that is enhanced by smoke and barbecue sauce.

The Pig's chalkboard menu usually includes both standards and specials.
*Photo by Jes Gearing*

One side of The Pig's chalkboard menu changes frequently. On the day I visited, it featured pimento cheese fries, a pastrami on rye sandwich, an andouille sausage and chicken gumbo, a shitake mushroom po' boy sandwich, and a lamb merguez (sausage) bowl containing locally raised lamb. The more permanent side of the menu includes fried chicken, fried catfish, and homemade bologna, in addition to the chopped barbecue, other smoked meats, and side dishes.

The place is friendly to vegetarians. The popular pickle plate includes pickled beets, string beans, tomatoes, cukes, and eggs. Beets are also featured in an attractive salad, where they're topped with blue cheese crumbles. The "PLT" (a sweet potato, lettuce, and tomato sandwich) is another tasty veggie favorite.

Desserts include banana pudding, chocolate layer cake, and coconut cake, plus occasional specials. Bottled beer, juices, and soft drinks are available.

The restaurant isn't large. It has about a dozen small tables, a few seats at the counter, and a compact kitchen and food preparation area. All in all, the place provides customers with a cozy, cheerful vibe. The prices are definitely on the high side—but hey, it's Chapel Hill, after all. The extra touches seem to furnish good value for the money.

## Allen & Son Bar-B-Que

5650 U.S. 15-501 North
Pittsboro, N.C. 27312
919-542-2294
Lunch and dinner, Tuesday through Saturday

Established by Henry Hearne in 1950, this place became the first location of Allen & Son Bar-B-Que after James Allen purchased it from Hearne in the early 1960s. Recently, it has often been referred to as the "other" location, particularly since James's son Keith began attracting customers to his Chapel Hill Allen & Son by insisting—unlike this restaurant—on cooking barbecue over pure hickory coals.

Although it has a Pittsboro mailing address, this place is actually located in the community of Bynum, halfway between Chapel Hill and Pittsboro. Since the pork shoulders are now roasted on a gas-fired pit, the old, original pit is used only for burning trash. Still, the place has its share of enthusiastic supporters and was listed as a top spot for barbecue in a 2001 issue of *Travel* magazine.

The takeout window, which faces U.S. 15-501, is where much of the action takes place, especially among customers ordering barbecue sandwiches and the restaurant's popular milkshakes. Some customers, though, prefer to come inside to what a wooden sign identifies as the "Dinning Room," located toward the rear of the building.

The barbecue here is actually pretty doggone good, despite the changeover to cooking with gas. Lacking the intense hickory flavor that characterizes the meat at the Chapel Hill restaurant, the chopped pork is nonetheless tender and moist. The sauce, which has no tomato paste, leaves a nice peppery aftertaste and best complements the meat when sprinkled on a sandwich topped with coleslaw. (In fact, the sauce may be practically the same as that used by Keith Allen at his place.) The homemade, skins-on French fries are a tasty treat as well.

Frankly, the prices seem pretty steep, especially compared to those at other res-

Allen & Son Bar-B-Que,
Pittsboro

taurants that use labor-saving gas or electric pits.

The Allen & Son name is a proud one in North Carolina barbecue circles, but the Bynum restaurant seems to be trading on the reputation established here earlier by James Allen and continued by Keith Allen in Chapel Hill. If you're in the neighborhood, though, it's definitely worth checking out.

## Hursey's Pig Pickin' Bar-B-Q

http://hurseysbarbecue.com
Lunch and dinner, Monday through Saturday

1834 South Church Street
Burlington, N.C. 27215
336-226-1694

Second location:
1234 South Main Street (N.C. 87)
Graham, N.C. 27215
336-570-3838

Hursey's has been a big name in the barbecue wholesale business for decades, servicing restaurants, supermarkets, and institutional customers, both directly and through several major meat distributors. The family didn't have what could be called a high-profile barbecue restaurant until 1985, when Charles Hursey opened his place on the corner of South Church Street and Alamance Road near downtown Burlington. There, from atop a knoll, the smoke from Hursey's wood-fired pits and the enchanting aroma of roasting pork still float down over a busy in-

tersection, mesmerizing drivers with images of savory barbecue and causing them to turn obediently into the parking lot in front of Hursey's cheerful country-style brick building. Another Hursey's is located on N.C. 87 in Graham, this one a large, barnlike structure run by Hursey's son Chuck.

Inside the Burlington restaurant, the domain of a younger Hursey son, Chris, the photographs, newspaper articles, and awards displayed around the foyer reflect the family's generations in the barbecue business. This is one of only a handful of North Carolina restaurants east of Greensboro where barbecue is slow-cooked over real hardwood coals most of the time, although Hursey's does have electric pits to help during busy periods. Hursey's continues to build on a solid reputation for both quality restaurant fare and efficient catering. The place is normally packed at peak periods, particularly at lunchtime. Meanwhile, the wholesale business, located in a facility just north of Burlington, continues to prosper, keeping alive a tradition begun in 1949, when Charles's mother, Daisy, obtained the first barbecue wholesaler's license granted in North Carolina.

Charles Hursey relates that the family tradition began when his grandfather started to cook hogs in his backyard as a hobby. Hursey's father, Sylvester, learned the basic technique as a child, but the business didn't really get started until Sylvester was a full-grown adult. Charles, a sober, churchgoing man whose children all graduated from Alamance Christian School, tells the story—a little sheepishly—this way: "When my daddy was in his thirties or so, he was in his backyard with some friends, and they was drinkin' a little bit, so they decided to cook some hogs. Well, people were wanting to buy the meat, and they sold all of it, in advance, before those hogs were even done. So he said, 'If I can do that drinkin', I know I can do it sober.' "

Sylvester built a little tin building maybe fourteen feet by eighteen feet in the backyard, put up a swing nearby so the parents could keep an eye on Charles and his younger brother, Larry, and started cooking one hog per week. During that time, Sylvester used a sauce recipe he got from his father. But one night, according to Charles, Sylvester won the recipe for a competitor's sauce in a poker game. Sylvester decided to combine the two recipes, thus creating the Hursey's sauce that is still used today.

It wasn't long before the business outgrew the backyard pit, so the Hurseys bought a little café in the town of Gibsonville, near Burlington, and built two barbecue pits in the back to handle the growing volume. In addition to the café trade, the Hurseys built a sizable wholesale business, with Daisy Hursey using a station wagon to make deliveries all over the region.

Charles began learning the business by helping his parents after school and during the summer. As soon as he graduated from high school in 1960, he plunged full-time into the family enterprise, quickly taking over the operation of the Gibsonville restaurant and the wholesale business. In 1966, he also began running the takeout barbecue counter in Burlington that his father had opened several years earlier.

In 1960, one of Charles Hursey's first acts as manager of the Gibsonville café was to welcome blacks through the front door as regular customers. At that time, most similar restaurants still followed Jim Crow customs that required African-Americans to place takeout orders around back. Later, when he began running the Burlington takeout stand, which was located in a predominately black neighborhood, his reputation for equal treatment preceded him, and his place was one of only a few spots in town where black and white customers regularly rubbed elbows. When ugly racial incidents broke out at nearby Williams High School in the late 1960s, the unrest spread. One evening, a virtual riot occurred in the neighborhood around Hursey's barbecue counter. The next morning when Charles returned to work, nearly every store in the neighborhood had been vandalized and had windows smashed, but his place was untouched. He later heard that word had been passed among the rioters to spare Hursey's, possibly so neighborhood residents would have someplace to eat the next day. Today, Hursey is proud of this legacy of equality. "We treated everybody fair and right, like it's supposed to be," he says.

Although Charles's father and grandfather cooked whole hogs in the early days, the Hursey restaurants follow the prevailing Piedmont custom and roast pork shoulders. The menu offers both chopped and what Hursey calls "pig-pickin' barbecue"—hunks of meat that have been either sliced or pulled by hand from the shoulder. The regular barbecue is just a little too finely chopped for my taste—although many customers prefer it that way. However, the "pig-pickin'" meat has a substantial texture that invites a real bite, as well as being extremely tender and full of flavor.

The sauce is a mild but interesting blend between the hot vinegar of the east and the sugar-and-tomato-added sauces popular around Lexington. This isn't surprising, considering Burlington's location almost on the dividing line between the two barbecue styles. The sauce has achieved a loyal following. Hursey tells of a young fellow from Burlington who accepted a job with a company in Japan and was invited to dinner one evening by his boss, a Japanese businessman. As the evening progressed, the boss leaned across the table and murmured that he was getting ready to bring out something he unveiled only on special occasions. Expecting some sort of wine or liquor, the young man was

Interior of Hursey's Pig Pickin' Bar-B-Q, Graham

flabbergasted to see the businessman reverently produce a bottle of Hursey's Barbecue Sauce—made right in the employee's North Carolina hometown.

Between the meat coming off the grill and the sauce going on the meat, Hursey's came up with the right taste combination to be judged the winner of the 1984 North–South Carolina Barbecue Bowl competition, held in Washington, D.C. But its biggest claim to fame has come from serving barbecue to Bill Clinton, George Bush, and Ronald Reagan. The barbecue that went to President Clinton and President Reagan was delivered by presidential staffers, who considered their own meals at Hursey's so good that they wanted to take some barbecue back to their bosses in Washington. President Bush ate his Hursey's barbecue during the 1992 campaign. While Bush was in Burlington for a campaign stop, Hursey's delivered a large order of barbecue directly to the president's train. After the Secret Service gave the box of barbecue and fixings the once-over, it was loaded on the train. Charles later heard that the president enjoyed his barbecue before the train even reached Raleigh.

In addition to hardwood-cooked pork, the Hursey restaurants are known around the area for what they call "broasted" chicken, which is really fried chicken cooked in some sort of pressure cooker that's supposed to keep it from getting excessively greasy. Now, I firmly believe fried chicken should be cooked in a heavy skillet, but I can certainly attest in the most complimentary way possible that Hursey's chicken tastes pleasantly greasy, just

the way wonderful fried chicken is supposed to. My wife and I have agreed after several tailgate gatherings that it's our favorite take-out chicken.

While other barbecue places are known for their fruit cobblers or banana pudding, Hursey's serves firm, nicely browned, well-seasoned fried apple turnovers. Quite a few people pull through Hursey's "Pig Up" window just for a sack of the warm fried pies.

## Short Sugar's Pit Bar-B-Q

1328 South Scales Street
Reidsville, N.C. 27320
336-342-7487
http://shortsugarsbar-b-q.com
Breakfast, lunch, and dinner,
  Monday through Saturday

Second location:
  2215 Riverside Drive
  Danville, Va. 24540
  434-793-4800

Of all the barbecue restaurants in America, Short Sugar's must have the greatest name. Johnny, Clyde, and Eldridge Overby had planned to call their new business the Overby Brothers Drive-In. But two days before it was to open in June 1949, Eldridge was killed in an auto accident. Instead of using the original name, Johnny and Clyde decided to honor their brother, who had been known as "Short Sugar," by naming the place after him alone. Now, the stories vary as to why Eldridge had that particular nickname. It seems well established that he was short,

Short Sugar's Pit
Bar-B-Q, Reidsville

which takes care of the first half. But as for "Sugar," time has muddled people's recollections of whether it was because Eldridge was exceptionally friendly and had an attractive laugh or whether it was because the ladies considered him kind of cute. In any case, even though Eldridge didn't live to see the restaurant open, his nickname has certainly been immortalized, since it's the one thing no one ever forgets about the place.

Today, Short Sugar's sits at the same location and still looks like a 1950s-style teenage hangout, which is exactly what it became on the first day it was open. It even has drive-in parking spaces where customers still can get curb service just by tooting their horns. And although Short Sugar's may not be a hot gathering spot for the current students of Reidsville High School, the folks who grew up in town during the 1950s, 1960s, and 1970s still flock to the place, as do seekers from all over central North Carolina who've heard about the barbecue and had their interest piqued by the name.

As a reporter for WFMY-TV in Greensboro during the 1970s, I was assigned to cover Rockingham County for a while, which meant that I made frequent lunch stops at

both Short Sugar's in Reidsville and Fuzzy's in Madison—the two spots that anyone would tell you had the best barbecue in the northern Piedmont. Part of the job of covering the largely rural county involved keeping up with the local daily and weekly newspapers. I'd sometimes spend part of a slow day sitting in Short Sugar's reading the *Reidsville Review* and listening for local gossip that might develop into a story.

Reidsville was a tobacco center. Unfiltered Lucky Strike cigarettes were manufactured at the big American Tobacco Company factory in the middle of town for more than fifty years. The town's minor-league baseball team during the 1940s and 1950s was even called the Reidsville Luckies. Fans used to marvel over the exploits of players like home-run slugger Leo "Muscle" Shoals as they enjoyed their barbecue sandwiches at Short Sugar's. Now, both the team and the company that inspired its name are gone, and the plant—operated for a while by Brown & Williamson—is defunct. Reidsville is struggling to stay afloat and diversify its economic base. It's sobering to think how the community's spirits might sag if anything ever happened to Short Sugar's.

At a time when the world seems to be shifting beneath their feet, it must be comforting for Reidsville natives to grab a stool at Short Sugar's counter and see things just as they have been for many decades. Breakfast preparation cranks up by three-thirty in the morning six days a week—biscuits, bacon, sausage, and grits. And do the folks here ever know how barbecue ought to be prepared! Short Sugar's chops or slices only what pork it needs at the moment, so the meat will taste fresh. The restaurant pit-cooks its barbecue (hams for sliced, shoulders for chopped) over hickory coals in two small pits located near enough to the counter so that everyone can watch when it's time to turn the meat or spread more coals. The barbecue is served with a thin, dark sauce that's mixed according to the original recipe by owner David Wilson. Short Sugar's sauce, said to be the key reason for the barbecue's reputation, seems to have less ketchup or tomato paste than some of the popular Piedmont "dips." The definite presence of both sugar and Worcestershire sauce adds a heated pungency to the mixture. The sauce and the meat obviously blended well on the judges' palates during the 1982 Barbecue Bowl cookoff between North and South Carolina, held in Washington, D.C., since Short Sugar's was the first restaurant from either state to be crowned champion. (In a maddening bit of political correctness, the inaugural event the previous year had been declared a tie.)

While Short Sugar's is justly famous for both its sliced and chopped barbecue—both of which are lean, tender, and smoky

tasting—I can't quite understand the community's taste for "minced" barbecue. This is pork chopped ultrafine and served swimming in sauce—a sort of barbecue chili, if you will. The only other place I've encountered minced barbecue is Bridges Barbecue Lodge in Shelby, and I can't say I really enjoyed pork served in this form at either place. Now, if you're a local who's fond of this particular specialty, well, God bless. But if you aren't already hooked, I'd suggest you enjoy Short Sugar's notable barbecue in its most delicious and appetizing forms—either chopped or sliced.

The hot dogs and burgers at this place are immensely popular as well.

## Fuzzy's Pit-Cooked Bar-B-Q
407 North Highway Street (U.S. 220 Business)
Madison, N.C. 27025
336-427-4130
Lunch and dinner daily

Fuzzy's has been serving authentic hickory-cooked barbecue since 1954, when it was opened by T. H. "Fuzzy" Nelson. Because of its out-of-the-way location twenty-five miles north of Greensboro in Madison, it hasn't developed the statewide reputation enjoyed by some of North Carolina's other barbecue restaurants, but it is a household name to barbecue lovers from the Triad area and the northern Piedmont.

Coincidentally, two fairly well-publicized attempts to market North Carolina barbecue in New York City both happened to involve Fuzzy's. Neither venture was successful, but the restaurant never missed a beat among its fans in the local area. It continues to be very much a part of the ebb and flow of ordinary life in western Rockingham County.

"Barbecue in *New York City*?" you can almost hear North Carolinians snarl. Well, it seems that New York talk-radio host Barry Farber, a native of Greensboro, got the idea back in 1977 that North Carolina barbecue would sweep New Yorkers off their feet, if only a way could be found to properly introduce them to the delicacy. Obviously, pit-cooking pork in the middle of Manhattan was out of the question, so the next best thing was to find a supplier in North Carolina who would prepare the barbecue, then ship it overnight to New York. Farber remembered

Fuzzy's from his Greensboro days and talked a friend who owned a Times Square building into flying down for a taste test. The friend fell hard for the barbecue. The would-be importers found that Fuzzy's had an existing wholesale branch that could easily handle the preparation and shipment. The problem was that the friend's ground-floor space on Times Square was leased to a proprietor selling Greek specialties and bagels. The building's owner basically coerced his tenant, who was behind on his rent, into adding North Carolina barbecue to his menu. However, the reluctant restaurateur was apparently content to serve the alien chopped pork on cold buns, often with no coleslaw. Outraged Tar Heels living in New York complained that the place was giving North Carolina barbecue a bad name. The experiment came to an abrupt end

Fuzzy's Pit-Cooked Bar-B-Q, Madison

when Farber took a friend by for a sandwich and the two were served barbecue—pork barbecue!—on a bagel.

Ten years later, veteran magazine and television model Zacki Murphy, a Hillsborough native and unabashed barbecue lover, hired vendors to sell North Carolina barbecue sandwiches from a pushcart on Fifth Avenue. Between modeling assignments, she even occasionally donned suspender overalls to fill in for the cart operators. Like Farber, Murphy arranged for Fuzzy's wholesale operation to cook the barbecue over an open pit, but the chopped pork was then mixed with her own special Lexington-style sauce before it was fast-frozen for shipment to New York. The vending-cart operation was short-lived. Although Murphy later tried selling her trademark barbecue from a small storefront-type restaurant, the venture was plagued by problems with unreliable help and high overhead.

It may be that a barbecue place, with its unhurried pace and atmosphere of conviviality and trust, just isn't suited for the mean streets of a place like New York. But through the years, Fuzzy's seems to have done just fine back home in Madison. Aside from some minor remodeling and refurbishing, the restaurant remains basically unchanged. The exterior still looks much as it has for the past forty years or so, the same curb service is available, local businessmen in suits still crowd the counter at lunchtime, and the pork hams and shoulders are still cooked for long hours over hickory wood. Sheriff's deputies and highway-patrol troopers who have eaten regularly at Fuzzy's for a quarter-century still occupy their favorite booths and stools several days each week. One of those officers told me with a straight face that if a felon in custody begged for a last meal at Fuzzy's, he'd bring the miscreant in for one final sandwich before carting him off to jail.

Chopped barbecue is prepared from shoulders at Fuzzy's, while the whiter meat from pork hams is preferred for sliced barbecue, which is fairly popular in these parts. The chopped barbecue is cut very fine, the way you'd expect to find it in the eastern half of the state. But the similarity ends there, because unlike its eastern cousin, Fuzzy's chopped barbecue is as heavily moistened by sauce as any I've encountered in North Carolina. The sauce, which has always been considered the real secret to the barbecue at Fuzzy's, is a mild and fairly sweet Lexington-style blend with tomato ketchup added to a vinegar base. Now, if I were mixing up the barbecue, I might not stir in quite as much sauce as do the folks who run Fuzzy's, but they certainly know their customers' tastes better than I do. Ah, well . . . I believe this moist barbecue would go better on a nice, soft bun—topped with some of Fuzzy's tart, peppery coleslaw—than in a plain barbecue tray, which is what I ordered on my last visit. Next time, I'll order a sandwich and just enjoy the extra sauce as a special local touch. When in Rome . . .

You'll like the fresh-tasting hush puppies at Fuzzy's. Or perhaps I should say the hush *puppy*. As it has been for years, the batter is squeezed by hand from a pastry bag into the hot cooking oil in one long swirl, so you end up with a single serpentine coil of fried corn bread, which you can make into as many hush puppies as you like. The mix contains tasty bits of onion, but the pups still taste straightforwardly of cornmeal and are not overly sweet.

If you visit Fuzzy's on a Wednesday, you'll more than likely find the place packed to the rafters, and a bowl of pinto beans sitting in front of virtually every customer. The beans, as you might imagine, are perfectly seasoned with pork—what else? The kitchen staff swears they just can't cook enough to feed everyone who wants some. Another distinctive side dish added by the present owners is a tasty sweet potato casserole. A baked potato topped with barbecue and cheese has also become popular.

Final notes: be sure to try the warm banana pudding, which comes with a rich, golden meringue topping, and don't miss out on Fuzzy's famous sweet tea.

## Country Barbeque

4012 Wendover Avenue
Greensboro, N.C. 27409
336-292-3557
Breakfast, lunch, and dinner, Monday through
  Saturday

A cardiologist recommended this place to me, pronouncing it "the best barbecue in Greensboro." Praise for a barbecue joint from a cardiologist is pretty unusual. Now, I won't go as far as proclaiming it the best barbecue place in the Gate City, since I'm a big fan of Stamey's authentic wood-cooked barbecue across town. However, I will say that Country Barbeque manages to keep its chopped barbecue chunky and moist, whereas some people have told me they feel the pork at Stamey's is machine-chopped too finely and thus becomes dry.

Seeing no sign of a real pit or a woodpile around Country Barbeque's plain brick

Country Barbeque, Greensboro

building, I can only deduce that the barbecue here is cooked on electric- or gas-fired pits. Although the meat is not noticeably smoky tasting, it's tender, moist, and well seasoned. It is served with an excellent Lexington-style dip. In addition, I tried the three-times-per-week barbecued chicken and found it to be tender and flavorful without being overcooked, as this dish often can be.

The typical Lexington-style barbecue coleslaw served here is tasty and well put together. However, the hush puppies are the frozen variety, which is an unfortunate concession to convenience. Customers can also order hamburgers and hot dogs.

For dessert, I tried the homemade peach cobbler. Although I certainly thought it was good, a cute and precocious toddler in the booth next to mine rated it even more highly, exclaiming several times, "It's just the *best* peach cobbler I've ever tasted."

Country Barbeque opens for breakfast at six in the morning. For those who don't want to leave their car, a drive-up window is available for takeout orders.

## Stamey's Old Fashioned Barbecue

http://www.stameys.com
Lunch and dinner, Monday through Saturday

2206 High Point Road
Greensboro, N.C. 27403
336-299-9888

Second location:
2812 Battleground Avenue
Greensboro, N.C. 27408
336-288-9275

I moved to Greensboro in 1972 as a young television reporter for WFMY-TV. One of my most vivid recollections from my early days there is of Steve Campbell, our autocratic, five-foot-three-inch assignment editor, sitting at his U-shaped work station and barking orders into the mobile radio microphone. One day around noon, Steve had just dispatched one news crew to an accident he had picked up on the police scanner and had instructed another to head toward a high school to check out reports of a large fight. A call came in from a hungry news photographer saying he had finished a shooting assignment and wanted to take his lunch break. Steve loved to use police lingo, so he grabbed the microphone and asked the fellow's "10-20," or location. When he found that the news car was eastbound on High Point Road near the coliseum, he barked, "Pull into the drive-through at Stamey's, get two barbecue sandwiches, and head straight downtown to cover the city council meeting." Since no protest came back over the squawky radio receiver, I suppose the cameraman—probably just as green as I was—meekly followed instructions.

Some things you just didn't argue about in those days, and Stamey's reputation for having the best barbecue in Greensboro was one of them. At that time, the rambling white-frame restaurant across from the Greensboro Coliseum was the end result of several remodelings and additions made since the original drive-in opened in 1953. Traffic on High Point Road wasn't as heavy back then, and crowds from the Big Four and

Stamey's Old Fashioned Barbecue, Greensboro

ACC basketball tournaments used to line the boulevard, waiting for breaks between oncoming cars so they could dash across the avenue to Stamey's between games. Occasionally, newspaper and television reporters and photographers from around the Triad shared a table at the restaurant. I can clearly remember sipping iced tea and listening to a young New York native rejoice about landing a reporting job back in North Carolina, where he had attended college. "Man, I've eaten barbecue and hush puppies here every day since I got back," he exclaimed proudly.

Today, Stamey's occupies a newer lodge-style building, constructed on the same site in the 1980s. It's fitting that its quarters are probably the most impressive among all the barbecue restaurants in North Carolina. Stamey's is, after all, one of the proudest names in the business. Its founder, Warner Stamey, taught the secrets of the barbecue craft to the operators of some of the Piedmont's best-known barbecue establishments. A portrait of Warner Stamey hangs just inside the front door of the restaurant. Not far

from the portrait are two smaller black-and-white pictures that present a fascinating contrast to the polished brass, brick, and wood of the cathedral-ceilinged building. The aging photographs show the emporiums of the two men who popularized Lexington-style barbecue and taught the process of its preparation to Warner Stamey. One picture shows a semipermanent tent set up as a barbecue stand in the 1920s by Jess Swicegood, while the other reveals a tiny café built a few years later by Sid Weaver, who had originally set up a barbecue tent right beside Swicegood's just a few yards from the county courthouse in Lexington. From those humble beginnings grew dozens of restaurants across the North Carolina Piedmont, all serving the same slow-roasted, chopped pork shoulders and tangy-sweet vinegar-and-tomato sauce perfected by Swicegood and Weaver and passed along through Warner Stamey.

The real monument to Stamey is not the restaurant but the pit building, which is by far the largest and best equipped in the state. Warner constantly experimented with the design of the wood-fired pits used to cook pork shoulders. While the pits in early photographs were essentially open-top rectangular boxes with metal covers that could be raised and shut, the ten pits at Stamey's—built in the late 1960s—are basically a series of large brick ovens forming a solid wall along each side of the rectangular building. Fireplaces for burning wood down to coals are also built into the walls. The wood is thrown into the fireplaces through an exterior door beside the woodpile, while coals are shoveled from doors inside the building and into the pits. Each pit has two steel doors—one providing access to the metal cooking racks, the other to the floors of the pits, where the hickory coals are spread twenty-four inches below the roasting shoulders. Smoke from the pits is vented through chimneys, rather than emerging directly into the pit building as it does at several establishments. Thanks to its dull red brick, its arched fireplaces, and its black steel doors, the place has the look and feel of a nineteenth-century foundry—a look of permanence and solidity perfectly matching the reputation of Warner Stamey.

A succession of employees—now mostly Vietnamese Montagnards and Cambodians—have presided over the pits for many years, drawing coals from the fireplaces with long-handled shovels, scattering them evenly beneath the meat, and, when the time is right, bending from the waist and leaning into the smoky pits to turn the heavy shoulders with three-foot forks. The pits are kept fairly hot at Stamey's, with the result that small shoulders are done in six hours or so. That means all the meat can be put on early in the morning, rather than having to be cooked overnight. The smaller shoulders are done in time for lunch, while the larger ones—up to around eighteen pounds—are finished early in the afternoon after nine or ten hours on the pits, in time to be prepared for the dinner crowd.

Keith and Charles Stamey, Warner's sons, ran the restaurant for nearly thirty years. Keith, the restaurant's unofficial spokesperson and the more visible of the two brothers, left a ten-year military career and joined his brother in the business in 1970, three years after Warner Stamey passed along its ownership. Charles retired in 1996. His son, Chip, and Keith were partners until Keith's death in 2000. Chip has run the business since.

The restaurant is a large, cheerful, bustling place that's always crowded at peak periods. A second location on the north side of town also does a thriving business. Its barbecue is cooked on the pits at the main restaurant, then trucked to the satellite location.

The tender, smoky pork is served chopped or sliced—although "sliced" in most Piedmont barbecue places, including this one, means broken up into appetizing, juicy pieces, rather than cleanly sliced like ham or rare roast beef. Due to the heavy volume at Stamey's, the chopped barbecue is cut by machine. The only minor complaint I have is that this implement chops the meat a little too finely for my personal taste. The overall texture, flavor, and tenderness are superb nonetheless.

Stamey's sauce seems just a bit sweeter than most other Lexington-style versions. It is not thick at all. When a small amount is ladled over a serving of chopped barbecue, the liquid seeps down and moistens the meat from top to bottom, rather than resting atop the barbecue like ketchup or a thick commercial barbecue sauce.

Since my family comes from eastern North Carolina, nearly all the barbecue and fixings I ate during my childhood and adolescence came from that region. When I moved to Greensboro, the Piedmont-style barbecue meal served by Stamey's looked decidedly odd, its reddish green coleslaw and thin, crescent-shaped hush puppies far different from what I had theretofore encountered. However, I quickly grew to love Stamey's hush puppies, which were sweet and light and didn't fill me up while waiting for my barbecue to arrive. I later found out that Stamey's uses a head on its hush-puppy machine that was originally designed to form miniature doughnuts; it's been modified so that it cuts the cornmeal "doughnuts" in half as they drop into the deep fryer. I also discovered that, at least in the Piedmont, Warner Stamey is usually credited with the introduction of serving hush puppies with barbecue during the 1950s. For many years before he did so, barbecue was served with dinner rolls or even with plain white bread. Balls or crescents of fried corn bread were customarily eaten only with fried fish at the Piedmont's many "fish camps."

Stamey's unquestionably serves the tangiest coleslaw in North Carolina. The cabbage is chopped into fine bits about the size of air-rifle pellets and dressed with a peppery sweet-and-sour sauce that has considerably more kick than the restaurant's barbecue sauce. The mild, sweet coleslaw of the east may serve to soothe the palate between bites of tart, pepper-flavored barbecue, but at Stamey's, the slaw has a definite bite, waking up the sweet, smoky barbecue in the same way ground horseradish wakes up roast beef. I personally consider Stamey's slaw to be a bracing accompaniment to the 'cue, but some first-timers find that it takes getting used to. While every single customer may not like this side dish, no one ever forgets it. Chip Stamey says that Miss Dell Yarborough, the sister-in-law of Lexington barbecue pioneer Sid Weaver, used to work for Warner Stamey and should be credited for the slaw recipe.

No one ever forgets the fruit cobbler at Stamey's either. You'd be hard-pressed to find a complaint about this dish among the customers. Keith Stamey used to be downright fussy about the peach cobbler, which he told me outsold the cherry version by about ten to one. When I was invited to discuss North Carolina barbecue as a guest on ABC's *Good Morning America*, I asked Keith Stamey to make a peach cobbler that I could add to the table of barbecue, hush puppies, coleslaw, and other dishes I was getting together for the segment. He actually made four cobblers before he ended up with one he thought looked good enough for national television. The others cooked over and had juice running down the sides of the dish, which to me is exactly the way they're supposed to look. Ironically, Keith's perfect cobbler looked great on the air, but time constraints kept me from even mentioning it on that occasion. Now, however, I finally feel I've done it justice.

A 1996 poll published in *The State* (now *Our State*) magazine named Stamey's one of North Carolina's two best barbecue restaurants. Personally, I'd have a great deal of trouble narrowing my choices to two, but there's no question that Stamey's is right up there at the top. Whenever I'm on the west side of Greensboro, I enjoy simply riding by the place, watching the smoke billow from the pits, and breathing in the enchanting aroma that spreads for blocks around.

Clark's Barbecue, Kernersville

### Clark's Barbecue

1331 N.C. 66 South
Kernersville, N.C. 27284
336-996-8644
http://www.clarksbarbecue.net
Breakfast, lunch, and dinner, Monday through Saturday

The town of Kernersville, located off Interstate 40 between Greensboro and Winston-Salem, is best known for being a fast-growing bedroom community and for Körner's Folly, an odd, twenty-two-room structure built in the late 1800s by decorator/designer/painter Jule Körner. Körner was famous for painting Bull Durham Tobacco bulls on buildings across the Southeast. Inside the "Folly," eccentric nooks and crannies, trapdoors, and child-sized rooms alternate with or open into elegant, high-ceilinged spaces. It's said that no two doorways are exactly alike.

I'm happy to report that Clark's Barbecue will transport you from the fanciful to the down-to-earth. This is evident from its location in an unprepossessing rectangular brick building on N.C. 66 south of Kernersville, between the business and bypass sections of Interstate 40. The interior decorations and ambiance are equally unremarkable, although the décor had been recently spruced up when I visited. But the owner of Clark's certainly resembles the imaginative young Körner in that no two spellings of the word *barbecue* are alike on the restaurant's premises. It's *Bar-B-Q* on the sign atop the building, *Barbeque* on the sign behind the counter, *Barbecue* on the menu, and *BBQ* on the label of Clark's own brand of sauce. Four different spellings at a single barbecue joint must represent some kind of North Carolina record.

That said, I got a deep, solid feeling about Clark's when I made the obligatory swing around the building before parking and saw the neatly stacked woodpile. That feeling was reinforced during midafternoon, when wisps of smoke were still drifting from the brick pit's chimneys. Although the pork shoulders go on the pit before dawn, they don't reach the perfect state of doneness until around 6 P.M. Randy Gentry, son of the founder, says, "Until they can figure out another way to get the flavor in the barbecue, we're going to keep cooking with wood, even though it's a lot of extra work."

My barbecue sandwich was good, solid, middle-of-the-road Lexington-style fare. The meat was lean and chopped to the right consistency, the smoke flavor from the pits was very much in evidence, and the Lexington dip and barbecue coleslaw were pretty much textbook offerings.

Clark's now offers pit-cooked ribs Thursday through Saturday. Some of the home-style sides include cabbage, corn, pintos, limas, green beans, baked beans, black-eyed peas, stewed potatoes, potato salad, and mac 'n' cheese.

The place gets good reviews from the online barbecue blogs, from traveling salesmen, and from employees of the giant Roadway Express truck terminal next door. What more could you ask for?

## Prissy Polly's Bar-B-Que

729 N.C. 66 South
Kernersville, N.C. 27284
336-993-5045
http://www.prissypollys.com
Lunch and dinner, Monday through Saturday

Okay, I know you're probably wondering, so let's get it out of the way right up front. This place got its name from the nickname pinned on owner Loren Whaley's mother.

Whaley must have figured that a place called Prissy Polly's would fit right into the fabric of life in Kernersville, home of the annual Honey Bee Festival and something called the "Spring Folly."

Whaley is originally from eastern North Carolina. When he opened Prissy Polly's in 1991, the idea was to create a niche market by serving strictly eastern-style barbecue in the heathen territory of the Piedmont. Whaley studied the preparation of eastern North Carolina 'cue under the tutelage of Doug Sauls, who operated barbecue places in several towns over the years and whose namesake restaurant is now located in Nashville, not far from Rocky Mount. Whaley obviously made a course correction along the way, because nowadays his place serves both authentic eastern-style barbecue and a very credible version of Lexington-style, or Piedmont-style, pork-shoulder barbecue—even though the sauce is a little too red and thick to win Lexington credentials as genuine "dip."

Prissy Polly's is now located in much larger quarters than the original tiny restaurant. The cheerful dining area—brightened by red-checked tablecloths and sunlight from big windows—is spacious enough, in fact, to allow the restaurant to host live music on Thursday and Saturday evenings.

Loren's daughter Debra Whaley told me that the restaurant has added fried chicken and beef brisket to the menu, which already included barbecued ribs. One thing that hasn't changed is the tasty, authentic Brunswick stew prepared at Prissy Polly's. It contains chicken, beef, white corn, butter beans,

Prissy Polly's Bar-B-Que, Kernersville

tomatoes, onions, and potatoes, plus seasonings, and is definitely one of the better restaurant Brunswick stews anywhere in the state. It deserves special kudos in light of the fact that many otherwise fine barbecue restaurants serve Brunswick stew that should cause embarrassment to the owners, in my opinion. Not this place.

Prissy Polly's offers a nice selection of vegetables, including both white and Piedmont-style coleslaw, green beans, squash, fried okra, barbecued beans (containing three different bean varieties), boiled potatoes, Red Bliss potato salad, collards, and mac 'n' cheese. A couple of specials I noticed on my most recent visit included Moravian chicken pie and an appetizing-sounding pork tenderloin wrap.

Homemade desserts include Prissy Polly's

"Crazy Good" lemon pie, "Nuts About Fudge" pie, pecan pie, "Unbelievable" Key lime pie, and banana pudding.

One unusual touch is that the place offers circular hush puppies resembling onion rings or small fried doughnuts. They're crisp and tasty. In an earlier review, I mistakenly attributed the unusually shaped pups to Clark's Barbecue, located just up the road, and Prissy Polly's was quick to point out the error when I stopped in most recently.

Prissy Polly's is definitely worth a stop if you're nearby. As a bonus, you'll get a kick out of answering if someone asks where you had lunch or dinner.

## Stratford Bar-B-Que

630 South Main Street
King, N.C. 27021
336-983-0623
http://www.stratfordbbq.com
Breakfast, lunch, and dinner are served Monday through Saturday. Breakfast and lunch are offered on Sunday.

Stratford Bar-B-Que, housed in a white-sided, red-roofed structure resembling a barn, makes much of the fact that the barbecue here is cooked with hickory wood. The area behind the restaurant does indeed boast a big pile of hickory slabs.

However, I should point out that four key factors are involved in preparing great barbecue: tenderness, consistency, wood-smoked flavor, and seasoning. Since smoked flavor can carry you only so far (and since some people don't like it anyway), it's important to make sure the meat is cooked long enough and at a low-enough temperature for the barbecue to stay moist and for the meat

fibers to relax into a perfect state of tenderness. Many pit masters wrap the shoulders in foil for the last two or three hours on the pit, which works wonders in tenderizing the meat and holding in moisture. After the meat is cooked, it's important to pull it from the bones and to add enough seasoning so it has some flavor aside from the sauce.

During my most recent visit to Stratford, I found the barbecue not only totally lacking the smoke flavor I had previously encountered there but also a little dry. Furthermore, it lacked salt or any other seasoning. I found no evidence of sauce having been applied either. What I got was a generously sized, bland roast pork sandwich—not a barbecue sandwich.

I also noticed that the service was exceptionally slow that day (a Friday). While a lot of people stood around out front waiting for their orders to be filled, it seemed a few people were standing around in the kitchen not doing much of anything. Someone had just

Stratford Bar-B-Que, King

ordered nine or ten barbecue plates to go, which seemed to throw everyone out of their normal routine.

It could very well be that my experience was an anomaly, which can happen anywhere. If Stratford's management is willing to go to the trouble to cook with wood, I'll certainly cut the restaurant some slack for having a less-than-perfect day. I'm sure I'll be making another visit.

The restaurant serves a complete breakfast featuring its famous tenderloin biscuit and tenderloin platter. It also offers a complete selection of sandwiches, as well as plate lunches and dinners, including some seafood. But aside from the pit-cooked barbecue, the place's biggest claims to fame are probably its hot dog and foot-long hot dog. It also has some really good homemade cakes, including chocolate cake and pound cake. I saw people enjoying some mighty good-looking peach and cherry cobbler, too.

The restaurant now advertises live music on Tuesday nights.

## Hill's Lexington Barbecue

4005 North Patterson Avenue
Winston-Salem, N.C. 27105
336-767-2184
Breakfast, lunch, and dinner daily

When founder Joe Allen Hill opened his Winston-Salem restaurant in 1951, he was the first to use the term *Lexington barbecue*, in honor of his hometown. At the time, none of the small barbecue places in the actual town of Lexington were using it as descriptive of their particular style of barbecue, so Hill appropriated it in Winston-Salem.

Hill got a big boost in starting the restaurant from Paul Meyer, who had enjoyed success in the barbecue business in Winston-Salem in the late 1930s and early 1940s. Meyer actually came to work with Hill and his wife, Edna, to help them get the operation going. But everyone says the biggest asset to the business for many years was Edna, whose portrait hangs behind the cash register.

Gene Hill, Joe and Edna's son, helped his

Hill's is famous for its meringue-topped banana pudding.

mom and dad run the place for decades. Now, Gene's son, Eugene (also known as J. R.), takes care of much of the management, although Gene is still active in greeting customers and being an elder statesman. You'll recognize Gene by the white hair and jaunty mustache.

Hill's serves chopped, pulled (or "blocked"), and sliced barbecue from shoulders pit-cooked over hardwood coals. All of it has good, tender texture and a deep, smoky flavor. During my visit, I especially enjoyed the "blocked" barbecue (big chunks of pulled meat) and the sliced, which Gene Hill claims is as good as steak. His "dip" is a closely guarded secret. Gene made it for years, and J. R. carries on with the task today.

I also enjoyed some of the best barbecued chicken I've ever had, cooked on the same pits as the pork shoulders. It was notable because of its deep color and char. Rather than falling apart at the touch, it had suitable firmness—a big plus for me personally—yet it offered no real resistance to the teeth.

Customers can choose between a white coleslaw and a red "barbecue" slaw that's sweet-tart and has a peppery kick. I also sampled baked beans, turnip greens, and potato salad and enjoyed all three.

Believe it or not, seafood is a popular specialty at Hill's. After hearing several customers praise the fried flounder, I tried it somewhat skeptically. I wasn't the least bit disappointed. The breading was light and crispy, the fish wasn't even remotely greasy, and the flavor of the flounder came through cleanly.

In my opinion, Hill's serves some of the best banana pudding in North Carolina. The secrets are the rich egg custard, for which there are just no shortcuts, and the perfectly browned meringue. Served warm, this is a truly authentic version of a classic dessert.

## Little Richard's Barbecue

http://eatmopig.com

4885 Country Club Road
Winston-Salem, N.C. 27104
336-760-3457
Lunch and dinner are served Monday through Saturday. Curb service is available from 4 P.M. to 9 P.M.

Second location:
5353 Gumtree Road
Wallburg, N.C. 27373
336-769-4227
Lunch and dinner, Monday through Saturday

Richard Berrier, who gained his barbecue experience in Lexington, started his first restaurant in Winston-Salem in 1991. He decided to open his establishment to keep people in Forsyth County from having to drive to Davidson County to get real Lexington-style barbecue.

Some confusion surrounds the Little Richard's name. Aside from the original location on Country Club Road in Winston-Salem and a restaurant in Wallburg, there's also a place called Little Richard's in Clemmons. There used to be another on South Stratford Road in Winston-Salem. Without delving too far into details of ownership and franchising gone awry, all you have to remember is that *great* barbecue, slow-cooked on real wood-burning pits, awaits you at the restaurants on Country Club Road and Gumtree Road. The Clemmons restaurant is under different ownership.

By any measure, Richard's place on Country Club has to be regarded as one of the best barbecue restaurants in North Carolina. Rocking with music played at a higher-than-normal volume, it's decorated with old signs advertising cigarettes, soft drinks, and the like. The restaurant is laid-back, comfortable, and nearly always crowded. One of the most important decorations is a 1999 "Certificate of Barbecue Excellence" from the North Carolina Barbecue Club.

The barbecue is pure Lexington-style. It's pulled from pork shoulders, which are slow-roasted over wood coals for twelve to fourteen hours. It has both a robust smoky flavor and the bewitching taste and aroma that come when juice drips onto coals spread directly beneath the meat. This process produces small clouds of aromatic steam that give the golden brown meat a grilled taste that complements the overall smokiness. Whether it's coarse-chopped, chopped, or sliced, the meat at Little Richard's is so tender that it practically falls apart without being chewed. The red barbecue slaw has just the right amount of zing to perfectly balance the sweet, pliant meat. On top of all that, the hush puppies are outstanding.

Little Richard's Lexington dip deflates the common misperception among easterners that Piedmont barbecue basically consists of "a hunk of dead hog meat with tomato sauce on it," as the Raleigh *News & Observer*'s Dennis Rogers once wrote. Typical of many Lexington dips, Richard's blend is still strongly vinegar-based, with a bracing dose

Little Richard's Barbecue, Winston-Salem

of pepper. True, it has enough tomato to give it a soft red color, but not nearly enough to turn it thick. Just enough sugar is added to cut the power of the vinegar slightly. An additional hint of onion flavor will not lessen the taster's inevitable conclusion that the differences between eastern North Carolina sauce and Lexington dip are subtle indeed. As the label advises, the dip at Little Richard's reaches its peak flavor when heated, which is how it's served at the restaurant.

Little Richard's is also known for great burgers and a wide selection of other sandwiches. However, in my opinion, the barbecue is just too good here for anyone to venture too far into other areas. As Little Richard's sauce label asserts, "Pit Connoisseurs Can't Be Wrong."

## Mr. Barbecue

1381 Peters Creek Parkway
Winston-Salem, NC 27103
336-725-7827
Lunch and dinner, Monday through Saturday

Mr. Barbecue occupies a brick building with brightly painted red-and-white accents. Since 1962, it has cooked barbecue over real wood coals, letting customers know that an old-fashioned interaction between pig and fire is going on—at least some of the time. Mr. Barbecue has added a couple of electric pits to augment the wood-burning ones, so the degree of genuine pit-cooked taste probably depends on the day and the hour you're there. The paper wrappers for the barbecue sandwiches don't make a distinction about how they're prepared—they're all imprinted with the words, "Real hickory wood barbecue."

Personally, I don't quite understand why a restaurateur wouldn't make a decision to either stick with wood-burning pits all the way or convert entirely to the electric version. Some places use electric pits only as backup when they get extremely busy, but that means that even on the same day, some customers get a different-tasting product from others. The same customer is also likely to have two entirely different experiences on different occasions. And if barbecue customers value one thing, it's knowing what to expect and what they can truthfully recommend to others. If cooking with wood is worth the trouble at

Mr. Barbecue, Winston-Salem
*Photo by Bill Stancill*

all, it's worth doing all the time. On the other hand, an owner who thinks the public really can't tell the difference might just as well go with electricity and be done with it.

I sampled a coarse-chopped sandwich and thoroughly enjoyed it. The meat was tender and the dip mild and appealing. I experienced a delightful peppery aftertaste but didn't encounter a great deal of smoke flavor, especially considering that I had just seen a woodpile behind the restaurant.

Mr. Barbecue has tasty ribs and a choice of fried or barbecued chicken. It is also known for its terrific hot dogs. My peach cobbler had a lazy man's "dump cake" crust—made basically by sprinkling a dry cake mix on top of the fruit filling—but it was still worthwhile. I noticed several people ordering the homemade banana pudding with meringue topping.

At its best, Mr. Barbecue offers delicious, tender, *smoky* barbecue. At other times, it serves moist, tender barbecue with little pit-cooked flavor. Maybe it would make an impression on the owner if we all started asking right up front whether the barbecue we're getting at that moment is from the wood-burning pits or the electric ovens.

## Pig Pickin's of America

3650 Reynolda Road
Winston-Salem, N.C. 27106
336-923-2285
Lunch and dinner are served Monday through
    Saturday. Lunch is offered on Sunday.

Pig Pickin's used to be a local chain of three barbecue restaurants established by the son of the founder of Mr. Barbecue on Peters Creek Parkway in Winston-Salem. The original Pig Pickin's opened on Deacon Boulevard in 1985, but that location and another on South Stratford Road no longer exist. In 2008, new ownership took over the third and only remaining location, on Reynolda Road. Owner Alan Willard is doing some nice things with the business.

The barbecue here is cooked on an electric smoker that uses wood chips or pellets. The smoke flavor still comes through very well—although one layer of flavor is lost from not having juices dripping directly onto live coals. (In electric- and gas-fired smokers, the heat source and the wood are offset to the side of the meat.) After cooking, the barbecue is fairly heavily sauced with a Lexington-style dip and held in a steamer to continue to cook at low temperature in the sauce. As a result, it's a "wet" barbecue and has what I would call a shredded rather than chopped consistency. I found lots of attractive, tasty brown bits in the 'cue. I think the idea of holding the meat in a fairly heavy amount of sauce actually goes a long way toward solving the problem that all barbecue restaurants experience in keeping it flavorful and moist between the time it's cooked and the time it's consumed. The barbecue is served chopped, sliced, or in chunks. Available sauces include not only the Lexington-style dip but a thicker Texas-style sauce containing molasses, as well as a sauce flavored with Cheerwine, the iconic cherry-flavored North Carolina soft drink bottled in Rowan County.

Pig Pickin's is also known for its tasty ribs, brisket, and smoked chicken, all of

Pig Pickin's of America,
Winston-Salem

which receive frequent customer reviews as being fall-off-the-bone tender.

The Piedmont-style red coleslaw is finely minced and very sweet—which I like—and not as peppery as some versions. It makes for a nice, well-balanced barbecue sandwich. Pig Pickin's also seems to have come up with the secret of producing memorable hush puppies. Nearly every one of the restaurant's online reviews mentions them in a highly complimentary way.

In case you're searching for ways to in-corporate more fat and calories into your diet, try the "Dogzilla" or the "Hogzilla." These are, respectively, a foot-long hot dog and a big ol' burger, each topped with a couple of pieces of bacon, garnished with a copious helping of chopped barbecue, and doused with barbe-cue sauce. Somebody he'p me!

Desserts at this pleasant little restaurant include peach cobbler, ice cream (including a Cheerwine float!), deep-fried apple pie 'n' ice cream, and meringue-topped banana pudding.

The "Dogzilla" at Pig Pickin's is a foot-long hot dog topped with bacon, barbecue, slaw, and barbecue sauce.

## Snook's Old Fashion Barbecue

109 Junie Beauchamp Road
Advance, N.C. 27006
336-998-4305
www.letseat.at/snooks
Lunch and dinner, Tuesday through Saturday

Snook's is located in an unusual gaggle of buildings on U.S. 158 just southwest of Hillsdale, which in turn is southwest of Clemmons and Winston-Salem. An old country store—apparently closed—is in one building, a kitchen and enclosed takeout window in another, a dining room in a third, and restrooms in a fourth. Various storage buildings and sheds and a barbecue pit complete with woodpile are also on the premises. It seems the present kitchen-and-takeout building is located in what was the original barbecue pit, built over fifty years ago. The present owner constructed a new pit and, rather than undertaking major renovations, simply added small freestanding buildings and sheds as needed. Once patrons receive their orders from the takeout window, they go outside and either enter a separate room containing counters, stools, and dining tables or eat al fresco at one of the picnic tables scattered around the grounds.

This picturesque complex is located on a busy corner. The food enjoys a strong reputation among local residents—although during my visit one lady mused that she thought the barbecue prepared twice a year by the nearby Advance Fire Department is "just a little better."

Well, let's admit it: no commercial establishment is ever going to win a barbecue face-

Snook's Old Fashion Barbecue, Advance

off with *any* local fire department. But suffice it to say that Snook's Old Fashion Barbecue serves excellently flavored wood-cooked barbecue, plus lots of other goodies. Dozens of Day-Glo signs tacked up outside the takeout window advertise every conceivable type of sandwich, among which the burgers are the biggest sellers (next to barbecue, of course). The management is proud of the fact that the burgers are made of freshly ground local meat, with no frozen processed stuff from who knows where. A wide, appetizing selection of fresh vegetables is available in season. All the desserts are homemade, including strawberry cream cheese pie, chocolate cream cheese pound cake, and chocolate meringue pie, among others.

Snook's is across the road from an interesting-looking store featuring antiques and collectibles, so customers have the opportunity of a quality dining and shopping experience. The restaurant is well worth a slight detour. Take Exit 180 off Interstate 40 and turn west on U.S. 158 at Hillsdale. Snook's is on the left after 2.3 miles.

## Deano's Barbecue

140 North Clement Street
Mocksville, N.C. 27028
336-751-5820
http://www.deanosbarbecue.com
Lunch and dinner, Tuesday through Saturday

Dean Allen, proprietor of Deano's in downtown Mocksville, earned his spurs working for two of the best-known barbecue experts in Davie County: the late Buck Miller, who owned Buck's Barbecue, and the late Odell "Bony" Hendrix, who built Hendrix Barbecue on U.S. 64. Allen actually ran both places for a number of years after their owners retired, so his barbecue credentials are solid.

Deano's is located in a new building, which can send a shiver of apprehension up the spine of someone searching for old-time barbecue. But never fear—the place has a real, honest-to-goodness pit and a reassuring pile of hardwood outside. A nice, natural-wood exterior and a pleasant front porch equipped with picnic tables and rocking chairs (a touch you'd think more barbecue restaurants would consider) welcome customers. Inside, old advertising signs and appliances are reminders of "the golden age" of North Carolina barbecue during the 1940s and 1950s. Among the novelties are an old Merita Bread screen door, an antique Dr. Pepper cold-drink box, a Sinclair gas pump (emblazoned with the silhouette of a dinosaur), and an old soda fountain.

Deano's seems to specialize in young, friendly waitresses with something of a gift of gab, a welcome touch in an age when so many of their counterparts either refuse to make eye contact (a defense against having to acknowledge patrons' existence) or deliver a clear, though unspoken, message that they dislike their jobs and would prefer to be somewhere else.

The barbecue at Deano's is finely chopped and mild, albeit with a distinctive

The wood stacked around back is an essential part of the operation at Deano's.

wood-cooked flavor. Personally, I found it a bit more interesting with a little Texas Pete added, but as they say, it's easier to add it than to take it out. I selected tasty homemade French fries and a nice peach cobbler to go with my meal. Overall, I would rate the food quite highly.

That goes as well for an unusual offering at Deano's: the bison burger. Bison meat is supposed to be quite a bit healthier than beef because of its lower fat and cholesterol content, but it is also drier. I tried a burger with lettuce, tomato, and mayonnaise (the latter of which overrode the health benefits, I suppose) and found it enjoyable. I was surprised that the bison burger was priced at only three dollars, compared to two dollars for a regular hamburger.

Deano's also features daily specials—barbecued chicken each Friday, plus occasional offerings of chicken 'n' dumplings and bar-

becued stew beef with pinto beans and corn bread.

## Red Pig Bar-B-Q House
7136 N.C. 801 South
Mocksville, N.C. 27028
336-284-4650
Breakfast, lunch, and dinner daily

The Red Pig is the last holdout at "Greasy Corner" (or Davie Crossroads), the intersection of N.C. 801 and U.S. 601 south of Mocksville that once was home to several barbecue joints. This place has been around since 1972, and it's hard to miss—a long tan-and-brown building with a large, eye-catching barbecue pit and a wood yard filled with bundles of split hardwood slabs bound with metal strips. So far, so good.

The inviting interior features large front

Red Pig Bar-B-Q House, Mocksville

and back rooms. The front dining area is decorated with shelves of old kitchen jars, farm implements, and kitchen gadgets. The comfortable booths around the walls and in the room's center are painted in a soothing color scheme of dark and light green.

I ordered a simple barbecue tray. During the rather long wait for the food to arrive (hmmm, I noticed a couple of others waiting quite awhile, too), I had time to check out the lengthy menu. Breakfast is available, as is a large selection of sandwiches (including a local favorite, fried bologna). You can find just about any dinner plate you might desire, including chicken, shrimp, and hamburger steak. Quite a few daily specials are offered. The day I visited (Saturday), the menu included country-style steak, fried chicken, baked ham, and chicken livers, with sides of pintos, creamed potatoes, baked apples, white beans, and beets.

The barbecue here is cooked seven days a week. When my order finally arrived, I found it *well* worth waiting for. My chopped barbecue was exceptionally tender, smoky-tasting, mild, and sweet, although the sauce was just a little too far on the thick and red side for my taste. (It's my firm conviction that, nearly without exception, the sauce grows thicker the farther west one travels.) The barbecue was slightly mild for my personal taste, but a dash of hot sauce made it perfect. All in all, this has to be described as really good pit-cooked barbecue.

The impressive chopped pork was accompanied by coarsely chopped barbecue slaw, which was mild but tasty. The round, golf-ball-sized hush puppies were excellent—light, crisp on the outside, not too sweet, and with a clean cornmeal flavor.

The Red Pig is a relaxing, unpretentious local hangout with a menu full of comfort foods. After all, it has survived at the place known as "Greasy Corner" while its competitors have faded. That alone makes it worth adding to your list of places worth visiting.

I was in Sanford to review a restaurant called The Steele Pig, so named because of its location on Steele Street in the downtown area.

Chef-owner Chad Blackwelder's attractive sixty-five-seat restaurant features contemporary Southern cuisine, with plenty of grilled and smoked meat on the menu, including steaks and enormous pork chops. Blackwelder previously worked with James Beard Award–winning chefs Louis Osteen in Charleston and Ben Barker at Durham's Magnolia Grill. He was also executive chef at Brightleaf 905 in Durham, named by *Esquire* magazine's John Mariani as one of 1999's top twenty-five new restaurants in the United States.

As a small crowd of Blackwelder's family members and friends gathered to observe the filming, I prepared to sample some of The Steele Pig's house-smoked items, including an inventive smoked North Carolina rainbow trout appetizer, homemade tasso ham (an ingredient in a wonderful shrimp-and-grits dish), and—most visually impressive—a huge beef rib served with the house specialty, smoked tomato barbecue sauce. Videographer Allen Brown and I set up a close-up shot in which I would describe the beautifully browned, crusty rib while artfully anointing it with a rivulet of the thick, reddish brown sauce prior to cutting a bite for tasting. The sauce, which was in a plastic squeeze bottle, contained small bits of bell pepper. One of the vegetable fragments apparently lodged in the tip of the bottle, blocking the opening. Unbeknownst to me, pressure began to build

up behind the blockage as I squeezed harder.

All of a sudden, the sauce bottle erupted, violently blowing the offending bit of pepper and the pent-up sauce out the tip and all over the table, my face, my glasses, and, most obviously, my light-colored shirt.

"Hey, Mr. Garner, it *explodes* with flavor!" wisecracked someone off-camera.

My snickering cameraman alertly kept rolling as the room burst into laughter.

I couldn't help thinking back to the time many years earlier when I experienced a copious on-camera nosebleed while anchoring the 11 P.M. news at WFMY-TV, Channel 2, in Greensboro. The nosebleed actually began a minute or two before we went on the air. Throughout the first half of the eighteen-minute news portion of the program (not including sports and weather), I was able to keep it staunched during the off-camera intervals offered by film and videotape news stories. After the first commercial break, however, things went south in a hurry.

Our news film projector and both of our videotape machines went on the blink at once, leaving the director with no choice but to keep me on camera long enough to fix the problem. In that era before teleprompters, I began reading some "fill" stories ripped from the Associated Press wire-service teletype, waiting for a signal from the floor director that we could get back to the normal rundown of stories I had prepared. But the fervently hoped-for signal didn't materialize, and I felt a drop of blood roll out of my nostril, over my lips, and down my chin. I tried to cue a commercial by miserably intoning,

I had to change into a restaurant T-shirt to finish the review at Sanford's The Steele Pig after I splattered myself with barbecue sauce on camera.
*Courtesy of UNC-TV*

"We'll be back in just a moment." But since the videotape machines were inoperative, the director was unable to go to commercial either. The floor director waved off the attempted break and pointed inexorably at me.

Having no option except possibly the blessed relief of instant death, I lowered my head slightly and kept reading. Spatters of blood, spraying off my lips as I spoke, began to appear on the teletype pages clenched in my fingers. I experienced an intense longing to vanish through an imaginary trapdoor beneath my studio swivel chair.

That long-ago incident—viewed by many thousands—seared my sensibilities and provided a rock-solid assurance that nothing worse could *ever* happen during my career in broadcasting, however long it might be. I was never nervous after that, no matter what. And thus the slapstick barbecue-sauce explosion seemed merely amusing. It

wasn't *live* TV, after all, and even if it had been, the potential humiliation was infinitesimal compared to that of the fateful nosebleed.

After several minutes of hilarity and photo-taking at The Steele Pig, I accepted the offer of a restaurant T-shirt, made a quick wardrobe change, and finished the segment, joking that I would "do anything to get a free shirt."

Of course, I kept the footage of the accident in the edited segment, figuring that viewers would probably enjoy the disaster more than they did the review itself. I was apparently right, because UNC-TV received more positive feedback on that particular piece than practically anything else I have ever produced. *North Carolina Weekend* producer David Hardy insisted on including the saucy segment in a New Year's Eve highlight program.

It almost made up for the nosebleed. But not quite.

## Kepley's Barbecue

1304 North Main Street
High Point, N.C. 27262
336-884-1021
http://www.kepleysbarbecue.com
Breakfast (beginning at 8:30 A.M.), lunch, and
dinner (ending at 8:30 P.M.), Monday through
Saturday

Kepley's is still located in the corrugated-metal building perpendicular to High Point's North Main Street where it opened for business in 1948. The paneled, L-shaped interior has seen a multitude of customers over the years, and Kepley's has attracted the long-time loyalty of most of them.

Just about everyone who talks about how good the barbecue is at Kepley's makes some reference to its having been a big part of their growing up in High Point, or they remark that it has been their favorite since they were children. Furthermore, it seems that at least half the customers who come in for takeout orders tell owner Bob Burleson (who, with his wife, Susan, has been around for all but six years of the restaurant's existence) that they've gotten barbecue from Kepley's their entire lives. Burleson does a big business selling barbecue by the pound for entertaining at home and says he ships to quite a few customers in distant locations.

All of this goes to show the power of pleasant childhood associations, or it could be due to the genial, white-haired Burleson's kindly air, because by the area's standards (Lexington is just a few miles away, after all), the barbecue at Kepley's is rather unremarkable, to my taste. Not that there's a thing wrong with it, mind you. Despite being called "pit-cooked barbecue," it tastes like it's cooked on an electric or gas cooker, with nothing memorable added in the way of seasoning. The overall taste of the barbecue and sauce is quite vinegary, compared to the sweeter aftertaste of most Lexington 'cue. In fact, Kepley's chopped pork could almost be labeled an eastern-style barbecue, except that it's prepared from shoulders and hams, rather than the whole hog. The slaw, too, is vinegar-based and not as sweet as some versions, while the hush puppies are cooked to a deep

Kepley's Barbecue,
High Point

brown and have a grainy texture on the outside. You'll have a pleasant barbecue meal at Kepley's, but not a mountaintop experience.

Well, you certainly can't argue with success, and Kepley's has earned plenty of that over the years. I'm sure Bob and Susan Burleson are proud of their legion of loyal fans. There's a lesson here about the importance of a pleasant atmosphere in shaping customers' perceptions about the food itself.

## Kerley's Barbecue

5114 Old U.S. 52
Welcome, N.C. 27374
336-731-8245
Breakfast, lunch, and dinner, Monday through
    Saturday

It's difficult to imagine that a town the size of Welcome could support a barbecue restaurant, but Kerley's has been in business quite awhile. The first thirteen years were in a previous, smaller location, also on Old U.S. 52.

The large brick building that currently houses the restaurant was built in 1991.

Welcome, along with Lexington to the south and Winston-Salem to the north, is smack-dab in the middle of NASCAR country, and the interest in racing is evident at Kerley's. For one thing, the restaurant helps sponsor the Richard Childress team; the waitresses wear shirts imprinted with the name and logo. Then, too, one of the two dining rooms is completely decorated with framed NASCAR posters. (The other is hung with prints of rural scenes painted by Dempsey Essick, a local artist who has a gallery in Welcome.)

Although a brick pit and a woodpile are outside Kerley's, my sliced barbecue sandwich, while certainly tasty, had little or no smoke flavor. It contained a slice of very white meat, obviously from the ham, which is unusual in an area best known for cooking pork shoulders, which have slightly darker meat. The sandwich was dressed with a mild, well-balanced Lexington-style dip.

Kerley's Barbecue,
Welcome

Kerley's occasionally has baby back ribs on special. It offers plenty of other specials as well, including pork chops, meat loaf, and country-style steak, all available with seasonal vegetables cooked up the old-fashioned way. A large breakfast selection is also available every day except Sunday, when Kerley's is closed.

## Blue Mist Bar-B-Q

3409 U.S. 64 East
Asheboro, N.C. 27203
336-625-3980
Breakfast, lunch, and dinner daily

Blue Mist has been around since 1948 and is a landmark stopping place on U.S. 64, North Carolina's mountains-to-coast highway. Old-timers say that, for a long time, it was the most popular stop between the western Piedmont and the capital, and that many Charlotte parents used it as a halfway point to meet and visit with their children attending college in the Raleigh–Durham–Chapel Hill area.

A second location that operated for a while in Randleman has closed. The original Blue Mist is a cheerful, bustling place with booths lining the front window and an extra-long counter. A back dining room is available for meetings and large groups. Little touches—such as a lost-dog poster taped beside the cash register—make patrons feel right at home. Breakfast is served any time of day. In addition to barbecue, Blue Mist offers a complete selection of sandwiches and burgers, steaks, chicken, meat-and-three-vegetable combinations, and seafood.

The restaurant advertises "Randolph County's only pit-cooked barbecue." Blue Mist has in fact remained true to the old ways in slow-cooking pork hams and shoulders over real coals. The place goes through

Blue Mist in Asheboro is definitely a wood burner.

around fifteen hundred pounds of hams and shoulders each week, served chopped or sliced.

On one occasion, I had a sliced barbecue plate. While at some restaurants "sliced" denotes a chunk of meat pulled loose with the fingers, Blue Mist served me a real sharp-edged slice of pork obviously cut from the ham, given its extreme leanness and nearly white color. (Meat from the pork shoulder is the "dark meat" of a pig. It ranges in color from gray to reddish brown and is suffused with tiny pockets of fat.) The meat had a smoke flavor and was served with a more-sweet-than-sour Lexington-style sauce, but it could have been more tender. (Pork hams sometimes get done faster than shoulders and are removed from the pit before the meat has really "relaxed" into its most tender stage.)

On another visit, I ordered a sliced sandwich and got large chunks of meat, this time seemingly from the shoulder. While the meat was very tender, it had no discernible smoke or wood-cooked taste. From the look of the well-used pit house and the pile of hardwood slabs and split wood around back, Blue Mist is going to considerable trouble to cook its pork over wood coals. But at least some of the time, the extra effort and traditional approach aren't getting enough of a smoke flavor into the meat.

Tiny hush puppies, a bit more firm than most, provided an interesting balance to the taste of the barbecued meat, as did the white coleslaw, which was served with less mayonnaise than most versions.

I also tried one of Blue Mist's special cheeseburgers, served on a grilled and slightly flattened bun. Even though the restaurant's ground beef patties are simply fried on a griddle, the one I sampled was cooked to perfection. It had a dark, crusty exterior and was topped with a slice of cheese and adroitly garnished with lettuce, tomato, and mayonnaise.

I noticed homemade persimmon pudding on the dessert menu, which is reason enough for me to swing by sometime soon and try this old favorite restaurant again.

## Troutman's B-B-Q
18466 N.C. 109 South
Denton, N.C. 27239
336-859-2206
Lunch and dinner, Monday through Saturday

The southeastern Davidson County community of Denton is home to the annual Southeast Old Threshers' Reunion, a festival celebrating farm machinery of bygone years. Its second claim to fame could well be Troutman's B-B-Q on N.C. 109, one of the two main thoroughfares through town.

Two other Troutman's are located in Cabarrus County, but there's no business connection between the owner of those establishments and Jimmy Troutman, who for years was the self-proclaimed "Boss Hog" of the Denton establishment. For my money, this Troutman's—now run by Heather Troutman Morris—is the best. Heather obviously thinks so, too, since she's bold enough to continue her father's claim that the restaurant

The most important physical feature at Troutman's in Denton is the woodpile that fuels the barbecue pits.

serves "the best barbecue in the world."

I don't know if it's the world's best, but it's certainly very, very good. You know you're in for a genuine barbecue experience the minute you drive up to the plain cinder-block building veneered in front with a layer of brick. Behind the modest structure, you'll see three big brick chimneys and a large woodpile. Inside the restaurant are two sheet-paneled dining rooms and a few counter stools. The menu confirms what the locals already know as an article of faith: that Troutman's cooks its barbecued pork shoulders over wood coals every day. And—this is a big deal—like nearly all the really good barbecue restaurants in the Piedmont, Troutman's still offers curb service.

The moist, tender chopped 'cue has a wonderfully robust wood-cooked flavor and lots of chewy bits of outside brown meat from the surface of the pork shoulder. Troutman's sauce is thicker than the typical Lexington-style dip. As a result, it tends to sit atop the chopped meat like sauce on spaghetti, rather than soaking into the barbecue. Personally, I would thin the sauce just a bit. But hey, there's no reason to tamper with success, and plenty of people are fond of it just the way it is. The barbecue is served with savory, fresh-tasting hush puppies and Troutman's signature barbecue slaw. A chunkier-than-normal side dish, the slaw is sold in containers in area grocery stores. It's some of the best slaw I've ever tasted.

Troutman's also offers a tender, flavorful barbecued chicken, which is smoked on a rotisserie rather than on the same pits as the barbecued pork shoulders and is anointed with a milder sauce than the one served over the barbecue. The sauce complements the attractively browned bird just perfectly.

Among the other favorites here are the small-sized cheeseburgers, which are often sold by the sackful and which are clearly su-

Troutman's B-B-Q, Denton

perior in taste and texture to fast-food burgers, as well as being reasonably priced.

You can finish off your meal with an absolutely enormous bowl of homemade banana
pudding topped with whipped cream, rather
than the more common egg-white-and-sugar
meringue. Or you can choose homemade
peach cobbler with vanilla ice cream, or even
strawberry cobbler in season.

This is a place that doesn't put on airs
but is absolutely excellent by any standard.
Next time you're in the vicinity of Lexington,
Asheboro, or High Point, drive the fifteen to
twenty extra miles to Denton and check out
Troutman's.

## Bar-B-Q Center

900 North Main Street
Lexington, N.C. 27292-2694
336-248-4633
http://www.barbecuecenter.com
Breakfast, lunch, and dinner are served Monday
    through Saturday.

If you're approaching Lexington from
High Point or Greensboro and determine

you need barbecue *immediately*, Sonny Conrad's Bar-B-Q Center is the answer to your
prayers. Not only is it the first of twenty or
so restaurants you'll come to, it's one of the
few places in town that still cooks entirely
with wood; Sonny even has a printed hand-
out he'll give you explaining exactly how the
process is carried out. Although it's been
seven generations since the Conrads came
to this country from Europe, a touch of German thoroughness such as this proves that
barbecue, like most everything else, benefits
from new blood once in a while. Because of
Bar-B-Q Center's authenticity, its efficiency,
and most of all its favorable location within
a stone's throw of the main Lexington exit, I
feel entirely justified in naming it an official
"Emergency Barbecue Treatment Center"
and conferring upon it all the privileges of
that title.

Most of the time, the cooking at Bar-B-Q
Center is done on a couple of pits built onto
the kitchen. But on special occasions like the
day before the annual Lexington Barbecue
Festival, the restaurant's older outside pits
are fired up. These "special" pits are now enclosed in a metal shed; the shelter's doors are

Rachel Jones prepares one of
Bar-B-Q Center's banana splits.

The media coverage for the Lexington Barbecue Festival is intense. Sonny's place is usually the spot where TV folks, including crews from the national shows, go to do their stories on advance preparations for the festival, since it's the easiest location in which to shoot without having to traipse through the kitchen and get under everyone's feet. Locals also flock to Bar-B-Q Center during the festival. The entire time the meat's on the fire, a knot of observers is usually standing with their hands in their pockets, sniffing the incomparable aroma of pork roasting over wood coals and hoping to be offered a crunchy nibble pulled from the outside of one of the shoulders.

Conrad came by his barbecue skill honestly. One of his grandfathers used to cook shoulders on a backyard pit every Friday during the mid-1940s. His other grandfather, a tobacco farmer, was known for cooking chickens over a pit. "We always ate big at corn shuckings and tobacco curings," remembers Conrad. However, it was through his wife's family that he happened to go into the barbecue business. His brother-in-law, who at one time worked for Warner Stamey, used to operate a dairy bar and barbecue restaurant farther up Main Street; in 1961, he built what is now Bar-B-Q Center. When Sonny got out of the service in the early 1960s, he came back and worked with his brother-in-law. And when his brother-in-law died in 1967, Conrad bought the place. He's been running it ever since, with family help, and has passed along his mastery of pit cooking Lexington-style barbecue to his sons Cecil and Michael.

usually thrown open so the smoke rolls out across the parking lot and onto North Main Street, reminding everyone on that end of town of what lies in store when the festival kicks off the next day. The festival's several sponsoring restaurants, including Bar-B-Q Center, cook some fifteen thousand pounds of extra barbecue among them, which is sold at a furious pace in three large tents on the courthouse square. That's not counting the large amount of meat that has to be cooked for each individual restaurant, since festival day brings every place in town its biggest volume of the year.

Like so many barbecue spots, this one was built as a drive-in. The original shelter is still in place over the parking spots where curb service was once available. Although Bar-B-Q Center no longer employs carhops, you'll still find a drive-in ambiance here, since Sonny's is one of the few places around town where you can get a genuine, hand-dipped banana split, the kind that takes about fifteen minutes to make. A big neon sign advertises this specialty. Families bring their kids in, especially in the summertime, to be entertained by the girls who make the desserts.

As for the barbecue, it's good, solid, genuine stuff straight from the heart of the Lexington tradition, cooked for nine hours or more over glowing hickory coals. Served chopped or sliced, the meat is tender and naturally sweet, and the standard red slaw and hush puppies set it off to perfection. Bar-B-Q Center isn't one of Lexington's largest restaurants, but as Conrad is quick to point out, "this is one town where the little boys aren't automatically eaten up by the big boys the way they are other places."

From I-85 Business (also U.S. 29/70), follow the signs for downtown Lexington, which will lead you directly onto Main Street. If you're approaching from the north, you'll see the restaurant almost immediately on your right.

## Cook's Barbecue

366 Valiant Drive
Lexington, N.C. 27292
336-798-1928
http://www.cooksbbq.com/
Lunch and dinner, Wednesday through Sunday

All right, stick with me now, because this may get confusing. Doug Cook, who opened this rustic place off N.C. 8 in the Cotton Grove community during the late 1960s, doesn't own it anymore, but it still bears his name. Cook now owns Backcountry Barbecue, another out-of-the-way place, but one that *doesn't* bear his name. Actually, Cook doesn't even live in North Carolina any longer. He raises horses in Colorado but comes back to Lexington to check on things from time to time.

Cook was one of the first to play around with the idea of opening a chain of barbecue restaurants, but apparently it never worked out. He was also one of the first to experiment with electric cookers that had a chamber in which you could put green wood to smolder and produce smoke. Cook's Barbecue, which really isn't Cook's, used such an electric smoker at one time, but now it has gone back to cooking with real, honest-to-God hardwood in old-fashioned pits. Got all that?

Actually, it isn't as complicated as I make it sound. Doug's son Brandon and Brandon's wife run Cook's now. And it was Brandon's choice to return to the old ways at the original restaurant, while his dad prefers to keep using some form of electric-fired wood

Cook's Barbecue, Lexington

smoker over at Backcountry. Brandon, who worked at Cook's for years before taking it over, decided there's really nothing like old-fashioned wood cooking, God bless him.

All you really need to know is how to find this place (along with the fact that you *should* find it, because it serves really, really good barbecue). Getting here is an adventure, or at least it used to be before auto navigation systems became commonplace. When you pull into the parking area of what looks sort of like a hunting camp in the woods, you'll begin having that thrill of anticipation that something good is going to happen.

Inside the rough wood-sided structure is a small front room with unusual stainless-steel-topped tables, picnic benches, distressed wood paneling, and a fireplace. In the back is a larger paneled room, also with a fireplace. Doug Cook built the front room with the original restaurant and added the larger room later, when business warranted.

The presence of a salad bar indicates that Cook's has other offerings, but believe me, barbecue is the main deal. Pork shoulders are pit-cooked over oak and hickory coals until they're the shade of cordovan leather and falling-apart tender. The meat is then served chopped, coarse-chopped, or sliced, with a little cup of warm Lexington dip. The round hush puppies the size of cherry tomatoes and the finely chopped barbecue coleslaw both get good marks, but frankly they're almost beneath notice compared to the richly flavored, crusty meat. If you order sweet tea—and it's v-e-r-y sweet—the staff will bring you a whole pitcher of it, which is a nice touch.

As far as I know, Cook's is the only barbecue restaurant in Lexington to serve pit-cooked beef brisket in addition to pork shoulders. The brisket is smoky, tender, and very good, but it doesn't begin to compare to the pork, at least in my book. Brandon probably cooks brisket as well as anyone, but I believe pig is just naturally superior for barbecuing.

The restaurant also sells barbecued chicken, hamburger steaks, fish, salads, and sandwiches. The homemade cobblers include cherry, peach, and strawberry.

But the barbecue is the main deal here.

## Jimmy's BBQ

1703 Cotton Grove Road (N.C. 8 South)
Lexington, N.C. 27292
336-357-2311
Breakfast, lunch, and dinner, Wednesday through
  Monday

The popularity of barbecue grew out of the need to celebrate something—a special event such as a commencement, perhaps, or maybe the successful completion of a lengthy process, such as the harvesting of crops. But as you look at those barbecue restaurants that have been most successful over the years, you'll find that something else is celebrated there as well: family togetherness. It just seems that barbecue restaurants are meant to be run by families and handed down from one generation to the next. When the owner of a successful place sells out or appears to lose interest, it's often because he or she has no family member coming along who's interested in keeping the business going. In most cases, however, someone in the family wants to keep the tradition alive. It's amazing, really, how many children who grow up helping their parents operate barbecue restaurants end up going into the business themselves, even after attending college and exploring other career options. There's obviously a deep satisfaction in serving good food to people, even when it requires hard, dirty, unglamorous work and long, inconvenient hours. Restaurant work, particularly cooking barbecue, has been categorized among the world's most demanding jobs. But members of barbecue families speak less often about the hardships than about the fulfilling sense of continuity they find in preparing food the same way every day, or the satisfaction derived from constantly trying to improve service and quality.

If you want to see a portrait of a barbecue family in the flesh, stop by Jimmy's BBQ in Lexington. Founder Jimmy Harvey has passed on, but you're likely to find his sons Terry and Kemp, his daughters Kirksey and Karen, and his grandchildren Kemp and Jennifer in the restaurant at different times of the day. Even when they aren't working, which is seldom, the family members have traditionally vacationed together at the beach or nearby High Rock Lake. Considering all the pressures that drive families apart today, I'm convinced that the Harveys know something a lot of the rest of us don't. Maybe it's worth a trip to Jimmy's just to ask what it is, or to enjoy the pleasure of observing a family that works hard and sticks together.

Incidentally, the barbecue is pretty darned good at Jimmy's, too. The family ought to know what it's doing by now, since it's been at it since 1942 or thereabouts. Like

Jimmy's BBQ, Lexington

some other well-known barbecuers around Lexington, the late Jimmy Harvey started out working part-time, then full-time, for Warner Stamey. During those early years, he also had a chance to work with another barbecue pioneer, Sid Weaver. When he opened his own place in Thomasville in 1958, he already had sixteen years' experience in the business. By the time Jimmy's opened at its present Lexington location in 1970, he'd been cooking pork shoulders and all the trimmings for twenty-eight years.

Jimmy's serves true Lexington-style pork-shoulder barbecue, cooked long and slow, chopped by hand, and seasoned with a sauce that, even in its mild version, may be among the hottest in town. The 'cue isn't chopped superfine but has an appealing chunky texture. Outside brown meat is available by special order, either chopped or sliced. Since the "brown" typically has a deeper flavor and more toothsome texture than any other part of the shoulder, be sure to try this treat, which you'll find only at a handful of Lexington restaurants.

For a long time, the barbecue here was cooked entirely over wood coals because,

as Jimmy used to say, "smoke is one of the best advertisements in the world. People can smell it all the way out on the highway." But preserving the old ways is also a huge consumer of the family time the Harveys prize, so for a while now, the barbecue has not been cooked with wood.

Jimmy's regular sauce has more red and black pepper and less sugar than the typical Lexington versions you'll find at other spots around town. His "Hot, Hot Dip" is even more invigorating, although it's nothing to be intimidated about, especially when compared to full-bore eastern sauces like those at Scott's and Wilber's. Jimmy's sauce is thicker than either of those, though. You'll probably have to stir it around a bit after you put it on the barbecue in order to get the full effect.

Around Lexington, Jimmy's may be just about as well known for its barbecued chicken as for its pork barbecue. Jimmy's cooks chicken Thursday through Sunday only. On those days, you can bet that just about every one of his 125 seats will be full, at least during peak hours. The half-chickens are slowly grilled for hours until they're a deep, rich brown, then brushed with just enough sauce to soften the good, crispy skin. The chicken is moist and tender and has a wonderful, light flavor.

Jimmy's switch from wood cooking was foreshadowed by some of the founder's remarks several years earlier. Harvey—a gentle, genial man with eyes crinkled by years of smiling—used to grow serious when talking about the future of pit-cooked barbecue around Lexington. He believed events like the annual Lexington Barbecue Festival, for which Jimmy's is one of the sponsoring restaurants, would help maintain a market for the regional specialty. But he also thought a combination of rising costs, environmental regulations, and changing tastes would cut down on the number of places willing to go to the trouble to cook with wood (although I'm not sure he realized at the time that their number would include his own establishment). "There's a shortage of people who will even bring you wood, and when you can get it, it's tripled in price from what it used to be," he pointed out. "The folks with wood can make more money having it chipped up for sale as landscaping mulch."

Wood or no wood, the parking spaces outside Jimmy's stay full. It's worth noting that at least one of the other popular barbecue places in Lexington, Speedy's, has also foregone real wood cooking and remains popular, particularly among locals. The Harvey family members now running things at Jimmy's attribute their success to across-the-board consistency. They may just be on to something.

# Hendrix Barbecue

3664 N.C. 8
Lexington, N.C. 27292
336-357-2364
Breakfast, lunch, and dinner, Tuesday through Sunday

Other locations:
1624 West Innes Street
Salisbury, N.C. 28144
704-645-8040

2488 Statesville Boulevard
Salisbury, N.C. 28147
704-633-9838
Breakfast, lunch, and dinner are served Monday and Wednesday through Saturday. Breakfast and dinner are offered on Tuesday.

614 North Salisbury Avenue
Spencer, N.C. 28159
704-638-0542

The original Hendrix Barbecue has been in Salisbury since 1954, although it's been owned by several families—and even rented out—during portions of its existence.

The most recent Hendrix location is in Lexington, in the former Whitley's Barbecue building. That's where I had an opportunity to sample the current Hendrix approach to barbecue. A second location in Salisbury and one in Spencer, together with the Lexington restaurant, make a total of four barbecue joints now owned and operated by Billy Garris and his brother Timmy. The two have a pretty deep barbecue pedigree. Billy and Timmy grew up in Lexington near the legendary Old Hickory Barbecue, dating back to the 1950s. Both brothers began racking up

Hendrix Barbecue, West Innes Street, Salisbury

barbecue experience at Old Hickory in their early teens. Both also worked at Speedy's in Lexington, Timmy for seventeen years. Shortly after Billy bought Hendrix Barbecue in Salisbury in 1989, he brought in his brother as co-owner. The two have grown the business together since then.

Hendrix was voted number one in the 1997 Salisbury Taste of the Town competition, so I was anxious to see what the two brothers had put in place and how they would compete in North Carolina's Piedmont barbecue capital, Lexington. Chris Harris, Billy's nephew, was the manager of the Lexington location at the time I visited.

When I pulled around to the back of the Lexington restaurant upon arrival, I saw a pile of hickory wood and a gas tank standing side by side, which provided an immediate and accurate foreshadowing of the cooking method at this location. The Garris brothers cooked for years on old-fashioned pits, but their restaurants now use gas or electric smokers. In Lexington, a gas flame heats a firebox full of

hickory, and the pork shoulders spend hours on racks rotating through a larger chamber filled with the aromatic smoke. This cuts down on the number of hours someone has to stay with the meat while it's cooking, and it produces a pleasant, clearly recognizable smoke flavor, if not a second "grill" taste that results when meat juices are allowed to drip onto the coals.

Still and all, the hefty, piled-high barbecue sandwich I sampled at Hendrix was delicious. The meat was tender and moist and was served with a mild, warm dip that didn't have as much vinegar tang as I'd been led to expect, based on scouting reports from other Hendrix locations. (Salisbury's barbecue culture tends toward more vinegar and less tomato taste, whereas Lexington leans more toward the red stuff, which probably explains the differences in sauce at various locations under the Hendrix umbrella.) I also encountered a finely chopped red slaw on my sandwich in Lexington, whereas my correspondents tell me that the Hendrix barbecue slaw in Salisbury is coarser and has more tartness, which also conforms to the norms in that city.

I was encouraged to notice "Skin Sandwiches" and side orders of skin available—even a "Box of Skins," should you ever need such a thing. Pork skins are often discarded in the Piedmont, but a good, crisp "Skin Sandwich" is a nice change of pace once in a while.

The barbecued chicken at Hendrix in Lexington is not cooked in a hickory smoker, for an interesting and revealing reason. Hickory smoke tends to turn meat—and especially white meat—pink. Many customers are so conditioned to equate pink color in chicken with a lack of doneness that they send it back, refusing to listen to any explanation for the color, no matter how well done the meat actually is. Many barbecue restaurants using gas- or electric-fired smokers have encountered this headache. Hendrix decided to simply cook the barbecued chicken on an electric rotisserie and be done with it. It's still pretty good.

I was pleased to find vegetables including okra, squash, pinto beans, and green beans with whole potatoes on the menu at Hendrix in Lexington, along with local standbys such as bologna sandwiches, hot dogs, and hamburgers.

The restaurant was pretty crowded for three o'clock on a Sunday afternoon. I ran into several effusively complimentary customers. One couple remarked that the place served their "very favorite barbecue." One table called the manager out from the kitchen to praise the fried flounder, which the cus-

tomers said was "the best in the county—like cooking you get at home." The cook told me that Billy Garris had personally taught him how to bread fish so it fries up light, crisp, and fresh tasting.

Hendrix has homemade pumpkin pie in season, although the waitresses say they run out of it quickly. It also serves cobbler and banana pudding, as well as a different type of homemade cake each day; the most popular of these is the "Hershey Bar Cake," which also sells out quickly.

Hendrix's Lexington location is quite impressive, if simple and straightforward in its service and décor. It shares enough common touches with the other Hendrix locations to bode well for the overall brand.

## Lexington Barbecue

10 U.S. 29/70 South
Lexington, N.C. 27295
336-249-9814
Lunch and dinner are served Monday through
  Saturday. Curb service is offered.

The highway that passes within fifty yards of Lexington Barbecue's front door used to be a part of Interstate 85 between Greensboro and Charlotte. However, many years ago, I-85 was relocated so that it now bypasses Lexington several miles to the east. The former route mostly carries local traffic along the furniture corridor stretching from High Point through Thomasville to Lexington.

But owner Wayne Monk never lost a dollar's worth of business when the interstate was

Lexington Barbecue, Lexington

moved because, to the faithful, *all* roads still lead to Lexington Barbecue. Today, Monk, his son Rick, and the many family members who work with them are not only the undisputed barbecue chiefs of Lexington—a town with twenty or so barbecue places, depending on the day or week you're counting—they're also perhaps the most widely known of all North Carolina's barbecue restaurateurs.

Lexington has several fine barbecue restaurants, but none serve the town's famous wood-smoked pork shoulder in a more lean, moist, and tender, yet firmly textured, state than does Lexington Barbecue. The restaurant itself is bright and clean but unremarkable, and the side dishes, while perfectly rendered, are few. The meat is the thing here—enhanced to perfection by a dark, rather thin sauce, or "dip," that is neither too mild nor too fiery. The meat's reputation is reflected in the restaurant's unusual clientele. While all of Lexington's barbecue restaurants get their fair share of trade from local customers—who tend to stick with one favorite place—Lexington Barbecue attracts barbe-

cue pilgrims from across the state and even farther. Having left the interstate and driven several miles out of their way to reach this mecca, these people usually emerge from their cars with a gleam of purposefulness in their eye and move toward the restaurant with steps quickened by anticipation. Many of them have been here before, and it's the meat that has brought them back.

A fortuitous series of circumstances helped the place achieve its current position. But Monk, who still serves as chief spokesman, will tell you that the real luck came in the fact that he was a natural hard worker and that he chose the right man to imitate. In Warner Stamey—a pioneer in establishing Lexington barbecue—Monk found a mentor who exuded both pride in the craft of barbecuing and a strong drive to achieve excellence. Today, Lexington Barbecue is one of at least three venerable barbecue places in the Piedmont that owe their existence to Stamey's ideas.

Monk got his first restaurant job as a sixteen-year-old carhop at a Lexington barbecue joint. At the time, he was more interested in hot dogs and cheeseburgers and didn't really understand what attracted people to barbecue. During the next ten years, Monk "bounced around a good bit," working a variety of jobs. He spent several of those years working directly under Warner Stamey at his place in downtown Lexington. Monk began to absorb Stamey's vision of Lexington-style barbecue as a legitimate, distinctive regional specialty and gradually came to appreciate Stamey's talent for surrounding himself with good, reliable people who shared his enthusiasm for the product and its demanding method of preparation.

In 1962, with considerable experience under his belt for a man of twenty-six, Monk had a lucky opportunity to buy a prime roadside location beside U.S. 29/70—the same spot his restaurant has occupied ever since. Ironically, both Stamey and Holland Tussey, another former boss, had owned the parcel previously, but neither had ever done anything with it. Monk, on the other hand, has not only made a go of it but added on to the place five times over the years.

Monk's early good fortune held. Right after he opened the restaurant, it became popular as a teenage hangout. However, it wasn't long before he realized that spending late-night hours with a restaurant full of high-school kids was exhausting and not particularly profitable. With a fresh image in mind, Monk worked hard over the next several years to reposition the restaurant as a place catering to families and devoted to the slow, painstaking preparation of succulent meat—barbecue that would later have much

of the state beating a path to his door.

Lexington Barbecue is now the kind of place that's not only warm and inviting, but also one where first-time visitors are immediately put at ease by the helpful staff, who are prepared to cheerfully and quickly explain the delightful variety of ways in which barbecue can be delivered to the table. The restaurant's mode of operation is very much a reflection of the personality and magnetism of Wayne Monk, an animated, outgoing man with a youthful, elfin face. Although he spends much of his time working the counter and cash register at the front of the restaurant, where he can chat and joke with customers, he has largely passed the torch to his son Rick and his two sons-in-law, all of whom normally work in the kitchen. Other family members too numerous to keep up with also work at the restaurant.

While Monk is known as a man who looks out for his own and pays his employees well, he also demands a high level of performance. At peak periods, the kitchen looks a little like the bridge of a warship called to battle stations, with every position manned and every person alertly attending to his assigned details of food preparation and presentation. Waitresses, who tend to stay on for a long time once they're hired, must have, as Monk puts it, "the right appearance, attitude, and chemistry" to mix well with the families and older adults he wants to attract. Orders are quickly delivered to the tables, and tea glasses are kept full. On the pits at the back of the restaurant, pork shoulders roast for ten hours over mostly oak coals; hickory is added when available. Veteran attendants shovel fresh coals from the fireboxes and scatter them under the dripping meat every thirty minutes or so. They turn the shoulders so that the exposed meat side is facing up once it has roasted over the embers to a deep, dark brown.

Wayne or Rick Monk and any of the personally trained staff can take one of these beautifully browned, tender pork shoulders apart like the pieces of a puzzle. The skin lifts off in one piece and is discarded, and the excess fat is quickly trimmed. The "outside brown" is removed and set aside for special orders. Then the meat is pulled off the shoulder in large pinkish brown chunks and placed on a chopping board until needed. As the orders come in, the succulent pork is either sliced, chopped into coarse chunks, or chopped more finely, then piled on a plate, a tray, or a sandwich bun. Sauce is ladled over the meat just before it leaves the kitchen, so the barbecue comes to the table moist but not saturated.

If you want a little foretaste of heaven, order a tray of the sliced "brown"—the chewy outside meat that absorbs so much of the oak- or hickory-smoke flavor. While many barbecue places chop this portion of the shoulder into the other chopped meat, Monk's place serves it separately in order to satisfy all the customers who think, as I do, that it's absolutely the most delicious kind of meat on earth. You'll need to arrive early for lunch or dinner to be sure of getting some, since the restaurant usually runs out of "brown" early in every meal service.

The coleslaw and the hush puppies at Lexington Barbecue are as good as you'll find anywhere. The pups have a good, fresh cornmeal taste with little hint of sweetness or onion. Be sure to try the "Smokehouse Sauce," which has quite a bit more kick than the regular dip. I also recommend the pit-smoked, sliced turkey breast. Moist and deeply infused with the flavor of wood smoke, it's a new favorite among quite a few of Monk's regulars.

Frankly, though, the barbecue itself is so outstanding here that the side dishes assume a purely complementary role. In fact, the barbecue is good enough to have been served to world leaders. In 1983, Monk was asked by a politically connected local attorney if he would be interested in preparing barbecue for President Reagan. Not thinking much about it, Monk answered in the affirmative. The next thing he knew, he was booked by White House staffers to cater a meal for the heads of state of the world's seven leading industrial countries. A major economic summit meeting had been scheduled in Williamsburg, Virginia, and the president wanted to introduce his guests to genuine American cuisine. Monk was thus chosen to introduce the likes of England's Margaret Thatcher and France's François Mitterand to North Carolina barbecue. Undaunted, he flew to Williamsburg and served the meal without a hitch. It seems his luck continued to hold—the only out-of-town event he had ever catered before was in Williamsburg, so he was already familiar with the layout. He even had a former employee who lived there and was ready to pitch in as the local liaison.

However, Monk does not consider serving his barbecue to world leaders his greatest achievement by any means. He's actually sort of a homebody who doesn't like to get too far off his turf. Not surprisingly, then, he says his biggest satisfaction has come in adopting one local specialty and helping to make it great. And the way he says it leaves little doubt that he *does* consider Lexington barbecue great. In addition to being utterly sold on his product, he's really stubborn about the way it's prepared. While he shakes his head in mock disbelief over the number of Lexington restaurants that have switched to cooking with electricity, he acknowledges that in ten, fifteen, or perhaps twenty years, all those in town may have given up cooking over live coals because of the expense and the uncertainties of environmental regulation. "But I've got quite a few more years in me," he declares. "And as long as I'm the one making the decisions, we'll continue to cook and serve our barbecue the way we always have."

## Smiley's Lexington BBQ

917 Winston Road (N.C. 8 North)
Lexington, N.C. 27295
336-248-4528
http://www.smileyslexingtonbbq.com
Breakfast, lunch, and dinner, Tuesday through
    Saturday

This place opened in the 1960s as Smiley's, then went through a spell being called Southern Barbecue, and is now back to the original name. It's a great little place.

The barbecue here is the real deal, con-tinuing a fifty-year tradition of pit-cooking with wood. Offering a great deal of smoke and "grill" flavor (which comes from fat dripping onto coals), the meat is served chopped, coarse-chopped, or sliced, swimming in a delicious, tangy "dip." The barbecued chicken is absolutely wonderful as well; it literally falls off the bone. It is pink from the wood smoke (*not* from being underdone) and has its sauce served warm on the side. The red slaw, a little chunkier than some, is adroitly seasoned for near-perfect balance with the smoked meat. I have heard several customers offer testimonials to the effect that the barbecue at Smiley's is the best Lexington has to offer. While that's

Smiley's customers are greeted by a fanciful barbecue-choppin' pig.

Smiley's Lexington BBQ, Lexington

such a subjective judgment as to be of limited value, you can be pretty sure that dining at this modest little restaurant will put you near the top of the Lexington barbecue pyramid.

Smiley's also specializes in hot dogs, which are said by many to be the best in Lexington. Plenty of people always seem to be waiting for curb service or buzzing around the register inside, eager for hot dogs to go. A customer came in and bought twenty at one whack while I was there.

Pork-skin sandwiches are also a big deal here. Hamburgers and cheeseburgers (the favorite comes "Carolina-style," with chili and slaw), pimento cheese, grilled cheese, ham and cheese, and country ham are other popular sandwich offerings. Locals rave as well about the battered potato wedges, served with homemade ranch dressing. They're said

to be ideal even when rewarmed in the oven at home.

Many customers speak positively about the quick, smiling service at Smiley's, including the prompt curb service.

## Smokey Joe's Barbecue

*North Carolina Classic*

1101 South Main Street
Lexington, N.C. 27292
336-249-0315
Breakfast, lunch, and dinner, Monday through
Saturday

Located in a freestanding flat-roofed building that has a bit of a 1950s look inside, Smokey Joe's Barbecue is right on Lexington's main drag. Old photographs from the town's early days as a barbecue center, along with framed Lexington Barbecue Festival posters, give some idea of the weight of tradition and expectation that rests on the shoulders of Scott and Kaffee Cope as the owners of one of Lexington's premier establishments. The Copes are so dedicated to barbecue that in addition to the pits at the restaurant, they have large brick pits at their home, where they help cook extra barbecue for the city's huge annual festival in October.

The day begins early with Smokey Joe's full breakfast, which includes eggs and hotcakes. But the lunch and dinner traffic brings the place its true renown. The establishment's reputation has been boosted by recommendations in *Southern Living* and *USA Today*, to say nothing of word-of-mouth praise from hundreds of thousands of barbecue lovers.

As the sign says at Smokey Joe's, the barbecue is "pit cooked the old fashioned way." While many Lexington-area barbecue places can make that claim, I believe Smokey Joe's has, hands down, the most tender slow-roasted pork shoulders in town—as well as the sweetest iced tea I've ever tasted.

I like to order coarse-chopped barbecue, which usually arrives cut into cubes roughly one inch square. At Smokey Joe's, these moist, flavorful bites, lightly kissed by the restaurant's peppery dip and subtly flavored by wood smoke and the steam from fat dripping onto coals, melt onto the tongue without having to be chewed at all. The meat is so tender and enjoyable that the restaurant's well-balanced barbecue slaw and crisp hush puppies go almost unnoticed.

Smokey Joe's pit-cooks barbecued chicken on Thursday, Friday, and Saturday and also offers whole pit-cooked pork shoulders. Rather than buying several pounds of chopped barbecue to feed a large group, I'd suggest buying a whole shoulder, which will feed around fifteen people, and chopping and seasoning it yourself, perhaps with some of Smokey Joe's delicious dip, which is offered for sale. Remember to salt the chopped meat lightly before moistening it with the sauce.

Smokey Joe's Barbecue, Lexington

Daughter-in-law Jessica Garner, the 2010 North Carolina Teacher of the Year, presented a signed copy of *North Carolina Barbecue: Flavored by Time* to President Obama during a visit to the White House.
*Courtesy of the White House Photo Office*

My daughter-in-law, Jessica Garner, was selected as the 2010 North Carolina Teacher of the Year. One of the perks was a trip to Washington and a chance for her and her husband, my son Nelson, to visit the White House for a Rose Garden recognition ceremony. Each of the fifty state Teachers of the Year would have an opportunity to meet President Barack Obama one on one in the Oval Office, after which each would be introduced to the gathering in the Rose Garden prior to the president's remarks to the entire group.

A few weeks before the trip, Jessica called to ask me to autograph a copy of my first book, *North Carolina Barbecue: Flavored by Time*, as a gift for the president and first lady. The teachers had not been instructed to take gifts to the chief executive, but Jessica thought the book was appropriate as a keepsake from North Carolina and simply took matters into her own hands, as she is wont to do.

When her turn came to meet the president, Jessica presented the book, which I had inscribed with a comment about *Barack* having become another favorite *b* word to many North Carolinians, along with *basketball* and *barbecue*. President Obama graciously accepted the gift and made a comment about having recently eaten North Carolina barbecue at Asheville's 12 Bones restaurant during a presidential visit to the state. (He also sampled the fare at Cape Fear Barbecue in Fayetteville during the 2008 campaign.)

Leafing politely through the volume, he came upon my book-jacket photo, taken when I weighed around a hundred pounds more than I do today. The super-slender, athletic Mr. Obama grinned and remarked mischievously, "Well, it looks like he's enjoyed quite a bit of barbecue over the years."

Jessica confided the presidential comment to my son and my wife, but all three of them conspired to keep it from me for quite a while—until it finally slipped out one night after a couple of glasses of wine.

Nelson had been with the crowd in the Rose Garden, waiting for Jessica to emerge from the Oval Office and onto the Portico for her formal introduction to the group. He said he knew some sort of conversation was taking place when it became obvious that Jessica was spending more time with the president than the few seconds allotted for a quick handshake and a photograph.

After all the teachers had completed their private Oval Office receptions, the president emerged to speak to the entire group of honorees. At the conclusion of some brief remarks, Mr. Obama waved goodbye and turned to head back to the Oval Office. Then he turned back to the podium, waved once again to the crowd, and called out, "And thanks for the barbecue book!"

I, too, am grateful to that first book for opening several new chapters in my life.

## Speedy Lohr's BBQ of Arcadia

8000 N.C. 150 North
Lexington, N.C. 27295
336-764-5509
Breakfast, lunch, and dinner, Monday through Saturday

The mailing address is Lexington, but Speedy Lohr's is actually in the community of Arcadia on N.C. 150 some distance from the Piedmont barbecue capital. It's run by Roger Lohr, son of the legendary Paul "Speedy" Lohr, founder of Speedy's in Lexington, with able assistance from Speedy's grandson, also named Paul. For a while, the place was known as Arcadia BBQ, but now the name reflects the legacy of one of Lexington's leading barbecue figures, with all the promise that implies.

Speedy Lohr learned his craft working at Stamey's and at Old Hickory Barbecue in Lexington. Later, he bought Tussy's Drive-In and renamed it Speedy's. The restaurant still operates under that name in Lexington, although it was sold years ago to the Dunn family. But that's another story. Suffice it to say that any place bearing Speedy's name is a good bet.

Speedy Lohr's in Arcadia is the real deal—pork shoulders cooked for hours and hours in traditional pits over hardwood coals. The coarse-chopped meat and sliced meat from the shoulder are my favorites, although the regular chopped barbecue would be at the top of the pyramid in practically anyone's rating system, I imagine. You'll get all the complex, bewitching pit-cooked flavor you

Paul Lohr, grandson of Speedy Lohr, helps man the pits at Speedy Lohr's BBQ of Arcadia.

can imagine from any of these choices, and you'll find the experience heightened considerably by the simple enhancements of the Lexington-style "dip" and the red coleslaw. Goodness, it's good!

Speedy's in Arcadia now offers pit-cooked ribs (at a good price, too) on Wednesday and barbecued chicken on Thursday. The fact that the place regularly sells out of both specials early in the day should tell you all you need to know. I didn't get to sample either, but when someone knows how to cook pork shoulders to this degree of excellence, you can bet they know how to prepare ribs and chicken just as expertly.

The Arcadia restaurant also draws rave reviews for its skin sandwiches. Employee Brittany Walker told me the skins are so good because they're pulled immediately from the shoulders and fried up crispy as quickly

as possible. Between the appealing, crunchy texture and the mesmerizing smoke flavor, the sandwiches are addictive, if a bit sketchy from a health perspective.

The restaurant could do better than the one dessert it offered on my visit: an uninspiring, instant-pudding-type banana pudding. On the other hand, maybe we need a reminder that this little restaurant isn't actually heaven—only a close facsimile.

## Tarheel Q

6835 U.S. 64 West
Lexington, N.C. 27295
336-787-4550
Breakfast, lunch, and dinner, Tuesday through Saturday

Established in 1984, Tarheel Q is located in a neat white stucco building beside a service station on a rural stretch of U.S. 64. Out back, the large brick pit and the neatly stacked woodpile present ample evidence that the owners intend to compete seriously for their share of the barbecue market in the Lexington area, despite being located off the beaten track. A 2010 fire damaged the building, but the owners quickly brought Tarheel Q back.

Considering that this rural restaurant is seven miles west of downtown Lexington, almost at the Yadkin River, I was surprised to find it crowded at three o'clock on a Saturday afternoon. However, my surprise evaporated once my order was brought to the table.

Advertising "old-style pit barbecue," Tarheel Q delivers the goods as well as any restaurant in the target-rich environment around Lexington. My order of coarse-chopped "outside brown" barbecue was absolutely superb. It was crisp and chewy on the surface, reddish-colored from wood smoke, tender, and full of flavor. The sauce was a lit-tle milder and thicker than many of the local "dips," but it complemented the meat to perfection. The red barbecue slaw had just the right amount of bite to it (white slaw is available as well), while the hush puppies were just the way I like them best—tiny and crisp, with a pure cornmeal flavor and only a hint of sugar.

Lexington-area residents in the know speak highly of both the barbecued chicken and the baby back ribs at Tarheel Q. Unfortunately, I haven't had the opportunity yet to try either. The chicken is available Thursday through Saturday, while the ribs are a once-a-week treat on Wednesday night.

The locals also speak highly of breakfast at Tarheel Q, which begins at six o'clock. Actually, I have a hard time imagining a meal at this restaurant that doesn't include some of that wonderfully smoked pork barbecue.

A complete selection of sandwiches, salads, and dinner plates is also available.

Tarheel Q, Lexington

Stamey's Barbecue of Tyro

## Stamey's Barbecue of Tyro

4524 N.C. 150 South
Lexington, N.C. 27295
336-853-6426
Breakfast, lunch, and dinner, Monday through
Saturday

Owners Dan and Nancy Stamey are not relatives of the Greensboro Stameys, although both families trace their barbecue beginnings to Lexington. This restaurant in the tiny community of Tyro has no connection whatsoever to the larger, better-known Stamey's on Greensboro's High Point Road. Dan, who used to operate Hog City Barbecue in Lexington, relocated to Tyro on N.C. 150 in 1973. Dan, Nancy, their two sons, and a daughter-in-law operate the restaurant.

This attractive restaurant has an aesthetically pleasing setting, a nice little glassed-in porch on the front side, a cozy, paneled interior, and some interior neon accents. It has a reputation for quick service, for keeping beverage glasses full, and for generous—some call them enormous—helpings of reasonably priced food.

The barbecue here comes from pork shoulders pit-cooked over hardwood coals. The moderately coarsely chopped meat has perhaps a touch more fat and crispy skin worked into it than is the norm in this part of the state. But as I'm fond of repeating, the fat is the conduit of flavor—particularly the fat on the outside of the shoulder that absorbs the lion's share of the smoke and "grill" taste from the pit. While the concept of "lean and clean" barbecue is attractive to many, I personally think that a bit more fat vastly increases not only the flavor but also the

silkiness of the meat's texture. By way of comparison, it does for your tongue what a satin bed sheet does for your tootsies. You can also order coarse-chopped chunks of meat and sliced barbecue, both of which maintain a good level of smoky flavor.

The sauce is a bit thicker with tomato purée than the average dip found in Lexington, several miles to the east. A good bit of sauce is added to the barbecue in the kitchen, so that the 'cue is served fairly "wet." While the sauce isn't exactly fiery, it does have a little kick that manifests itself mostly in the afterglow. The mixture between meat and sauce is about right in the chopped barbecue. But if you're ordering coarse-chopped or sliced barbecue, you may want to ask for your sauce on the side, so as not to get too much.

Some customers stoutly maintain that the red barbecue slaw at the Stamey's in Tyro is even better and more memorable than the barbecue itself. Others are of the opinion that the acidity of the slaw overpowers the meat and the sauce either in a barbecue tray or on a sandwich. In my opinion, you'll have an en-

joyable meal if you simply approach the slaw with due respect, perhaps taking small bites of it in proportion to the pit-cooked meat itself.

## Backcountry Barbeque
4014 Linwood-Southmont Road
Linwood, N.C. 27299
336-956-1696
Breakfast, lunch, and dinner are served Monday through Saturday. Lunch and dinner are offered on Sunday.

There was a time when Doug Cook's Backcountry Barbeque was housed in a squat building with a spindly, tin-roofed overhang. It looked like a cross between a country store that had fallen on hard times and a place where dogfights might be held. However, the restaurant has been slicked up considerably in recent years, most recently after a fire. New red awnings are out front, a large second dining room is in the back, and a tasteful palette of fresh paints is visible throughout. When I

Backcountry has terrific barbecue. The twenty-ounce sirloin steak for two is one of its most popular specials.

visited, a sanitation rating of 101 brightened up the place even further.

Located well out in the country, the restaurant is decorated with Indian pottery and framed prints of Western scenes, a circumstance explained by the fact that Cook is an absentee owner who now spends most of his time in Colorado. However, his long years in the barbecue business (see the entry on Cook's Barbecue in Lexington) bode well for anyone able to find his or her way to this restaurant.

What can I say about the barbecue at Backcountry except that it's incredible? Dark, reddish brown, lean, moist, chewy, tender, and robustly flavored by the hardwood pit, the pork is accompanied by a delicious, fiery dip that's served warm. The meat also comes with a terrific barbecue coleslaw that has a lingering peppery aftertaste. The restaurant serves the same small, round hushpuppies as does Cook's Barbecue. They're as irresistible as fresh popcorn shrimp.

What do you have when you aren't eating barbecue at Backcountry? Well, breakfast, of course, and sandwiches—burgers mostly, although the pork-skin sandwiches are always

in high demand. Sirloin steak—the only cut of steak the restaurant prepares—is another choice. The overwhelming favorite among local customers (and one of the best food deals on the planet) is the twenty-ounce sirloin for two, which comes with two trips to the salad bar, two baked potatoes, and rolls for two. Easily enough food for three, it costs $16.95, plus tax. Unbelievably, the price has decreased by a dollar since I first wrote about this special place in 2002. I love this restaurant.

## College Bar-B-Que

*North Carolina Classic*

117 Statesville Boulevard
Salisbury, N.C. 28144
704-633-9953
Breakfast, lunch, and dinner are served Sunday and Tuesday through Friday. Breakfast and lunch are offered Monday and Saturday.

Plenty of super-enthusiastic College Bar-B-Que fans are out there—generally people who have lived in Salisbury all their lives and who say things like, "The barbecue and the hot dogs at College Bar-B-Que will

College Bar-B-Que, Salisbury

be what I want for my last meal on earth," or, "It's the best in the world!"

But owner Jay Owen knows that, subjective opinions aside, his place—like many—is more about people and continuity than simply about the food itself. Since its founding in 1963, College Bar-B-Que has become *the* comfortable and familiar place for many regulars to eat most or all of their meals—breakfast, lunch, and dinner. When the restaurant closed for six weeks for much-needed renovations in March 2011, Owen worried that his regulars, some of them elderly, would feel quite a disruption in their lives. Now that the place is back with its familiar exterior profile and signature green booths—but with a much improved roof, plumbing system, and kitchen—order has returned to the universe for a slice of Salisbury's citizenry.

To be sure, the wood-cooked barbecue here is exceptionally good. And I take comfort in the fact that the actual barbecue pits weren't changed at all during the renovation. College chops its 'cue a little more finely than other joints in Salisbury. But along with competitors like Hendrix, Wink's, and Richard's, it shares the Rowan County characteristic of saucing the meat with a dip that's less sweet and more vinegary than the sauce used in Lexington and elsewhere around the Piedmont. The red slaw is also a bit more tart than the common Lexington version.

The hush puppies at College are straightforwardly cornmeal-flavored, with noticeably less sweetness than many in the region. Footlong hot dogs are the second-most-popular item on the menu. As you would expect, most loyal customers order them "all the way"—loaded with mustard, slaw, onions, and the restaurant's homemade chili.

Alongside other, more standard beverages, College offers fountain Cheerwine and its own "Lemon Sun Drop" mixture.

For breakfast, patrons can order crispy livermush (try it with a couple dashes of Texas Pete!) to complement the standard bacon, ham, and sausage. The omelets, described as "massive," are available with a virtually endless supply of fillings.

## Richard's Bar-B-Q

522 North Main Street
Salisbury, N.C. 28144
704-636-9561
Breakfast, lunch, and dinner, Monday through
    Saturday

Richard's Bar-B-Q is a cozy place that's been in business since 1979 on downtown Salisbury's North Main Street. Its brick exterior with red awnings and its inviting interior are kept as neat as a pin. The main room, accented by toy trains, has an unusually long stainless-steel counter. Back behind the restaurant where the pit and the woodpile are located, the parking lot routinely stays full. It's obvious that Richard's is a popular gathering place, since people are usually waiting for booths, tables, and counter stools.

Presiding over this enterprise is Richard Monroe, who learned his craft working for Salisbury's famed T & F Barbecue. T & F opened for business in 1935 and for quite some time was known as "the Biggest Little Place in North Carolina." Remember, Salisbury is proud of its barbecue heritage. Some accounts say its barbecue history even predates Lexington's.

The barbecue here is closely akin to Lexington-style but has its own characteristic Rowan County vinegar tang. The pit-cooked pork shoulders are served chopped or sliced. Both have a lean consistency and a pronounced and pleasant smoky taste. The barbecue coleslaw is slightly less sweet than what is usually found in Lexington. Enormous hush puppies nearly the size of tennis balls round out a barbecue meal.

Richard's has a complete breakfast menu. Like all traditional places in the area, the selection includes that wonderful specialty brought to the area by settlers of German ancestry—livermush. This romantic-sounding stuff is a mixture of ground pork liver, other ground pork, cornmeal, and seasonings. Throughout a large swath of the Piedmont, livermush is served sliced and fried, either as a breakfast meat or in sandwiches.

Richard's Bar-B-Q,
Salisbury

Richard's also offers barbecued chicken, a salad bar, and a wide sandwich selection. Dinner specials include homemade chili beans and homemade spaghetti, both of which are available after four o'clock.

## Wink's: The King of Barbecue

509 Faith Road
Salisbury, N.C. 28146
704-637-2410
Breakfast, lunch, and dinner are served Monday through Thursday. Dinner is offered on Friday and Saturday.

For many years, Wink's occupied a modest red-painted building on U.S. 52 just east of its intersection with I-85. People used to comment that while the building wasn't much to look at, the hickory-wood smoke would grab your nose a half-mile away.

The old building was torn down years ago because of road improvements, and Wink's moved to its present location not far from the original site. I was gratified to see the wood-burning pit and the pile of wood at the present facility. Hopefully, the aromatic smoke from the pit will drift back over the spot where Wink's used to stand, reminding everyone that the business is still cooking barbecue the old-fashioned way just a short distance up the road.

The new building couldn't be more different from the original. Instead of one dark, low-ceilinged room, Wink's now has two large dining rooms with high ceilings. Lots of light-colored diagonal wood paneling and modern decorating touches are in evidence.

At the average barbecue joint, radical changes in the physical environment can cause serious apprehension about how the

Wink's, Salisbury

barbecue itself may have changed. ("This place is nice ... too nice.") I'm happy to report that the 'cue at Wink's is still very, very good. It's smoky, sweet, tender, and, atypically for the region, served with white slaw, rather than the red barbecue variety.

Since the present digs are a touch too elegant for barbecue alone, it's appropriate that you can get just about anything you want at Wink's. The extensive breakfast menu has that Piedmont favorite, livermush. You can also choose from a menu that includes seafood, steak, prime rib, salads, and a wide sandwich selection. Among the desserts are homemade oatmeal cream pie, double chocolate cake, coconut crème cake, peanut butter pie, persimmon pudding (in season), pumpkin pie, banana pudding, and blackberry, peach, and cherry cobblers.

## Keaton's Barbecue

17365 Cool Springs Road
Cleveland, N.C. 27013
704-278-1619
http://www.keatonsoriginalbbq.com
Lunch is served Tuesday and Wednesday. Lunch (until 2 P.M.) and dinner (until 8 P.M.) are offered Thursday through Saturday.

Here's a wonderful rural hole in the wall, halfway between Mocksville and Statesville, where the pork barbecue takes a backseat to the barbecued chicken, and where the barbecued chicken isn't actually barbecued but deep-fried, then immersed in a memorable, mysterious barbecue sauce. No matter. Keaton's is an absolute must-stop. If its mention

here and the fulsome write-up in the January 2002 issue of *Gourmet* aren't enough to convince you, then maybe the guest book signed by visitors from all over the world will be. The *Charlotte Observer* has ranked Keaton's number twelve among the Tar Heel State's top twenty-five restaurants.

The late B. W. Keaton, a large, jovial-looking black gentleman whose portrait shows him dressed in an apron and with a cigarette dangling from his lips, began the business as a neighborhood grill in 1953. The original place had a cement floor inside and wood-burning barbecue pits outside. Unlike most barbecue places, it served beer, just as it does today. Keaton is said to have kept his place from turning into a typical beer joint by insisting his patrons behave themselves. To this day, signs warning against loud talking and the use of profanity are prominently displayed.

Along with pit-cooking pork barbecue, Keaton experimented to come up with a unique way of preparing chicken. He finally settled upon cooking half and whole chickens in a deep fat fryer, then dipping them for a few seconds in either a mild or spicy barbecue sauce. Developing just the right sauce took quite awhile, and Keaton said later that the dogs ended up eating a lot of his chicken during the trial-and-error period. Once he perfected the sauce, though, his business soared. He was quoted as saying there was now little left for the dogs but clean-picked bones. Keaton kept his sauce recipe a secret, turning down an offer of ten thousand dollars to divulge it not long before his death.

Keaton's Barbecue, Cleveland

Keaton's is notable for chicken that's fried, then marinated in barbecue sauce.
*Photo by Kristin Garcia*

Today, Kathleen Murray, a niece of B. W. Keaton's, runs the restaurant. The original, modest barbecue pit and chicken shack have been expanded to include a plain but comfortable dining room. But customers still line up at the counter to order and pay before being sent to numbered booths to await the ar-

rival of their orders. Besides barbecued pork sandwiches, the only items on the menu are half and whole chickens; side dishes of beans, coleslaw, and macaroni and cheese; beverages; and desserts (banana pudding and "Cherry Yum-Yum").

A customer standing next to me in line

recognized me from television and was so delighted that I intended to write about the place that he insisted on buying my entire dinner. I ordered a barbecue sandwich (for research purposes) and found it to be moderately good, the electric-pit-cooked pork chopped fine and mixed liberally with a sweet sauce. My attention was soon drawn, though, to the half-chicken, its crisp skin gradually softening after the split bird had been immersed in a dark, spicy sauce with an absolutely tantalizing aroma. As I expected, the chicken was moist and bursting with a superb flavor that—as one customer described it— "penetrated all the way to the bone." A serving of rich, chewy macaroni and cheese and a half-pitcher of excellent iced tea accompanied my world-class chicken.

You'll be surrounded by miles of orderly western Piedmont farmland on your way to Keaton's. From I-40, take Exit 162 (the Cool Springs exit) between Mocksville and Statesville and turn west on U.S. 64. After passing a Texaco station on the left and crossing a narrow bridge, turn left onto Woodleaf Road, which before long turns into Cool Springs Road. The restaurant is located on the right two to three miles from the intersection. Be sure to sign the guest book, and remember, no loud talking or profanity!

## Gary's Bar-B-Q

620 U.S. 29 North
China Grove, N.C. 28023
704-857-8314
Lunch and dinner, Monday through Saturday

Growing up in China Grove, Gary Ritchie always wanted to own a barbecue place. In 1971, he opened Gary's Bar-B-Q in a renovated service station and garage. Today, the parking lot is nearly always full. Inside, warm wood paneling, cheerful yellow booths, and a colorful collection of thousands of cigarette advertisements and soft-drink signs, the majority for Coke and Pepsi, help create a homey, inviting atmosphere.

At one time, Gary's Bar-B-Q pit-cooked its pork-shoulder barbecue over wood coals. Long after he switched from the old-fashioned pits to electric cookers, Ritchie kept a pile of wood outside just for appearance. The wood turned so gray and weathered that it didn't fool anybody, so the decorative pile of split logs is no longer there.

But people's memories are incredibly powerful. Even though today's chopped barbecue at Gary's is, in my opinion, not so

Gary's Bar-B-Q, China Grove

memorable, many present and former residents believe it is now and always has been the best barbecue they've ever eaten. Who's to say they're wrong? Even though China Grove is on the western side of the North Carolina Piedmont, one former resident gushed, "There's nothing like eastern Carolina barbecue, and no place like Gary's to get it!" *Salisbury Post* editor Elizabeth Cook told me years ago that Gary's was her favorite barbecue place in the area. And since Salisbury and the surrounding communities have quite a proud barbecue tradition and a good number of pretty fair barbecue restaurants, that's no faint praise.

Gary's barbecue is lean and not too finely chopped. It's served with the hotter version of Piedmont dip characteristic of Rowan County. The red barbecue slaw is a bit more tart than the usual Lexington-style slaw, and the hush puppies are loose and grainy.

The inviting atmosphere at Gary's is conducive to forming pleasant memories,

and that's obviously Ritchie's chief gift to the community.

## M & K Bar-B-Q & Country Cookin'
215 North Salisbury Avenue (U.S. 52)
Granite Quarry, N.C. 28146
704-279-8976
Breakfast, lunch, and dinner are served
Monday through Friday. Breakfast and lunch
(until 3 P.M.) are offered on Saturday.

The "M & K" comes from Moran and Kathy Thomas, who have seen their Granite Quarry restaurant prosper during the past several years. Occupying a former service station and garage, the restaurant used to have a large overhang, or portico, out front, with the dining room occupying what once was the waiting room. The barbecue was cooked out back in the former garage bay. Now, the portico area has been enclosed, doubling the dining space. And the owners have built an

M & K Bar-B-Q & Country Cookin', Granite Quarry

entirely new, modern pit house designed so the pork shoulders don't have to be turned during the ten or more hours it takes to cook them. One thing that hasn't changed, though, is the practice of cooking the barbecue over oak and hickory slabs. Moran Thomas claims that his is the last place in Rowan County that cooks barbecue entirely over wood, with no backup help from electric or gas pits.

Moran learned the art of barbecue from his father, who passed along secrets learned from *his* father. Moran's grandfather reportedly sold open-pit barbecue off rough board tables to railroad workers and passengers in the town of Spencer during the early 1900s, perhaps even before legends-to-be Jess Swicegood and Sid Weaver set up their famed barbecue stands in Lexington. After driving a truck for a number of years, Moran returned to his roots, establishing M & K Bar-B-Q & Country Cookin'. He continues to pit-cook

the lean, tender, smoke-flavored barbecue that has been an important part of his family's history for nearly a century.

As to the "Country Cookin' " side of the business, M & K has plenty to offer— country-style steak, hamburger steak, stew beef, country ham, pork chops, and tempting vegetable selections such as okra, squash, pintos, cabbage, and macaroni and cheese.

This is also a fabulous place to get a good, messy, old-fashioned hamburger or cheeseburger—the kind that's practically guaranteed to leave grease stains on the front of your shirt. The cooks at M & K hand-patty the hamburgers and sausage, rather than using frozen patties. Thomas says he goes through five hundred to six hundred pounds of top-grade hamburger each week. Even though I didn't have an opportunity to try a burger, someone is obviously doing something right if those numbers are any indication. However, I can personally attest that the Lexington-style barbecue and fixin's at M & K earn a letter grade of A.

## Log Cabin BBQ

2322 U.S. 52 North
Albemarle, N.C. 28001
704-982-5257
Lunch and dinner, Monday through Saturday

As you might expect from its name, Log Cabin BBQ is located in a rustic, brown-painted log building. When I first visited the restaurant on the northern outskirts of Albemarle several years ago, I found the pit master working at outdoor, wood-burning pits. The pits have been enclosed since then, taking away some of the atmosphere—but none of the taste of pork shoulders and chicken pit-cooked over real hickory wood.

Inside this roomy, cheerful restaurant is a long, attractive, dark-stained wood counter with a blue Formica top. This color scheme is repeated in the booths lining the walls. As you might expect in this region of the state, quite a few NASCAR posters are in evidence. But the large picture of golden brown pork shoulders roasting on a pit showcases the real attraction at Log Cabin.

Because of family connections, some similarities exist between this restaurant and Whispering Pines BBQ, located just down the street toward town. Both serve intensely flavored, wood-cooked barbecue and an unusually peppery sauce that resembles a lively eastern sauce more than the Lexington-style dip prevalent in the Piedmont. The iced tea at both restaurants isn't overly sweet. At Log Cabin, a full pitcher of the flavorful nectar can be found on every occupied table.

Log Cabin has a recipe for hush puppies that's different from that at Whispering Pines. Here, they're golf-ball-sized and have a smooth, golden brown exterior, as compared

Log Cabin BBQ,
Albemarle

to the grainy, crusty pups at Whispering Pines. I enjoyed the creamy, white coleslaw at Log Cabin, a contrast to the tart barbecue slaw at the other restaurant.

Log Cabin offers specials every day. On the Wednesday I visited, I tried the pit-cooked barbecued chicken, which came to the table with a wonderful, smoky aroma wafting up from the plate. The chicken was as tender and delicious as it appeared.

A good selection of homemade desserts is available. During my visit, these included chocolate pound cake, "Lemon Sun Drop Cake," and chocolate brownies.

This is, quite simply, one of the best barbecue restaurants in this part of the state. It's worth driving quite a bit out of the way to give it a try.

Whispering Pines BBQ, Albemarle

## Whispering Pines BBQ
1421 U.S. 52 North
Albemarle, N.C. 28001
704-982-6184
Lunch and dinner, Tuesday through Saturday

Located in a tiny building with a steeply pitched roof, Whispering Pines BBQ looks a little like a mountain chalet perched beside U.S. 52 North in Albemarle. The tall, triangular sign, emblazoned with a pine tree, tells passersby the place has been here since 1945. Inside the compact, pine-paneled dining room are eight or ten stools at the counter and maybe a half-dozen booths painted bright green and yellow.

While its physical dimensions aren't

large, Whispering Pines is known for some of the biggest servings of barbecue in the entire state. Lonnie Doby started out cooking on wood-burning pits at the end of World War II. Although the restaurant eventually passed to Lonnie's wife and then to his son, it has stuck with the old ways, producing pork barbecue that's smoky and flavorful. It's also some of the leanest barbecue you'll find anywhere. It's rather different from what's normally found in the Piedmont, in that it's salty and served with a fiery sauce containing lots of ground red pepper and little, if any, sweetener or tomato ketchup. Hand-chopped with a dull cleaver that breaks the meat down into tender fibers, it's absolutely delicious.

The coarse-grated red slaw is tart, rather than sweet, and contains bits of red and green bell pepper. The hush puppies are the "shaggy dog" type—they're grainy-textured on the outside and have a fresh flavor that doesn't include too much onion or sugar. The iced tea is that most elusive of North Carolina brews—one that's not overly sweetened. I found it refreshing after the mild wallop my taste buds got from the saucy barbecue.

Whispering Pines offers burgers, sandwiches, barbecued chicken, a few dinner plates, and some homemade desserts. But what bring the crowds in are the big servings of some of the best wood-cooked barbecue around.

## Troutman's Bar-B-Q

362 Church Street North
Concord, N.C. 28025
704-786-5213
Open for breakfast, lunch, and dinner on Tuesday, Wednesday, Saturday, and Sunday; for lunch and dinner on Monday and Friday; and for lunch on Thursday

Second location:
1388 Warren Coleman Boulevard (U.S. 601)
Concord, N.C. 28027
704-786-9714
Breakfast, lunch, and dinner daily

Troutman's has been around downtown Concord for a long, long time. The Church Street restaurant still has the metal framework of its original drive-in canopy out back, and customers still park in the spaces on either side of the center concrete walkway, where the curb hops used to hustle barbecue sandwiches, hot dogs, and hamburgers.

There's no covering on the rusting canopy, but you get the idea of the kind of busy place this must have been in the 1950s and 1960s.

The original barbecue pits are out back as well, and they're still in use, although Troutman's now cooks barbecue only two days per week, except during the busiest times of the year, like Christmas. But when it does cook, it does it in the most traditional way possible. The place cooks pork shoulders and chicken (for the weekends) over 100 percent hickory wood. The coals are scooped from a big fireplace at one end of the pit building and scattered under meat cooking on up to seven pits, so the slow-roasting temperature stays around two hundred degrees.

Sandy Torrence, who has a culinary degree from Johnson & Wales University in Charlotte, is the part-time pit master when he isn't pursuing his full-time job with the fire department. He comes in and gets the big hickory fires going early in the morning, then puts the meat on the pits, where it cooks for around ten hours in the case of shoulders or three hours for barbecued chicken. After they're completely cooked, the pork shoulders remain on the grates overnight while the coals slowly die out, which gives the meat an even deeper smoky flavor.

Troutman's hickory-smoked barbecued pork is served moderately finely chopped and very lean. The tasty, kicky, authentic sauce resembles the eastern North Carolina variety more than the Lexington-style dip you might expect. Also available is a "mild" sauce that's thick and red and has added Liquid Smoke; don't waste your time on it. The slaw is the

Sandy Torrence mans the pits at Troutman's in Concord.

"barbecue" type, although it isn't really red or nearly as sweet as most barbecue coleslaws you'll encounter. The meat and slaw go together to make a high-quality sandwich, and the serving size is generous.

Troutman's is also well known for its breakfast (and the "Liar's Club" that assembles every morning), as well as its country-style specials, down-home vegetables, and homemade desserts.

I sense from comments I've heard that Troutman's may have experienced a "down" period of indeterminate length, when the quality of the barbecue and the service suffered, at least in the estimation of some. But the restaurant is clearly making an effort to bring things back up to a high level. I found the barbecue to be authentic and tasty, and the service on the day I visited was quick and cheerful.

## Lancaster's BBQ

http://www.lancastersbbq.com

9230 Beatties Ford Road
Huntersville, N.C. 28078
704-394-1464
Open daily

Other locations:
515 Rinehardt Road
Mooresville, N.C. 28115
704-663-5807
Open daily

In Duckworth's Food Market
558 River Highway (N.C. 150)
Mooresville, N.C. 28117
704-799-1222

I visited the newest Lancaster's, on Beatties Ford Road in Huntersville. I understand it's considerably smaller than the three-level original location on Rinehardt Road in Mooresville. From what I can tell, the Mooresville location considers itself "the Stock Car Capital of the World," filled as it is with NASCAR memorabilia. That's not surprising when you consider that Mooresville is a town with a big racing presence. The Huntersville restaurant is just the right size and is attractively decorated in dark green and dark blue on a theme that pays homage to bygone gasoline and service-station brands.

The specific locations don't really mat-

Lancaster's, Huntersville

ter. All the barbecue for the three Lancaster's is cooked at the same place, and it's done up right, I can assure you.

The "meal that made us famous" at Lancaster's is the pork dinner, featuring whole-hog barbecue with an eastern North Carolina "pig-pickin'" taste. The 'cue looks more pulled than chopped—maybe *shredded* is the right word—with a nice mixture of dark and light meat, as well as appetizing chunks of chewy, well-browned outside meat. It's fresh-tasting, suitably moist, and nicely textured, meaning the meat is not the least bit limp or soggy. The delicious eastern-style sauce has a strong vinegar presence, although it's really more of a pig-pickin' sauce, meaning a little tomato and some sugar have been added without compromising the essential nature of the stuff. Also available is a thicker western-style sauce, which would go well with the ribs at Lancaster's.

This place serves coleslaw strictly reminiscent of the coastal plain. The cabbage is finely grated, plenty of sugar is added, and a surprisingly strong presence of mustard is in evidence—something you'd be more likely to find in an eastern tobacco-market town like Rocky Mount. It complements the generous servings of pork perfectly.

The alternate name of this enterprise is Lancaster's Bar-B-Que & Wings. I found the wings to be much to my liking. They're served in all types of sauces with varying degrees of heat, but I stuck with the basic Buffalo wings, which had a nice, buttery sauce that was interesting but not overwhelming. I particularly liked the texture of the meat, which was firm enough to provide a pleasant bite but plenty tender as well.

For one side dish, I enjoyed a pretty doggone authentic Brunswick stew that had a robust, savory flavor. It could have been a little thicker, and the green beans definitely didn't belong in it (in my opinion), but otherwise the ingredients seemed to be traditional, and the balance was nice. My other side dish was nearly perfectly fried medium-sized pods of whole okra. The battering was light and

Lancaster's, in Mooresville, has a decided NASCAR ambiance.

evenly applied, and the pods had a pleasant, firm texture without a hint of the sogginess or even sliminess that sometimes afflicts okra.

To finish off my high-grade dining experience, I sampled a rich, homemade chocolate cake made by a local lady in Mooresville. Wonderful!

Lancaster's is definitely worth a visit if you're anywhere in the area.

## Bubba's Barbecue

4400 Sunset Road
Charlotte, N.C. 28216
704-393-2000
http://www.bubbasbarbecue.com
Lunch and dinner daily

Not long after banker-turned-restaurateur Ralph Miller bought the venerable Spoon's Barbecue on Charlotte's South Boulevard in 1986, he changed the name to Bubba's. In 1994, Miller moved Bubba's to the present location on Sunset Road, just off Interstate 77 north of the city. (After the move, the original owner of Spoon's came out of retirement and now operates the lunchtime-only Bill Spoon's Barbecue at the original South Boulevard location.) The marketing approach employed by Miller, first at Spoon's and now at Bubba's, is offering whole-hog eastern-style barbecue in a city where the Lexington version is dominant.

Bubba's is located in a new, one-story frame building decorated inside with cheerful, yellow-checked tablecloths and a red-and-white Bubba's Barbecue sign. Outside are two stationary pigs that appear to be grazing on the lawn, which drives home the point that Bubba's serves whole-hog barbecue. The menu at Bubba's advertises barbecue "slow-cooked for over ten hours using hickory wood." Actually, there's no evidence of an

The concrete pigs at Bubba's remind customers that the restaurant features eastern North Carolina–style whole-hog barbecue.

old-fashioned pit or a woodpile at Bubba's. The whole pigs are cooked in two electric pits, with a little hickory wood added during the last two hours.

As you might expect, the barbecue at Bubba's is finely chopped and has little smoky taste. But I have to admit that those characteristics put Miller's product right in line with how *most* eastern-style barbecue can be described these days. This is good, average, middle-of-the-pack eastern barbecue. While

it isn't *distinguished* barbecue, it will certainly satisfy your everyday need for a pig fix. The house sauce is a typical vinegar-based mixture, while an alternate sauce for chicken and ribs is thicker and sweeter and has a touch of added Liquid Smoke. The slaw is the yellow eastern variety. Brunswick stew is available to accompany the chopped pork (and to make any eastern fan's heart glad). The Luzianne iced tea is extremely tasty.

Besides whole-hog barbecue, Bubba's

offers ribs, barbecued chicken, chicken and dumplings, sandwiches, and some plate specials, including meat loaf and beef tips and rice.

While Bubba's isn't the slightest bit fancy or unique, it is a pretty good place to do exactly what its slogan recommends: "Pig out with the locals."

## Mac's Speed Shop

http://www.macspeedshop.com
Lunch and dinner daily

2511 South Boulevard
Charlotte, N.C. 28203
704-522-6227

Other locations:
19601 Liverpool Parkway
Cornelius, N.C. 28031
704-892-3554

2414 Sandy Porter Road
Charlotte, N.C. 28273
704-504-8500

Mac's has 'cue, brew, and bikes, all in abundance. It's housed in a former Charlotte transmission shop and car wash. While it isn't really a place that serves traditional North Carolina barbecue, it does cook up some fine pulled pork in a wood smoker. It's flavorful, it's lean, and it can be enhanced with one of the house sauces—including one with a good vinegar tang—plopped into a sandwich, and topped with slaw. Only a real hairsplitter would complain about that.

The *Charlotte Observer* has called Mac's

one of the top ten destinations in the city, and the Kansas City Barbeque Society has opined that it has the best barbecue in Charlotte. That's probably because Mac's serves *all* the KCBS categories—pulled pork, ribs, chicken, and brisket, the last three of which are not generally referred to as "barbecue" in the Tar Heel State, not that we don't eat and enjoy them under their actual names. A North Carolina traditionalist will find something good to eat here. Other, more adventurous barbecue enthusiasts, including expatriates from other barbecue regions, will find even more things to enjoy.

Despite the constant parade of bikes and hot rides of all types pulling into and out of the parking lot at the South Boulevard location, Mac's actually sports a fairly preppy, Uptown Charlotte–type crowd that shows up to sample the wide selection of beers and ales as well as the barbecue.

The beef brisket at Mac's has gotten a lot of over-the-top reviews. Rick Brown of *Barbecue America* on PBS, who's also the author

Beer, bikes, and barbecue are the draws at Mac's Speed Shop.

Mac's Speed Shop,
South Boulevard, Charlotte

The bar at
Mac's Speed Shop,
South Boulevard, Charlotte

of a guidebook/cookbook of the same title, says Mac's serves the best brisket he's ever had. And he isn't the only one to praise this particular offering. The brisket slices are cut very thick at Mac's, almost like steaks, and indeed have outstanding moisture, texture, appearance, and flavor—all the things a good judge looks for in evaluating brisket. I found it to be pretty special stuff.

The barbecued chicken is actually a beer-can chicken (no surprise at a beer mecca like Mac's), finished off on the grill with a nice crust and good all-around color. The indirect-smoker cooking and the beer "steaming" that goes on in the cavity of the bird give it a multilayered, smoky, yeasty flavor and plenty of tenderness without allowing it to become soft and mushy.

The ribs come to the table well glazed with thick sauce, an even appearance, and a pleasing texture. They're cooked for at least six hours on the smoker, yet they don't get too soft. The ribs provide a pleasant chewing sensation when you bite into them.

I liked the green bean casserole at Mac's, which may be the first version of this dish I've run into in any kind of barbecue joint. I also liked the fairly traditional Brunswick stew, despite the fact that it had slices of carrot in it, which would draw frowns of disapproval in the northeastern part of the state. In Charlotte, which is really sort of a different country anyhow, all bets are off. The stew actually measured up pretty well, despite being served with Texas toast, of all things.

Mac's also serves smoked turkey, smoked chicken wings, chili, and fried pickles. You'll have fun here, so go with an open mind.

## Old Hickory House Restaurant

6538 North Tryon Street
Charlotte, N.C. 28213
704-596-8014
Lunch and dinner, Monday through Saturday

In business since 1956, this restaurant is a Charlotte landmark. However, the location on North Tryon just a couple of miles south of Harris Boulevard makes it somewhat out of the way for most people these days.

On the outside, the building isn't all that inviting. Inside, however, the restaurant is warm and attractive, featuring wagon-wheel light fixtures mounted with replicas of kerosene lamps. Large cuts of meat are kept on a small wood-burning pit behind the counter, where they sizzle and hiss, creating smoke and wafting tantalizing smells throughout the room. Chances are, the meat that's actually being served is kept wrapped in aluminum foil back in the kitchen to prevent it from drying out.

I should make it clear that, while the Old Hickory House specializes in pit-cooked barbecue and Brunswick stew, it isn't exactly the North Carolina–style barbecue or the stew most of us have come to expect. Instead, the menu here has distinct Georgia and Alabama roots. The recipes were brought to Charlotte in the mid-1950s by the Carter family, which still runs the place today.

The chopped pork at the Old Hickory House is delicious, with lots of crusty brown outside meat, a reddish hue from the pit, and a good, strong smoky flavor. Served hot in ramekins, the thick, red sauce is definitely more of a Memphis- or Texas-style sauce than a Lexington dip. It's still appealing, with a good deal of onion flavor and little bits of barbecued meat mixed in. The white coleslaw is quite good and not much different from the North Carolina norm, except that it contains bits of dill, rather than sweet, pickle. The crispy, round hush puppies have lots of onion and complement the crusty, smoky pork very well.

Darker and more robust than the typical eastern North Carolina Brunswick stew, the Old Hickory House's version is intriguing. It contains a lot of pepper and has no baby lima beans, an ingredient in every Brunswick stew I'd ever tasted before trying this recipe. Despite those differences, the stew was so tasty and different that I bought a quart to take home. As I enjoyed it during the next several days, I struggled to identify another ingredient that had to do more with giving

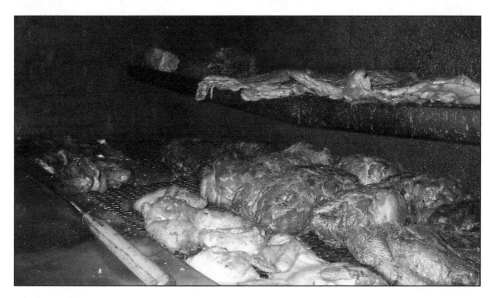

Shoulders, ribs, chicken, and brisket on the dining-room "holding pit" at Old Hickory House Restaurant

the stew a smooth, thick texture than with the taste itself. It finally came to me that what this stew contains is stale bread, which pretty well dissolves in the hot liquid but thickens the stew and makes it smooth and pleasant on the tongue. Brunswick stew is said to have begun in Brunswick County, Virginia, in the early 1800s. Ironically, the original version is said to have contained squirrel meat, onions, and—you guessed it—stale bread. The Old Hickory House's Brunswick stew may thus be closer to the original than our modern-day North Carolina version, which ordinarily contains chicken, pork, tomatoes, lima beans, corn, onions, and seasonings. No matter how much of a purist you may be about Brunswick stew, I recommend you put aside your preconceptions and give this a try, because it is very, very good.

Even though it's grounded in a slightly different tradition, the Old Hickory House definitely belongs in any comprehensive list of top North Carolina barbecue places.

### Carolina Bar-B-Q

213 Salisbury Road
Statesville, N.C. 28677
704-873-5585
http://carolinabar-b-q.com
Lunch and dinner, Monday through Saturday

The distinguishing physical characteristic at Carolina Bar-B-Q is the restaurant name displayed in large white letters, along with a sizable pig cutout, on the steeply pitched, Carolina-blue roof. You'll notice the full parking lot, the brick pit chimney, and

Carolina Bar-B-Q, Statesville

a good-sized woodpile, all of which are encouraging signs.

You won't be disappointed. The late Charles Kuralt mentioned this place in his book *Charles Kuralt's America*, although the reference was actually a tongue-in-cheek criticism that the barbecue didn't have the amount of fat and skin Kuralt was used to in barbecue joints down east. Indeed, owner Gene Medlin proudly told me, "We remove all the fat and gristle." The chopped pork is in fact as "lean and clean" as anyone could ask for, and maybe even more than some folks prefer.

The barbecue served here is actually closer to eastern North Carolina whole-hog barbecue than it is to the Lexington-style, or Piedmont-style, barbecue you would expect in this part of the state. It's fairly finely chopped and is served with a faint vinegar flavor. You can choose from two very different sauces—a hot version, which has the definite vinegar-and-pepper attitude usually found in the east, and a mild sauce that

is thick, red, and influenced by overtones of Liquid Smoke. I'd stick with the hot. The smoky flavor of the barbecue, though, is real. I couldn't help pondering how much both regional styles of barbecue are improved, at least in most cases, by cooking over real wood coals. Everything—the slaw, the barbecue, and the huge, round hush puppies—goes together harmoniously.

I also sampled the tender barbecued chicken, which had a good smoky taste but came with a fairly generic, thick sauce.

Gene Medlin is proud of Carolina Bar-B-Q's fresh-baked fruit cobblers. I sampled a serving of blackberry, which Gene insisted I try with ice cream. While I was much too full to finish it all, it was terrific. The iced tea is worth mentioning as well, since it's flavorful, not too sweet, and garnished with two lemon slices, just the way I like it best.

One item I didn't sample, although I wanted to, was what's billed as "the World's Best Foot-Long Hot Dog."

Medlin does a lot of catering in the

Statesville area, which no doubt helps stimulate some of the trade at the restaurant. However, I have a feeling that even without the extra exposure catering brings, the clean, attractive surroundings and the quality food at Carolina Bar-B-Q would still pack in the customers.

## Alston Bridges Barbecue
620 East Grover Street
Shelby, N.C. 28150
704-482-1998
Lunch and dinner, Monday through Friday

The barbecue business is so physically demanding and time consuming that the bonds of family are usually required to hold it together through the years. Today, few are willing to accept the long hours and exhausting work necessary to run an outstanding barbecue restaurant. Those who do usually possess a sense of continuity and pride that has been passed down through the generations, as well as a direct stake in the financial rewards such a business can provide. At Alston Bridges Barbecue in Shelby, a third generation is carrying on the family barbecue tradition. In this case, it's a tradition tied directly to Warner Stamey, the man who taught virtually all of today's outstanding Piedmont barbecuers their craft.

Stamey learned how to roast pork shoulders to perfection from Jess Swicegood and Sid Weaver in Lexington, where he went to high school in the late 1920s while living with a sister. After building up a nest egg, Stamey moved back to Shelby, his hometown, in 1930. There, he ended up teaching his newly acquired barbecue skills to his wife's brother, Alston Bridges, as well as to Red Bridges (no relation), who would later own Bridges Barbecue Lodge across town from Alston's place. Before long, Stamey moved back to Lexington, then on to Greensboro. But in the 1950s, he opened a Shelby restaurant in partnership with Alston Bridges. Bridges eventually bought the site from Stamey and opened his own place in 1956.

Kent Bridges, Alston's son, was with his father from the beginning, giving him nearly forty years behind the counter at the restaurant. During that time, Kent's four children literally grew up in the business, often playing in the restaurant's basement while their father and his wife, Linda, tended to business upstairs. Mabel Bridges, Alston's widow, taught the children to count money and make change; she sometimes asked to see the bills in their wallets and gave them a bonus if she found the presidents' heads turned in the same direction. As they got older, the children learned to wash dishes and do other jobs around the restaurant. Now, the reins of leadership have largely been handed over to Jay, Reid, and Michelle, the three oldest children. They all made the decision to enter the family business full-time after exploring other career options in college. Laura, the fourth child, decided to go into nursing.

Two walls of the restaurant on Grover Street are dedicated to family photographs. One features portraits of Alston and Mabel Bridges; the other contains the Christmas

Alston Bridges Barbecue, Shelby

card photos of Kent and Linda Bridges, their children, and their grandchildren. In one photo, the Bridges family members are posing with baby pigs, while in another, they're surrounded by cows ("since we serve beef, too").

There have been some changes since the early days. Instead of coming in at midnight to get the pork shoulders on the pits so they'll be ready for the next day's lunch crowd, the third-generation Bridges family members now arrive early in the morning. That's because the restaurant instituted a shortened cooking process in which the shoulders spend their first few hours in an electric cooker before being finished over hardwood coals on the pits. Kent and the children decided on this change together. They all say Alston and Mabel Bridges would have applauded what the younger generation sees as a realistic balance between the demands of work and the responsibility of spending time with family.

In any case, customers who grew up on the slow-cooked pork of Alston Bridges claim that the barbecue continues to live up to its lofty reputation. On one occasion, I ran into a couple in the parking lot who had just driven fifty miles from Morganton for the sole purpose of enjoying a plate of barbecue, something they did several times a year. That brought to mind a moment in Joe Murphy's fine documentary on Southern barbecue, *Slow Food for Fast Times*, when a customer remarked that a particular restaurant's barbecue was "a good thirty-mile barbecue," meaning he was willing to drive that far one way to eat it. A fifty-mile barbecue is obviously pretty special.

One of the main reasons customers go to such lengths to enjoy the barbecue at Alston Bridges is that the pork shoulders aren't removed from the pits until they're slow-roasted to the peak of tenderness. And tenderness is not a factor the Bridges family takes lightly. One particular fork, prized above all the others, is almost always used to test the shoulders to see if they're done. The "magic fork," as it's known, has a bent tine and a broken shaft that's been welded together. Apparently, no other fork provides exactly the same feel. On several occasions when the fork was lost, the Bridges children pawed through the garbage dumpster to reclaim it. Perhaps the implement is more of a superstition than anything, since the years have taught the family members to tell when a shoulder is done simply by looking at it. Still, they always reach for the magic fork. You don't toy with success.

The pit-cooked offerings at Alston Bridges are more diverse than those at most Piedmont barbecue places, perhaps because the restaurant's customer base extends well into the nearby Blue Ridge Mountains, where an entirely different barbecue tradition has taken root and spread westward. The unofficial motto at Bridges is, "If it can be cooked on a pit, we'll cook it (within reason)." The menu features not only the mainstay, barbecued pork shoulder, but also pork ribs, beef brisket, and even chicken. However, make no mistake—the pork barbecue at Alston Bridges is the genuine article, squarely in the center of the Piedmont tradition.

The sauce at Alston Bridges Barbecue is not overly sweet, leaning more to the peppery, spicy-vinegar side than most "dips" in this part of the state. Unlike at many places, the sauce isn't premixed into the meat; instead, it is ladled over the barbecue just as it's served. The regular barbecue, which has a delicate but unmistakable wood-smoke flavor, is hand-chopped a little more finely than most. However, the staff is so accom-modating that you can get the meat brought to your table just about as finely or as coarsely chopped as you like simply by asking. (The family members are constantly amazed at the inventive requests of customers. But they say, "We're here to serve barbecue—period.") The restaurant also sells a great many sandwiches containing extremely tender *slices* of barbecued pork, topped with finely chopped coleslaw. I think these sandwiches would be my favorite if I were dropping in on a regular basis (and I wish I were).

Few genuine North Carolina–style barbecue places serve racks of barbecued pork ribs that are actually pit-cooked over hardwood coals. Alston Bridges is one of them. Even though ribs are popular among North Carolinians, they're normally considered to be in a class of their own, outside the normal definition of *barbecue* (unless they're pulled from a whole roasted pig). However, the ribs at Alston Bridges are prepared much in the Lexington style—they're slow-cooked for hours in an enclosed pit over hardwood coals, without first being boiled or baked, and without being basted with sauce while they're cooking. After the ribs are removed from the pit—with the meat so tender it's barely clinging to the bone—they're immersed for an hour or so in "Boss Sauce." A creation of Kent Bridges, this sauce has a sweeter, more complex flavor than the regular barbecue sauce, and it sets off the natural sweetness of the rib meat to perfection. These are memorable ribs. If you're able to make only one visit to Alston Bridges, I strongly suggest you either include ribs in your order or have the restaurant pack up a batch you can take along with you.

In North Carolina, baked beans are not widely served with barbecue. But at Alston Bridges, you'd be well advised to step outside the normal coleslaw-and-hush-puppies routine to try this particular recipe. The beans simmer for several hours in a thick, tangy tomato sauce with lots of chopped bacon, onion, bell pepper, and brown sugar. Their rich, sweet flavor provides a delightful counterpoint to the wood-smoked taste of the barbecued pork. Brunswick stew is on the menu as well. Like the signature Alston Bridges sauce, it has a bit more connection to the barbecue culture of eastern North Carolina than to the common Piedmont practice.

Lunchtime in particular is extremely busy at Alston Bridges Barbecue. A glassed-in area is set aside strictly for takeout orders. On a cold day, you're liable to find yourself packed into the tiny vestibule with twenty or thirty others, like commuters on a rush-hour subway train, as you wait for your order. Meanwhile, all the seats at the counter will likely be full, with customers waiting two deep behind each stool. The dining-room tables will be jam-packed as well. But the service is extremely efficient. Even during peak periods, you probably won't have to wait longer than fifteen minutes. Whatever you do, don't get impatient and leave, because this place is well worth the wait.

## Bridges Barbecue Lodge

2000 East Dixon Boulevard (U.S. 74 Bypass)
Shelby, N.C. 28152
704-482-8567
http://www.bridgesbbq.com
Lunch and dinner (until the barbecue runs out),
    Wednesday through Sunday

The first thing you'll notice when you drive up to Bridges Barbecue Lodge on U.S. 74 Bypass just east of Shelby is that it has to be the neatest, cleanest barbecue place on the face of the earth. But what about the commonly held belief that the shabbiest exterior generally houses the best barbecue? For a minute, you may think you've stumbled upon one of those all-electric franchise barbecue places with the calico curtains and fake country furnishings. It's all just too *nice*. The parking lot, shaded by large trees, is immaculate. There's a white picket fence and a neat mailbox decorated with a pink pig. Then you'll spy the woodpile out back, which is just about as large as the restaurant. That's a good sign, but wait . . . What is it about that woodpile? The logs are neatly stacked according to length and diameter, and the whole thing looks like it's just been dusted. It is no man's woodpile, all tumbled over with the logs lying every which way. This woodpile—in fact, this restaurant—has a *woman's* touch all over it.

Bridges is still known to some folks around Shelby as Red Bridges' Barbecue Lodge. But Red's widow, Lyttle (pronounced "Light-ul"), otherwise known as "Mama B," was the heart and soul of the place for many years from Red's passing until shortly before her death in 2008. Now, Red and Lyttle's daughter, Debbie Bridges-Webb, is in charge, with the help of her daughter, Natalie Ramsey, and her son, Chase Webb.

The current restaurant is actually the second building at this location, the first having burned during the 1960s. Bridges celebrated sixty-five years in business in 2011. For nearly the last four decades of that time, Mama B steadfastly carried on the business her late husband learned from Warner Stamey in the 1930s. Red Bridges established his own place in 1946. No doubt, Mama B and her husband both had red hair when they started out. But following Red's death in the mid-1960s,

Mama B was the one the staff referred to as "the redhead." When I first visited Bridges in 1996, the waitresses were sporting fiftieth-anniversary sweatshirts adorned with a red-headed female cartoon pig and this verse:

> Mama B for 50 years
> Served her pork to all you dears.
> She will serve for 50 more
> The barbecue you all adore.

The succeeding years of fulfilling that promise have fallen to the second and third generations of the family. Debbie is a striking woman who returned in the mid-1970s

Debbie Bridges Webb *(l)*, her son, Chase Webb, and her daughter, Natalie Webb Ramsey, comprise the leadership team at Bridges Barbecue Lodge.
*Courtesy of the* Shelby Star

to help her mother run the business after spending several years as a professional model. As a matter of fact, this is a good-looking family all around. Various studio photographs of Debbie's children, Chase and Natalie, at different ages are proudly displayed on the dining-room walls, as are several photos of Lyttle and a portrait of Red Bridges himself, looking sharp in a fedora hat.

Debbie says that, at age five, and at her father's urging, she used to dance on the restaurant's tables, back when all the booths were outfitted with individual jukebox terminals. Although she no longer dances on tables, the bantering between Debbie and her mother and now with her children has been entertainment enough over the years for the diners who sit up front around the curved counter near the kitchen. Whether you settle onto a stool there, just inside the front door, or find a table or booth in the wood-paneled dining room, you'll find that the stock in trade is, of course, Piedmont-style pork shoulder, slow-roasted over hardwood coals and served up in a sandwich or on a barbecue tray or barbecue plate. Sandwiches come wrapped in aluminum foil, loaded with meat and topped with coleslaw (if desired), and with the buns toasted crispy on top. Trays are simply a serving each of meat and slaw, while plates come with barbecue and slaw plus French fries.

The barbecue is available minced, chopped, or sliced—or, in fact, just about any way you'd like it. The minced barbecue is finely chopped and mixed with a heavy dose of sauce, whereas the chopped comes in varying degrees of chunkiness (it can be coarse-chopped at the customer's request) and is laced with crusty bits of outside brown, with just a hint of sauce. The rather mild vinegar-to-mato dip has the distinction of being served warm. Bridges is one of the few barbecue restaurants in the state to do that; you'll get an extra Styrofoam cup of sauce with your order. The meat itself is some of the best I've ever tasted anywhere in North Carolina. It's moist, sweet, and incredibly tender, while still maintaining its body. I always notice the grain and texture of barbecued meat—the way it bites, if you will—and the pit men at Bridges obviously know how to get the 250 or so shoulders they cook every week just about perfect. Since I believe subjecting meat this good to mincing can't help diminishing its best characteristics, I recommend ordering your barbecue chopped or sliced, either of which will virtually melt in your mouth. The outside brown meat that's available by special order is as good as you'll find anywhere.

Bridges has been featured in many national publications, but a mention in the 1994 issue of *Gourmet* magazine was especially interesting. Itinerant food writers Jane and Michael Stern had stopped by—attracted, they said, by the number of police cars in the parking lot (which is considered a sign of either trouble or a good eating spot—in this case the latter). Of all the glowing comments in the Sterns' piece, the Bridges family and staff got the biggest kick out of a description of their coleslaw as having "a pearlescent cinnabar hue" and being "a handsome complement to your pork of choice." Whew! But the Sterns were right—it is attractive slaw, with just the right crunch and sweet-tart balance to perfectly showcase the rich, moist meat.

The hush puppies at Bridges are unusual. For one thing, they're a little longer and larger in diameter than the norm for this part of the state. Then, too, they have a grainier texture and slightly darker color than the average Lexington-style pups, which usually come with a rather smooth outer crust and a light gold color. Let's see, maybe these are more of a shaggy, robust hush puppy—a spaniel, rather than a terrier. They're satisfyingly crunchy and hearty, their flavor a marriage of cornmeal and a touch of onion.

One thing I especially enjoyed at Bridges was the individual iced-tea pitcher brought to the table with my order. It held enough to provide several delicious refills and was accompanied by a healthy chunk of lemon to help balance the overwhelming sweetness barbecue lovers apparently demand in their tea.

It's obvious that Debbie Bridges-Webb, like her mother before her, derives not only her income but also a great deal of her social contact and her overall sense of satisfaction in life from operating the restaurant. Lyttle used to say the biggest challenge was "to become the best," but she unhesitatingly added that she thought she had achieved that goal with the help of her coworkers, several of whom had been with the business for a long time. "I've always liked to work hard," she used to say, but she pointed out that she tried to maintain a level of excellence by providing the staff a good balance between work and rest. Debbie has maintained the practice

of closing the restaurant each Monday and Tuesday, in addition to closing for a week in July and the week after Christmas. Of course, Debbie is at the restaurant during those breaks, as was Lyttle, who said she kept herself busy "lifting up everything in the restaurant and cleaning underneath it."

During my original visit, Lyttle Bridges wouldn't let me leave without inspecting what she called "the cleanest floors in the barbecue business." She didn't make me eat off them to prove her point, but I probably could have. "I've been cleaning up my whole life," she used to say in mock exasperation, making it clear she loved every minute of it. Under the leadership of Debbie, Natalie, and Chase, the floors are as clean as ever, the ambiance and spirit of the place are relatively unchanged, and the barbecue is as close as it has ever been to perfection.

## The Flying Pig
901 East College Avenue
Shelby, N.C. 28152
704-487-0087
Lunch and dinner, Monday through Saturday

This out-of-the-way place near Shelby has absolutely terrific barbecue. It's no surprise that many of the recreational fliers who land at the Cleveland County airport down the road do so, at least in part, to have lunch or dinner at The Flying Pig. Here, you'll find incredibly tender chopped Boston butt, meaty pork ribs, competition-grade beef brisket, and barbecued chicken, all with a complex

The Flying Pig, Shelby
Photo by Randy McNeilly

flavor that results from smoking with a mixture of hickory, pecan, and oak wood.

Owner Terry Bridges, a former auto glass installer, was a barbecue hobbyist for many years—the kind of guy everyone said should open a restaurant someday. His wife, Beth, is also a skilled cook and a curious, inventive "foodie." When arthritis began to make installing windshields nearly impossible for Terry, the couple decided to turn their love for barbecue into a full-time business. The restaurant has been open since 2006. While it's a modest little place, it's homey and has the feel of an undiscovered treasure.

The Boston butts are cooked with no dry rub or seasoning, and the chopped barbecue isn't seasoned or sauced at all, or even salted, before it's served. I found the barbecue to be extremely tender, moist, and clean, with no visible or otherwise discernable fat or gristle, although the relatively high fat content of the upper part of the pork shoulder naturally gives the meat a juicy, silky texture. I mistakenly thought the meat may have been

seasoned with salt, pepper, and a little sugar, but the flavors I tasted apparently came from the wood smoking itself. For me, the chopped barbecue needed no sauce whatsoever. Whole, smoked Boston butts are available with a two-day advance notice.

The beef brisket at The Flying Pig is, quite simply, among the best I've ever tasted—beautifully smoked, tender without being overdone, and glistening with retained juices. Members of competition barbecue teams will tell you that of the four categories in which most compete—pork, ribs, chicken, and brisket—brisket is the most difficult to cook because of the danger of its drying out when cooked long enough to become properly tender. In my opinion, The Flying Pig's brisket would definitely be in the championship category in any barbecue competition because of the texture, flavor, moisture, and appearance of the sliced meat. Terry and Beth's daughter, Tracy Knight, emphatically declared, "I used to be married to a guy from Texas, and our brisket is much better than anything I ever had out there." Having eaten a fair amount of Texas brisket, I agree that the Lone Star State has nothing on this tiny corner of Cleveland County when it comes to top-drawer beef barbecue.

It turns out that serving brisket was the idea of Beth Bridges. Despite living near Shelby all her life, Beth is conversant with the specialties and traditional foods of other regions of the country. She calls it having "bees in my bonnet about different interesting foods." She advised Terry to add brisket to the menu at the new restaurant. "I told her I didn't think anyone would know what it was," Terry admits, "but it's turned out to be probably our most popular specialty."

The pork ribs, believe it or not, are of the same caliber. Terry Bridges buys meatier racks of ribs than most restaurants serve. The meat has a wonderfully yielding but sufficiently firm texture, so that it comes free cleanly when you take a bite, with the surrounding meat remaining in place rather than sliding off the bone. The smoke flavor is exquisite, and the sweet rib meat is as juicy as could possibly be desired.

Terry and Beth Bridges offer three different tomato-oriented sauces. While none of their smoked meats requires any sauce at all, the condiments offer interesting and quite different enhancements to the deep flavor of the meats themselves. The choices are a fairly middle-of-the-road sweet sauce, a fascinating, Asian-influenced "sour" sauce, and a "hot" sauce that actually doesn't pack a lot of heat but has a clearly discernable jalapeño flavor profile. Most people will like all three,

some will enjoy mixing them, and some will decide that the pork, ribs, and brisket are too delicious on their own to be compromised with any type of sauce, no matter how tasty.

I didn't have an opportunity to sample the smoked half-chickens, but the word around town is that they're very, very good. The Flying Pig also sells smoked turkeys during the holidays.

Curiously, this foothills restaurant serves a tasty, authentic Brunswick stew of the type more commonly found in the coastal plain, and particularly in the northeast quadrant of the state. Rather than containing the mélange of vegetables found in some Piedmont stews, The Flying Pig's version has only the traditional tomatoes, potatoes, butter beans, and corn. It does use all of the restaurant's smoked meats, a slight departure from the eastern practice of using chicken almost exclusively. That being said, this Brunswick stew is excellent and well balanced and would be eagerly consumed in any eastern North Carolina restaurant. The Brunswick stew was also Beth's idea.

The Flying Pig is around eight miles outside Shelby. The rural location and building size suggest it will probably always be a fairly small business. However, it has room for some well-deserved growth. This is unquestionably a place that deserves a spot on the "A" list of North Carolina's best barbecue restaurants. From now on, I'll definitely detour to visit Terry, Beth, Tracy, and staff whenever I'm anywhere in the vicinity.

## Brushy Mountain Smokehouse and Creamery

201 Wilkesboro Boulevard
North Wilkesboro, N.C. 28659
336-667-9464
http://www.brushymtnsmokehouse.com/wilkes/
aboutus.htm
Lunch and dinner are served Monday and
Wednesday through Saturday. A lunch buffet
is offered on Sunday.

Second location:
Brushy Mountain Café
2958 N.C. 16
North Millers Creek, N.C. 28651
336-667-4870
http://www.brushymtnsmokehouse.com/
millerscreek/aboutus.htm
Breakfast and lunch are served Monday
through Wednesday and Saturday. Breakfast,
lunch, and dinner are served Thursday and
Friday.

I was impressed with Brushy Mountain Smokehouse and Creamery not only because of the regular smokehouse menu but because of the Sunday buffet, which drew a big and obviously enthusiastic crowd the day I visited. Everything I tasted was good, the staff was friendly and efficient, and the big, barn-like building provided a cheerful, inviting, and airy atmosphere.

The pork barbecue is slow-roasted in electric-fired wood smokers. It's lean and has a discernible smoky taste. I found plenty of chewy "outside brown" bits chopped into the mixture. Customers can go either the vinegar or the tomato route with the sauces. All in all, this is representative, mainstream North Carolina barbecue. One interesting oddity is

the "Barbecue Cruncher," which consists of chopped barbecue rolled up in a flour tortilla, which is then deep-fried to give it an especially crisp exterior. I don't know that the crispy tortilla will ever take the place of a nice, soft bun, at least as far as my personal taste is concerned, but I imagine that this way of serving our iconic pork will attract its fans.

The smoked pork ribs are especially good. One customer offered an unsolicited testimonial, telling me that he hadn't been a fan of ribs until he tasted those served by Brushy Mountain. Now, he says, "I'm here every week for another fix." The smoke-flavored, dry-rubbed ribs have a deep reddish brown color, and while the meat is exceptionally tender, it doesn't slide off the bone when you take a bite but stays in place. As an occasional barbecue judge, I've been taught that this should earn high ratings, and indeed, these ribs would do well in a competitive cookoff.

Brushy Mountain Smokehouse and Creamery also does a nice job with its smoked chicken and its barbecued, thin-sliced pork loin. The chicken is served with an attractive and crispy crust, but it's also moist and tender without being overcooked. The same deep, smoky flavor that characterizes the chicken finds its way into the pork loin, which is brushed with a moderately thick barbecue sauce after it's plated for service.

Although I was primarily focused on the barbecue and smoked meats, I noticed that the Sunday buffet had really good-looking country-style steak and gravy, an appetizing-looking selection of country-style vegetables,

Brushy Mountain Smokehouse and Creamery features bright, open space and a cheery staff, in addition to terrific barbecue, ribs, and homemade ice cream.
*Photo by Mike Oniffrey*

some perfectly breaded fried shrimp, and, surprisingly, eastern North Carolina–style fried corn sticks, which are hardly ever found west of the coastal plain.

The creamery portion of the enterprise does a booming business in homemade ice cream. I observed that the staff members build a mean banana split, as well as making their own waffle cones. I sampled a perfectly delicious fried apple turnover, crusted with sugar and cinnamon and served with a scoop of wonderfully textured, creamy vanilla ice cream. This rich, frozen treat goes so well with barbecue that it's surprising more barbecue joints don't market the homemade stuff.

I'll definitely plan to make Brushy Mountain a regular stop when I'm passing through the North Wilkesboro area.

## Smoky Mountain Barbecue

1008 South Jefferson Avenue
West Jefferson, N.C. 28694
336-246-6818
Lunch and dinner, Monday through Saturday

Featuring a well-dressed pig consulting a pocket watch, this restaurant's logo has the slogan, "We will serve no swine before its time." Cute.

In this case, it's also accurate. Owner Byron Jordan wood-smokes his whole pigs for twenty hours before chopping and seasoning the hams, shoulders, loin, and side meat into lean, moist eastern North Carolina–style barbecue. In deference to his location in mountainous Ashe County in the state's far northwest corner, Jordan also offers a thicker western-type sauce on every table, along with a vinegar-pepper sauce. But without any additional sauce at all, this

Along with pork from the whole hog, fried chicken and country ham are specialties at Smoky Mountain Barbecue.
*Photo by Mike Oniffrey*

tender barbecue practically squeals "whole hog from the coastal plain."

When Jordan and his wife, Nancy, planned a permanent move to Ashe County from the Triangle area, they already had the notion of offering eastern-style barbecue once they settled into their new home. Jordan received his instruction on the finer points of cooking eastern 'cue in Sampson and Bladen counties. It's obvious that whoever did the teaching knew their business well.

And if its delicious, traditional chopped pork isn't enough, Smoky Mountain Barbecue also has a widespread and well-earned reputation for serving absolutely superb fried chicken. Permanent residents and vacation-

home owners around West Jefferson tell me they've willingly stood in line at Smoky Mountain Barbecue for up to thirty minutes for takeout fried chicken dinners. Fried chicken, of course, is all about crisp skin and a satisfying crunch on the outside, lots of juice on the inside, and a deft touch with salt and seasoning. This chicken gets top marks in all those categories.

Jordan also does a nice job with wood-smoked baby back ribs. The thick, dark red sauce with which they're slathered before serving might look a little off-putting to some North Carolinians, but the dressing actually has a nice, well-balanced vinegar tang and doesn't go overboard on molasses or spices. The ribs are exceptionally tender.

Smoky Mountain Barbecue's Brunswick stew is another pretty authentic eastern North Carolina transplant that's surviving nicely in Christmas-tree-growing country. The stew has a flavorful tomato sauce and the traditional ingredients of lima beans, corn, potatoes, and onions (and a few random green garden peas), plus chicken, beef, and pork. It has enough sweetness to perfectly complement the piquancy of the barbecue.

The country green beans, cinnamon-flavored baked apples, crispy hush puppies, and biscuits are all top-drawer. I also sampled a delicious, tart blackberry cobbler with a cakelike crust.

The Jordans also own the A. B. Vannoy Ham Company, which produces old-fashioned, climate-cured country hams with much deeper and more complex flavor than the quick-cured country-ham varieties that predominate in the marketplace nowadays. These wonderful hams, sold whole and sliced at Smoky Mountain Barbecue and online, are aged for a full nine months in the couple's West Jefferson ham house, so that the changing seasons, salt, brown sugar, and fresh air do the curing. No nitrites or nitrates are used in the process.

The same thing is true of the ham that is said of the barbecue: no swine is served before its time. Smoky Mountain Barbecue is well worth a stop for one or the other—or both.

## The Woodlands Barbecue & Pickin' Parlor

8304 Valley Boulevard (U.S. 321 Bypass)
Blowing Rock, N.C. 28605
828-295-3651
http://www.woodlandsbbq.com
Lunch and dinner daily

The word *Pickin'* in this restaurant's name refers to what musicians do here with banjos and guitars every Saturday night, rather than what the guests do at a whole-hog barbecue in the coastal plain. After all, this is western North Carolina, where the custom of slow-cooking barbecue never caught on until fairly recently. Even then, it was practiced mostly as a way to attract and feed tourists. For decades, when mountaineers got ready to slaughter hogs, they thought primarily in terms of making sausage and curing country hams.

That said, Woodlands should definitely be rated one of the best barbecue places in the North Carolina mountains. While its beef brisket and pork ribs may be influenced by establishments west of North Carolina, the chopped pork qualifies not only as authentic North Carolina barbecue, but as doggone *good* North Carolina barbecue.

In addition to barbecued pork, beef, ribs, and chicken, the menu includes home-style Mexican dishes.

In 1991, a fire did extensive damage

Interior of The Woodlands Barbecue & Pickin' Parlor, Blowing Rock

to the original location, but the owners rebuilt on the same spot without losing their customers' loyalty. Like many places in the mountains, Woodlands' new building is a mixture of Bavarian kitsch and hillbilly humor—wooden floors, rough wood paneling, picnic tables and benches, lots of cutesy pig pictures and figures, and even a send-up of the *Mona Lisa* featuring Miss Piggy.

## Okie Dokies Smokehouse

2375 U.S. 70
Swannanoa, N.C. 28778
828-686-0050
http://www.okiedokiesbbq.com
Lunch and dinner, Monday through Saturday

Second location:
  801 Smoky Park Highway
  Candler, N.C. 28715
  828-633-0777
  Lunch and dinner, Monday through Saturday.
    Takeout only.

What is today a restaurant serving some of western North Carolina's best barbecue had its origins in 1999 in a little red truck. In an early version of the food trucks so popular today, Steve Dunning sold sandwiches and barbecue plates on the side of the road in different western North Carolina communities, showed up at local festivals, and catered private parties. The day he met Jody, now his wife, at a casual gathering of friends, she volunteered to help him upfit his mobile kitchen. In 2007, the couple bought a two-story building in Swannanoa, intending to

use the downstairs as a catering kitchen and rent the upstairs to a delicatessen. Within a short time, the deli announced it was leaving. Finding themselves without a renter at a time when the economy was beginning to tank, the Dunnings swallowed hard, renovated the top floor, and opened a restaurant.

And a very popular restaurant it is. Okie Dokie's features pulled pork, ribs, beef barbecue, and chicken, all smoked for hours over hardwood coals. Although the meat has the tenderness, depth of flavor, and attractive appearance to stand alone without any sauce, the Dunnings offer four different sauces—a mild sauce, a sweet version, a hot sauce, and an eastern North Carolina–oriented vinegar-based sauce—to enhance, rather than to define, the meat.

"We make what we like to eat, and actually do eat, every day," says Steve Dunning. "We feel like if we continue to enjoy our food, all our customers will as well."

The Dunnings have amassed a collection of trophies from barbecue competitions, have won several other awards, and have been featured in *Southern Living Off the Eaten Path*. Travelers to the Asheville area from other parts of North Carolina have been taking favorable reports back to the Piedmont and coastal plain, resulting in quite a buzz around the state about this modern but unpretentious restaurant. The couple has also continued to expand its Grill House catering business, which offers not only barbecue but finer dining touches as well.

Okie Dokies' pulled pork, which comes from the shoulder, not only looks attractive, thanks to its good, deep color, but has a nearly perfect feel on the palate—a lightly firm, yet yielding, texture. There's plenty of smoke taste, but it doesn't overpower the natural sweetness of the slow-roasted pork. On a soft bun, topped with either creamy white coleslaw or the spicier red "barbecue" version, and with any or none of the sauces, this 'cue makes one terrific sandwich. Perhaps most importantly, customers in the Asheville area seem to feel that the pulled pork represents authentic North Carolina–style barbecue, in contrast to the offerings from several other western North Carolina barbecue joints.

The pork ribs are prepared with a precook rub and are served "dry," meaning they aren't glazed with sauce. If you'd like a little sauce in which to dip these full-of-flavor, tender ribs, any of Okie Dokies' four versions will suit you admirably. But absolutely no sauce is required, since the wood smoke and the spices adhering to the meat's surface, plus the natural sweetness of the rib meat, provide all the flavor "pop" you can possibly imagine.

In a process becoming popular at a number of barbecue places around the state, Steve and Jody and their staff turn out delicious chicken wings that are first smoked, then deep-fried with no coating other than the natural skin. These are lightly glazed with sauce after they're fried but aren't the least bit gooey, and the skin maintains a satisfying crunchiness. The wonderful smoke flavor goes all the way to the bone.

Okie Dokies also serves a tasty smoked boneless chicken breast that is sliced not quite all the way through and lightly sauced.

I enjoyed black-eyed peas and collard greens with my barbecue. Other sides include mac 'n' cheese, fried okra, new potatoes, cheese grits, baked beans, and potato salad.

Okie Dokies Smokehouse, Swannanoa

A must-have appetizer at this place is the tart, deep-fried pickle chips. They have a crunchy, savory coating and are served with a barbecue ranch sauce for dipping. Fantastic! You can also enjoy either jalapeño or sweet hush puppies, which are golf-ball-sized, crunchy, and full of good, solid corn taste.

Okie Dokies' barbecue truck is out and about on a regular schedule in several nearby locations, including Candler and Burnsville. Call the restaurant for exact days and times.

# GONE BUT NOT FORGOTTEN

## Bob Melton's Barbecue—Rocky Mount

Bob Melton's—now totally gone—was thought to be the oldest real sit-down barbecue restaurant in North Carolina. It was nestled on the same shady spot beside the Tar River for nearly eighty years. The ramshackle white-frame building, so familiar to the generations that remained faithful to the place, was eventually replaced by a newer dining room built on its foundation. Inside, the wood floors and light wood paneling of the original eatery were closely reproduced, so the feel of the place was similar to what it had always been. And the peaceful view of the river didn't change at all over the years. That is, the peaceful view didn't change except when the floods came, which ultimately led to the demise of Melton's after countless instances of water damage, repair, and rebuilding. It was, after all, constructed in a flood plain. While that didn't matter when the place was just a shack next to a crude barbecue pit, it did once it became a full-fledged restaurant. Finally, the insurance company refused to cover the place any longer. A short-lived move to an inland, nondescript spot off U.S. 301 was a final embarrassment to the memory of one of the most legendary barbecue spots in the South and probably the entire nation.

Even before Melton's closed its doors for good, it had made some major changes in the way the barbecue and other dishes were prepared. But a lot of old-timers vowed

Bob Melton's provided a peaceful meal setting. Its windows overlooked the shady Tar River.
*Photo by Mike Burke*

that everything still tasted the same, which may have been due largely to both pleasant memories and the management's ability to maintain much of the original atmosphere of the eastern North Carolina institution.

I clearly remember visiting Melton's in the 1950s, when it seemed far outside town. It was reached by an unpaved road that formed a steep, eroded gully through the woods until it emerged in Melton's dirt parking lot. Wooden steps led up to an un-screened, creaky wooden porch that rambled around two sides of the building, while an old-fashioned screen door provided access to a main dining room that contained long wooden tables and a well-worn board floor. Later, the kitchen and takeout area occupied the old parking lot, once a paved lot was built on the opposite side of the restaurant. But the exterior was still white clapboard (well, okay, vinyl siding), and the first view of Melton's new layout provided a comforting feeling of familiarity.

Bob Melton, who died years ago, prob-ably did more than any other man to popu-larize eastern-style barbecue. Like so many other famous barbecuers, this farmer, mer-chant, and horse trader got into the barbecue business as a part-time venture. Melton start-ed out with some barbecue pits and a sim-ple shed in 1922. So many people made their way down to the riverbank to buy his barbe-cue to take home that he decided to open a sit-down restaurant in 1924. According to a wall-mounted menu board from 1929, a plate of barbecue and boiled potatoes cost forty-five cents (forty cents without the potatoes),

while a barbecue sandwich was fifteen cents. All soft drinks were a nickel. A large admoni-tion printed in red across the bottom of the sign warned, "No Whiskey Allowed."

However, the premises were still wet from time to time, due to the floods. But business never slowed much even during high water, as customers made their way to Melton's door in boats. (Flood-control meas-ures in later years lessened the problem, but of course hurricanes and other major storms couldn't be controlled. It was a hurricane that struck the final blow.)

For at least ten years, Melton's was one of only a handful of barbecue restaurant in eastern North Carolina. While nearby Wil-son has some barbecue establishments across the street from its largest tobacco market by the early 1930s, quite a few Wilsonians still traveled the eighteen miles between the two towns to eat at Melton's. In the early 1930s, Adam Scott opened his famous restaurant on the back porch of his home in Goldsboro, eventually leading to quite a rivalry between Rocky Mount and Goldsboro—really be-tween Melton's and Scott's—for bragging rights as to which city produced the best barbecue. In 1958, the year Melton died, Rocky Mount appeared to have gained an edge in this competition when *Life* maga-zine referred to Melton as "the king of south-ern barbecue."

Bob Melton and Adam Scott built their reputations by cooking whole hogs laid out on metal rods over beds of oak and hickory coals. At Melton's, one added innovation was the placement of a layer of sheet tin just above the roasting pigs, so coals could be shoveled on top as well as underneath, providing heat from both above and below the meat. It's ironic that although both men deplored the practice of preparing barbecue on gas cookers, the later management of their restaurants eventually switched to that cooking method for reasons of cost and efficiency.

What's more, Melton's also switched to cooking pork shoulders, rather than whole hogs. Tommy Smith, the last owner before the restaurant closed, stated unequivocally that he thought Melton's barbecue was better in the later years—over gas—than it ever was previously. There's no question that the majority of his customers accepted the premise that it was at least as good as always. Apparently, most patrons thought the tenderness and seasoning of the meat made up for any lack of wood-smoked taste, which can no longer be considered a prime characteristic of eastern-style barbecue. One lady, who told me before the restaurant closed that she had eaten at Melton's at least once a week for forty-five years, said, "It's just the same as it's always been."

Now, at least in former customers' memories, Melton's will always be the zenith of eastern-style barbecue.

## Scott's Famous Barbecue— Goldsboro

Scott's is now open only Thursday and Friday, and then only for lunch between 10:30 A.M. and 2:30 P.M. But even though it was never one of those half-dozen or so places whose names sprang immediately to the tongue whenever North Carolina barbecue was discussed, it was in fact one of the state's oldest barbecue restaurants, as well as a thriving black-owned enterprise. Many outside Goldsboro are familiar with the family name through the visibility of Scott's Famous Barbecue Sauce, a quintessential eastern North Carolina–style vinegar-based sauce sold commercially in several grocery chains in North Carolina, South Carolina, and Virginia. The yellow label features the red silhouette of a pig and the legend, "It's The Best Ye Ever Tasted."

A portrait of the late reverend Adam W. Scott hangs just inside the front door at Scott's Famous Barbecue. It's the image of a man with an intriguing twinkle in his eye. Scott was a preacher in the Holiness Church and the inventor of the sauce—well, sort of. Adam was a young man working as a janitor and elevator operator in Goldsboro when he first tried his hand at cooking barbecue. His early efforts were so enthusiastically received that he began to cater occasional parties and receptions. A number of years later, he began regularly cooking pigs in a backyard pit on weekends. By 1933, he had enclosed the back porch of his home to make it into a dining room. Over the years, many of the state's most prominent citizens, including Governor J. Melville Broughton, visited Scott's to sample some of his famous barbecue.

An enigmatic aura just naturally surrounds any good barbecue man's sauce, but Adam Scott perhaps carried the mystery to new heights when he announced that the recipe for his sauce had come to him in a dream. That original recipe was served in Scott's restaurant for many years until Adam's son, A. Martel Scott Sr., spiced up the mixture a bit before obtaining a patent on it in 1946. Since all eastern North Carolina barbecue sauces, including Scott's, start with a base of vinegar, salt, red pepper, and black pepper, what must have come to Adam Scott as he lay slumbering were all the ingredients lumped together on the label under the general classification of "spices." Those spices form two inches of sediment at the bottom of the reddish liquid before it's shaken thoroughly, in accordance with the directions on the label. In addition to several types of ground black and red pepper, it contains some lighter-colored grains, something that might be onion or garlic powder. . . . But trying to guess the ingredients is really sort of pointless, the kind of game you play to pass the time while waiting in pleasant anticipation for your plate of barbecue to arrive. This is a robust, lively sauce that should be enjoyed for the sum of its parts, rather than any one or two unknown ingredients. Suffice it to say that the overall taste sensation is of spicy, salty vinegar, that the coarse-ground pepper and spices impart a pleasant grittiness to the tongue, and that the heat is kept moderately under control. Personally, I enjoy taking an occasional swig straight from the bottle as I pass my kitchen pantry. And as for lifting a forkful of barbecue that's still glistening from an anointing of Scott's sauce, well, that is a dreamlike experience.

Scott's founder Adam Scott (*portrait in the background*) claimed his sauce recipe came to him in a dream.

In 1989, Scott's Famous Barbecue Sauce was awarded second place in a national competition among thirty-one vinegar-based barbecue sauces sponsored by *Food & Wine* magazine. Fewer than one-fourth of the barbecue sauces on the market today are of the vinegar-based variety, so Scott's, in its award-winning eminence, stands as a lonely but sturdy reminder of eastern North Carolina's barbecue heritage. If it had been available in the nineteenth century, maybe

Scott's closed completely at one point but has reopened for lunch on Thursday and Friday.

no one would ever have tried adding toma-toes to barbecue sauce. Who knows?

While handing out well-deserved praise, I shouldn't neglect to note that this stuff can blister your skin if you work around it too long without wearing rubber gloves. One night in 1957, someone saw a man breaking into Scott's restaurant and called the police. When the officers arrived and searched the premises, they found a broken window but no burglar. As they were preparing to leave, they heard a sound from the storeroom. When they investigated, they found the would-be thief hiding in a fifty-five-gallon drum half full of Scott's sauce. His rapidly growing dis-comfort had caused him to stir inside the barrel, which led to his discovery. The police lifted the man out of the drum and carted him off to jail, where he spent the night in a cell without benefit of a shower to wash the sauce from his skin and clothing. The next morning, Martel Scott showed up at the po-lice station. When he realized the man had spent the night marinating in Scott's Famous Barbecue Sauce, he declined to press charges, saying the unfortunate intruder had already suffered enough.

Scott's has served its share of the rich and famous over the years. Adam Scott was invited to the White House on one occasion to serve barbecue to Franklin and Eleanor Roosevelt. He took along his children and even some of the grandchildren for the his-toric event. In the late 1940s, Adam Scott turned the restaurant over to his son Martel Sr. and moved to Winston-Salem to serve as the personal barbecue chef for R. J. Reynolds Jr., Bob Hanes of Wachovia Bank, and James Hanes of the textile family. He continued traveling with the Reynolds family and cooking barbecue for high-society functions until 1976, when he returned to Goldsboro.

Adam died a number of years ago, but a third generation of Scotts operates the restaurant—albeit only very part-time—as well as the sauce business. A. Martel Scott Jr. is a quiet, modest man who seems to have a markedly different personality from his colorful grandfather. But the continued successful operation of the family business was cause for Scott's to be featured in a 1992 article in *Entrepreneur* magazine.

Its vastly reduced hours notwithstanding, Scott's is a cheerful, sunlight-filled place with chrome-and-Formica tables and comfortable booths upholstered in light green vinyl. The fairly extensive menu includes a lot of non-barbecue items, along with a couple of unusual twists. For one thing, Scott's whole-hog barbecue is offered not only chopped, which in eastern North Carolina is de rigueur, but also sliced or "chunked" into tender, one-inch cubes. For another, barbecue plates are accompanied by a complimentary serving of crisp pork skin and a few ribs. These are the ribs pulled from the roasted whole pigs and are different from the spareribs offered on the menu.

Scott's switched from hardwood to gas for cooking its barbecue sometime in the mid-1970s, so the meat has no smoky taste. On the other hand, both the white meat from the hams and loins and the dark meat from the shoulders and sides are cooked for hours at the precisely controlled low temperatures that are possible with gas cookers. This creates barbecue that is moist and juicy.

No sauce has been placed on the barbecue when it's brought to the table, so what you're served is mild, naturally sweet, tender roast pork waiting to be turned—by a liberal dose of Scott's Famous Barbecue Sauce—into what your taste buds will recognize as barbecue. Even though Scott's is now open only a couple of lunch hours per week, if you'll think of the barbecue as the canvas and the sauce as the paint, you'll leave having created a minor masterpiece.

## A & M Grill—Mebane

A & M Grill was in business from 1948 to 2011. If I had assigned ratings, this place would have rated five out of five little pigs, sauce bottles, or whatever other icon I might have devised to indicate absolutely excellent barbecue. Located within the city limits of Mebane but only a hundred yards into Orange County, A & M turned out what was unquestionably the best pit-cooked barbecue in the Greensboro-to-Hillsborough stretches of Interstate 40/85 and U.S. 70.

Ironically, when I began producing UNC-TV features on outstanding North Carolina barbecue restaurants, A & M's owners wouldn't allow me to come and do a story. Even though it would have meant free publicity, they weren't any too polite about declining either. When I first approached them with the idea, I think they assumed I was trying to sell them something. Although I explained a number of times that no charge was involved, they were unmoved, telling me, "We

A & M Grill, Mebane

just really don't want to talk to anyone."

So just to have some fun, a crew and I ended up doing what we referred to—tongue in cheek—as an "undercover barbecue" report, complete with dark glasses and a miniature hidden camera. With no hard feelings whatsoever, I was happy to report that A & M didn't have time to leave the serious work of cooking great barbecue long enough to fool around with any bothersome TV guys. That was obvious when I walked into the small original dining room and heard the hollow thunk of barbecue being hand-chopped with a cleaver. The place proved so popular that a larger room was added. Out back, the brick pits, chimneys, and large pile of split wood let me know I had arrived at an old-fashioned, uncompromising, pit-cooking barbecue place.

Anyone ordering a small "sliced" tray received an absolutely huge serving of "pig-picking," or pulled, meat. The pork was falling-apart tender, had a robust, smoky flavor, and was practically as good as it ever gets—anywhere.

I noted one amusing geographic oddity about A & M. Eastern North Carolina coleslaw was white or yellow, moistened with mayonnaise or mustard, while Lexington-style "barbecue" slaw—also known as red slaw—contains vinegar, sugar, ketchup, and red and black pepper. Orange and Alamance counties are in a sort of in-between nether region. They follow the Piedmont practice of cooking pork shoulders rather than whole hogs, but they don't feel quite comfortable serving barbecue slaw. The dividing line for Lexington slaw seems to be around Greensboro. A & M and a few Alamance County joints solved this split-personality problem by serving pink slaw, boasting both mayonnaise and ketchup. It actually tasted as though it contained Thousand Island dressing.

I greatly miss A & M.

## Dillard's—Durham

For nearly sixty years, Dillard's was a minority-owned place on Durham's south side where blacks and whites alike gathered to eat what was arguably the Bull City's best barbecue and soul food. The late Sam Dillard, a native of Mississippi, founded the restaurant in 1952. Although he died in 1997, his family continued to operate the place for almost fifteen years much as it had always been run. Because Dillard was a devout man, the sign outside reminded diners who took the trouble to look up Deuteronomy 8:3 that, as good as the food was at Dillard's, "man does not live by bread alone."

Food was served cafeteria-style. Once customers filled their trays, they moved to comfortable booths in a dining room decorated with pennants from ACC schools and the state's historically black colleges and universities.

Getting through Dillard's serving line ranged from an exercise in self-restraint to an episode of caution-to-the-wind recklessness. Succulent, juicy fried and barbecued chicken took its place beside tender, meaty pork ribs; tangy chopped pork barbecue; falling-apart pork chops in gravy; slow-cooked country-style steak; fresh, crispy fried fish; and, at the end of the week, pork chitterlings, or "chitlins." The seasoned vegetables included all kinds of snap beans and peas, collard greens, country-style cabbage, squash and onions,

Dillard's, Durham

fried okra, fresh corn, sweet potatoes, mac 'n' cheese, fried apples, and much more, depending on the season.

It has long been my observation that barbecue customs among North Carolina's African-Americans often cross or ignore the established boundaries between eastern and Piedmont-style barbecue. For example, Dillard's served barbecue that was nicely seasoned and fairly heavily moistened with a sauce that included not only vinegar and red pepper but also tomato paste and mustard. This is not characteristic of either eastern or Lexington-style sauce, but rather of the sauces found in South Carolina and elsewhere. The pork was cooked in electric pits without benefit of smoke flavor from wood coals, but the signature sauce somehow managed to make up for that shortcoming. By the way, Dillard's sauce is still sold in Durham-area grocery stores, where it's popular for use on both pork and chicken.

For years, Dillard's was well known for selling pork ribs at the old Durham Bulls ballpark, where they were advertised as costing "a buck a bone."

## Barbecue Inn—Asheville

The late Gus Kooles, founder of the now-shuttered Barbecue Inn, had run another restaurant in Asheville for several years when a friend suggested he try barbecue. Gus replied that as far as he knew, barbecue was nothing but "roast pork with ketchup on it." The friend then hooked him up with an acquaint-ance in Goldsboro and arranged a summer visit. The idea was for Kooles to learn the secrets of preparing eastern-style barbecue and bring the delicacy back to the Asheville area.

After first being mistaken for an efficiency expert by the Goldsboro restaurant employees, Kooles settled in to learn the art of cooking pork for long periods of time at low temperatures, in order to make the meat tender, moist, and juicy. He came back and established Barbecue Inn in West Asheville in 1961. The place served coastal-plain barbecue to mountaineers and visitors for fifty years before closing in 2011.

As a promotional stunt during the restaurant's early days, Kooles offered a free meal to any customer who brought him a decorative pig unlike any other he owned. The pigs, foreign and domestic, arrived by the hundreds—made from wood, metal, jade, ceramics, and other materials. Kooles ended up giving away a lot of barbecue. By the restaurant's later years, it boasted a couple of thousand pigs, arrayed on every available shelf. There were so many, in fact, that visitors often referred to Barbecue Inn as "the Pig Restaurant."

Second-generation family members Woodie, Martha, and Charles Kooles operated the laid-back restaurant for many years following the founder's passing. The place featured unusual order pads that customers marked themselves. Barbecue Inn served eastern-style barbecue moistened with its vinegar-based sauce. Over time, the restaurant supplemented the eastern tradition by adding pork ribs, sliced and chopped beef,

beef ribs, and fried chicken. Customers usually anointed the ribs and beef barbecue with a tomato-based sauce that was sweeter and thicker than the vinegar-based version. Although the backbone of the business was barbecue, Barbecue Inn also served Italian-style spaghetti with homemade sauce practically from the beginning; the dish was a longtime favorite. The Kooles were also proud of their quarter-pound hot dogs, served with their own special chili sauce.

Barbecue Inn was a western North Carolina institution, and the Internet wept for days when barbecue lovers began to hear of its demise.

For years, Keith Allen of Allen & Son in Chapel Hill has been known for splitting his own hickory wood.
*Photo by Mike Burke*

# POSTSCRIPT

Barbecue obviously enjoys a high—and rising—level of appreciation as a cultural symbol in North Carolina, but there's no getting around the fact that the old ways are dwindling. The veterans who've fired the pits for decades at some places are aging, and they'll be difficult to replace once they're gone. Restaurants whose owners have no family members waiting in the wings are being sold. When ownership changes, restaurants sometimes have to switch from pit-cooking to gas or electricity in order to get insurance coverage. Wood is becoming increasingly expensive and difficult to obtain. And for many people, the desire to reduce fat intake makes foods like barbecue, hush puppies, and fried chicken practically off limits.

That's the bad news. But all is not gloomy. Traditions are being handed down from one generation to the next at some restaurants. And new blood enlivens the atmosphere at the oldest, most tradition-rich barbecue establishments. New places utilizing centuries-old cooking methods *are* opening, despite the guarantee of increased labor and other costs. High technology and dizzying social change make us anxious to cling to cultural connectors like barbecue that evoke associations with family, roots, and agrarian self-sufficiency. Technological developments such as the explosion in cable TV channels, social media, and video-sharing sites like YouTube help sharpen awareness of barbecuing and barbecue traditions. And the high rate of in-migration in North Carolina helps, since new residents are anxious to explore and absorb the cultural characteristics of their adopted home state. Nostalgic events such as pig-cooking contests and festivals help keep barbecue and its traditional practices in the public eye. And more than ever, people want to eat in places that have a little character and local color.

Since barbecue is a part of our heritage that can't be preserved in a museum or a book but must be experienced firsthand, I believe a smaller, tougher band of traditional barbecue practitioners will survive, prosper, and replicate itself, and that patrons will continue to beat a path to their doors. As long as people remain dedicated to keeping the fires alive, a lot of us will want to make sure we don't let this three-hundred-year tradition begin to simply drift away and disappear . . . like smoke.

BBQ

# Index

A & M Grill, 14, 30, 309-10

A.B. Vannoy Ham Company, 298-99

ABC's *Good Morning America*, 62-63, 223-24

Adams Roadside Bar-B-Q, 147-49

Adams, Scott, 147, 148

Addleton, Larry, 180

Addleton, Phyllis, 180

Advance, N.C., 234-35

Albemarle, N.C., 275-77

Allen & Son Bar-B-Que (Pittsboro), 210-11

Allen and Son Barbeque (Chapel Hill), 31, 35, 204-7

Allen, Chris, 172

Allen, James, 210, 211

Allen, Keith, 35-36, 204-7, 210, 211, 314

Alston Bridges Barbecue, 12, 287-90

Anderson, Jeff, 139

Applewhite, James, xxiv

Arcadia BBQ. See *Speedy Lohr's BBQ.*

Arkansas barbecue, 38

Asheboro, N.C., 242-43

Asheville, N.C., 312-13

Ayden, N.C., 6, 132, 136-40

B.J.'s Grill and BBQ, 144-45

B's Barbecue and Grill, 23, 125-29

Backcountry Barbecue, 265-66

Backyard BBQ Pit, 197-99

Banana pudding, 30, 87-88

*Barbecue America*, 282

Barbecue beans recipe, 85

Barbecue Cruncher, 296

Barbecue hash, 37

Barbecue Inn, 312-13

Barbecue judges' training, 56

"Barbecue Man, The," 39-43

"Barbecue Month," 60

Barbecue Presbyterian Church, 5

Barbecue: coarse-chopped, 28; cook entire pig (easy method), 77-80; cook entire pig (traditional), 69-77; cook pork shoulder, 66-69; "dip", 21; east vs. west debate, 18-19; Eastern-style barbecue, 19-28; how to prepare your own, 65-80; Lexington (Piedmont)-style, 28, 31; minced, 29; "outside brown," 28; outside N.C., 36-39; "pick the pig," 77; pit cooking, 31-36; politics, xxiii, 32; sauce recipes, 83-84; tobacco culture, 24-28; use of tomatoes, 21

Barbecued potatoes. See *Boiled potatoes.*

Bar-B-Q Center, 245-47

Barker, Ben, 158, 238

Barker, Karen, 158

Barnes, Keith, 26-27, 184-85

Barrett, Anna, 92

Beef brisket, 38

Belk, Henry, xxii-iii

Berrier, Richard, 229

Bill's Barbecue and Chicken, 116-20

"Black dip," 38

Blackwelder, Chad, 238

Blackwelder, John, 29-30

Bladen County, xx

Bledsoe, Jerry, xxiii, 14, 96

Blizzard, Ann, 104-5

Blizzard, Sid Jr., 104-5

Blizzard, Sid Sr., 104-5

Blowing Rock, N.C., 299-300

Blue Mist Bar-B-Q, 242-43

"Bob Garner Eats," 193

Bob Melton's Barbecue, 14, 33, 113, 303-6

Bob's Bar-B-Q, 175-78

Boiled potatoes, 22-23, 82, 85

*Bon Appetit*, 160

Braswell Plantation, ix, 82

Braswell, David, 27

Braswell, Doug, 27

Braswell, Herbert, 27

Braswell's Barbecue, 26, 27

Brewer, Henry Parker, 122

Bridges Barbecue Lodge, 12, 31, 290-93

Bridges, Alston, 12, 287, 288, 289

Bridges, Beth, 294, 295

Bridges, Jay, 287

Bridges, Kent, 287, 288, 289

Bridges, Linda, 287, 288

Bridges, Lyttle "Mamma B.," 290, 291, 292, 293

Bridges, Mabel, 287

Bridges, Michelle, 287

Bridges, Red, 12, 287, 290, 291, 292

Bridges, Reid, 287

Bridges, Terry, 294, 295

Bridges-Webb, Debbie, 291, 292, 293

Brightleaf 905, 238

Broughton, J. Melville, 7, 306

Brown, Allen, 238

Brown, Rick, 282-83

Brunswick stew, 22, 87

Brushy Mountain Smokehouse and Creamery, 296-97

Bubba's Barbecue, 280-82

Bullock, Tommy, 199

Bullock's Bar-B-Cue, 199-200

Bum's Restaurant, 132-36

Bunn's Barbecue, 109

Burgoo, 38

Burleson, Bob, 240, 241

Burleson, Susan, 240, 241

Burlington, N.C., 211-14

Bush, George, 214

Buzz, 106-7

Byrd, William, 4-5, 37

Cabarrus County, 243

Campbell, Steve, 220

Cape Fear Barbecue, 166-67

Carden, Charlie, 165, 166

Carden, Kim, 165, 166

Carolina Bar-B-Q, 285-87

Carthage, N.C., 167-69

Cary, N.C., 188

Center Brick Warehouse, 25

Chapel Hill, N.C., 204-9

Charlie's BBQ & Grille, 165-66

*Charlotte Observer*, 270, 282

Charlotte, N.C., 280-85

Cherry's Barbecue and Seafood, 120-22

China Grove, N.C., 272-73

Christian, Spencer, 62, 63

Claiborne, Craig, xix, xxi, 15

Clark's Barbecue, 224-25

Clayton, N.C., 165-66

Cleveland County airport, 293

Cleveland, N.C., 270-72

Clinton, Bill, 115, 214

Clyde Cooper's BBQ, x, 181-82

Cobb, Jack, 131

Cobb, Rudy, 131, 184

Coleslaw: eastern-style, 24, 84; Lexington-style, 30, 84-85

Collard Capital of the World, 135

Collard Festival, 133

College Bar-B-Que, 266-67

Competitive cooking, 54-58

Concord, N.C., 277-78

Conrad, Cecil, 247

Conrad, Michael, 247

Conrad, Sonny, 245, 246

Cook, Brandon, 247, 249

Cook, Doug, 247, 265, 266

Cook, Elizabeth, 272

Cook, Mrs. Brandon, 247

Cook's Barbecue, 247-49

Cooper, Clyde, 181

Cooper, Matt, 98

Cope, Kaffee, 259

Cope, Scott, 259

Corn sticks, 23

Cornelius, N.C., 282

Council, Mildred "Mama Dip," 42

Country Barbeque, 219-20

Country-style barbecued chicken, 156

Creedmoor, N.C., 175-78

Crispito, 130

Danny's Bar-B-Que, 188-90

Danville, Va., 214

Davis, Elmer, 149

Deano's Barbecue, 235-36

Deen, Paula, 80-81

Dennis, Bettie, 134

Dennis, Bill, 134
Dennis, Bobby, 134
Dennis, Jessica, 135
Dennis, John Bill, 133, 134
Dennis, Larry, 134-35
Dennis, Latham "Bum," 134, 132-36
Dennis, Leah, 135
Dennis, Skilten M., 6, 134
Dennis, Susan, 134
Dennis, Teresa, 135
Denton, N.C., 243-45
Dillard, Sam, 311
Dillard's, 311-12
Doby, Lonnie, 276
Dogzilla, 233
Doug Sauls' Barbecue and Seafood, 115-16
Drach, Judy, 126, 127
Dry ribs, 38
Duke University, 62, 63
Dunn, Emily, 135
Dunning, Jody, 300, 301
Dunning, Steve, 300, 301
Durham, N.C., 197-202, 311

Eason, David, 145, 146
Eason, Ken, 145, 146
Eason, Teresa, 147
Edge, John T., 158
Edmisten, Rufus, 96
Egerton, John, xxi-ii
Eilers, Cathy, 115
Eilers, David, 115
Eilers, Kim, 115
Ellis, Bill, 116-20
Ellis, Regina, 174
Empire Eats, 188
Esquire, 238
Essick, Dempsey, 241
Eure, Thad, xxiii
Evans, Henry, 5-6
Everett, Bob, 51, 53
Everett, Fate, 50-51
Everett, Jayne, 51

Everett, Tad, 51
"Everybody's Day," 9, 58-59

Farber, Barry, 16, 217-18
Farmville, N.C., 131-32
Farrior, David, 96
Fayetteville, N.C., 166-67
Ferris, Marcie Cohen, 160
Fish stew, 147
Flay, Bobby, 92-93
Flowers' Tavern, 162
Flying Pig, 293-95
Forsyth, Skipper, 174
Fox, Matt, 202, 204
Freeze, Gary, 5
Fried cabbage, 120
Fuller's Old Fashion BBQ, 169-71
Fuzzy's Pit-Cooked Bar-B-Q, 16, 30, 216-19

Gardner, Ava, 163
Gardner's Barbecue, 112-13
Garner, Deryll, 56
Garner, Everett, 92, 93, 94-96, 178, 179
Garner, Jessica, 260-61
Garner, Nelson, 106, 260
Garner, Ruthie Everett, 40, 50
Garris, Billy, 251, 252, 253
Garris, Timmy, 251, 252
Gary's Bar-B-Q, 272-73
Gentry, Randy, 225
Gilliam-McConnell airport, 167
Godley, Tammy, 126, 127
Goldsboro, N.C., 6, 7, 9, 15, 151-56, 305
Gourmet, 160, 270, 292
GQ, 157
Grady, Gerri, 157
Grady, Stephen, 156-57
Grady's Barbecue, 156-67
Graham, N.C., 211-14
Granite Quarry, N.C., 273-75
Gravy, 188
Greasy Corner, 236-37
Great Wagon Road, 2

Green, Ike, 153-54
Green, Tom, 94-96
Greensboro, N.C., 13, 219-24
Greenville, N.C., 125-30
Grill House catering, 300
*Guinness Book of World Records*, 10, 57

Hanes, Bob, 308
Hanes, James, 308
Hardy, David, 239
Harris, Chris, 252
Harris, Kirksey, 249
Harrison, Ted, 40
Harvey, Jimmy, 35, 249, 250, 251
Harvey, Terry, 249
Hatem, Greg, 186, 188, 193
Hearne, Henry, 210
Heath, J.D., 163
Henderson, N.C., 174-75
Hendrix Barbecue, 251-53
Hendrix, Odell "Bony," 235
Hertford County, 4
High Cotton Barbeque, 98-99
High Point, N.C., 240-41
Hight, Louise, 26-27
Hill, Edna, 228
Hill, Eugene "J.R.," 229
Hill, Gene, 228-29
Hill, Joe Allen, 228
Hill's Lexington Barbecue, 30, 228-29
Hillsborough BBQ Company, 202-4
Hillsborough Hog Days, 201
Hillsborough, N.C., 202-4
Hog Heaven Barbecue, 201-2
Holy, Cleveland, 163
"Holy Grub," 96, 182
Honey Bee Festival, 225
Hookerton, N.C., 140-42
Hughes, Karin, 249
Hunter Hill Café & Catering, 113-15
Huntersville, N.C., 278
Hurricane Floyd, 116, 117
Hursey, Charles, 211, 212, 213

Hursey, Chris, 211
Hursey, Chuck, 211
Hursey, Daisy, 211, 212
Hursey, Larry, 212
Hursey, Sylvester, 211, 212
Hursey's Pig Pickin' Bar-B-Q, 16, 211-14
Hush puppies, 23, 85
Hyde County oysters, 100

J.B. Dennis Café, 134
Jack Cobb & Son Bar-B-Que, 131-32
Jackson's Big Oak Barbecue, 108
Jimmy's BBQ, 35, 249-51
Johnson, Greg, 59
Johnson, Mark, 201
Johnston, Gene, 15-16
Jones, Bruce, 138, 140
Jones, Jeff, 138, 139, 140
Jones, Rachel, 246
Jones, Samuel, 138, 140
Jones, Walter B. "Pete," 3, 32, 137, 138
Jordan, Byron, 297, 298
Jordan, Nancy, 298
Julian, Alexander, 17

Kansas City Barbeque Society, 57, 58, 282
Kapp, Chancy, 40
Keaton, B.W., 270, 271
Keaton's Barbecue, 270-72
Ken's Grill, 145-47
Kentucky barbecue, 38
Kepley's Barbecue, 240-41
Kerley's Barbecue, 241-42
Kernersville, N.C., 224-26
King, N.C., 227-28
King, Frank Sr., 143
King's Barbecue & Chicken, 142-44
Kinston, N.C., 142-44
Kirby, James, 77
Kitty Hawk, N.C., 98-99
Knight, Tracy, 294, 295
Knightdale Seafood & Barbecue, 180-81
Knightdale, N.C., 180-81

Kooles, Charles, 312
Kooles, Gus, 312
Kooles, Martha, 312
Kooles, Woodie, 312
Kuralt, Charles 30, 286

La Grange, N.C., 144-47
Lamm, Kevin, 122-23
Lancaster's BBQ, 278-80
Lexington Barbecue Festival, 14, 58-61, 245-46, 251, 259
Lexington Barbecue, 13, 253-57
Lexington, N.C., 9, 32, 245-59, 261-65
*Life*, 7, 305
Linwood, N.C., 265-66
Lippard, Eric, 122-23
Little Richard's Barbecue, 229-31
Livermush, 268
Locklear, Fuller, 169
Log Cabin BBQ, 275-76
Lohr, Paul "Speedy," 261
Lohr, Paul, 262
Lohr, Roger, 261
Lucy, 107
Lumberton, N.C., 172-74
Lynch, John "Jack", xxi

M&K Bar-B-Q & Country Cookin', 273-75
Mac's Speed Shop, 282-84
Madison, N.C., 216-19
Mallard Creek Presbyterian Church, 5, 50
Mariani, John, 238
Marshall, Brandon, 99-100
Marshall, Brian, 99
Marshall, Justin, 99
Marshall, Martelle, 99-100
Marshall, Veronica, 99
Martelle's Feed House, 99-100
Massengill, Raymond, 164
McCall, Randy, 149, 150
McCall's Barbecue and Seafood, 149-51
McLawhorn, Bill, 127
McLawhorn, Donna, 126, 127

McLawhorn, Peggy, 125-27
Mebane, N.C., 309-10
Medlin, Gene, 286
Melton, Bob, 7-9, 98, 305
"Memphis in May," 37-38
Meyer, Paul, 228
Miller, Buck, 235
Miller, Ralph, 280, 281
Mitchell, Ed, 77, 158-60
"Mmm-mmmm" exclamation, 39, 41
Mocksville, N.C., 235-37
Monk, Rick, 254, 255, 256
Monk, Wayne, 12-13, 16, 28, 35, 202, 253-57
Monroe, Richard, 268
Moore, Big John, 101
Moore, Jerome, 126
Moore, Tommy, 57, 101-2
Moore's Olde Tyme Barbeque, 57, 101-2
Mooresville, N.C., 278
*More North Carolina Country Cookin'*, 106-7
Morning Times, 188
Morris Barbeque, 140-42
Morris, Ashley, 140, 141, 142
Morris, Frankie "Nannie," 140
Morris, Heather Troutman, 243
Morris, William Jr., 141, 142
Morris, Willie McKinley "Pop," 140
Morrisville, N.C., 190-91
Mr. Barbecue, 231-32
Murphy, Joe, 288
Murphy, Zacki, 16-17, 218
Murray, Kathleen, 271
Mutton barbecue, 38

Napier, John, 15
Nashville, N.C., 115-16
National Barbecue Association, 201-2
*National Geographic*, 15, 137
Nelson, T.H. "Fuzzy," 216
Nelson's Barbecue, 171-72
New Bern, N.C., 101-2
*New York Times*, 160
Newport Pig Cookin' Contest, 54

*News & Observer*, 182, 230
*North Carolina Barbecue: Flavored by Time*, 40-41, 260-61
North Carolina Championship Pork Cook-off, 54, 60
"North Carolina Classic" barbecue restaurant, 97
*North Carolina Country Cookin'*, 106-7
*North Carolina Now*, 40
*North Carolina Pig Pickin', A*, 94-96
North Carolina Pork Council, 56, 58
*North Carolina Weekend*, 183-85, 239
North Wilkesboro, N.C., 296-97
North–South Carolina Barbecue Bowl, 16, 214, 216

Oakwood Barbecue, 103-4
Obama, Barack, 166, 167, 260-61
Official North Carolina State Barbecue Championship, 58
Oink Express, 144
Okie Dokies Smokehouse, 300-302
Old Hickory House Restaurant, 252, 284-85
Old Hickory Pits, 151
Osteen, Louis, 238
*Our State*, 193, 224
Overby, Clyde, 214
Overby, Eldridge, 214, 215
Overby, Johnny, 214
Overton, Buck, 98
Owen, Jay, 267
Owensboro, Ky., 38

Pacini, Jennifer, 249
Parade of Pigs, 60
Parker, Graham, 122
Parker, Linwood, 163, 164
Parker, Ralph, 122
Parker's Barbecue (Greenville), 129-30
Parker's Barbecue (Wilson), 34, 122-25
*Paula's Home Cooking*, 80-81
Peach cobbler, 30, 90-91
Peters, Meta, 50
Pig in a Puppy, 144

Pig Pickin's of America, 232-34
Pig picking, 44-54
Pig, The, 208-9
Pik N Pig, 167-69
Pit Authentic Barbecue, The, 186-88
Pork backbone, 120
Pork ribs, 37
Price, Andy, 171, 172
Price, Nelson, 171
Prissy Polly's Bar-B-Que, 225-26

Raleigh Times, The, 188
Raleigh, N.C., 186-88
Ralph's Barbecue, 110-12
Ramsey, Natalie, 291, 292, 293
Randolph County, 242
Reagan, Ronald, 16, 214, 256
*Real Barbecue*, 59
Red Pig Bar-B-Q House, 236-37
Reidsville Luckies, 215
Reidsville, N.C., 16, 214-16
Reynolds, R. J. Jr., 7, 308
Richard's Bar-B-Q, 268-69
Richlands, N.C., 103-4
Ridenhour, George, 9-11, 59
Ridge, Alan, 17
Ridgewood Barbecue, 37
Ritchie, Gary, 272
Roberts, Grady, 121
Rocky Mount, N.C., 7, 9, 112-15, 303
Rogers, Dennis, xxiii, 94-96, 182, 230
Roosevelt, Eleanor, 308
Roosevelt, Franklin, 308
Roux-en-Y surgery, 192-94
Russell, Grace, 109
Russell, Randy, 109
Russell, Russ, 109
Russell, Wilbur, 109

Saintsing, Kay, 59
*Salisbury Post*, 272
Salisbury, N.C., 29, 251, 266-70
Sauls, Doug, 225

Scott, A. Martel Jr., 7, 309
Scott, A. Martel Sr., 7, 307, 308, 309
Scott, Adam W., 6-7, 305, 306
Scott, Bob, 94-96
Scott's Famous Barbecue Sauce, 306, 307-8, 309
Scott's Famous Barbecue, 33, 306-9
Sechriest, Vernon, xxii-iii
Sedgefield Hunt, xvi
*Sharecroppers: The Way We Really Were*, 46-48
Shelby, N.C., 287-93
Sheppard family, 167
Shirley, Wilber, 33, 152-56, 171, 193
Shoals, Leo "Muscle," 215
Short Sugar's Pit Bar-B-Q, 16, 214-16
Sid's Catering, 104-5
Silver Moon, xiv
Simmons, Melvin, 197, 198
Sink, Joe Jr., 59
Sitti, 188
Skillet corn bread, 86-87
Skipper Forsyth's Bar-B-Q, 174-75
Skylight Inn, 3-4, 15, 23, 32, 136-40
*Slow Food for Fast Times*, 288
Smiley's Lexington BBQ, 257-58
Smith, Sadler, 99, 183
Smith, Tommy, 306
Smith, Van, 92
Smithfield, N.C., 161-62
Smithfield's Chicken 'N Bar-B-Q, 161-62
"Smoke ring," 37
Smokey Joe's Barbecue, 258-59
Smokey's BBQ Shack, 190-91
Smoky Mountain Barbecue, 297-99
Snook's Old Fashion Barbecue, 234-35
South Carolina barbecue, 37
*Southern*, 15
*Southern Barbecue*, xviii
Southern Culture on the Skids, 63
Southern Foodways Alliance Symposium, 158-60
*Southern Living*, 259
*Southern Living Off the Eaten Path*, 300
Spearman, Walter, 30
*Spectator*, 181

Speedy Lohr's BBQ of Arcadia, 261-62
Spoon's Barbecue, 280
Stamey, C. Warner, 11-14, 221, 222, 223, 250, 254, 255, 287, 291
Stamey, Charles 222
Stamey, Chip, 222
Stamey, Dan, 264
Stamey, Keith, 62, 63, 222, 223
Stamey, Nancy, 264
Stamey's Barbecue of Tyro, 264-65
Stamey's Old Fashioned Barbecue, 13, 30, 220-24
Stann, Tommy, 202, 204
Statesville, N.C., 285-87
Staton, Vince, 59
Steele Pig 238-39
Stephenson, Andy, 195, 196
Stephenson, Lynn, 196
Stephenson, Paul, 195
Stephenson, Wayne, 195
Stephenson's Bar-B-Q, 195-97
Stern, Jane, 292
Stern, Michael, 292
Stith, Raymond, xviii
Stone, Dewey, 173
Stratford Bar-B-Que, 227-28
Stroupe, Mark, 185
Suchoff, Sam, 208
"Sugar Pig's chess pies, 99
Sutton's, 26
Swannanoa, N.C., 300-302
Sweetie Pies, 147
Swicegood, Jess, 11, 61, 221, 287

T&F Barbecue, 268
Tarheel Q, 262-64
Taylor Grocery, 158
Taylor, Roy, 46-48
Texas-style barbecue, 37, 38-39
*The State. See Our State.*
Thigpen, B.J., 144
Thigpen, Darrell, 144
Thomas, Kathy, 273
Thomas, Moran, 273, 274

Thompson, Morris, 103-4
Thorp, Will, 98, 99
Timberlake, Bob, 42
Torrence, Sandy, 277
*Travel*, 210
Trillin, Calvin, xxi, 158, 160
Troutman, Jimmy, 243
Troutman's Bar-B-Q (Concord), 277-78
Troutman's B-B-Q (Denton), 243-45
Tryon, N.C., 58
Tussey, Holland, 255
Tussy's Drive-In. See *Speedy Lohr's BBQ*.

UNC-TV, 40
*USA Today*, 259

Vilas, James, 22
Village Inn Bar-B-Que and Seafood, 172-74

Walker, Brittany, 262
Waters, Wayne, 184
Weaver, Sid, 9-11, 59, 61, 221, 287
Webb, Chase, 291, 292, 293
Welcome, N.C., 241-42
Weldon, N.C., 110-12
West Jefferson, N.C., 297-99
Westbrook, Worth, 149, 150
Wet ribs, 38
WFMY-TV, 40, 51, 215, 220, 238
Whaley, Debra, 225
Whaley, Loren, 225
Whispering Pines BBQ, 276-77
White Swan Bar-B-Q & Fried Chicken, 162-65
Whitfield, Bobby, 175, 176
Whitfield, Nita, 175, 176, 177
Whitt, Bob, 176, 177
Wicker, Tom, 35
Wilber's Barbecue, 15, 32, 151-56
Willard, Alan, 232
Williams Memorial Presbyterian Church, 5
Williams, Donald, 122
Williamsburg, Va., 16, 256
*Wilmington Morning Star*, 108

Wilmington, N.C., 108
*Wilson Daily Times*, 185
*Wilson Mirror*, 26
Wilson, N.C., 116-20, 120-25, 305
Wilson, David, 216
Windsor, N.C., 109
Wing Tip Farm, 94
Wink's: The King of Barbecue, 269-70
Winston-Salem, N.C., 228-33
WITN-TV, 144
Woodlands Barbecue & Pickin' Parlor, 299-300
Woodward, Bobby, 122
Woodward, Karen, 120
Woodward, Robbie, 120

Yarborough, Dell, 223